CLEAN BREAKS

500 NEW WAYS TO SEE THE WORLD

PUBLISHING INFORMATION

This 1st edition published August 2009 by
Rough Guides Ltd, 80 Strand, London WC2R 0RL
14 Local Shopping Centre, Panchsheel Park, New Delhi 110017, India
Distributed by the Penguin Group
Penguin Books Ltd, 80 Strand, London WC2R 0RL
Penguin Group (USA) 375 Hudson Street, NY 10014, USA
Penguin Group (Australia) 250 Camberwell Road, Camberwell, Victoria 3124, Australia
Penguin Books Canada Ltd, 10 Alcorn Avenue, Toronto, Ontario, Canada M4V 1E4
Penguin Group (NZ) 67 Apollo Drive, Mairangi Bay, Auckland 1310, New Zealand
Typeset in Century Schoolbook and Berthold Akzidenz Grotesque to an original design by Diana Jarvis
Printed and bound in China

© Richard Hammond and Jeremy Smith 2009

No part of this book may be reproduced in any form without permission from the publisher
except for the quotation of brief passages in reviews.

392pp includes index

A catalogue record for this book is available from the British Library

ISBN: 978-1-84836-047-1

1 3 5 7 9 8 6 4 2

CREDITS

Editor: James Rice **Contributing editor**: Lucy White **Managing editor**: Jo Kirby
Design and layout: Diana Jarvis **Picture research**: Nicole Newman **Cartography**: Ed Wright
Cover design: Chloë Roberts & Diana Jarvis **Production**: Rebecca Short **Proofreader**: Janet McCann
Additional design input: Scott Stickland, Dan May, Michelle Bhatia, Cosima Dinkel, Joseph Freiberger, Edward Steer, Emily Taylor, Mark Thomas

PUBLISHER'S NOTE

This book is printed on paper produced from environmentally sustainable sources certified by the forest stewardship council (ⓦwww.fsc.org). All inks used are vegetable-based and derived from renewable resources. The carbon emissions associated with the plane, train, bus, car and boat trips taken during the production of this book have been offset by the authors and Rough Guides, including a donation to the World Land Trust.

CONTACT US

If you think you've got an experience worthy of consideration as a Clean Break – or want to give your own take on one of the experiences included – we'd love to hear from you. If you want to submit photos of your experience, all the better.
Send in suggestions to ⓔmaill@roughguides.com.

CONTENTS

Introduction 6

Great Britain and Ireland 8

Western Europe 46

Mediterranean Islands 76

Scandinavia 92

Eastern Europe and the Aegean 110

Northern Africa and the Middle East 124

Southern Africa 156

North America 188

Mexico, Central America and the Caribbean 218

South America 250

Central and East Asia 276

Southeast Asia 292

The Indian Subcontinent 316

Australia, New Zealand and the South Pacific 346

Make the most of your trip 372

Index 385

Features

Green festivals in the UK 44
Take the train to the slopes 74
Rail and sail to the Med 90
Going green 108
Miscellany 122
The New Travellers 154

Carbon offsetting 186
Mapping your world 216
Eco labels and awards 248
Live with the locals 274
Volunteering 290
Local voices 314
Travelling by cargo ship 344

INTRODUCTION

Kayaking around the Scottish isles, snow-shoeing in the Pyrenees, wild swimming in Finland, learning to dance in Rio, walking across the Serengeti... these are just some of the hundreds of Clean Breaks featured in this book – unusual, alternative and incredible experiences that also make a difference to the lives of local people and the planet.

So what makes a Clean Break? Essentially it's about minimizing your environmental impact – on your journey and at your destination – by choosing carefully how you travel and the nature of the place you choose to stay at. It's also about having a positive impact in other ways – by contributing where you can to the conservation of wildlife and local heritage, and supporting local economies. And the good news is that this doesn't mean you have to sacrifice any notions of comfort or adventure: the experiences we've selected are (hopefully) ones that you'd love to do anyway – the difference is that you can rest assured that your presence in some way benefits the locality. Many of the properties we review are as stylish and innovative as they are environmentally aware, from beautifully crafted treehouses in the South of France and luxury yurts in Andalucía to eco-chic hotels in Thailand.

We've also included experiences that provide a closer connection with local culture. Seeking out less touristy places has always been at the heart of Rough Guides, and in this book we feature local markets and festivals as well as tours that employ native guides, which make for more rewarding encounters. After all, the most inspiring person to take you on safari is likely to be a local guide whose ancestors have lived on the land for thousands of years; your dinner tends to be better when the cook has grown and harvested the ingredients; and the most suitable person to take you to meet remote tribes is someone who understands their culture, speaks their language and is committed to their welfare.

Along the way, consider taking more time: often the best travel experiences are as much about enjoying the journey as the destination itself, in contrast to fly-and-flop "we could be anywhere" holidays. Wherever possible information is given on how to travel by public transport to the starting point of all the experiences featured. For further tips on how to plan your next Clean Break, turn to the back of the book to the section called "Make the Most of your Trip", where we provide a list of online resources for trip planning, including transport options, details of ethical tour operators and how to link up with "couch surfers", local guides and "greeters".

Finally, a note of caution: while many progressive travel companies are putting environmental and social issues at the heart of their business, there are also lots of unscrupulous businesses that are jumping on the eco bandwagon – meaning it can be difficult to tell the green from the greenwash, or environmental spin. We have done our best to make sure all of the experiences featured in this book show a tangible commitment to environmental and social responsibility and reflect a new, progressive way to see the world. We hope you enjoy the journey.

Richard Hammond and Jeremy Smith

SCOTLAND

035
046
003
005
048
025 030
044

NORTHERN
IRELAND

042
016
026

REPUBLIC
OF IRELAND

034
033

032
055 036
049

050
008

WALES

015
029
002 031
040
009 004 038 006
018

ENGLAND

014 010
047
019

020 021
022 023

027
001
007

012 013 039

041 037
028 043
017 011
052 051
024

045

053

054

GREAT BRITAIN AND IRELAND

001 Ride the National Cycle Network
002 Spend a week at Ecocabin, Shropshire
003 Get out into the wilds of Scotland at Alladale
004 Spend a weekend "Under the Thatch" in Wales
005 Sleep out in a remote bothy
006 Stay in a bunkhouse barn in the Brecon Beacons, Wales
007 Huntstile Organic Farm, Somerset
008 Bushey Heath Farm, Buxton, Derbyshire
009 Caerfai Campsite, Pembrokeshire
010 Deepdale Campsite, Norfolk
011 A day at The Eden Project, Cornwall
012 Hunt a Geocache
013 Eat out at Brighton Beach
014 Retreat to Lincolnshire
015 The Centre for Alternative Technology, Wales
016 Cycle the Kingfisher Trail, Ireland
017 Eco-steering at Lusty Glaze, Cornwall
018 Photograph seabirds on Skomer Island, Pembrokeshire
019 Milden Hall, Suffolk
020 London Wetland Centre
021 The Duke of Cambridge pub, London
022 Acorn House restaurant, London
023 Create some energy at Club Surya, London
024 Train and ferry to the Scilly Isles
025 Take the sleeper train from London to the Scottish Highlands
026 Volunteer on a National Trust working holiday
027 A long weekend on Lundy Island, Devon
028 Down on the farm at Higher Lank Farm, Cornwall

029 Mountain biking at Coed Llandegla Forest, Wales
030 Bag a Munro on Rannoch Moor, Scotland
031 Ludlow Food Festival, Shropshire
032 Autumn in the Lake District at Southwaite Green
033 Rail and sail from London to Dublin
034 Action and adventure at Delphi Mountain Resort, Ireland
035 Go Wwoofing
036 Full Circle Yurts, Lake District
037 Cornish Yurt Holidays
038 Larkhill Tipis, West Wales
039 Barefoot Yurts, Sussex
040 Fforest, Wales
041 Cornwall Tipi Holidays
042 Orchard Acre Farm, County Fermanagh, Northern Ireland
043 Tamar Village Tipis, Devon
044 Ardfern Tipis, Scotland
045 Yurt Village, Dorset
046 Camping and kayaking in the Summer Isles, Scotland
047 Eco-chic at Strattons Hotel and Restaurant, Norfolk
048 Wild camping on the Knoydart Peninsula, Scotland
049 Explore the North Pennines
050 Go easy on yourself and the planet at Titanic Spa, Yorkshire
051 Stay in an eco cottage on the Trelowarren Estate, Cornwall
052 Surfing in Cornwall
053 Whale-watching in Cork
054 See the light on Sark
055 Wild swimming

001 RIDE THE NATIONAL CYCLE NETWORK

Despite Britain's cyclists' success at the Beijing Olympics, the British have always lagged behind most other Europeans when it comes to a national cycling culture. Sustrans – the Sustainable Transport charity – is trying to change all that. In 1977, it helped establish the National Cycle Network and, with the help of thousands of volunteers, has since developed over 20,000km of cycling lanes throughout the UK, along disused railway lines, converted bridle paths and canal towpaths, through forests and open countryside and along the coast.

As part of a programme known as "Art and the Travelling Landscape", Sustrans has commissioned over 350 permanent sculptures to line some of the flatter, more family-friendly cycling paths. The idea is that they reflect some aspect of the local community and landscape. Examples of where you can find the artworks are:
The Water Rail Way A 50km route from Lincoln to Boston, which meanders alongside the River Witham crossing open fenland. Artworks by Belgian architect Paul Robbrecht. (National Cycle Network Route 1)

(Clockwise from top left) The Collier's Way; *Hi Views* designed by Paul Robbrecht on the Water Rail Way, Lincolnshire; Close-up of *Hi Views*; The Collier's Way; *Lincoln Red Shorthorns* by Sally Matthews on the Water Rail Way

The Collier's Way A 13km route across northeastern Somerset, passing Dundas Aqueduct, Radstock and Frome. Artworks: *Enamel Signs of Old English Apple Varieties* by Liz Turrell and Imi Maufe; *Stone Column* by Jerry Ortmans; *Fussell's Railings* by Jez Pearson; *Simplicity Bench* by Yumiko Aoyagi. (National Cycle Network Route 24)

The Spen Valley Greenway A 13km route along a disused railway line running near the River Spen between the towns of Cleckheaton, Dewsbury and Heckmondwike in the north of England. Artworks: *Forty Giant Steel Hoops* by Trudi Entwistle and *Giant Pedal & Cycle Seats* by Alan Evans. (National Cycle Network Route 66)

In 2008 Sustrans won £50 million from The People's Millions Lottery (a scheme whereby the British public gets to vote for projects that will benefit local communities), which it intends to use to fund the development of walking and cycling networks throughout the UK. So expect to see a massive extension of the National Cycle Network over the next few years... and a few more healthy faces.

Need to know *For information on Sustrans projects and route maps see ⓦwww.sustrans.co.uk; ☏+44 (0) 845 1130 065.*

---

002 SPEND A WEEK AT ECOCABIN, SHROPSHIRE

Nowhere is 100 percent green, but Ecocabin – in the South Shropshire Hills, 25km from Ludlow – comes close. This single-storey lodge is a model of sustainability, from its design and construction to the way it is run. The timber frame is made from local Douglas fir and larch, the flooring is finished with native ash and eco-friendly paints, there's sheep's wool for insulation, solar power for hot water and electricity, and wood pellets for the stove. Most of the furnishings are from a community recycling scheme, the 1950s kitchen cabinet was plucked from a junk shop and the kitchen work surface is made from recycled yogurt pots.

Inside, the floor plan is simple: a small kitchen-dining area with large windows to let plenty of light in, a cosy lounge with a sofa and stove, one double bedroom and one twin-bed room, and a utility room with a washing machine.

But back to that list of eco features: the barbecue is stocked with locally made charcoal, there's an "honesty" shop in a side room with essentials such as Fairtrade chocolate, and – as it's self-catering – you can order a delivery of local organic food. And on the website, there is a list of "what there is not", such as a TV, microwave and reliable mobile phone signal.

The only minor complaint you could have is that Ecocabin is in such a remote setting you do have to jump in the car if you want to see any of the local sights other than those you can reach in a day's walking. Unless of course you come by bike or hire one locally. Hopton Castle and Black Hill forest tracks are just a 10min ride away.

In fact, everything seems to have been so well thought through that you can't help trying to find a flaw. Maybe there are plans for a helipad on the farm? Maybe pigs can fly.

Need to know *The nearest mainline train station is Craven Arms, from where you can arrange to be collected by the owner. Further info, including rates and availability, at ⓦwww.ecocabin.co.uk; ☏+44 (0) 1547 530 183. Rented bikes can be delivered to the cabin by ⓦwww.wheelywonderfulcycling.co.uk.*

Ecocabin: made from local Douglas fir and larch and fitted with a rainwater collection butt

003 GET OUT INTO THE WILDS OF SCOTLAND AT ALLADALE

On a clear day, standing on top of Glen Alladale, you can see the east and west coasts of Scotland. This is the narrowest point in Britain and also one of its most remote: an hour and a half from Inverness, itself the northernmost city in the UK. But then, you don't come to stay in the lodge and cottages of the 93-square-kilometre Glen Alladale Wilderness Reserve for the nightlife.

Wildlife, however, is another matter. You can watch (or catch) salmon as they swim and leap their way upstream to spawn. The sky is patrolled by buzzards, peregrine falcons, ospreys and even golden eagles. And amid the heather and pine-covered terrain, along with the many deer, there are wild boars, pine martens, otters and a couple of elk.

Glen Alladale, a part of the Scottish Highlands being "rewilded" with lynx, bears and elk

Elk? And soon hopefully to be joined by wolves, lynx, bears and other mammals that were hunted to extinction in Britain over the last few centuries. The estate's "rewilding" project involves reforesting this vast area to resemble the great Caledonian forest that once covered these hills and then restocking it with the animals that used to inhabit it. Guests, who stay in either the richly decorated rooms in the imposing greystone main house or in the more intimate converted bothy cottages, get a chance to see this project develop first-hand on guided trips out into the estate with some of the gamekeepers.

In the long run, it's hoped that the estate will also serve as a catalyst to revitalize this region, one of the poorest in the UK, and perhaps persuade other landowners to follow suit. For now, it offers the chance to get away from it all into one of the last pieces of real wilderness left in the UK.

Need to know *The sleeper train from London Euston goes to Inverness each night (ⓦwww. firstgroup.com/scotrail), from where staff can collect you (by arrangement). For more information on rates and activities see ⓦwww.alladale.com; ☎+44 (0) 863 755 338.*

004 SPEND A WEEKEND "UNDER THE THATCH" IN WALES

In its heyday in the nineteenth century, thatch played an important role in protecting British homes from the weather. But new technologies since have led to a rapid decline in thatching, and many of the genuine thatched cottages that remain have been modified beyond all recognition by developers or have run into disrepair, a rather poignant reminder of a bygone age. An enterprising Welsh company, however, is trying to breathe new life into some of the last traditional thatched cottages in western Wales by restoring them and letting them out as holiday homes.

"Under the Thatch" is run by restorer Greg Stevenson, who lives in his own thatched cottage in Ceredigion. An architectural historian by training, his renovations are authentic. He uses lime instead of cement; paints that are natural oil-based rather than synthetic; and local thatched materials, such as wheatstraw (rather than imported reed).

All the cottages are in stunning locations around southwest Wales. One of Greg's most famous commissions was from Griff Rhys Jones to renovate his cottage Trehilyn Uchaf, near the beautiful Strumble Head peninsula in Pembrokeshire, which became the subject of the TV series *A Pembrokeshire Farm*. (It's now let through "Under the Thatch" whenever Rhys Jones is not there.) Heated by a wood-pellet central heating system (so no oil used), the cottage is insulated with Welsh sheep's wool rather than fibreglass.

Unlike most holiday homes, the cottages are let all year round – chiefly because Greg prices them lower than many holiday properties, but also because he further drops the price of any he judges might not be taken – he'd prefer that properties are rented just above cost price than not used at all. And with that comes a bargain or two: it's not unusual for a property to go for as little as £35 a night. Consequently occupancy for properties with "Under the Thatch" is at 95 percent (the average in Wales is 35 percent).

Its success has meant that Greg has been able to buy up more derelict cottages and bring them back into the community. Greg has also diversified from offering only thatched cottages: he now lets out a range of unusual accommodation dotted around western Wales, including a converted train carriage, a Scandinavian-style log cabin and two gypsy caravans. Most of his thirty properties are run using environmentally friendly technologies, including solar panels, reed-bed sewage systems, wood-chip boilers and recycled furnishings. Greg also provides guests with the opportunity to pre-order a food hamper from a local producer (ⓦwww.welcome-box.co.uk).

But most importantly, what the cottages all have in common is that they bring back life to local communities. Spend a weekend "Under the Thatch" rather than in a holiday home, buy local food and visit nearby pubs and restaurants, and you'll be contributing to the local economy rather than to its decline.

Old thatched cottage tea rooms, Cenarth, Ceredigion

Need to know *For full information on each of the cottages, including local amenities, rates and availability, see ⓦwww.underthethatch.co.uk; ☎+44 (0) 1239 851 410.*

At home in the wilderness: a bothy near Corrour

005 SLEEP OUT IN A REMOTE BOTHY

The fire crackling in the old hearth provides the only light against the thick darkness outside, as the smell of smouldering wood fills the small stone dwelling where you've broken your hike. Britain may be one of the most crowded islands on earth, but it's nevertheless still possible to trek for days through some truly remote areas, mainly in the north of Scotland and the Welsh hills. Scattered across these moors and valleys are old stone bothies (the word comes from the Gaelic "bothan", meaning hut), once lived in by farm workers and estate staff. Nowadays they lie empty except for a supply of firewood, awaiting the next walkers keen to rest and warm themselves at the end of a long day's ramble.

The Mountain Bothy Association maintains around a hundred of them across the British Isles. They are very simple places: no water, perhaps a wood-burning stove and at best a platform upon which to roll out a mat to sleep.

There's no booking system, no room key and no charge – you simply turn up, sleep the night, tidy up and move on.

This sense of collective responsibility is at the heart of the bothy code, which lays out guidelines for their use – leave no rubbish, bury any human waste and cut no living wood. They are only kept in a habitable state through the conduct of those who use them, and the Mountain Bothy Association organizes volunteer groups to spend time repairing and restoring them. Thanks to their efforts the bothies' future is safe – and there can be few better ways to soak up the sense of solitude while out in the wilds.

Need to know *Bothies are only to be used for short stays and are too small for groups any larger than six. The Mountain Bothy Association (Ⓦwww. mountainbothies.org.uk) costs £20 to join and members will be issued with details of where the various huts are located.*

006 STAY IN A BUNKHOUSE BARN IN THE BRECON BEACONS, WALES

As in all of the UK's national parks, the Brecon Beacons has plenty of hostels that offer budget accommodation for a single night. But there's also a network of locally run "bunkhouse" barns, which provide facilities for a longer stay. The concept of bunkhouses began in the Yorkshire Dales in the 1980s, where redundant agricultural barns near long-distance footpaths were converted into basic lodgings for hikers. The idea soon caught on in the Beacons, and there are now 24 bunkhouses in some of the park's most scenic areas, from Abergavenny in the east (where the Brecon Beacons Way begins) to Builth Wells in the north and Llandeilo in the far west.

A bunkhouse should provide all you'll need for several days in the outdoors, such as a drying room for wet kit, storage facilities, cooking equipment and hot showers. As the term "bunkhouse" suggests, the buildings can be as basic as just a collection of bunk-beds in a restored barn (such as the Wain House next to the medieval ruin of Llanthony Priory) but others are more sophisticated, with single and double beds in a cottage (like Perth-y-Pia, high up on Table Mountain near Crickhowell). Each bunkhouse is stocked with information on local walks and cycling paths as well as details of operators who run adventure activities nearby.

One of the most scenic bunkhouses is Trericket Mill near Talgarth, at the northern edge of the park. It's in secluded woodland across from the old mill, where you can treat yourself to dinner in the beautifully restored building. From Trericket you can walk along a path that follows the River Usk to Glasbury, where there's a good selection of food served in the boathouse. The owners also rent out canoes so you can paddle all the way to Hay-on-Wye, home to Britain's largest collection of secondhand books.

Need to know *Booking is advisable and in some cases essential. For details of each bunkhouse, including rates, see Ⓦwww.hostelswales.com/bunkhouses.htm. Twelve bunkhouses have joined together to coordinate information – for details, including local attractions and activities, see Ⓦwww.bootsbikesbunkhouses.co.uk. For canoe hire at Glasbury see Ⓦwww.wyevalleycanoes.co.uk; ☎ I 44 (0) 1497 047 213. More information on the park is at Ⓦwww.visitbreconbeacons.com.*

Bar and rooms at Llanthony Priory ruins; a welcome rest overlooking the Fan Hir escarpment, Brecon Beacons National Park

CAMPING

Tucked up inside a sleeping bag in your tent, camping pits you against the elements and is about as green a holiday as you can imagine. Once you've packed up camp, apart from the change in colour of the patch of grass where you were pitched, you're likely to leave the place as untouched as you found it. Large commercial campsites, however, can be a much less green proposition. When fields are packed with hundreds of campers all wanting to eat outdoors, use the toilet, shower and wash dishes, then the ecological footprint – as well as the rubbish – soon begins to build up. Here is a selection of campsites that go that bit further to make sure your camping holiday is as kind to the planet as it is to your wallet.

007 Huntstile Organic Farm, Somerset

A small campsite (only five pitches) on an organic farm in the foothills of the Quantocks. With so few other campers, it's possible to have a decent hot shower courtesy of solar power, plus you can enjoy the peaceful setting while barbecuing on a wood-burning stove. There are maps of farm walks to see wildlife ponds and their own "stone circle", but make sure you're back in time for the cream teas with home-grown organic strawberries. Nearby there are opportunities for mountain biking and horseriding.

Baslow Edge, Derbyshire

Need to know *Large "ecotents" (for up to twelve people) are available for hire in a separate part of the valley. For rates and further details see Ⓦwww. huntstileorganicfarm.co.uk; ☎+44 (0) 1278 662 358. Quantock Hills: Ⓦwww.quantockhills.org.uk.*

008 Bushey Heath Farm, Buxton, Derbyshire

A small, family-oriented campsite surrounded by woodland in the heart of the Peak District National Park. Rainwater is harvested to flush the toilets and a wind turbine provides all the electricity. There's also a bunk barn (with a ground-source heat pump for all heating and hot water), a static caravan and a bothy (see p.14), which were developed thanks to grants from the Sustainable Development Fund and the Low Carbon Buildings Trust. The farm shop sells free-range eggs, Fairtrade snacks, drinks and a selection of vegetarian frozen foods. The owners also keep a variety of animals, including Suffolk and Swale ewes, hens, guinea pigs, rabbits and chicks plus three Chilean alpacas in the field at the back.

Need to know *The nearest train stations are Dove Holes and Hope. For more details of the accommodation options and local information see Ⓦwww.busheyheathfarm.co.uk; ☎+44 (0) 1298 873 007. Peak District National Park: Ⓦwww. visitpeakdistrict.com.*

009 Caerfai Campsite, Pembrokeshire

Take a peek out of your tent and you'll see the beautiful Caerfai Bay and beyond that the rocky coastline of St Brides. Three fields at this organic (mostly dairy) farm near St David's on the Pembrokeshire coast are given over to camping, from Whitsun (around mid-to late May) until late September. The showers are heated by solar-thermal panels, there's a wind turbine to help power the lights in the toilet block, drinking water comes from the farm's own borehole and there are full recycling facilities. At the entrance to the campsite is a small shop, which sells organic cheeses and milk from the farm as well as other camping food essentials. The campsite is on the Pembrokeshire Coastal Footpath – one of Britain's best walks – and it's just a short walk down to the sheltered, sandy beach at Caerfai Bay.

Need to know *A twenty percent discount is offered if you arrive on foot. The nearest train station is Haverfordwest (about 25km away), from where you can take a taxi or catch bus 342 to within 1km of the campsite. Ⓦwww.cawscaerfai. co.uk; Ⓣ+44 (0) 1437 720 548.*

010 Deepdale Campsite, Norfolk

A quiet, family-friendly campsite in the north of Norfolk famous for its bird reserves and flat, open country ideal for cycling. There are

Relaxing under canvas

five "paddocks" for pitching tents, which are separated by landscaped trees planted by the owners. The campsite has a strict eco-policy: the toilet block is solar-powered and though you should expect to share the campsite with camper vans (there's also a backpackers' hostel on site), it is free from caravans and noisy generators. A few kilometres along the coast is Holkham Beach, used by the monarchy when they stay at nearby Sandringham. It's a wonderfully open beach with long dunes backed by a tall, shady pine forest and is one of the largest nature reserves in the country.

Need to know *The nearest train station is King's Lynn, from where you can catch the Norfolk Coasthopper bus (Ⓦwww.norfolkgreen.co.uk) to the campsite. For availability, rates and local attractions see Ⓦwww.deepdalefarm.co.uk; Ⓣ+44 (0) 1485 210 256.*

011 A DAY AT THE EDEN PROJECT, CORNWALL

Home to over a million plants and more than five thousand different species from around the world, the iconic "biomes" (gigantic greenhouses) at the Eden Project are the focus of the UK's premier green attraction. Built on the site of a former clay quarry, the Rainforest Biome houses plants from tropical islands, Malaysia, West Africa and South America, while the smaller biome displays citrus, olives, herbs and vines from the Mediterranean, the rich variety of proteas and aloes from southern Africa, drifts of colourful Californian poppies and lupins, and shrubs of the chaparral. Visitors are guided along the walkways by species labels and explanatory notes that describe how the plants are used for medicine, food and biofuel, and how a vision of a sustainable future is pinned to their survival.

Each year over a million people visit the Eden Project, many of whom arrive by bike, bus or train. It is by far the most successful visitor attraction in the southwest of England, largely thanks to the vision of chief executive Tim Smit (the man behind the Lost Gardens of Heligan) and also the ideas and labour of over five hundred staff, most of whom come from the local area.

On most days throughout the summer the Eden Project hosts attractions and events including theatre, workshops, art displays, gardening talks, children's events and music festivals. All the facilities are managed with sustainability in mind. The food in the cafés is local and organic; food waste is composted and used in the gardens; rainwater is harvested and used to irrigate the plants and flush the loos; and you get a discount if you arrive on foot or by bicycle.

Need to know *The nearest train station is St Austell, from where there's a shuttle bus to the Eden Project. Admission is free for children under 15. ⓦwww.edenproject.com; ☎+44 (0) 1726 811 911. Green places to stay nearby include Cornish Tipi Holidays and Cornish Yurt Holidays (see p.34), Higher Lank Farm (see p.29) and Trelowarren (see p.40).*

Top: the Mediterranean Biome at the Eden Project; Bottom: Tim Shaw's sculptures related to the wine god Bacchus at the Eden Project

012 HUNT A GEOCACHE

The GPS device gave the coordinates of the stash of goodies by the side of the lake, but it didn't reveal where exactly. That was down to the group of young sleuths who were following a map and instructions carefully as they walked around the water's edge. Then the instructions started making sense: the fallen log, the path off to the right and then the pile of stones under the oak tree. "Found it! Found it!" shouted one of the children. Within seconds the other kids had run over to share the goodies.

It's all part of the "geocaching" craze, the ultimate treasure hunt for children (and more adults than would like to admit it). Plastic boxes are packed with goodies by geocachers and hidden outdoors all over the country: by lakes, in woodland, at the top of hills, even in city parks. There are over half a million geocache locations worldwide and apparently over 25,000 in the UK alone.

Here's how it works: you choose where you'd like to go, download the coordinates of the nearest geocache from the website and set off. All you need is a GPS and the hope that the treasure really is there when you get there. It's a great way for children to become familiar with the outdoors and it'll keep them occupied for hours while you enjoy the fresh air.

Need to know *The name and description of the geocache described above has been kept sufficiently vague so as not to give the game away. Go find one yourself: ⓦwww.geocaching.com.*

013 EAT OUT AT BRIGHTON BEACH

The view from Due South looks out: through the converted fisherman's arch that houses the restaurant, over Brighton's pebbled beach, past its iconic West Pier and across the grey-blue English Channel to France. But the menu, which changes monthly depending upon what's in season, looks back to Britain: eighty percent of the ingredients are sourced from within 30km.

This could mean limited options, but instead Due South offers an innovative menu filled with such delicacies as quail, skate, asparagus and rabbit. Foods that remind you just how exciting English cooking can be, along with a varied European-only wine list that includes some rather excellent whites from Sussex. Due South may be surrounded by the piers, postcard sellers and fish-and-chip joints that symbolize the beach holidays of Britain's past, but by serving up the best of UK produce, its menu looks confidently to the future.

Need to know *Due South is located on the beach beneath West Street's Odeon cinema, at 139 Kings Road Arches. The best tables are outside or upstairs by the window. ⓦwww.duesouth.co.uk; ☏+44 (0) 1273 821 218.*

014 RETREAT TO LINCOLNSHIRE

It's back to basics at this small, self-catering lodge in Old Leake, Lincolnshire. Surrounded by woodland, there are just two rooms (each with two beds), an open-plan living area and a small kitchen. It's ideal as a get-away-from-it-all bolthole, a peaceful place where you can take a stroll in the nearby woods, go birdwatching in the Fenland sea marshes or cycle along the Hull-to-Harwich cycle route.

"Ecolodge" is a much overused title but here it is credible. Owners Geri and Andy (a woodsman) built the lodge using timber from land around their home. Electricity comes from a large wind generator and solar panels, plus there are compost toilets, filtered rainwater for washing and a wood-burning range. If you want to learn more about eco-living, the owners run workshops on charcoal-making and will gladly tell you how they live and breathe sustainability. The lodge even provides a shiatsu masseur to help it all sink in.

Need to know *The nearest train station is Boston (on the Nottingham to Skegness line), from where the owners can collect you by arrangement; a ten percent discount is offered if you arrive by train or bike. For rates and links to local producers and activities see ⓦwww.internationalbusinessschool.net/eco-lodge.htm; ☏+44 (0) 1205 871 396.*

The hydro-powered lift; a poppy growing in 30cm of soil on top of slate waste; interactive wind tunnel; a demonstration greenhouse

015 THE CENTRE FOR ALTERNATIVE TECHNOLOGY, WALES

When a small group of scientists and engineers founded the Centre for Alternative Energy in Powys in 1973, their ambitious outdoor project was regarded by many as a fanciful experiment rather than a means to investigate applicable, cutting-edge technology. For the founders, however, it was a vital focal point for them to test theories as well as create a showcase of their work for anyone who cared to take an interest. That was in the days when going green was considered extreme. Thirty years on, many of the fringe technologies that CAT has helped develop are now mainstream.

Pride of place is the hydro-powered lift that takes you from the ticket-office fifty metres up to the Centre, where exhibitions cover just about every eco technology under the sun, from solar thermals to wind turbines and vast woodchip boilers. The potential of wind power for Britain's energy requirements, for example, is one of CAT's key messages, and a vast multi-blade windmill has been modified into a "wind seat" so you can feel the full force of wind power. "Britain receives 40% of Europe's wind energy", says the signage, as if anyone in gale-battered Britain didn't already know.

But CAT isn't solely about demonstrating the power of alternative energy. There's an Eco-House, where you can learn how to decrease your home's carbon footprint, and a "Mole-Hole" – an underground cave with model organisms that are highly magnified to illustrate how many creatures in the soil are killed by pesticides.

And of course, energy-wise, CAT practises what it preaches. Not only does it run its restaurant, offices, conference centre and lifts using wind, solar and hydro power, it also creates so much surplus electricity that it sells it to the national grid. That would be impressive for a

small ecolodge, but CAT is a sprawling visitor attraction and research station that pulls in over sixty thousand visitors a year.

We could go on, but go see for yourself. Whether you go to CAT for a week-long education course, an intensive weekend or just to stroll about for an afternoon, it's likely you'll leave, scratching your head, thinking "I could do that".

Need to know *The nearest train station is Machynlleth, 5km south of the visitor centre. Admission is half price if you arrive by public transport. Further info on getting there, as well as courses, membership and local accommodation is at Ⓦwww.cat.org.uk; ☎+44 (0) 1654 705 950.*

016 CYCLE THE KINGFISHER TRAIL, IRELAND

Ireland's mountains might put off all but the hardiest cyclist, but choose your route carefully and you can enjoy days of pedalling along relatively flat cross-country terrain. The Kingfisher Trail is Ireland's first long-distance cycle route and covers some 370km across the vast network of lake-lands through the border counties of Fermanagh, Leitrim, Donegal, Sligo, Monaghan and Cavan.

The trail is designed as two loops in a figure-of-eight so you can explore the trail from a few days up to a week. There are thigh-busting sections over the Drumlins, but you can also choose to pedal alongside canals, through forests, across windswept heath, over sandy beaches and along meandering country lanes. The northern loop encircles the Lower Lough Erne, while the southern loop runs between Upper Lough Erne and Lough Allen. There are also shorter circular routes for day-trippers and young cyclists.

The trail is administered by Greenbox, an organization that develops ecotourism projects and sets standards for green accommodation and activities across the Emerald Isle.

Need to know *The Kingfisher Trail is Route 91 of the National Cycle Network. For maps and details of where to hire bikes along the route see Ⓦwww. cycletoursireland.com. The nearest train stations to the trail are at Sligo and Carrick-on-Shannon. Greenbox: Ⓦwww.greenbox.ie.*

017 ECO-STEERING AT LUSTY GLAZE, CORNWALL

It's billed as an eco-adventure, but getting "back to nature" is the last thing on your mind when you peer over a 10m cliff and see how far you have to jump into the sea below. As you step off the rock, be sure to jump out as far as you can, leaning forward with your legs tucked together and your body upright. When you hit the water your buoyancy aid lessens the impact but you can still turn a full somersault underwater. You'll emerge bobbing like a buoy and grinning like a dolphin.

Cliff jumping is just one of the activities you do on a day's "eco-steering" at Lusty Glaze Outdoor Adventure Centre in Newquay. It's a green spin on the coasteering craze, which involves swimming along the coast (in a wet suit and with a helmet), scrambling up barnacle-covered rocks and throwing yourself from a height into water. On an eco-steering trip, the emphasis is as much on education as it is on adrenaline. You're given an insight into the marine life that lives among the sea caves, blowholes and rocks along a stretch of spectacular Cornish coastline. So expect to get up close to slimy molluscs, identify seabirds that perch in the steep cliffs and learn about the seals, dolphins and basking sharks that visit the waters of southwest England. And expect to get exhilarated in the process.

Need to know *For details of activities at the Adventure Centre, as well as accommodation and dining options, see Ⓦwww.lustyglaze.co.uk; ☎+44 (0) 1637 872 444. The centre is a member of CoaST, the Cornwall Sustainable Tourism Project, which organizes various initiatives linking tourism with the local environment: Ⓦwww.cstn.org.uk.*

(Clockwise from top) Bluebells on Skomer; guillemots; puffin; curlews.

018 PHOTOGRAPH SEABIRDS ON SKOMER ISLAND, PEMBROKESHIRE

The sky is perfect blue and the ground covered with wild flowers; overhead, flurries of kittiwakes circle while gulls wheel and dive among the cliffs. The National Nature Reserve of Skomer Island – a 20min boat ride off the Pembrokeshire coast – is one of the best places in Britain to view seabirds, especially puffins. Though their numbers have dwindled elsewhere, a visionary sustainability project at Skomer has raised the puffin population here: there are now some six thousand breeding pairs on the island. So if you're after that elusive picture of a puffin with a silver sand eel clamped in its beak, this tiny island merits a stop.

Skomer is the second largest of the Pembrokeshire islands and also home to guillemots, razorbills and Manx shearwaters (to list just a few), as well as insects and small mammals, including the elusive Skomer vole. There are day-visits out to the island from Martin's Haven, but stay the night and you'll be treated to the nightly call of thousands of Manx shearwaters as they fly home under the cover of darkness.

Farmhouse accommodation on Skomer has recently been given a green makeover by the Wildlife Trust of South and West Wales, with tourist income put towards the island's conservation. Rainwater is harvested and hot showers come courtesy of a combination of wind and solar power – with enough electricity to keep batteries charged so you can review your day's pictures for as long as you want.

Need to know *From St David's catch the No. 400 Puffin Shuttle bus to Marloes and Martin's Haven, from where the ferry runs to Skomer (1 April–31 Oct). Ferry info: ⓦwww.dale-sailing.co.uk; ☎+44 (0) 1646 603 110. Further information on Skomer Island and accommodation is at ⓦwww.welshwildlife.org/skomerIntro_en.link.*

019 MILDEN HALL, SUFFOLK

Your first impression as you turn off the main road up the long drive to Milden Hall is of a typically grand country house in the heart of Suffolk. And that's what it is, but with a twist: the fifth-generation owner Christopher and his wife Juliet have turned their sixteenth-century estate into a sprawling, back-to-nature, family-friendly playground.

Each of the three period rooms in the main farmhouse caters for two on a B&B basis. The farmhouse is a listed building so the rooms – large and beautifully furnished with antiques, prints and pencil drawings – share the same bathroom. All have wide views of the walled garden and wild-flower meadows of the estate. Meanwhile, groups of up to 22 can self-cater in a wonderfully eccentric restored Tudor cartlodge, where you eat at a huge banquet table and sleep in Tudor oak beds.

In the farmhouse, a vast wood-burner fuelled by coppiced wood heats the large but surprisingly cosy living room as well as the bedrooms. There's a comprehensive compost and recycling programme, and the excellent breakfast (bantam eggs, sausages, fruit compote) is sourced either from the farm or local suppliers.

Juliet, an ecologist, has a "family activity pack" with over fifty suggestions for things kids can do, such as pond-dipping, leaf-sewing, moth-identifying and den-making in the woods. She also runs one- or two-hour guided nature trails on the estate. Adults, meanwhile, can forage for mushrooms, play tennis and explore the nearby medieval villages of Lavenham, Long Melford and Kersey.

Need to know *Bikes can be rented free of charge. The nearest train station is Sudbury, from where it's a 15min taxi ride to Milden (clarify that you want The Hall at Milden and not the town of Mildenhall). For rates, availability and more on activities and getting there see ⓦwww.thehall-milden.co.uk; ☎+44 (0) 1787 247 235.*

GREEN LONDON

It may not immediately seem a green city, but London has a burgeoning eco-movement, from barge communities to organic delis and farmers' markets. You'll see plenty more people on their bikes in the city centre these days too – although it's not for the faint of heart. Below is one possible itinerary for a greener day out in the English capital: a visit to a wetland centre, lunch or dinner with an eco-twist and then a buzzing clubbing experience where you can generate your own electricity.

020 London Wetland Centre

One of London's largest green spaces, the London Wetland Centre is a vast network of wetland habitats that's just 25min on the train from central London. It's run by the Wildfowl and Wetlands Trust and though it's a must-see for birders, it's also a great place to while away a few hours away from the crush of Oxford Street. You can wander the lakeside pathways and visit ponds, reed-bed marshes and wetland meadows, climb up a three-storey bird hide or just watch images of the birds from the more remote areas of the reserve that are beamed back to TV monitors in the visitor centre. Kids will like it too – there's a Discovery Centre with water games and an adventure playground with a zip wire, giant "water vole" tunnels and a safe climbing wall.

Need to know *The nearest train station is Barnes. There are free guided tours and bird feeds twice a day. ⓦwww.wwt.org.uk; ☎+44 (0) 208 409 4400.*

The London Wetland Centre

021 The Duke of Cambridge pub

A short walk from where Islington's farmers' market is held on a Sunday, "The Duke" has been going strong since it opened in 1998. Guests come as much for the mellow ambience – the soft lighting and wide wooden tables – as they do to sip organic ales, taste over forty organic wines (including twelve available by the glass) and feast on the excellent, seasonal, mainly British food (such as honey-pressed ham and braised beef) served in the main room of the pub or in the glass-roofed conservatory out the back. The restaurant's fish-purchasing policy has been approved by the Marine Conservation Society and the entire pub has been certified organic by the Soil Association. Expect to hear "Mine's a pint of Eco Warrior".

Need to know *The nearest tube station is Angel. See the website (*Ⓦ*www.dukeorganic.co.uk) for directions, bookings, sample menus and drinks lists.* Ⓣ*+44 (0) 207 250 3066.*

022 Acorn House restaurant

It's not often you get to eat a gourmet meal directly underneath where the ingredients are growing – and certainly not in London's King's Cross area, within walking distance of the Eurostar terminal. But from its rooftop vegetable garden using compost from leftovers to its fleet of biodiesel-powered delivery vans collecting fresh organic produce from local farms, Acorn House has been turning London dining upside-down since it opened in 2006.

Many restaurants still find that being bound by the seasons means limitations and an awful lot of root vegetables. But at Acorn House, the menu shows what's possible. Depending on the time of year this can mean wild mushrooms, quinces, scallops, asparagus and even lobster. And unlike most restaurants, where a second visit means revisiting the same menu, a return to Acorn House is a chance to discover the products of a whole new season.

Need to know *Acorn House Restaurant is located at 69 Swinton Street (nearest tube is King's Cross).* Ⓦ*www. acornhouserestaurant.com;* Ⓣ*+44 (0) 207 812 1842.*

023 Create some energy at Club Surya

At the Club for Climate night at Club Surya, in King's Cross, guests who can prove they've come by public transport get in free for a night of electro, hip-hop, techno and soul. But this is more than just a nice gimmick to attract eco-conscious Londoners wading through the listings for the capital's nightlife, as a closer inspection of the venue itself shows.

Club Surya is set apart by what's going on behind the scenes, and most of all, beneath your feet. Thanks to an innovative technology fitted into the dancefloor, the more clubbers shake their stuff, the more energy is transferred into a dynamo powering the club, with any surplus being donated free to the surrounding buildings.

Aside from this, the whole club is like a demonstration of how buildings can be designed with the environment in mind: it runs on solar and wind power, is fitted with low-energy plumbing and air-conditioning systems, and even the walls are made out of old mobile phones. And seeing how they benefit from any surplus electricity generated, it may be the first time in history that a nightclub's neighbours are asking the punters to keep dancing.

Need to know *Club Surya is on Pentonville Road, within walking distance of King's Cross.* Ⓦ*www. club4climate.com/surya.*

A hearty lunch at the Duke of Cambridge pub, Islington

024 TRAIN AND FERRY TO THE SCILLY ISLES

It's all very well choosing to travel by train as an environmentally friendly alternative to flying, but it's not much fun if you have to hang around in a soulless station waiting for an onward connection that never comes. Thankfully, travelling to the Scilly Isles involves an easy transition from train to ferry. There's a sleeper train service to Penzance in Cornwall, from where it's a short walk to the ferry terminal building at Penzance Quay. The *Scillonian III* ferry to the Scilly Isles is scheduled to leave about an hour after the train arrives, so there's plenty of time to pause for a pasty before you board. It takes just 2hr 40min to cross to the bustling harbour of St Mary's – from where you can head to the botanical gardens on Tresco, the laid-back island of Bryher, the Turk's Head inn on St Agnes, the white sands of St Martins…

Need to know *For timetables and fares for the Night Riviera sleeper train from London Paddington to Penzance see* Ⓦ*www.firstgreatwestern. co.uk. Sailing timetables, fares and general info on attractions in the Isles of Scilly at* Ⓦ*www. islesofscilly-travel.co.uk.*

The main harbour at St Marys, Scilly Isles

025 TAKE THE SLEEPER TRAIN FROM LONDON TO THE SCOTTISH HIGHLANDS

Board the Caledonian sleeper train one evening at Euston station and the following morning you'll wake up in the heart of the Scottish Highlands – a slow, subconscious teleport out of the urban grit and grind into the mountainous fresh and wild.

After leaving Euston at 9.15pm the train reaches Crewe just before midnight; it's then a long trundle overnight up to Scotland. The train has one- and two-bed cabins plus a lounge car with comfy chairs and a bar. If you wake up early, take a peak through the curtains and you'll see the vast, desolate heath bogs of the Central Highlands before the train passes over Spean Bridge and arrives at Fort William around 10am at the foot of Ben Nevis, Britain's highest peak.

From here you can join the second leg of the West Highlands Railway, one of the most brilliantly engineered and scenic train journeys in Britain. The track winds all the way to the coast in just under an hour and a half. From Fort William, the train crosses the Caledonian Canal over a swing bridge at Benavie before travelling

along the shores of Locheil and passing over the impressive 21-arch viaduct at Glenfinnan. There are wonderful snapshots of the Small Isles and Skye as the train runs past the silver sands of Morar before pulling in to Mallaig – a small fishing town and ferry port that's the gateway to the Outer Hebrides.

Need to know *Single travellers share sleeping berths only with passengers of the same sex. The sleeper runs daily except Saturday nights, year-round. Book early and you might be one of the lucky few to snap up a "Bargain Berth" ticket, from £19 single; otherwise tickets cost from £112 return. www.firstgroup.com/scotrail; tel: +44 (0) 845 755 0033.*

026 VOLUNTEER ON A NATIONAL TRUST WORKING HOLIDAY

Join a working holiday organized by the National Trust and do your bit for conservation while enjoying exclusive access to some of the UK's most secluded, beautiful and historic locations. These voluntary holidays are no longer just about hedge-laying and dry-stone walling; many of the Trust's four hundred working weekends and week-long breaks include learning a specific skill, from surfing to making cider, building a yurt or running an outdoor concert. Here are three of our favourites:

Work and Surf, Devon Spend five days helping wardens repair the coastal footpaths around Morte Coastal Estate, then receive two days' surfing lessons from a professional surf instructor on Woolacombe Beach.

Strangford Lough, Northern Ireland Explore the shoreline and islands of the largest sea-lake in Britain and Ireland, which is Northern Ireland's first marine nature reserve and home to some eighty islands. You'll help with conservation projects on the estate – typically by clearing scrub and planting trees – while staying at Castle Ward, a former gamekeeper's cottage in a wood alongside "the narrows", an 8km-long channel at the southern end of the lough.

Tidy up the North Yorkshire Moors Help clear vegetation on The Bridestones Nature Reserve and restore footpaths along the coast. The North York Moors National Park covers an area of almost 1500 square kilometres and contains the largest extent of heather moorland in England and Wales. It's a vast, beautiful and quiet place, with windswept heather, towering sea cliffs, protected beaches and grassy dales. You'll stay at Lockton Youth Hostel, one of the few accommodations in the UK to have earned the EU Flower, an eco label awarded to environmentally friendly places to stay. From the hostel there are some lovely walks in Cropton Forest and Levisham Beck, or you could extend your stay and cycle along the Moor to Sea cycle route – 130km of forest tracks, green lanes, minor roads and dismantled railway lines linking inland Pickering with the coastal towns of Scarborough and Whitby (Ⓦwww. moortoseacycle.net).

Need to know *Full information on all available working holidays at Ⓦwww.nationaltrust.org. uk/volunteering; ☎+44 (0) 844 800 3099. For photos, interviews with volunteers and a useful brochure that includes working holidays not on the website, contact Alison Dalby (alison.dalby@ nationaltrust.org.uk; ☎+44 (0) 1793 817 780).*

Volunteers repairing a dry-stone wall on Exmoor, north Devon

027 A LONG WEEKEND ON LUNDY ISLAND, DEVON

Two hours by boat off the north Devon coast, Lundy is perfect for a long weekend's mini-adventure, scrambling down steep banks to explore rock pools and coves on the protected east coast, or taking blustery walks along the exposed west coast where a Georgian cannon and Britain's highest lighthouse sit atop the cliffs. Lundy was once famous for its resident puffin population, and though numbers have dwindled in recent years, the island is still home to a handful of breeding pairs. The rugged coastline is also a magnet for climbers, attracted to the island's many challenging rockfaces.

Lundy is England's only marine reserve, established to protect the huge variety of aquatic life around the island, including sea fans, branching sponges and cup coral. A marine warden runs wildlife-watching trips in summer: you can snorkel or dive to see the island's resident grey seals, and you might even spot one or two basking sharks off the coast.

On land, it's a quiet and gentle place – free from cars and city lights – where wild ponies, Soay sheep and Sika deer roam among moorland and heath. The only inhabitants are the few people who look after the island's buildings – a church, a small convenience store, a pub and over twenty properties, managed by the Landmark Trust, which it has restored as holiday lets. These include cottages, dormitory-style barns, a lighthouse, a late-Regency house (for twelve people) and a thirteenth-century castle. The remote Tibbetts is the only one that has no electricity, while the Old Schoolhouse, a cottage for two overlooking the sea, is just a short walk from the pub, where you can enjoy good, home-cooked food and island-brewed beer by a large wood fire.

Need to know *For accommodation: Landmark Trust (Ⓦwww.landmarktrust.org.uk; ☎+44 (0) 1628 825 925); for boat tickets to the island: Lundy Shore Office (☎+44 (0) 1271 863 636). See also Ⓦwww.lundyisland.co.uk for more on activities, wildlife and the island's history.*

Walkers on Lundy's exposed west coast

Braving the snow, Coed Llandegla Forest

028 DOWN ON THE FARM AT HIGHER LANK FARM, CORNWALL

This one is for families. In fact, you can only stay at Higher Lank Farm, a listed fifteenth-century working farm near Bodmin, if you have at least one child under five. It might sound like age discrimination, but anyone who has a pre-school child will understand the benefits of staying in a place that not only tolerates the little darlings but actually focuses your stay around them.

B&B is in the main farmhouse building or there's self-catering in a seventeenth-century en-suite barn called "Bo Peep Cottage". Many things you might need for your stay are provided so that you can travel there light. There are books, games and jigsaw puzzles, hundreds of DVDs, highchairs and booster seats, baby carriers and spare buggies. The owners even offer a trial of real nappies and wash them free of charge throughout your stay.

The "nursery rhyme" barns have their own underfloor heating and wood-burning stoves. There are stair gates, fire- and cooker-guards and children can sleep in cots or hand-made miniature beds with bed-guards. Outside, there's a separate children's play area with its own toddler-proof gate, toy rides and a sandpit. After breakfast, kids are taken to feed the chickens, ducks, geese and guinea fowl, then lots of other activities are arranged, including a "tractor and trailer adventure" to the Camel River to look for eels and baby salmon. If you have older children, they can help put the animals to bed and give the orphan lambs a bedtime bottle (if you're there in spring). Nursery teas begin at 5.30pm, after which, if you still have any energy left, you can slope off to the pub while the babysitters take over.

Need to know *The nearest train station is Bodmin Parkway, from where staff will collect you by arrangement. Babysitting costs £10 per hour per family. For more on accommodation prices and availability, local attractions and activities see ⓦwww.higherlankfarm.co.uk; ☎+44 (0) 1208 850 716.*

029 MOUNTAIN BIKING AT COED LLANDEGLA FOREST, WALES

If you fancy a day outdoors, then how about this: start the day with what has been officially recognized as the best breakfast in Wales, then hurtle across forest trails, up and over a maze of muddy tracks in the fresh country air before returning to the One Planet Adventure Café for a snack of home-made soup and organic bread. Sound good?

Coed Llandegla is a purpose-built mountain-biking centre, 11km from Wrexham, in the heart of a forest that has been certified by the Forestry Stewardship Council. There are over 30km of graded mountain-bike trails, from green routes for beginners and families to red and black runs for experienced riders. Mindful of the potential damage mountain biking can cause, the owners carried out an environmental impact assessment before they designed the cycle circuit. In addition to this, the log-cabin visitor centre is powered by solar panels and geothermal energy, and rainwater is used to flush the loos and wash the bikes. So you can pedal for all you're worth and need only worry about hidden roots or low-hanging branches.

Need to know *For bike rental costs, opening hours, trail routes and how to get there, see ⓦwww.coedllandegla.com; ☎+44 (0) 1978 751 656. Details of mountain-bike courses at Coed Llandegla are at ⓦwww.oneplanetadventure.com.*

(Clockwise from top left) Hiker surveying the wild landscape near Loch Ossian; red deer stags on Rannoch Moor; Loch Ossian Youth Hostel; Rannoch Moor and The Black Mount

030 BAG A MUNRO ON RANNOCH MOOR, SCOTLAND

It's just a three-minute walk from Corrour train station before you find yourself in the middle of nowhere. A single path winds round the back of the station's café (which does a good breakfast of bacon butties) and after a few hundred metres, the train tracks are obscured by a grassy embankment. Pan round 360 degrees and all you'll see is the wild expanse of Rannoch Moor, a plateau of bog and heath flanked by shadowy mountains in the heart of the Scottish Highlands.

Corrour Station is a request stop on the West Highland line from Glasgow to Fort William (if you're travelling up from London you can catch the Caledonian Sleeper all the way – see p.26). Though remote, after a couple of kilometres' walk you'll reach Loch Ossian Youth Hostel, which is tucked between a clump of birch and rowan trees and is the only visible property on the bank of the spectacular loch, a long stretch of water flanked by high peaks with forest at the far end. A single-storey building with twenty beds in two dorms, the hostel has a fully equipped self-catering kitchen, electricity courtesy of a wind turbine and solar panels, and a multi-fuel stove for heating. There are compost toilets and a reed-bed filtration system for waste water, though there are no laundry facilities or bed linen, so bring a sleeping bag.

It makes a great base from which to explore the wildlife and mountains of Rannoch Moor. Otters live on the loch, over a hundred species of birds have been logged by the hostel's warden, and roe deer, red squirrels and pine martens are regularly seen on the mountainside and in the surrounding forests. There are eight Munros (hills over 3000ft) within walking distance of the hostel, including Carn Dearg ("Red Hill") at 3080ft, Stob Coire Sgriodain ("Peak of the Corrie of Scree") at 3211ft and the region's highest mountain, Beinn Eibhinn ("Rough Hill"), at an intimidating 3611ft.

From the top of any of these Munros you can see as far west as Ben Nevis and north beyond the River Spean, across lochs, glens and moor. Rannoch Moor is certainly remote, but it proves the rule that the best places are often the hardest to reach.

Need to know *Book a bed or the entire hostel for a group at ⓦwww.syha.org.uk/SYHA/web/ site/Hostels/LochOssian.asp; ☏+44 (0) 870 155 3255. Information on the Caledonian Sleeper at ⓦwww.firstscotrail.com; ☏+44 (0) 8457 550 033.*

031 LUDLOW FOOD FESTIVAL, SHROPSHIRE

For the sausage lover, there's no more apt place of pilgrimage than the annual Ludlow Food Festival. Each year in this medieval town in the Welsh Marches, whose high street of timber-fronted shops is one of Britain's most striking, the town's six independent butchers compete to produce the best new variety of banger. Willing participants on the Sausage Trail sate themselves by walking from shop to shop, sampling and voting on each one.

Established in 1995, Ludlow has grown to become the UK's most famous food fair – a celebration of local cuisine and a means to protect the livelihoods of small producers and the environment they work in. It's a great place to discover what the Slow Food movement is all about: visitors can try out breadmaking courses and tasting sessions of some of the finest real ales, ciders and perries in the country. Ludlow is also the UK headquarters of Città Slow, a Slow Food spin-off dedicated to promoting quality of life, local produce and diversity in small towns. Of course, if you've just eaten six sausages, all this slowing down should come fairly easily.

Need to know *The food festival, featuring more than 150 independent food producers, takes place in September each year. More at ⓦwww. foodfestival.co.uk.*

032 AUTUMN IN THE LAKE DISTRICT AT SOUTHWAITE GREEN

Most of the ten million annual visitors to the Lake District come in the summer. But go in the autumn and you'll enjoy the fabulous combination of heritage, lakes and fells when it's a more mellow place: the air is fresher, mist hangs low over the water and the thick forests are iridescent with the colours of the season.

Southwaite Green is a collection of four self-catering eco cottages in the heart of the eastern lakes, 40min from Wordsworth's birthplace in Cockermouth and near some of the best walking country in the Lakes. The cottages overlook Lamplugh Fells and are near to the dramatic Western Lakes of Crummock Water and Buttermere, from where you can walk over the high, narrow ridge at Whiteless Pike to the beautiful Derwent Water, bordered by woods and towering crags, and known locally as the "Queen of the Lakes". From Derwent Water you can catch a ferry to Keswick, where there's a bus back to Cockermouth, or you can take the easier option

of spending the day strolling along the woodland path around Lake Buttermere and enjoying the views of Fleetwith Pike and Haystacks. After a day in the fresh air, amble back to Southwaite for a hot bath and – arranged by the owner – a local pasty and traditional Cumbrian beer.

The eco cottages are the vision of owner Marna Mcmillin, whose day-job is to help run a company that funds community-owned renewable energy schemes. Her aim is to provide luxury accommodation in traditional Cumbrian farm buildings but with an environmentally sensitive design. So although the cottages are made with local stone and slate roofs supported by high beams, the walls have super-thick insulation, there are solar thermal panels for water heating, a bio-digester to deal with waste water and an innovative ground-source heating system beneath the slate and oak floors.

The grounds of the cottages are being landscaped with trees, organic fruit beds and wild-flower meadows. It's sufficiently far away from the crowds at Cockermouth and if you're there out of season you'll feel like you have the Lakes to yourself.

Need to know
Southwaite Green donates ten percent of its profits to Action Aid and Third World Organics, and there's a ten percent discount if you arrive by public transport. The nearest train station is Penrith, from where you can catch the X4/X5 bus service to Cockermouth; the owner will pick you up there by arrangement. For more on the cottages, rates and sites of local interest see Ⓦwww. southwaitegreen.co.uk; Ⓣ+44 (0)1900 821 055.

Wooden jetty on Derwent Water

033 RAIL AND SAIL FROM LONDON TO DUBLIN

The schlep across land and sea to Dublin used to be more of a chore than a holiday. The cold, trundling train across Wales, the characterless waiting room at Holyhead and then the slow, stomach-churning, pitch-and-roll ferry ride across the Irish Sea. No wonder the no-frills airlines have had a ball.

But times have changed. You can now travel by train across the English and Welsh countryside on a fast, direct service from London Euston that'll whizz you to Holyhead in just over four hours. The clean and modern ferry building there has an efficient check-in system (so you don't have to haul your bags around the ferry) and the departure times now tie in with the train's arrival so there's little time for waiting-room boredom. What a difference joined-up transport makes – and it's cheaper than flying too: the return route from London to Dublin should cost you only a little more than £50 even if booked at short notice. The fast ferry across to Dublin takes less than two hours – just enough time to watch a film in the on-board cinema or have a meal in the restaurant before you coast in to Dublin port and head for a pint of the black stuff in Temple Bar.

Need to know Tickets can be booked via websites such as Ⓦwww.raileasy.co.uk or Ⓦwww.sailrail.co.uk.

034 ACTION AND ADVENTURE AT DELPHI MOUNTAIN RESORT, IRELAND

It's not unusual to experience four seasons in one day in the west of Ireland. As they say in these parts: "If you don't like the weather, wait a minute." So it's no surprise that there's an activity to suit every kind of weather at Delphi Mountain Resort, an outdoors activity centre in the Connemara forests in Galway.

There are over twenty different activities to choose from, including cycling, canoeing, archery, hill-walking, rock-climbing and raft-building. You can sea-kayak around Ireland's only fjord, learn to surf at Cross Beach and if the weather takes a turn for the worse, you can scramble up the walls in the indoor climbing centre. Afterwards you can soothe aching muscles in the spa, treat yourself to a therapeutic massage or take a dip in an organic seaweed bath.

As well as this, the resort has a strong emphasis on sustainability. The water is sourced from a spring, it has its own waste-water treatment plant and the heating comes from two woodchip boilers that use wood from the surrounding forest.

Need to know The nearest train station is Westport, from where the owners can collect you by arrangement. For directions, rates, local attractions and details of activities, spa treatments and accommodation, see Ⓦwww.delphimountainresort.com; ☎ +353 (0) 9542 208.

035 GO WWOOFING

There's no such thing as a free lunch, but thanks to WWOOF (World Wide Opportunities on Organic Farms) there is such a thing as a free stay while you help grow other people's lunch. WWOOF is an international organization that puts you in touch with organic farms and smallholdings looking for a helping hand in return for board and lodging. Often they're run by people living alternative lifestyles in some fantastic locations – in the UK you can stay in a croft in the Outer Hebrides, a commune in Pembrokeshire and a small farm in the remote Irish countryside. It's a great way to travel around on a budget and learn a thing or two about organic living, but be warned – it's not for slackers.

Need to know More information on volunteering opportunities throughout the world at Ⓦwww.wwoof.org.

YURT AND TIPI CAMPS

Yurt and tipi camps have been springing up all over Britain. They range from a single canvas structure pitched in a farmer's spare field to multi-tent sites spread over tracts of woodland and with all the activities and facilities you'd expect at a modern campsite. Indeed, many are now designed for luxury camping: they have floorboards and supported walls and are spacious enough to house a double bed, comfy chairs, basic cooking equipment and a stove to keep you snug under a sheepskin blanket. Here are our top ten favourites:

036 Full Circle Yurts, Lake District

Three Mongolian yurts in the beautiful grounds of Rydal Hall, a historic house between Grasmere and Ambleside. The yurts are made by a Mongolian yurt-maker in Ulan Bator and have been shipped to the UK by the owners. Each yurt has a wood stove, a gas cooker, a bookcase and several beds (double and single pull-out mattresses on wooden stacks) around the perimeter. The estate also manages its own campsite on the grounds and guests have access to all the usual amenities, such as a shower block and dishwashing facilities which draw on the local spring water.

Need to know *The nearest train station is Windermere; from there you can take a Stagecoach bus (nos. 554 to 556). For further info on the yurts, location and rates see ⓦwww.lake-district-yurts.co.uk; ☎+44 (0) 1539 821 278. There's also an excellent "Hawk Walk": spend an afternoon walking in the nearby woodland with a falconer who carries bait for the hawk as it follows you overhead. (☎+44 (0) 7960 159 167; costs £150).*

037 Cornish Yurt Holidays

Two handmade, stylish yurts tucked among oak and hawthorn trees on the western edge of Bodmin Moor. The camp has no electricity, but a wood-burning stove in each yurt provides lots of heat and there are lanterns to help you find your way around the futons and huge floppy cushions. There's a small compost toilet yurt and a cosy bathroom yurt, where you can soak in a roll-top bath by the heat of a crackling wood fire under the night sky.

Full Circle Yurts: a taste of Mongolia in the Lake District

Need to know *Open March to October. The nearest train station is Bodmin Parkway, from where the camp is a 25min taxi ride. Cyclists can follow the National Cycle Route 3 (the Camel Trail) to St Breward. Campcraft courses available for children in summer school holidays. For more info, including prices and availability, see Ⓦwww.yurtworks.co.uk; ☎+44 (0) 1208 850 670.*

038 Larkhill Tipis, West Wales

A wind- and solar-powered yurt and tipi camp on a smallholding in Carmarthenshire. Three tall tipis, each with several futons around a central wood fire, are positioned in their own landscaped terraced area surrounded by a wild-flower meadow, while two mushroom-shaped canvas yurts – made from local ash and oak – are tucked away in woodland. There's also a solar-powered log cabin for hot showers.

Need to know *Tipis open from April to October; yurts closed in February and March only. The nearest train station is Carmarthen, from where the owners will collect by arrangement. For more on prices, availability and the surrounding area see Ⓦwww.larkhilltipis.co.uk; ☎+44 (0) 1559 371 581.*

039 Barefoot Yurts, Sussex

Two modern Mongolian yurts (accommodating one group between them) at the edge of woodland near Rye in the Sussex countryside. One has an ornate handmade oak bed and wood-burner, while the other is the sitting room, with a large table, sofa and a central stove. Next door is a log cabin with a shower and a fully equipped kitchen, which has a cooker, barbecue, fridge, sink and running water. The owners provide home-grown fruit and veg, and you can order a box of local dairy products.

Need to know *For bookings, rates, directions and local attractions see Ⓦwww.barefoot-yurts.co.uk; ☎+44 (0) 1424 883 057.*

Best of the rest

040 Fforest, Wales

Swedish Kata tipis, geodesic domes and tunnel tents (all pitched on elevated decks) at a modern campsite near Cardigan Bay. Ⓦwww.coldatnight.co.uk; ☎+44 (0) 1239 623 633.

041 Cornwall Tipi Holidays

Britain's first and biggest tipi camp: forty North American tipis scattered throughout a wooded valley near Port Isaac on Cornwall's north coast. Ⓦwww.cornishtipiholidays.co.uk; ☎+44 (0) 1208 880 781.

042 Orchard Acre Farm, County Fermanagh, Northern Ireland

A single 6m tipi on a small farmholding near Lower Lough Erne. Organic hampers can be ordered. Ⓦwww.orchardacrefarm.com; ☎+44 (0) 286 862 1066.

043 Tamar Village Tipis, Devon

Three tipis on a working farm overlooking the Tamar Valley, decorated with traditional Native American artwork. Ⓦwww.tamarvalleytipis.co.uk; ☎+44 (0) 845 456 0302.

044 Ardfern Tipis, Scotland

Three tipis on a hill by Loch Craignish on the west coast. Ⓦwww.ardferntipis.co.uk; ☎+44 (0) 1852 500 715.

045 Yurt Village, Dorset

Six Mongolian yurts (with double and single futons) in woodland, 1.5km from a beach. Ⓦwww.yurtvillage.co.uk; ☎+44 (0) 192 942 2932.

(From top) The blue bedroom at Barefoot Yurts; Cornish Tipi Holidays; Cornish Tipi totem

046 CAMPING AND KAYAKING IN THE SUMMER ISLES, SCOTLAND

The protected sandy beaches and shallow shores of the Summer Isles are perfect places to land a kayak and pitch a tent for the night. If you like the idea, canoeing tours organized by Wilderness Scotland make for an excellent choice: there can't be many trips that leave so little trace behind them.

The journey begins and ends at Inverness train station, where you're taken by minibus across the northwest of Scotland to Achiltibuie, the launchpad to the Summer Isles. Paddling 12–14km daily for five days, guests are led along the rugged coastline of this remote archipelago, under sea arches and over water surges between narrow channels of rocks. You pass the dramatic sandstone cliffs of Eilean Flada Mar and its outlying skurries, the dramatic peaks of Assynt, the island of Eilean Mullagrach and the wildlife reserve of Isle Ristol.

Along the way, you may see dolphins, whales, seals and a huge variety of birds, including golden eagles. After setting up camp late in the afternoon on one of the many islands, dinner is prepared and eaten in a communal tipi before retiring to your tent under a clear night's sky.

Sea kayaking enables you to get to remote places like the Summer Isles that you wouldn't otherwise be able to reach. Yet these fragile ecosystems can easily be ruined if you ignore a few simple guidelines on how to respect the great outdoors. Head guide Myles Fairbank, an experienced kayaker, has one simple rule of engagement with the wilderness – leave it as you found it. Group size is limited to just eight kayakers, which minimizes impact and also means you're more likely to see wildlife en route.

Myles insists that all rubbish is carried away from each campsite, so you become far more conscious of how much food you cook; the last thing you want to carry in your canoe is half a

Kayaking in the Summer Isles

saucepan of stodgy porridge. Tents are pitched only on tough vegetation (rather than fragile turf, such as moss and lichen) and you are even taught how to dig a toilet deep into the soil so your waste won't pollute the ecosystem. But perhaps the most important thing you learn is how to build a "mound fire" that won't leave a mark after you've left camp – typical of the attention to detail that has won Wilderness Scotland several awards for sustainable tourism.

On the final day, just before the approach to land, Myles suggests that you lay down your paddle and spend a few minutes drifting on the water in quiet contemplation. It's an opportunity to appreciate the silence and solitude of the Summer Isles one last time and remember what it has been like to experience true wilderness. A sensitively managed pitch-and-paddle trip like this helps keep it that way.

Need to know *Wilderness Scotland offers a range of guided and non-guided activity holidays across Scotland, including walking, sailing and mountain biking. For details of these see Ⓦwww.wildernessscotland.com; ☏+44 (0) 131 625 6635. Kayaking trips to the Summer Isles run from April to September.*

047 ECO-CHIC AT STRATTONS HOTEL AND RESTAURANT, NORFOLK

The market town of Swaffham in Norfolk is hardly cutting-edge, yet its most celebrated hotel, Strattons, sets a worldwide standard for green accommodation. Equally surprising is that this family-run hotel is not your usual socks-and-sandals eco-retreat. It's a smart country house that's as much a Bohemian bolthole as it is a green escape.

Strattons' owners have transformed a Grade II-listed Queen Anne villa into an eclectic mix of ostentatious art and modern living. There are busts and statues along the walkways and murals and paintings crammed on the walls. Among the

ten stylish, individually decorated rooms, "Stalls" has lip-stick-patterned pillowcases and a fluffy carpet, the "Boudoir" has wallpaper splashed with Renaissance art print and the theatrical "Red Room" includes a four-poster bed and fireplace.

Guests come as much for the award-winning food as they do for the luxury accommodation. It serves only local, seasonal and organic food wherever possible (which is genuine). For dinner, there are local delicacies such as smoked Narborough trout, cheese from Swaffham's market and beer from the Brecks; for breakfast, there are kippers from Cley Smokehouse, organic porridge and fruit juice from nearby Ashill Fruit Farm.

Behind the scenes, the owners are waging a private war on waste. Once guests have checked out, staff swoop in to rifle through the bins to see what can be recycled, given to charity or composted. Almost everything is given a new home: magazines are sent off to doctors' waiting rooms, carrier bags are given to local market traders, organic food waste is used to fertilize the vegetable garden. What's left is then weighed to assess how much rubbish is produced. It may sound obsessive, but it works. According to the owners, just two percent of the hotel's total waste is sent to landfill.

A country house, a boutique hotel, a green escape. Strattons is all three. It's surprising how well eco and chic blend together here, and it leaves the lasting impression that being green can be simple and stylish.

Need to know *Ten percent discount offered if you arrive by public transport: take the train to King's Lynn then the local X-1 bus to Swaffham Market Place. Info on rooms, rates, availability and local activities at Ⓦwww.strattonshotel.com; ☏+44 (0) 1760 723 845.*

(From top) The grade II-listed Queen Anne villa and well-manicured gardens at Strattons; a resident cockerel; the grand entrance to one of Norfolk's most opulent guesthouses

048 WILD CAMPING ON THE KNOYDART PENINSULA, SCOTLAND

Few places on mainland Britain are as remote as the Knoydart peninsula in the West Highlands. Bounded on either side by Loch Nevis and Loch Hourn and facing across to the Inner Hebrides, you can only reach Knoydart by taking the train up to Mallaig and then the ferry across Loch Nevis – or by walking in along a rough 25km trek from the end of the road at Kinlochourn; there are no roads across the intervening hills.

You're free to pitch a tent almost anywhere in Scotland thanks to the Land Reform Act (Scotland) 2003 – as long as you're well away from dwellings and roads. There isn't a formal campsite anywhere on Knoydart, but there are plenty of places to pitch a tent in the wild: on moorland, in wooded areas and by the beach. You won't have any of the usual campsite amenities to hand, but without running the risk of sharing the experience with other rowdy campers you'll be that much closer to nature.

Rangers from the Knoydart Foundation (whose office is in the village of Inverie) can suggest some good places to pitch your tent. One of the best places to camp is a level area just behind the "long beach", a short stroll round the bay where the ferry drops you off at Inverie harbour. You can also arrange with the Knoydart Foundation to hire a boat for fishing or go on one of their guided walks to explore the sea lochs and bays around the islands, including Folach waterfalls and Sandaig bay.

After a day exploring the Knoydart wilderness, spend the evening in Inverie village at The Old Forge (recognized by the *Guinness Book of Records* as mainland Britain's most remote pub), where you'll have to compete with the motley collection of folk musicians, friendly locals, kayakers and campers for the pub's excellent range of fresh food, including freshly caught scallops, Loch Nevis langoustine, Loch Nan Uamh rope mussels, Isle of Rhum lobsters and Skye oysters.

Need to know *The Caledonian Sleeper train travels from London to Fort William, from where you can then take the local train up to Mallaig (ⓦwww.scotrail.com; ☎+44 (0) 845 601 5929). The ferry from Mallaig to Knoydart is operated by Bruce Watts Cruises (ⓦwww.knoydart-ferry.co.uk; ☎+44 (0) 1687 462 320). Knoydart Foundation Ranger Service: ⓦwww.knoydart-foundation. com; ☎+44 (0) 1687 462 242. The Old Forge Pub: ⓦwww.theoldforge.co.uk; ☎+44 (0) 1687 462 267. Helpful guidelines on outdoor camping are provided by The Mountaineering Council of Scotland: ⓦwww. mountaineering-scotland.org. uk/leaflets/ wildcamp.html.*

049 EXPLORE THE NORTH PENNINES

The North Pennines, which covers an area of two thousand square kilometres, is the second-largest Area of Outstanding Natural Beauty (AONB) and one of the last remaining protected areas of wilderness in England. It's an upland

Surveying the Knoydart Peninsula

plateau at the northern limit of the Pennine Mountains with heather moorland and blanket peat, hay meadows, rivers and waterfalls. Following a terminal decline in traditional lead-mining, tourism is one of the few industries left that is helping to stem the loss of rural services.

One of the greenest places to stay in the North Pennines is Langdon Beck Youth Hostel in the heart of Teesdale. A wind turbine and photovoltaic panels generate more than sixty percent of the 31-bed hostel's power, while solar panels heat the water. Sheep's wool and recycled newspapers provide the insulation and rainwater is collected from the roof. The hostel also serves dinner and stocks a range of local ales and organic wines. Langdon Beck is also near to the "High Force" – England's highest waterfall, with a 21m drop.

Need to know *Cycling, birding and walking guides for the North Pennines can be downloaded from ⓦwww.northpennines.org.uk, which also covers accommodation options. The nearest train station to Langdon Beck Youth Hostel (ⓦwww.yha. org.uk; ☎+44 (0) 845 371 9027) is Darlington. From there you can take the Arriva 75/76 bus to Middleton-in-Teesdale, then the Upper Teesdale bus link 73 to the hostel.*

050 GO EASY ON YOURSELF AND THE PLANET AT TITANIC SPA, YORKSHIRE

Is it really possible to indulge in a luxury wellness treatment while doing the planet a favour? The masseurs, therapists and beauticians at Titanic Spa certainly think so. They call their health-and-wellbeing retreat in the heart of Yorkshire – complete with steam and ice rooms, a sauna, hammam, mud-chamber and foot-bath – "the UK's first eco-spa".

The world of luxury travel is littered with spas that claim they are environmentally friendly, but more often than not they do little more than provide organic products in the treatment rooms

and Fairtrade food in the bistro. As for the rest, the huge amounts of energy required to power a spa and the colossal amounts of water waste they generate mean their businesses are about as "holistic" as a hole in the wall.

Titanic Spa, however, genuinely addresses the environmental challenges that are fundamental to running such a resource-intensive business. It's based in a converted textile mill (built in 1912, the same year as the Titanic ocean liner was commissioned) in the village of Linthwaite, close to Huddersfield at the edge of the Pennines. It comprehensively insulates its rooms, supplies its own electricity using solar panelling and heats its water via a biomass-generator that uses woodchips from sustainable forests. Water is provided from its own borehole – the original water source for the mill, proudly on display in front of the building – which provides drinking water and supplies the chlorine-free pool and showers.

Relaxing at Titanic Spa

But all this doesn't come at the expense of unconditional pampering. You can "Relax, Detox, Flow and Tonic" your whole body or just your little toe. Titanic, at least, is one of the few spas doing its bit to help leave your conscience as clean as your skin.

Need to know *The nearest train station is Huddersfield, from where it's a 15min taxi ride. ⓦwww.titanicspa.com; ☎+44 (0) 1484 843 544.*

051 STAY IN AN ECO COTTAGE ON THE TRELOWARREN ESTATE, CORNWALL

The daily dilemma at Trelowarren is whether to stay within the privacy of the estate (where there are several woodland walks, an award-winning restaurant, a Cornish arts exhibition, tennis court, outdoor heated swimming pool and walled garden) or leave the historic grounds to explore the surrounding Lizard Peninsula, the most southerly tip of the British Isles and an Area of Outstanding Natural Beauty.

Trelowarren is one of Britain's oldest estates. It is mentioned in the Domesday Book and has

One of the new wooden eco cottages at Trelowarren; Kynance Cove

been owned by a local Cornish family – the Vyvyans – for six centuries. The vision of Trelowarren's owner, Sir Ferrers Vyvyan, is to turn the estate into a luxury, self-catering holiday village that is carbon neutral. With this in mind he has planted over 100,000 trees, restored seven barns and cottages adjacent to the main estate building, and nearby, a short walk along a woodland track (created for a visit by Queen Victoria), has built eight wooden cottages, available to buy as a timeshare or to rent for self-catering.

The cottages (each with two or four bedrooms) are designed with an impressive raft of eco-features. The walls and roof are made of timber from sustainable sources, the paints and waxes are non-toxic, the walls are insulated with recycled newspaper and the water comes from the estate's own source. But Trelowarren's most substantial eco-initiative is its seven-tonne woodchip Binder boiler, fuelled by wood from the estate's coppiced forest, which ensures the heat for all the cottages is self-renewable.

The main walk around the estate is about 6km long, but there are several other woodland trails, including an 8km round-trip to Tremayne Quay. Afterwards, you can cool off in the swimming pool and eat at the adjacent New Yard Restaurant, which sources ninety percent of its ingredients from within a 15km radius. Expect locally caught fish, clams from the Helford River and game, herbs and fruit sourced from the estate.

If you can drag yourself out of Trelowarren's comfort zone, there are some fabulous beaches to explore around the coastline of the Lizard, such as Kennack, Pentreath, Polurrian and Mullion. One of the most picturesque is the National Trust-owned Kynance Cove, accessible only by foot, east of the Lizard Point. Just behind the cove there's a beach café run on solar power, and the waters here are unpolluted thanks to an innovative biological waste-water treatment system. Inland, you can walk across the Lizard's National Nature Reserve at Goonhilly and spend a day at Tregellast Barton Farm near St Keverne, a working organic farm where the kids can help milk the cows and eat the famous Roskilly organic ice cream and fudge.

Need to know *For more on the estate, timeshare options and details of the self-catering cottages (including availability and rates) see ⓦwww. trelowarren.co.uk; ☎+44 (0) 1326 222 105. The nearest train stations to Trelowarren are Truro or Redruth, approximately 45min by taxi. Biodiesel taxi service: ⓦwww.biotravel.co.uk; alternatively, hire an electric car: ⓦwww.eco-drive.co.uk. Roskillys Organic Farm: ⓦwww.roskillys.co.uk; ☎+44 (0) 1326 280 479.*

052 SURFING IN CORNWALL

It's all about timing. As you feel the wave touch your toes at the back of the board, you push down with your hands and spring up onto your feet, looking straight ahead as the energy of the breaker thrusts you forward. You've a split second to adjust your balance: get it wrong and you'll be flung off the board into the tumbling surf; get it right and you can harness the power of the water to carve out a sweeping arc along the face of the curling wave. Either way, it's fun: all you need is a board and a bit of nerve.

Local surfers have long known that Cornwall's Atlantic coastline is something special, though only recently has it become internationally accepted as a first-class surfing location. Cornwall's economy has prospered as a result,

Surf's up at Chapel Porth Beach

yet this has come at a price: Cornwall's capital of surf, Newquay, now welcomes thousands of summer "surf tourists", but in their wake have come traffic congestion, amusement arcades and pollution.

Global Boarders is a holiday company that is trying to put the soul back into Cornwall's surfing. Based in Penzance, 80km west of Newquay on the south coast, it runs small-group and family-surfing holidays (with lessons for all levels) at alternative destinations throughout western Cornwall. Guests are encouraged to arrive by rail at Penzance, from where there's a free transfer to their large converted barn on the outskirts of town. Instead of following the crowds, you'll head in a minibus to some of the lesser-known beaches, such as Gwithian and Godrevy at St Ives, Porthcurno at St Levan and Sennen at Land's End.

After a day in the water, you're taken back to the barn overlooking the bay for a barbecue and chilled beers. Then it's a question of figuring out where's best to go surfing the following day, depending on which beaches suit the timing of the tide and weather conditions. That's what surfing is all about.

Need to know *With a wet suit you can surf any time of the year in Cornwall. Global Boarders organizes surfing holidays from April to October: ⓦwww.globalboarders.com; ☎+44 (0) 845 330 9303.*

053 WHALE-WATCHING IN CORK

The sheer thrill of sitting in a boat within a belly flop of a forty-tonne animal is what whale-watching is all about. If you're lucky, you may see one breach the water and flip its tail-fluke over in a sweeping arc before slapping it back down with a crashing thump. Naturally tour guide Nic Slocum won't guarantee that you'll see this display on one of his wildlife boat-tours off the southwest of Ireland, but with a viewing success rate of over eighty percent, your chances of seeing a whale up close with him are good.

Depending on the conditions, Nic's boat tours go past the Old Head of Kinsale or west beyond Cape Clear to the Fastnet Rock. The waters of West Cork are a popular summer feeding ground: on a good day you'll see several species of marine life, of which the most common are minke whales (May–Dec), fin whales (June–Jan) and humpback whales (Aug–Jan), while common dolphins and harbour porpoises can be seen all year round. There's also a chance you'll see killer whales, long-finned pilot whales and white-beaked dolphins.

Nic is a marine zoologist and a passionate marine conservationist; he operates his tours in accordance with guidelines proposed by the Irish Whale and Dolphin Group and the National Parks and Wildlife Service. He provides interactive commentaries using hydrophone and camera

Fin whales

equipment onboard his catamaran, and only takes small groups to ensure minimum disturbance. Because the tours form part of an "Education and Research" programme, you may also share the trip with student researchers gathering valuable marine data, which contributes towards the assessment of what impacts like boat traffic, unsustainable fishing practices and pollution have on the animals in Irish waters.

Need to know *Tours run up to three times daily in summer, leaving from Reen pier at Castlehaven harbour, West Cork. For sightings info, rates and booking details see Ⓦwww.whalewatchwestcork. com; ☎ +353 (0) 283 3357. Irish Whale and Dolphin Group: Ⓦwww.iwdg.ie.*

054 SEE THE LIGHT ON SARK

On a clear night, you can use the full moon to guide you across the narrow isthmus that connects Little Sark to the main island. And there won't be a city light in sight. Sark is the sort of place you'll probably end up recommending to anyone visiting the Channel Islands. It's the smallest and most unspoilt of the four main islands, and the only access is by ferry from Guernsey, so there are no cars – just a few tractors, bikes and horse-drawn carriages, the latter two available to hire.

The pick of several stunning beaches is the gloriously sandy cove at Le Grande Grêve, one of the most unspoilt in the Channel Islands. It's a small secluded bay flanked by steep cliffs, so you can enjoy a sheltered swim while the kids potter among rock pools and caves.

There are only a few places to stay on the island. The smart La Sablonnerie Hotel (the only place to stay and eat on Little Sark) serves produce from the hotel's own farm and gardens. You can also camp at La Valette campsite on the east side of the main island, where there are solar-powered showers. Because of the limited choice of accommodation, the island never gets crowded: that's part of its charm. Perhaps you shouldn't tell anyone about it.

Need to know The official website for Sark (ⓦwww. sark.info) has details on how to reach the island from Jersey or Guernsey, as well as full accommodation listings and details of attractions. La Sablonnerie Hotel ⓦwww.lasablonnerie.com; ☎+44 (0) 1481 832 061. La Valette campsite: ⓦwww.sercq.com; ☎+44 (0) 1481 832 202. Bike hire: ⓦatobcycles. sarkpost.com; ☎+44 (0) 1481 832 844.

055 WILD SWIMMING

Forget chlorinated pools, swimming lanes and locker tokens; take a dip in the wild. Britain has lots of clean rivers, lakes, ponds and coves where you can swim in the fresh air. All you need is a swimming costume (or not even that, if you're feeling brave) and perhaps a pair of goggles. Then off you plunge into crystal-clear waters where you can potter around a tree-lined lake, swim among lilies or be gently carried along by the river's flow...

Like camping, outdoor swimming in Britain has enjoyed a renaissance in recent years. Urbanites are flocking back to lidos – a halfway house between indoor swimming pools and the great outdoors. There's now an Outdoor Swimming Society, whose founder has recently published a book that lists many of the best places to swim outdoors in the UK.

You can even go on a dedicated swimming holiday with professionals. Swimtrek (ⓦwww. swimtrek.com; ☎+44 (0) 208 696 6220) organizes holidays in the Scilly Isles and the Scottish Inner Hebrides as well as overseas, including Croatia, Greece and Finland (see p.95). In each destination you'll swim several kilometres a day across lakes, rivers and sea under the eye of an experienced guide. For a taste of their holidays, try a weekend "short escape" in the Norfolk Broads, th River Wye or the Lake District, where you'll swim the dramatic Western Lakes of Crummock Water and Buttermere, and spend a full day crossing the isolated, picturesque Easedale Tarn.

The swing before the plunge

Need to know Outdoor swimming does have risks – that's part of its charm – but as long as you're not reckless it needn't be dangerous. The River and Lake Swimming Association (ⓦwww. river-swimming.co.uk) gives information and safety tips, while the website of the Outdoor Swimming Society (ⓦwww.outdoorswimmingsociety.com) has a map of excellent places to swim outdoors in the UK, along with swimming tips and events lists.

Green festivals in the UK

The festival ideal – people gathered together in a field, playing and listening to music, sleeping under canvas and letting time slip slowly past – sounds like a perfect green getaway. Unfortunately, the sheer size of many modern festivals often results in traffic congestion in small villages, piles of plastic packaging discarded by revellers, and large electricity demands from lighting rigs and sound systems. Take Glastonbury, the granddaddy of the festival scene. Though recognized for its commitment to environmental causes – it has long supported Greenpeace, Oxfam and Water Aid, encourages recycling and even hands out biodegradable tent pegs – the impact of well over 100,000 people descending on a small corner of Somerset is undeniable. There are, however, dozens of festivals that have revived the original Glastonbury ethos, creating smaller, greener events. They champion lift-shares, reusable and

biodegradable packaging, and even the occasional solar-powered sound system. A useful website on green festivals in Great Britain and Ireland is Ⓦwww.agreenerfestival. com, which has advice on how participants (mainly organizers and stallholders) can lower their impact at festivals. In 2008, it awarded three UK Festivals (Waveform, Shambala and Camden Green Fair) and two US festivals (Bonnaroo and Rothbury) with its "outstanding" mark. A further 24 UK festivals and eight international festivals were given its Greener Festival Award.

Cambridge Folk Festival

Aware that folk music aficionados tend to be keen on real ale, the organizers of the Cambridge Folk Festival have come up with an innovative way of avoiding mountains of plastic pint glasses. Visitors to this annual four-day event have to pay an initial deposit for a cup that they keep and reuse throughout the festival, plus everyone is given a bag for their recyclable rubbish on entry (and plastic bags are banned). The event itself mixes big names such as Joan Armatrading and Martha Wainwright with lesser-known bands who demonstrate the many ways folk continues to reinvent itself around the world.

Need to know *The festival takes place in Cambridge around the end of July and the start of August. For further info, including directions and a map, see Ⓦwww.cambridgefolkfestival.co.uk.*

Big Session Festival

Normally you'd expect "complete wasters" to be lying on the ground passed out in the middle of the day. But at Big Session, the Complete Wasters are likely to be the busiest people on site, since they're an organization responsible for sorting, recycling and composting as much rubbish as possible. This get-stuck-in ethos is central to the festival – for example, there's a session tent where anyone can bring along an instrument and join in. (The thirty different microbrewery ales on offer may help to give you the courage to participate.) Using its proximity to Leicester to promote the use of public transport and liftshares, Big Session also encourages people to take something green home with them after the weekend – offering a free energy-saving lightbulb to anyone who promises to use it.

Need to know *Big Session takes place in June each year at De Montfort Hall, a 15min walk from Leicester's train station. For further info see Ⓦwww. bigsessionfestival.com.*

Latitude

When Latitude appeared on the festival scene in 2006, it was clear it aimed to offer something more than the usual diet of rock and pop in a muddy field. Though a mid-size festival, it has already attracted some top names, including Arcade Fire, The Zutons and The Rapture. There is also a comedy stage that has hosted Bill Bailey and Jeremy Hardy, plus poetry events and a theatre arena powered by fuel-cell technology. Latitude also has a strong environmental focus: cutlery and plates at the food stalls are biodegradeable, pint glasses are reusable and plastic packaging is banned. And with unisex solar showers stocked with eco-friendly bath products, all but the most bashful will be keen to take time to get clean and green.

Need to know *Latitude takes place in mid-July on the grounds of Henham Park Estate in Southwold, Suffolk. For further info see Ⓦwww.latitudefestival.co.uk.*

End of the Road Festival

A small, five thousand-capacity festival set in the beautiful Larmer Tree Gardens in Dorset – complete with resident peacocks. The line-up in recent years has included Calexico, British Sea Power, Lambchop and Mercury Rev, and there's a 1970s-style light-up dance floor tucked away in the woods. The Bimble Inn, a bar and stage housed in an oversized tipi, is entirely powered by renewable energy.

Need to know *Festival buses connect Salisbury train station with Larmer Tree Gardens. For further info see Ⓦwww.endoftheroadfestival.com.*

The Big Green Gathering

For 25 years the Big Green Gathering was a lone beacon of environmental awareness, with solar-powered stages and organic food long before it was the fashionable thing to do. As such the crowd – hippies new and old among them – tend to be a pretty eco-minded bunch. Whereas most people go to the other festivals solely for the music, here many come because of the event's green focus – although there's also some wonderful (often fairly way-out) music, theatre and cabaret going on. With copious healing zones offering massages and alternative therapies it's like Glastonbury's Green Fields area becoming a festival all of its own.

Need to know *The Big Green Gathering takes place in early August near Cheddar in Somerset. For further info, including how to get there, see Ⓦwww.big-green-gathering.com.*

THE GREENER WAY TO A FESTIVAL

The single most effective thing festival-goers can do to reduce their carbon footprint is to cut down on the emissions caused by travelling to the event. Most festivals are accessible by public transport and many offer shuttle-bus services to and from the nearest train stations. Liftsharing sites are also a cost-effective and carbon-efficient way to travel to a festival. For a list of useful public transport websites and the best liftsharing schemes, see p.374.

WESTERN EUROPE

056 See Germany on two wheels

057 Explore Avignon and Ardèche

058 A day's sightseeing in Paris, by bike

059 Cocktails in Freiburg

060 A slice of Mongolia in Andalucía

061 Casanuova, Tuscany

062 Schwoich's banana lake, Austria

063 Chaumarty, the French Pyrenees

064 Le Camp, France

065 Feast your way through southern Italy

066 Take the train-hotel from Paris to Madrid

067 Hôtel les Orangeries, Lussac-les-Chateaux, France

068 Go walking with a donkey, France

069 Take the slow boat to Béziers, France

070 See Chamois in Chamonix, French Alps

071 Snow-shoe shuffling in the French Pyrenees

072 Winter work-outs in the Ammer Valley, Bavarian Alps

073 Hut to hut across the Spanish Pyrenees

074 Ski-touring in the Swiss Alps

075 Generate some watts in Rotterdam

076 Cycle mountain highs in the Alpujarras

077 Stay in an agriturismo in Le Marche, Italy

078 Walk in the Parc National des Pyrenees

079 Bathe in a natural spa

080 Canyoning in the Sierra de Guara

081 Take the train to the mountains

082 Party in the sun at Boom, Portugal

083 The alternative Algarve, Portugal

084 Feast at Salone del Gusto, Italy

085 Horse-riding in Tuscany

086 Pedal your way around Amsterdam

087 Food, glorious food, Amsterdam

088 Green spaces, Amsterdam

089 Stay on a canal boat, Amsterdam

090 Spot whales and dolphins on board the ferry to Spain

091 Tomorrow's tourism today in the Swiss Alps

092 Keycamp, northern France

093 Perché dans le Perche in northern France

094 Orion B&B, south of France

095 La Piantata, Italy

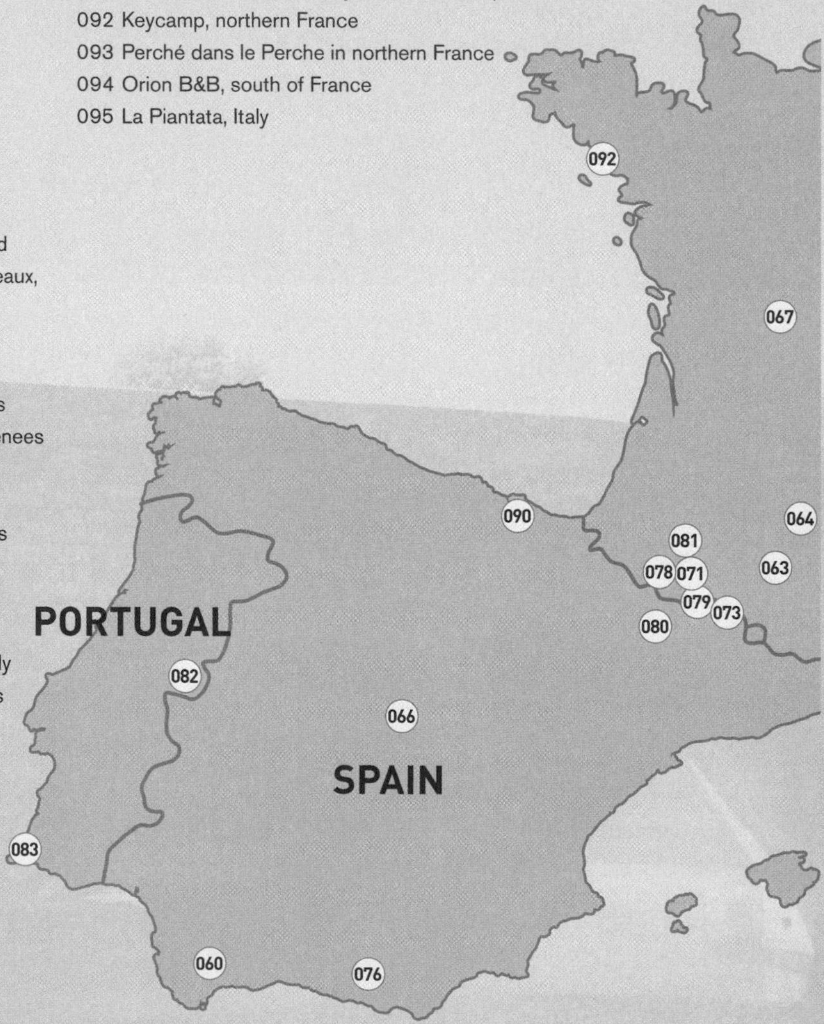

PORTUGAL

SPAIN

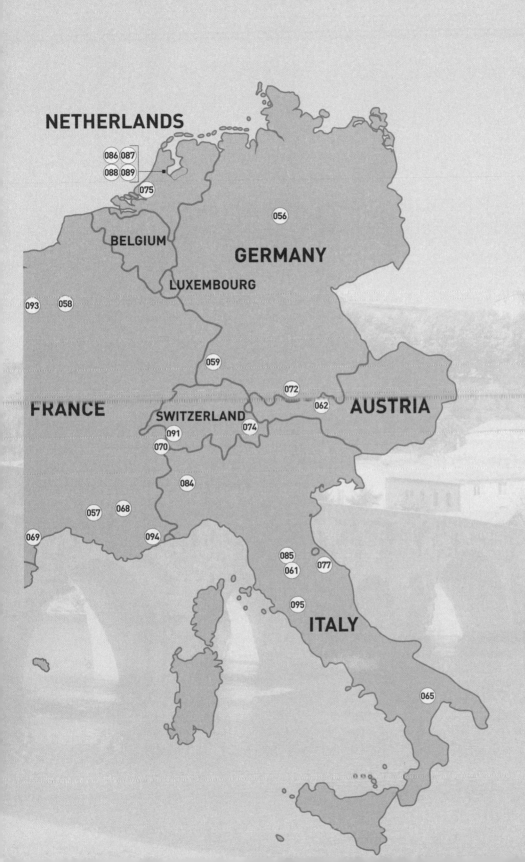

NETHERLANDS

086 087
088 089

075

BELGIUM

056

GERMANY

LUXEMBOURG

093 058

059

072

FRANCE

SWITZERLAND

062

AUSTRIA

074

091

070

084

057 068

069

094

085

061

077

095

ITALY

065

056 SEE GERMANY ON TWO WHEELS

Cycling in Germany is a national obsession. There are more than 150 long-distance cycle routes throughout the country (as well as numerous mountain-biking trails), while many of the country's major cities have a well-developed cycling infrastructure. The following three routes are among the best.

1) The 370km Green Metropolis Leisure Route is predominantly flat and mostly away from busy roads, running from Düren in North Rhine-Westphalia via Limburg in the Netherlands to Beringen in Belgium. For a map of the route (including a PDA-downloadable format) see Ⓦwww.gruenmetropole.eu. A whopping 63-page book of the circuit is available free from Aachen Tourist Service (☎ +49 (0) 241 180 2960).

2) The Tour de Fries is a 250km trail in Ostfriesland in the far northwest of Germany. It begins at Wilhelmshaven, where you cross by boat over Jadebusen and continue in the saddle to Bockhorn, Friedeburg, Wittmund, Schillig, Horumersiel and Hooksiel before stopping for a well-deserved beer in the brewery town of Jever. A six-day tour costs €259 per person, including B&B, maps, luggage transfer and a boat trip across Jadebusen Bay. For maps and detailed itineraries see Ⓦwww.friesland-touristik.de; ☎ +49 (0) 446 1919 1930.

3) If off-road biking is more your thing, head to the Solling Vogler Nature Reserve in northern Germany, where the terrain varies from valleys crisscrossed with streams and forested trails up to exposed wide ridges of the Grosse Blösse peak (528m). There are fifteen different circuits along 600km of trails (varying from easy to challenging) and one 160km trail around the entire park, which includes 2700m of climbing over two to four days. For itineraries and reservations contact the local tourist office: Ⓦwww.hochsolling.de (German only). There's also some info in English at Ⓦwww.germany-tourism.de.

Need to know *Several German cities have bike-hire schemes similar to the Paris Vélib (see p.50 & p.374). Berlin, Frankfurt, Cologne, Munich and Karlsruhe all run a scheme known as "Call a Bike". You first have to register with a credit card at Ⓦwww.callabike.de (German only, though has an English summary in menu bar), after which you're given a customer number and charged €5. When you've spotted a locked bike that you want to hire, you then call the number shown on the cycle's lock to get the code to release it. When you're done cycling, lock the bike to a traffic sign or cycle stand and call the service centre to let them know where you've left it.*

057 EXPLORE AVIGNON AND ARDÈCHE

Avignon is regarded as one of Europe's loveliest medieval cities: flanked by the Rhône and approached through tall stone ramparts, it has cobbled, shady squares, covered markets and quirky museums, the famous Palais des Papes (home to medieval popes), as well as the twelfth-century Pont St-Benezet, the fabled bridge featured in the French children's song *Sur le Pont d'Avignon*.

Avignon is also a bridge to the south of France: it is well connected by train and is the gateway to Provence and the Côte d'Azur. The direct TGV service from Paris takes just 2hr 40min and there's a direct Eurostar service from London to Avignon in the summer (5hr 53min; Sat only; Ⓦwww.eurostar.com). There's also a Eurostar service from London to Avignon year-round, which involves an easy platform change at Lille.

The TGV station is about 3km to the south of the town, where you can pick up pre-ordered hire bikes from Holiday Bikes (Ⓦwww.holiday-bikes.com; ☎+33 0810 809 609) or if you don't fancy negotiating the traffic-choked roads surrounding the city, a shuttle bus runs every 15min into town. In Avignon you can also hire bikes at Provence Bikes on Boulevard St Roch (Ⓦwww.provence-bike.com [French only]; ☎ +33 (0) 490 279 261).

Cycling through the Ardèche

While there are plenty of places to stay in the city (see ⓦwww.ot-avignon.fr), the surrounding region of the Ardèche is home to some hidden gems. Canvas Chic is a large yurt camp in a stunning setting near Mas de Serret above the Ardèche Gorge. There are twelve yurts: nine designed for families (with access to a conventional tent with a kitchen) and three intended for couples, a short walk into an oak forest in a more secluded part of the camp. The yurts provide the novelty, but the main feature here is the setting: a trail from the camp leads down the side of the gorge to an opening in the forest and out on to La Chataigneraie beach, where there's an idyllic natural bathing area surrounded by towering limestone cliffs.

For higher views of the Ardèche, stay at Les Roudils, a renovated three-room guesthouse near the village of Jaujac in the Ardèche Hills.

The house is built of chestnut wood and stone, heating is solar-powered and you can enjoy views of the Tanargue Range from the terrace over a breakfast of poached eggs, pancakes made with chestnut flour, honey cakes and home-made jams. There are lots of walks available to work off that breakfast: in the valley, along the riverbank or higher up in the hills.

Need to know *For Canvas Chic (ⓦwww. canvaschic.com; ☎ +33 (0) 475 384 277), take a bus from Ardèche to Vagnas (towards Aubenas) from where the owners can collect, by arrangement. There is no public transport to Les Roudils; for prices, directions and reservations see ⓦwww.lesroudils.com; ☎ +33 (0) 475 932 111. For B&Bs, holiday gîtes, hotels, restaurants and campsites in the Ardèche as well as ideas for where to go canoeing and riding see ⓦwww. ardeche.com.*

(Clockwise from top left) The wide paths by Notre Dame are perfect for cycling along; Whizzing past La Cinematheque; Jardin des Tuilleries; Organic market produce; Around Paris by vélib bike

058 A DAY'S SIGHTSEEING IN PARIS, BY BIKE

Though Paris is packed with iconic sights, it is not a large city. The main attractions – such as the Champs-Elysées, Notre Dame, the Louvre and the Avenue de l'Opera, the Marais, Pompidou Centre and Bastille – are all within walking distance of the principal train hubs: Gare du Nord (for those arriving on Eurostar), Gare de l'Est (for those arriving from the east) and Gare de Montparnasse (for those travelling up from the south).

The metro system can get you across Paris quickly, but the best way to see the sights in a day is from the comfort of a saddle. You can be more spontaneous: stop off en route at the shops and markets, cross one of the many bridges over the River Seine, or follow a dead-end alleyway that leads to that exquisite pavement café. You even begin to feel like a Parisian.

The city's self-service cycle hire scheme, "Vélib", which was introduced in the summer of 2007, has been a great success. It allows you to pick up and drop off bicycles throughout the city at over a thousand locations 24 hours a day, seven days a week. You need a credit card to hire the bikes (a €150 deposit is held as insurance) but it's free to use the bikes for the first half hour; thereafter it costs €1 for an additional half hour, €2 for another half hour and €4 for every 30min after that.

The bikes have a large front basket and a simple three-speed gear system so they aren't exactly speed machines but you can pedal at a decent pace, and you'll soon clock up the main sights of Paris. Once you've seen how easy it is to use, the metro feels dirty and inhibited. Vive Vélib.

Need to know *Parisians use the bikes as a means of travelling to work and as a cheap way of getting home after the metro closes, so expect a rush of hires immediately after work and late evening. Bike-hire pick-up locations are shown on the Google map on Vélib's homepage:* Ⓦ*www.en.velib.paris.fr.*

059 COCKTAILS IN FREIBURG

Sex on the Beach or Sex on the Rocks? Rusty Nail or Banana Banshee? These are among the hundred or so different cocktails to choose from at the Hemingway Café in Freiburg's Hotel Victoria, just 200m from the main train station in the heart of the city.

Of course, this being Freiburg – known for its eco-friendly buildings and extensive public transport system – the hotel is one of the most progressive in Europe. It may be affiliated with Best Western but it is independently owned and operated – in this case by a local German couple, Bertram and Astrid Späth, who have overseen the hotel's green makeover.

The entire hotel is powered solely by renewable energy: on a sunny day a 30-square-metre solar plant heats the water; a vast woodchip boiler powers the central heating (which the hotel says saves it fifty thousand litres of heating oil a year); and an innovative air-conditioning unit sucks up cool water from the ground and circulates it through pipes leading to each room. Oh, and guests are given a free public transport pass for the duration of their stay. We could go on, but the list is almost as long as the number of cocktails. Go try a Shirley Temple.

Need to know *To get a flavour of the cocktail menu see Ⓦwww.hemingway-freiburg.de. For prices and reservations at Hotel Victoria visit Ⓦwww.hotel-victoria.de; ☎ +49 (0) 761 207 340.*

060 A SLICE OF MONGOLIA IN ANDALUCÍA

It's one thing to plonk a yurt at the bottom of a field and call it luxury camping, but it's quite another to buy a private meadow in Andalucía, import yurts from Mongolia and Afghanistan, drill a well, install an outdoor swimming pool, and provide guests with three-course candlelit dinners with produce from your own garden. Then run it all off grid. Welcome to the remote,

Seclusion among the olive groves at the Hoopoe Yurt Hotel

ambitious and yes, luxurious, camp that is The Hoopoe Yurt Hotel.

There are five individually designed yurts, all in their own splendid isolation among shady groves of cork and olive trees. Each has a large double bed, sheepskin rugs, velvet cushions, wicker chairs, a power point, a compost toilet and a private garden, as well as a bamboo bathroom outside (including solar-powered hot shower). There is a small private garden just outside each yurt, but the rest of the meadow is left untouched to encourage the growth of wildflowers and visits from birds and butterflies.

Yoga, reiki, massages and aromatherapy are available in the nearest village, Cortes de la Frontera, plus you can go riding and walking in the nearby hills or go for a refreshing dip in the large rock pool at Cuevo del Gato near Ronda. After a day in the Andalucian countryside, return for a shower then dine in a lantern-lit pergola in the warm Mediterranean evening. There can be few yurt camps this side of the Urals that ooze as much style and shabby-chic sophistication.

Need to know *Take the Eurostar to Paris (Ⓦwww. eurostar.com) and then the train from Paris to Madrid (see p.55). Then cross the city to Madrid Atocha and take the Algeciras train to Ronda (4hr; Ⓦwww.srenfe.es), followed by the local train to Cortes de la Frontera (15min), from where you will be collected, by arrangement. For prices, directions and reservations see Ⓦwww.yurthotel.com; ☎ +34 (0) 660 668 241.*

NATURAL SWIMMING POOLS

Compared with a chlorinated hotel swimming pool, a dip in a natural pool feels like swimming in Evian – and thankfully European hoteliers are recognizing the draw of these natural, eco-friendly alternatives. Designs vary, but natural pools all work on the same premise: a wall separates a foil- or rubber-lined swimming area from an aquatic plant garden, whose marsh plants and sand act as a natural filter for oxygenizing and cleaning the water. Here are four of our favourites.

061 Casanuova, Tuscany

A family day out at Schwoich's Banana Lake; The wildlife-rich garden around the pool at Casanuova

On the large lawn by the water's edge at Casanuova, you can sunbathe to the sound of frogs croaking while butterflies dart among the reeds.

Then it's just a 200m towel-covered stroll back to the organic farm on the hills above the Valdarno, the valley of the Arno River. Plants and wildlife dominate the estate: ivy, wild vines and roses cover the walls while oleander bushes, oranges and bergamot grow everywhere. You can stay in one of fifteen rooms in the beautiful farmhouse or in two apartments, 800m from the main house on the edge of the small hamlet of La Bifolca; both will give you access to this wildlife oasis.

Need to know *From Florence take the train towards Rome/Arezzo to Figline Valdarno, from where it's a 5km walk to the house (or you can arrange to be collected). For prices, reservations and further info see Ⓦwww.casanuova.info; ☏ +39 (0) 559 500 027.*

062 Schwoich's banana lake, Austria

Below Mount Poelven at the edge of a pine forest, Schwoich's banana-shaped lake was Austrian Tyrol's first public natural bathing pool. From its wooden jetties and pebble beach you can enjoy a refreshing dip in the crystal-clear water with wonderful views of the surrounding mountain slopes. The average water temperature is 22°C, which is usually warm enough for young children. One of the best places to stay nearby is Ferienwohnung Steinbacher, a self-catering farmhouse apartment in Schwoich, where you can buy organic eggs and milk from the farm.

Need to know *Take the train from London and Paris (via Mannheim) to Kufstein and then the local bus to Schwoich (20min; €2.50). The lake is open daily from 10am to 6pm in the summer and costs*

€5 for adults and €2 for children. For more info see ⓦwww.kufstein.net; ☎ +43 (0) 537 258 113. For prices and reservations at Ferienwohnung Steinbacher ☎ +43 (0) 537 258 810.

063 Chaumarty, the French Pyrenees

Dragonflies hover overhead as the sun-warmed water laps against the pool's plant-lined rim. Beyond the rolling green hills, mountain peaks shimmer in the heat of the day. Here at Chaumarty, a three-room eco-gîte south of Toulouse in the approach to the Pyrenees, the *bassin de baignade* (natural pool) is exquisite: irises and papyrus surround it, plus there's a diving board and a smaller pool for children. Adjacent to the pools is a large terrace where you can admire the mountain panorama. Organic vegetables come from the kitchen garden, solar panels heat the water, and all the waste is separated, reduced and recycled religiously. Au naturelle.

Need to know Take the train from Toulouse to Auterive (27min), from where it's 15km to the gîte. For prices and reservations see ⓦwww.chaumarty. com (French only); ☎ +33 (0) 561 086 864.

064 Le Camp, France

Well what else would you call it? It is a campsite, after all, though expect more than just sleeping bags and roll mats. Hand-made beds, solar lighting and lazy chairs all come as part of the package at this luxury, five-yurt camp in oak woodland overlooking the green Aveyron Valley, about an hour northeast of Toulouse. Pride of place, though, is the 20m-long natural swimming pool, with a gently sloping beach that's a perfect distraction for kids – once they've grown tired of playing in the big sand pit, helping to feed the chickens and patting the resident pig.

Need to know Take the train from Toulouse to Lexos, where the owners can collect (by arrangement). ⓦwww.lecamp.co.uk; ☎ +33 (0) 563 654 834.

Making a splash at Le Camp

(Clockwise from top left)
Tasting the local Caneto wine;
The skyline at Matera, Puglia;
Café in Sasso Barisano
District, Matera; Grapes ripe
for harvest

065 FEAST YOUR WAY THROUGH SOUTHERN ITALY

Foodies who like a bit of exercise can now lace up their walking boots and enjoy the best of both worlds. Ferula Viaggi's five-day "Slow Foot, Slow Food" holiday, based in Matera – an enchanting city whose labyrinth of stone houses were carved out of a ravine – is a gastronomic tour of southern Italy that combines highlights of Italian cuisine with walking itineraries, so that you can feast on the best of the region's produce without having to worry about your waistline.

You'll taste bread from bakeries in Matera, wine from Aglianico and cheese from the mountains, then burn it all off as you cross the green meadows of the southern Apennines towards the small villages of the Lucanian hills and mountains in Basilicata. En route, you'll stay in an *agriturismo* and a locally run hotel, with workshops on slow food and cookery courses.

For the more adventurous, Ferula Viaggi also organizes cycling holidays in the region. Starting from Matera, you'll pass through the orchards and olive groves of the Bradano Valley, cycle around the wheat-covered hills surrounding San Giuliano Lake and climb up to the Lucanian Dolomites. Guests stay in *agriturismi* and three-star hotels and then return to Matera by minibus. The total cycling distance is 330km (you can also opt for an extra night in the mountains at Pollino and another by the sea at Maratea) and there are plenty of uphill and downhill stages, so remember to pack windproof clothing and a water bottle. Then help yourself to another salami.

Need to know *Take the train from Bari to Matera on the Appulo Lucane railway (Ⓦwww. fal-srl.it – Italian only). There are also direct bus connections from most main Italian cities to Matera (Ⓦwww.marinobus.it). For prices and booking for walking holidays see Ⓦwww.ferulaviaggi.it; ☎ +39 0835 336 572; for cycling holidays see Ⓦwww. bikebasilicata.it.*

066 TAKE THE TRAIN-HOTEL FROM PARIS TO MADRID

As you enter your private cabin, the train manager checks your tickets and asks you whether you'd prefer dinner at eight or ten o'clock. Choose 8pm – in the summer – and you can catch the sun setting over the French countryside as you sit down to a three-course meal and a glass of Rioja in the dining carriage. When you return to your cabin, the curtains will be drawn and the bed made. This is civilized travelling, and it's not even the Orient Express.

Welcome to the "Francisco de Goya" train-hotel – an intercity sleeper service from Paris to Madrid. During the night the train trundles through the southwest of France, the Pyrenees and northern Spain, and you're woken up in time to take a hot shower in your cabin, followed by breakfast before the train pulls into Madrid at 9.10am.

This, of course, is the luxury way to do it – in Grand Class. The next class down is Club Class (a private cabin with a washbasin), followed by Tourist Class (four-berth cabins with a washbasin) or if you're on a tight budget you can opt for just a reclining seat. Though prices can seem a bit steep, remember you're saving a night in a hotel, and the price for Grand Class customers includes an excellent meal and wine. There are similar train-hotels between several other European cities: "Joan Miró" links Paris with Barcelona, "Pau Cassals" links Zurich with Barcelona, and "Salvador Dalí" links Barcelona with Milan, plus you can join the train at selected cities en route.

Need to know *Trains depart daily from Paris Austerlitz at 7.46pm. Your passport will be taken as you board and is returned just before you arrive in Madrid. In Grand Class or Club Class you're given a key for your cabin, but in other classes don't leave valuables in unguarded belongings. For more details about the service, including a virtual tour of the trains, see Ⓦwww.elipsos.com. For reservations visit Ⓦwww.raileurope.co.uk; ☎ +44 (0) 8448 484 064.*

067 HÔTEL LES ORANGERIES, LUSSAC-LES-CHATEAUX, FRANCE

Start the day the French way: a morning dip in a 35m tree-lined pool followed by breakfast in a rose-filled garden with warm croissants and pain au chocolat, home-made orange jam, hot chocolate or strong coffee.

Hôtel les Orangeries is a wonderfully restored eighteenth-century house with well-tended gardens in an area renowned for superb cuisine and fine wines. Nothing unusual about that: you're in the heart of rural western France, after all. Yet Hôtel les Orangeries takes matters one step further with its commitment to "respect de l'environnement". It was the first French hotel to be awarded the European Ecolabel; it serves mainly organic and local produce; kitchen waste is composted and used on the garden; rainwater is harvested; and the power for hot water comes from solar thermal panels.

But most guests don't come to hear about kilowatt hours and management systems for water leakage. They come to stay in a magnificent hotel with French *art de vivre*, 21st-century style. There are four-poster beds, oak doors and insulated stone walls; on the top floor there's a large games room with two billiard tables, while downstairs is a smart dining room with antique sideboards. All is managed with typically polished service, though with a healthy dose of green panache that even the French aren't used to. "Tourisme durable", so they say.

The pool at Hôtel les Orangeries

Need to know Take the train to Poitiers (90min from Paris Montparnasse) then a 30min local TER (Regional Express Train) to Lussac-les-Chateaux, from where the owners will meet you (with a trolley) and walk with you to the hotel (5min). For train times see Ⓦwww.sncf.co.uk; for prices and bookings at the hotel see Ⓦwww.lesorangeries.fr; ☏ +33 (0) 549 840 707.

068 GO WALKING WITH A DONKEY, FRANCE

Here's one way to keep the kids happy. Based in the mountain village of Eourres, 35km west of the town of Sisteron in Haute-Provence, English-speaking company Bamboul'âne runs donkey-trekking holidays in the National Regional Park of the Baronnies, home to wild roe deer, chamois, buzzards and eagles. They'll teach you basic riding skills for the mountains as well as how to pack-saddle your donkey.

You can stay at Bamboul'âne's farm campsite and go on day-excursions with the donkeys, winding up along a rocky ridge among green pastureland and forests of ash and field maple before returning to a cooked meal using produce from the farm. If you have the confidence, you can choose to leave the farm and go on two- to ten-day circuits, staying in lodgings along the way or sleeping out in your own tent.

A two-day circuit includes walking up to pastures at 1600m, dining with shepherds in the evening and spending the following day with them as they tend their sheep. The six-day Jabron Valley Circuit is a daily 10–12km ramble and includes one night in the forest, two nights by the Jabron River, one at a mountain farm and a final night at a village on the Méouge River.

Need to know For prices, itineraries and bookings see Ⓦbamboulane.free.fr; ☏ +33 (0) 492 650 225. Alternatively, Itinerance (Ⓦwww.itinerance.net; ☏ +33 (0) 493 055 601) offers a one-week self-guided donkey trek in the Mercantour National Park. For a list of all other companies offering donkey hikes in France see Ⓦwww.ane-et-rando.com.

069 TAKE THE SLOW BOAT TO BÉZIERS, FRANCE

This is a unique chance to snuggle up on board a hotel-boat and cruise Languedoc via the Canal du Midi – the canal system built in the seventeenth century (now a World Heritage Site) that links the Atlantic with the Mediterranean in southwest France. Your home for a week is a renovated barge with two-berth cabins for up to fourteen people. The long hours of sunshine in this part of France power the boat's hot water and electric motor, though there's never much need to get out of the low gears. This truly is slow travel.

The trip starts with a night in a hotel in the medieval town of Carcassonne before you embark on the seven-day voyage to the town of Béziers, 75km away. En route you can choose to visit a wind farm, tour the vineyards of Minnervois and Ventenac or visit the Cathar castle at Lastours. The only slight cause for concern will be negotiating a "ladder" of seven lock gates before the final stretch to Pont Neuf in Béziers. But that's about as energetic as it gets. The rest of the trip is one long drift along this historic canal – gradual enough for you to appreciate the canal-side foliage or just nod off to sleep on deck.

Need to know *For programmes, prices and reservations see Ⓦwww.naviratous2.com (French only); ☏: +33 (0) 468 463 798.*

Béziers Cathedral; a solar-powered barge cruising along the Canal du Midi

FIVE NEW WINTER HOLIDAYS

What can beat the exhilarating freedom of the slopes, the first sip of a cold beer at 3000m and a fondue with friends at the end of a muscle-aching day? Yet the purpose-built resorts, chair-lifts, snow cannons and high-altitude infrastructure necessary to service downhill skiing hardly do the mountain ecosystem a favour. It's ironic, given that most skiers and snowboarders care passionately about the mountains, that by visiting most resorts they hasten the destruction of the wilderness they love. So here are five new ways to enjoy the winter wonderland – in the Alps and other mountains of western Europe – where you can enjoy the powder and fresh mountain air, but where your footprint will be only snow deep.

Snow-shoeing in the Alps

070 See Chamois in Chamonix, French Alps

Trek softly through off-piste, knee-deep snow on a pair of snow-shoes and you're more likely to encounter wildlife than if you're hurtling down a manicured slope on skis. You can also reach otherwise inaccessible places in thick forest and climb up to some of the most remote alpine summits. On a week's snow-shoeing and cross-country-skiing trip in the Chamonix Valley, with luck you'll see chamois or even the shy ibex. Afterwards head into town for Chamonix's legendary après-ski, which may be a bit of a shock to the system.

Need to know *For programmes and prices see ⓦwww.trekkinginthealps.com; ☏ +33 (0) 450 546 209. For a combined snow-shoeing and cross-country trek around the Mont Blanc massif visit ⓦwww.tracks-and-trails.com; ☏ +44 (0) 208 144 6442.*

071 Snow-shoe shuffling in the French Pyrenees

Join one of Mountainbug's tours, based in an eighteenth-century guesthouse in the central Pyrenean village of Barèges, and there's no need to bother with the usual ski equipment. Just strap on a pair of snow-shoes and away you go into the crunching virgin snow. Trekking four to six hours a day with a qualified International Mountain Leader, you'll spend a week exploring the spectacular peaks of the Cirque de Gavarnie, Pont d'Espagne and the Marcadau Valley. When it's over, soak for an afternoon in Barèges's baths at the highest thermal spa in Europe.

Need to know *For accommodation details, itineraries, prices and booking see ⓦwww. mountainbug.com; ☏ +33 (0) 562 921 639.*

072 Winter work-outs in the Ammer Valley, Bavarian Alps

Cross-country skiing is not for the faint of heart – there's no other work-out quite like it, as you push and glide (and huff and puff) across kilometres of flat tracks in the fresh winter air. One of the best places to put your body to the test is Oberammergau's Ammer Valley, in the foothills of the Bavarian Alps, where there are 100km of cross-country skiing trails. The King Ludwig Run, from Oberammergau to Linderhof, is a healthy 26km round trip, while the circular Ettaler Runde is a mere 4km, so you'll be back in time to have the sauna all to yourself. The most convenient place to stay near the ski area is the Oberammergau Youth Hostel, which has a mix of dormitories and family rooms, serves packed lunches (on request) and hires out sledges, snow-shoes and cross-country-skiing equipment.

Need to know *Take the train (ⓦwww.bahn.de) from Munich to Murnau (1hr), then change for the train to Oberammergau (40min). Oberammergau Youth Hostel: ⓦwww.oberammergau. jugendherbege.de; ☎ +49 (0) 882 292 2740; €17.70 per person B&B or €25.10 full board. For more information on the Oberammergau ski area see ⓦwww.oberammergau.de (German only); ☎ +49 (0) 882 292 2740.*

073 Hut to hut across the Spanish Pyrenees

Sunset at 2000m is worth every ounce of effort, especially when you have the satisfaction of having walked all the way up there on snow-shoes. On a trip with Pyrenean Mountain Tours you'll start on the French side of the Pyrenees (from the Valardies Valley), cross over the border to the Refuge de la Restanca at Encantats Nature Park and then stay in mountain huts for six nights, walking through pine forests and passing the many frozen lakes of Cirque de Colomers before circling back to Valardies.

Need to know *For itineraries, costs and suggested equipment see ⓦwww. pyrenees.co.uk; ☎ +44 (0) 1635 297 209.*

074 Ski-touring in the Swiss Alps

Ski-touring gives you the best of both worlds: synthetic "skins" attached to the underside of your skis give you traction to walk uphill into the wild hinterland, then once you've gained some height you strip them off and enjoy the thrill of skiing deserted descents. Going off-piste, though, is not without its dangers, which is why the Ski Club of Great Britain organizes guided ski-touring instruction holidays so you can better understand off-piste mountain conditions. You stay in mountain huts and learn the different techniques needed to ski on off-piste and glaciated terrain. Once you've mastered these, you can join one of their guided ski-touring safari holidays to regions including the French and Swiss Alps and the Dolomites. Then you can go it alone.

Need to know *Trips are run in allocated groups depending on your level of experience, from novice to expert. For prices and trip dates of all ski-touring trips see ⓦwww.skifreshtracks.com; ☎ +44 (0) 208 410 202.*

Ski-touring takes you to places other skiers cannot reach

075 GENERATE SOME WATTS IN ROTTERDAM

Enjoy the moment, or at least the momentum of the crowd, at Club WATT in Rotterdam – the first sustainable dance club in the Netherlands – which is designed to use the kinetic energy produced by people dancing to provide its electricity.

So how does it work? Well, according to the owners, each person produces between two and twenty watts of energy with each dance step (depending on their weight and how much they move). That may not sound much, but once several hundred clubbers collectively strut their stuff on the dancefloor then enough of a pulse is generated to excite the electromagnetic generator beneath. The generator converts movement into electricity, which is then used to power the flickering floor lights.

The club has four sections: a main hall with capacity for 1500 people and a 60-square-metre dancefloor; a basement for three hundred people; two rooftops; and a café at street level. Other green initiatives include a rainwater-flush system for the toilets, water-saving taps, LED lights, an efficient heating and cooling system, and drinks served in recycled plastic cups. The aim is to cut water consumption and waste production by fifty percent compared to a typical dance venue, and likewise to reduce the total energy consumption by thirty percent. Watt a great idea.

Need to know
For events and latest news about the club see ⓦwww.sustainabledanceclub.com; ⓣ +31 (0) 102 762 213. Take the train (ⓦwww.raileurope.co.uk; ⓣ +44 (0) 844 848 4070) to Rotterdam Centraal station and then change to Blaak station, from where it's a 5min walk to the club at Pannekoekstraat 106.

The dancefloor at Club WATT

076 CYCLE MOUNTAIN HIGHS IN THE ALPUJARRAS

Every day starts at an altitude of 1700m in the crisp morning air of southern Spain's Sierra Nevada mountain range. After a hearty breakfast of porridge, local honey and orange juice on the terrace, followed by a bike and kit check, you start the day's cycling with a gentle pedal across a 300m plateau, then either take the high mountain route or drop down into the verdant valleys of the Alpujarras.

Pure Mountains' cycling holidays are based at a remote stone farmhouse (*cortijo*) near the flat-roofed, whitewashed village of Bérchules. The rooms have large beds and open out onto a courtyard with a fountain and there's a large sitting room with a wood-burning stove. It is off-grid: solar power provides the heat and electricity, while water is supplied by a natural spring. The owners have also planted hundreds of poplar, chestnut and fruit trees, and there are glorious views across the meadows and terraces of the sprawling, wild landscape.

These holidays cater for both novices and more experienced bikers. Choose the "Easy Going" option and you'll spend the week cycling along mountain trails, picnicking by streams and whizzing down long descents – but with plenty of time to do your own thing back at the *cortijo* (including a Swedish massage). Pure Mountains' English owners have spent five years scouring the land and know the best routes and places to stop for lunch – where you'll be met by a Land Rover with all the necessary supplies, such as banana bread.

Choose the harder "Classic" cycling holiday and you'll be pedalling for six hours a day, negotiating rocky trails and climbing into the peaks above Granada. You'll cross the Veleta pass (3224m), following what was once Europe's highest road (until it fell into disrepair and became a mountain biker's adventure playground), followed by thrilling descents down to Trevélez, the highest village in Spain. Whichever route you choose, the scenery is nearly always dominated by the snowy peak of Mulhacén, Sierra Nevada's highest at 3497m.

Dinner at the farmhouse is usually simple, hearty fare (soup, fish pie, pasta), but there are evening trips to Alquería de Morayma – a local *agriturismo* and restaurant on an organic farm, where you can try local specialities such as thick stews and *migas* (breadcrumbs with garlic and meat). You can also visit some of the local fiestas (firecracker affairs) or just spend the evening on the terrace, enjoying the peace of the mountain wilderness and the fresh alpine air.

Need to know *Cost of bike hire is additional. For dates, itineraries, prices and reservations see Ⓦwww.puremountains.com; ☎ +34 (0) 958 061 052. Take the train (Ⓦwww.renfe.es) or bus (Ⓦwww.alsa.es) to either Almería or Granada then a local bus to Bérchules (2hr).*

077 STAY IN AN AGRITURISMO IN LE MARCHE, ITALY

Italy is the home of *agriturismi* – rural homes that provide accommodation for tourists, usually in the form of a farmstay. Depending on whether they are set up by farmers looking for extra income or as a separate business opportunity, they range from those that offer little more than a room at the back of the farm to those more like a boutique hotel. Locanda della Valle Nuova – on an organically run farm in the Le Marche region of northwest Italy – is somewhere in between.

Surrounded by ancient oaks, the 1920s farmhouse has been converted into a well-insulated, modern country house with six double rooms as well as a self-catering apartment for two. There are all the amenities you'd expect at a country hotel: an outdoor swimming pool (with wonderful views over rolling hills), en-suite rooms and five-course

Locanda della Valle Nuova

evening meals served in a lounge/dining area

Locanda della Valle Nuova is managed by Giulia, whose mother helps run the kitchen and whose father works the farm. They grow wheat, fruit and vegetables, raise cattle, pigs and poultry, and make their own bread and pasta, jams and wine. Water is purified, heating is solar-powered and there's a wood-fired stove fuelled by coppicing from the farm woods. In autumn you can go on truffle-hunting walks with Giulia's neighbour Giovanni, though if you want to guarantee seeing the king of truffles – the white truffle – go to the National Fairs of the White Truffle in Acqualagna and Sant'Angelo during the weekends of October and the first weekend of November.

The renaissance town of Urbino (birthplace of Raphael, and a World Heritage Site) is 12km away over the rolling hills. Just a few kilometres from the Locanda is Riserva Naturale Gola del Furlo, home to wolves and golden eagles. Giulia has leaflets of walks throughout the region, including information on trips to the beaches and rocky coastlines of Parco del Monte San Bartolo and Conero.

Need to know *There is no public transport to the Locanda and the only practical way there is by car. For directions (from Urbino, Rimini, Florence and Rome), prices and reservations see Ⓦwww.vallenuova.it; ☎ +39 (0) 722 330 303.*

GREEN PYRENEES

The Alps may be the mountain capital of Europe but the Pyrenees are no less dramatic and have something for everyone. Spanning 435km across the southwest of France, northern Spain and Andorra, the landscape varies from herb-scented Mediterranean slopes to dense broadleaf forests, deep river canyons, cool mountain lakes and snow-tipped peaks. What the Pyrenees lack in altitude, they make up for in inexpensive food and wine, hiking trails for all abilities and some of the best river sports in Europe. Here are a few suggestions for a different Pyrenean holiday.

078 Walk in the Parc National des Pyrenees

There are two famous long-distance walks across the Pyrenees: the GR10 (France: from the Atlantic to the Mediterranean) and the GR11 (Spain: from Roncesvalles to Andorra). But if you prefer to stay in one region, an excellent place to go is the Parc National des Pyrenees, where you can explore several stunning valleys: Aspe, Ossau, Azun, Aure, Cauterets or Luz. Throughout the park are "panda gîtes" – places to stay near walking routes, which have been awarded an eco label by the World Wide Fund for Nature. All provide binoculars, maps and guidebooks on the local plants and wildlife. Two of the best are La Bergerie and La Grange in the D'Azun Valley, which are smart, stone cottages each with a fully equipped kitchenette, living room and double rooms.

Need to know *Take the train from Pau to Lourdes then a local bus into the park. For prices and booking for panda gîtes see ⓦgites-france-pyrenees.fr. In each valley there is a National Park Centre, which gives advice on hiking routes. For suggested walking itineraries also see ⓦwww.parc-pyrenees.com.*

Gaube Lake and Vignemale Mountain, Parc National des Pyrenees

079 Bathe in a natural spa

On both sides of the Pyrenees, but especially in France, there are thermal spas where you can bathe in natural minerals and sulphurous water (the French have been doing so since the Roman times) – ideal after a day in the great outdoors. One of the largest geothermal spas is 150m underground at Bagnères-de-Luchon in the central Pyrenees (a 2hr train journey from Toulouse). There are several B&Bs and hotels along the town's main high street, but for a more homely break, stay 3km out of town in the small village of Juzet-de-Luchon at Le Poujastou, a converted eighteenth-century inn with five rooms where you'll dine on home-made stews. Other natural spa towns include Barèges in the west, Argelès-Gazost and Ax-les-Thermes in the central French Pyrenees, as well as Caldes de Boi in the Catalan region of the Spanish Pyrenees.

Need to know *For opening times, programmes and reservations for Luchon's spa see Ⓦwww. thermes-luchon.fr; ☎ +33 (0) 561 945 252. Le Poujastou: Ⓦlepoujastou.com; ☎ +33 (0) 561 943 288.*

080 Canyoning in the Sierra de Guara

Canyoning is one of the fastest-growing sports in the Pyrenees. It's a heady combination of scrambling, climbing, jumping off rocks in sculpted gorges then floating and swimming down ravines – and there are few better places in Europe to do it than the Parque de la Sierra y los Canones de Guara near Huesca. In this protected area the four main rivers (the Flumen, the Guatizalema, the Alcanadre and the Vero) have carved out a range of geological formations including caves, pits and spectacular canyons through the mountains.

One of the most popular stretches is the River Vero canyon, which is 8km long and has a drop of 250m (it takes 4.5–6hr to complete). En route you pass high cliffs, wall paintings and an underground passage known as Los Oscuros ("the

dark place"). If you catch your breath, you can peer into ancient cave dwellings, spot a variety of birds and enjoy spectacular water pools.

Need to know
Rafting season is from April to September. For details of where to go canyoning in the Sierra de Guara see Ⓦwww. caiaragon.com. For canyoning in France (near Barèges in the western Pyrenees) see Ⓦwww.mountainbug.com; ☎ +33 (0) 562 921 639.

Canyoning in the Sierra de Guara

081 Take the train to the mountains

Trains run at least into the foothills of the Pyrenees, after which you'll need buses to get higher. Access from the French side is from three main train stations: Pau, in the west, for Lourdes and the Pyrenees National Park; Toulouse in the centre, for Luchon, Foix and Andorra; and Perpignan, in the east, for the Mediterranean coast. On the Spanish side, there are few trains that run into the central Pyrenees – rail services mainly head into the mountains from the towns of the Atlantic (such as San Sebastián) and Mediterranean coasts (Barcelona and Girona).

Need to know *For train timetables and reservations in the French Pyrenees see Ⓦwww. sncf.fr; for the Spanish Pyrenees see Ⓦwww.renfe. es. All Pyrenean towns have a single main bus station, though services are drastically reduced on Sundays; local tourist offices will also have timetables. Accommodation options, hiking trails and general information on the French Pyrenees are at Ⓦwww.lespyrenees.net.*

24/7 partying at Boom Festival

082 PARTY IN THE SUN AT BOOM, PORTUGAL

Twenty thousand revellers each year come to Boom, Europe's greatest outdoor dance-music festival, which takes place for a week over the August full moon on a lakeside ranch about 60km from Lisbon. In true summer-of-love fashion it combines non-stop dance music with eco-idealism: here you'll find sustainability workshops, recycling and composting bins, a permaculture garden and generators powered on vegetable oil and solar power. In the meantime dancing goes on throughout the days and nights – on a beach, in a forest where an ambient music stage is set, or in the world music area based around a huge campfire.

For people wilting under the heat, the shallow hilltop lake provides the perfect place to cool off (and acts as a glistening mirror when the full moon rises). By late morning it's dotted with people lolling on inflatables or sitting half-submerged on deckchairs that they have sunk into the lake's bed. Further relaxation is on offer at various tents and stalls selling a range of massage, yoga and other alternative therapies to restore tired bodies and minds.

And when the week-long party is finally over, there's still the option of more to come – a three-day afterparty in the surrounding forested hills, where you can hike wooded paths or just lie back in the shade and wind down to ambient beats.

You won't see many wellies at this festival, however. There's little chance of it raining in Portugal in August, and even if it did people would be more likely to run out for a cool shower than hide in their tents. This is a party in the sun – and in this scorched part of Europe, that's about as guaranteed as it gets.

Need to know *For further info see ⓦwww. boomfestival.org; ☏ +351 277 208 138. Ticket prices vary depending upon when you buy, how long you come for and where you live. Shuttle buses to the festival run from Madrid, Lisbon and Porto; see website for details.*

083 THE ALTERNATIVE ALGARVE, PORTUGAL

It may be the Algarve, but come to Monte Velho Nature Resort – in the Costa Vincentina National Park overlooking the Atlantic swell – and you'll hardly see a soul. Near the small town of Carrapateira, the converted farmhouse (run mostly on wind and solar energy, with water from a well) has seven colourful rooms enlivened with paintings from local artists, plus a sitting room with country sofas and a wood burner for winter. Hammocks are strung outside your room, and you can have breakfast on a terrace with views over pine forest and dense scrubland to the sea.

Monte Velho's hilltop setting makes for a peaceful retreat (yoga courses are offered) but the main attractions here are the spectacular beaches and coastline. You can take a donkey ride down to the nearest beach at Carrapateira, or alternatively Praia da Bordeira – one of the best surfing beaches in Portugal – is just a few kilometres further to the north. A restaurant just back from the beach, O Sitio do Rio (☏ +351 (0) 282 997 119; closed Tues), uses largely organic produce for fresh soup, simple grills and stir-fried veggies. Another excellent beach, Praia do Amado, is 4km to the south, where you can take surfing lessons (equipment rental and courses from €40 a day; ☏ +351 (0) 282 624 560).

You can also go on guided mountain-bike trails through the park and along the coast. After a day tumbling in the surf, walking or cycling along the coast, it's great to be able to return for a massage in one of the resort's two Moroccan tents and then head out to one of the locally run restaurants. The crowded resorts further along the coast will feel like a thousand kilometres away.

Need to know *Carrapateira is 90km north of Faro. Other than an occasional weekday bus from Vila do Bispo, there's no public transport to Carrapateira so you will need to hire a car. For prices and reservations see ⓦwww.wonderfulland. com/montevelho; ☏ +351 (0) 282 973 207.*

084 FEAST AT SALONE DEL GUSTO, ITALY

Turn a corner and you're at one end of a long aisle, its sides lined with stalls selling nothing but chocolate. Turn a different corner and you enter another food-laden aisle, only this time dedicated to cheese, including matured Pecorino wrapped in walnuts, Norwegian Sognefjord geitost and Tcherni Vit green cheese from Bulgaria. There's no aisle for wine though – rather an entire area with some 2500 different labels to choose between. There's beer too. And vodka, whisky and a host of local liqueurs it would be rude not to try. And don't even start on the aroma of coffee wafting through some parts of the hall.

Imagine the world's largest farmers' market lasting five days, and you still wouldn't even be close to the Salone del Gusto (the "Exhibition of Taste") – the flagship event in Turin by Italy's Slow Food Movement. Having started as a local campaign to stop a McDonald's being built near the Spanish Steps in Rome, over the years the Movement has grown into the world's largest network of independent artisanal food producers. This is their biennial get-together, where you can meet a Tibetan farmer and taste his yak's cheese; or inhale the intoxicating aromas of Mexican Chinantla vanilla; or get a whiff of the sea with carrageenan jelly from Ireland. Everything you can imagine ever eating or drinking, and much more.

The Salone takes place in October in the Lingotto Fiere, the giant exhibition space created from the former Fiat car factory, and attracts 170,000 gourmets from all over the world. As well as the aisles dedicated to different foodstuffs and national cuisines, there are lectures that are a far cry from those at university. Book yourself in for a talk on the history of Bourbon, and rather than falling asleep at the back you'll be sampling six different types of whisky while one of New York's best cocktail barmen explains the story behind such drinks as the mint julep and whiskey sour.

This being the land of the long lunch and seven-course supper, some people still have room for more at the end of a day's grazing. For an extra fee, you can join them each evening at one of several hosted dinners in restaurants across the city and in castles, country houses and rural *trattorie* in the surrounding Piedmontese countryside, as some of Italy's finest chefs prepare their favourite local meals. Add a constant background of music from Cape Verde to Lake Baikal played live throughout the day, the chance to buy as much as you can carry on the train home for Christmas gifts and indulgent treats, and the city of Turin all around if you fancy a stroll around a gallery or two, and you have a recipe to satisfy almost every palate.

Need to know Turin has excellent rail connections throughout Europe (see Ⓦwww.bahn.de). Some of the most popular dinners, lectures and tasting events book up months in advance. See Ⓦwww.salonedelgusto.com for more information. For details on Slow Food events in your own region or anywhere in the world, go to Ⓦwww.slowfood.com.

085 HORSE-RIDING IN TUSCANY

Much of Tuscany's appeal lies in its simplicity of life: its isolated hill-towns, stone farmhouses, cypress-lined vineyards and rustic cuisine. If you don't want to break that spell by hiring a car to get around, one solution is to tour the region by horse on an eight-day riding tour with Equine Adventures.

Guests stay at a restored eighteenth-century farm estate in the hills between Dicomano and the summit of Monte Giove, in the Rufina part of the famous Chianti wine-growing area. Each day, you'll explore the region on horseback, crossing over the gentle rolling hills of the Mugello, along the River Sieve and through the wilderness of the Monte Giove National Park. En route, you'll stop at local restaurants for leisurely lunches then return in the evening to the estate, where you'll dine on typical Tuscan cuisine, including *crostini di fegato* (liver crostini), *tortellini al patate* (potato-filled pasta), *peposo al cinghiale* (wild boar stew), spit roasts, salads and cheeses.

The trip includes three full-day rides and two shorter half-day rides to give you some free time to relax by the pool on the estate or visit Florence (25km from the estate). This being one of the most famous wine-growing regions in Italy, there is an emphasis on tasting some of the local wine throughout the week, and the penultimate day includes a late afternoon ride through the Colognole Chianti vineyards, with the option to stop off for a wine-tasting tour at the fifteenth-century Villa Colognole, owned by Staletti, one of the most famous wine-growing families in Italy. Be prepared for a tipsy trot home.

Need to know *Tours start at Pontassieve train station (for prices and tickets see Ⓦ www.trenitalia. com), where you'll be collected and taken to the farm. For information about the farm and horses see Ⓦ www.simplesite.com/chiantitrails; Ⓣ +39 (0) 338 845 2755. For prices and booking visit Ⓦ www.equineadventures.co.uk; Ⓣ +44 (0) 208 256 5990. Further information about the wine and region of Colognole is at Ⓦ www.colognole.it.*

(Clockwise from top) Rolling hills of Le Crete Senesi, Tuscany; Horses for courses; Tasting wine in the Cantina Cantucci, Montepulciano

THE GREEN LIGHTS OF AMSTERDAM

There's always more to a city than meets the eye, and nowhere is this more so than Amsterdam. Explore a little beyond the main tourist attractions and you'll most likely find it an outdoorsy city with plenty of parks, canals and cycle lanes; a place where you can visit farmers' markets, see fringe theatre and art galleries, walk along litter-free streets dotted with street performers or just sit in one of its many green spaces and watch the world go by. Here are a few suggestions for how to spend a green day in this beguiling capital.

086 Pedal your way around

Amsterdam has an excellent network of trams, metro and buses, but cycling is usually the quickest, easiest and cheapest way to travel around the city. Nearly all the cycling lanes are separate from the road (with traffic lights especially for bikes), so it's a safe place to cycle, though you're advised to always lock your bike wherever you leave it.

Cycling past the International Budget Hostel

The main bike rental hubs are at Central Station, Leidseplein and Dam Square. Mike's Bike Tours (Ⓦwww.mikesbiketoursamsterdam.com; ☎ +31 (0) 206 227 970) are on the Kerkstraat, around the corner from Leidseplein. Macbike is one of the largest bike rental agencies – it has three outlets (Leidseplein, Central Station and Visserplein) and provides details for ten bike tours around the city, including a 2–3hr "Ring of Canals" route and a 10km "Filmtrip Amsterdam" itinerary, which visits locations in Amsterdam used for movies including *Ocean's Twelve* and *Diamonds are Forever*. It also arranges three guided tours (for groups of 10–15) all starting from Central Station East.

Need to know *For hire prices and a map of Amsterdam showing all Macbike's outlets and cycling itineraries see Ⓦwww.macbike.nl; ☎ +31 (0) 206 200 985.*

087 Food, glorious food

After all that walking and cycling, stop for lunch at The Noordermarkt (Amsterdam's main farmers' market) in the Jordaan district. You're bound to find something tempting among the local cheeses, eggs, fresh fish, bread, honey, herbs, spices, nuts, mushrooms and home-made cakes. For a slap-up organic feast go to the east side of town, home of De Kas, Amsterdam's renowned organic restaurant. Located in Frankendael Park, between the Rembrandt Tower and the nineteenth-century facades of Watergraafsmeer, De Kas is in an old greenhouse that belonged to Amsterdam's municipal nursery, which the maverick chef owner saved from demolition and converted into an 8m-high glass building. The menu changes each day depending on what local produce is available.

Need to know *For information on Noordermarkt see Ⓦwww.amsterdam.info/markets/noordermarkt. For opening times and reservations at De Kas visit Ⓦwww.restaurantdekas.nl; ☎ +31 (0) 204 624 562. For a list of organic restaurants, cafés,* groceries and markets in Amsterdam and throughout the Netherlands see ⓦ*www.biologica.nl* (Dutch only).

088 Green spaces

Amsterdam has more than thirty parks. The largest is Vondelpark in the museum square, which although popular with joggers and dog-walkers is a tranquil haven (except when it hosts open-air concerts in the summer). The largest woodland area is Amsterdamse Bos, home to the marshy areas at Nieuwe Meer, a nature reserve where you can hire a canoe or pedal-boat to explore Lake Grote Vijver.

In the centre of town, on Plantage Middenlaan, De Hortus is one of the oldest botanical gardens in the world, with more than four thousand plant species. A café in the orangery serves organic pastries, sandwiches and salads. Some thirty private gardens are opened to the public for three days in June; a €15 "Passe Partout" (with proceeds going to charity) allows you access to all the gardens.

Need to know *Information on the city's parks is at* ⓦ*www.amsterdam. info/parks. For opening hours and information on guided tours at De Hortus see* ⓦ*www.dehortus.nl;* ☎ *+31 (0) 206 259 021. For opening times, maps and directions for how to reach the Open Day gardens visit* ⓦ*www. canalmuseums.nl.*

089 Stay on a canal boat

There's no better way to get a flavour for the city's waterways than to spend a night on a houseboat. There are plenty available to hire for a weekend or longer – for a comprehensive listing see ⓦ*www.houseboathotel.nl.* Don't be put off by the anonymous numbering – many of these boats, if not their names, ooze character, such as BK09 – a small, cosy boat furnished in glossy wood, marble and copper, on the Amstel River (opposite De IJsbreker, a popular restaurant, theatre and café). If you're looking for a boat in a quiet part of town, try the Blue Wave boat, which you can rent from a local family; for prices and reservations see ⓦ*www.bluewavehouseboat.com;* ☎ *+ 31 (0) 650 667 760.*

A lazy day in Vondelpark; The canal at Herengracht

090 SPOT WHALES AND DOLPHINS ON BOARD THE FERRY TO SPAIN

From the deck of the *Pride of Bilbao* ferry it's not unusual to see striped, Risso's and bottlenose dolphins playing in the bow wave. Look further out to sea and you might spot any of various species of whale: fin, pilot, minke, Cuvier's beaked or even the enormous blue whale.

The Bay of Biscay is one of the best places in Europe to see whales and dolphins: so good, in fact, that a team of marine scientists from the Biscay Dolphin Research Programme boards the ferry every time it sails from Portsmouth to Bilbao in northern Spain. Since 1995, over 21 species have been recorded in these waters (more than a quarter of the world's total). On August 10 2007, 162 fin whales were spotted during just one trip.

On deck, a wildlife officer provides free presentations and inside the boat – in the Junior Crew Club – he gives a talk for children. He'll explain how different species are associated with different areas of the crossing; the common dolphins, for instance, spend their winters off the Brittany peninsula, while the beaked whale is often seen over the submarine canyons off Spain's north coast. And once you've enjoyed the natural history spectacle, you can disappear into the belly of the boat for all the usual entertainment: two casinos, a gym, saunas and a beauty salon as well as en-suite cabins.

The voyage leaves Portsmouth at 9.15pm and arrives in Bilbao at 8am two days later. Alternatively, you can cross the Bay of Biscay on a weekly service from Portsmouth to Santander (24hr) or from Plymouth to Santander (20hr). By the time you arrive, you'll probably have spotted some whales, enjoyed a range of onboard services and had a good rest. It may just take your mind off the pitch and roll.

Need to know Bikes can be taken on board ferries for an extra charge. For ferries from Portsmouth to Bilbao follow the link to P&O Ferries at ⓦ www.biscay-dolphin.org.uk – any tickets sold through this link will earn money for the Biscay Dolphin Research Programme. For prices and bookings of ferries to Santander visit ⓦ www.brittany-ferries.co.uk; ☎+44 (0)871 244 0744 (You can volunteer to spot cetacea on these crossings, see ⓦ www.orca.org.uk). From both Santander and Bilbao there are good onward connections throughout Spain by bus (ⓦ www.alsa.es) and train (ⓦ www.renfe.es).

091 TOMORROW'S TOURISM TODAY IN THE SWISS ALPS

For a glimpse of how ski accommodation might look in the future, check out Whitepod, an isolated resort at an altitude of 1600m, tucked beneath the Dents du Midi above the Swiss alpine town of Les Cerniers. This low-impact, hi-tech camp consists of domed "pods" made out of canvas and steel resembling roughly made igloos on wooden platforms. Each of the "expedition" pods has just one room with a double bed, thick duvet, washbasin, oil lamp, a wood-burning stove and a panoramic view of the alpine peaks. The larger "pavilion" pods have a separate bedroom on a mezzanine level.

If you can leave the super-insulated snug interior, you can ski over to a 600m private run (with two drag lifts) to practise your turns, or strap on a pair of snow-shoes and explore kilometres of virgin snow in off-piste woodland trails, then return for a soak in the sauna followed by dinner in the wooden chalet.

Need to know Trains go from Paris Gare du Lyon (via Geneva or Lausanne) to Aigle (ⓦ www.raileurope.co.uk; ☎+44 (0) 844 848 4070) where you can be collected, by arrangement. Groups can stay in the Alpage de Chindonne, a large refuge near the top of the ski run at 1800m. It sleeps sixty (in dorms) and includes access to the Whitepod activities (including yoga and gym) and ski run. For rates, reservations and details of activities see ⓦ www.whitepod.com; ☎+41 (0) 244 713 838.

A pod with a view at the unique Whitepod Camp in the Swiss Alps

THE HIGH LIFE OF A TREEHOUSE

Leaves rustle in the evening breeze; stars twinkle through the foliage; a barn owl hoots. A night up in the peaceful boughs of a tree and you feel not just close to nature but a part of it. Fortunately, treehouse designs have come a long way from makeshift shacks of flimsy wooden planks and rope ladders: the latest installations are stand-alone structures supported by stable, steel frames with spiralling staircases that wind up to a large open room and an outdoor terrace. In these modern arboreal abodes, you can enjoy all the creature comforts of a hotel, lots of natural light and a bird's-eye view of the world. And the kids are in den heaven. Below are our favourites.

092 Keycamp, northern France

Choose between three treehouses at Keycamp's family-friendly French campsites – at Carnac and Dol-de-Bretagne in Brittany and at La Croix du Vieux Pont near Disneyland Paris. The domed, thatched treehouses are wrapped

Choose between four stand-alone treehouses at Orion B&B in the south of France

around a treetrunk about 5m off the ground up a spiralling staircase. Each has one double and four single beds while on the ground there's a tent with cooking equipment, fridge and freezer. The kids can use all the campsite's facilities during the day – then when you've tucked them up, you can spend lamp-lit evenings on the terrace.

Need to know *For prices and bookings see* Ⓦ*www.keycamp.co.uk;* ☏*+ 44 (0) 844 406 0319.*

093 Perché dans le Perche in northern France

Nestled among a 200-year-old *châtaignier* (sweet chestnut tree) in the hills of southern Normandy, this treehouse at La Renardière offers splendid isolation. There are two double rooms (one has an extra single bed), a small kitchen and large shower room and you can order breakfast (organic bread, home-made jams, seasonal fruit, yoghurt) sitting out on a terrace looking out over green fields. The treehouse is surrounded by a nature reserve – watered by natural springs – that is home to wild boar, roe deer, badgers, foxes and hares, as well as various species of birds and butterflies. Perché dans le Perche is also a good base for hill-walking and mushroom-picking in the nearby Parc Naturel Régional du Perche.

Need to know *The treehouse is two hours' drive from Paris and ferry ports at St Malo and Caen. For prices, bookings and directions see* Ⓦ*www. perchedansleperche.com;* ☏*+33 (0) 233 255 796.*

094 Orion B&B, south of France

Swing from a hammock on a terrace perched 9m high in woodland near Nice. Each of the four cedar redwood treehouses at Orion has an en-suite double room with internet connection – "Shere Khan" has a round teak bath while "King Louie" has a footbridge over to the kids' bunkbed hideaway. Back on terra firma, soak up the sun on a lounger by a natural swimming pool. After breakfast on the garden-dining patio, the owner, Diane, will show you the short cut up to the pretty medieval village of St Paul de Vence and how to reach the beaches and nightlife of the French Riviera. Though venture too far and you'll miss the intimate Scandinavian-run La Brouette restaurant, a ten-minute uphill walk in the woods behind the treehouses. After smoked trout while the sun sets, stagger back down through the woods in torchlight to your nest in the trees.

Need to know *Take the train (🌐www.sncf. com) to Nice and then bus #400 to St Paul de Vence (☎+33 (0) 493 583 760 for bus times), from where it's a 20min walk to Orion. For prices and booking see 🌐orionbb.com (reservations by web only). To reserve a table at La Brouette (reservations essential) ☎+33 (0) 493 586 716.*

095 La Piantata, Italy

If you wake up not knowing where you are, you'll soon be reminded that you are 8m up a tree when breakfast arrives via a pulley. Situated among lavender hills, this treehouse for two is a short walk from an olive grove on an organic *agriturismo* (La Piantata) near the old Etruscan town of Tuscania. The treehouse is in the dense foliage of a century-old oak; there's a four-poster bed, bathroom, shower and terrace. La Piantata is also a horse-riding centre and it's just a few kilometres to Lake Bolsena, where you can hire sail-boats for the day.

Need to know *For prices, booking, itineraries and directions from Rome, Milan and Bologna see 🌐www.lapiantata.it; ☎+39 (0) 335 604 9630.*

(Clockwise from top) Splendid isolation at La Piantata; The horse-riding centre; Inside the treehouse; The gateway to La Piantata

Take the train to the slopes

Over a million skiers and snowboarders fly to the Alps each winter, yet many of the ski resorts in France, Switzerland, Austria and Italy are easily accessible by train. Cost-wise there's little difference to flying (once you've factored in transfers to and from airports) and travelling by train has many advantages: the check-in times are far shorter, there's free baggage allowance for your gear and the journey has a much smaller carbon footprint. In addition, the overnight service that leaves Paris on Friday evening and arrives early Saturday morning (returning the following Saturday evening) means you can fit in two extra days' skiing on the relatively quieter Saturday changeover days – without having to pay for extra nights' accommodation. Below are the options available.

Eurostar's **Ski Train** is a direct service from London St Pancras to Moûtiers, Aime la Plagne and Bourg St Maurice. The daytime service leaves on Saturdays at 10am and arrives at Moûtiers at 5.30pm, Aime la Plagne at 6.02pm and Bourg St Maurice at 6.20pm. The overnight service (which does not have couchettes) leaves on Fridays at 8.31pm and reaches the Alps early Saturday morning (6.27am at Bourg St Maurice). For prices, reservations and details of onward transfers by bus to the resorts (40–90min) see Ⓦwww.eurostar.com; ☏+44 (0) 8705 186 186.

RailEurope's **Snow Train** is an overnight sleeper service (with six-berth couchettes and a "bar disco" carriage) to the Alps on Fridays, returning Saturday evening the following week. It includes taking the Eurostar from London St Pancras at 5.35pm to Paris Gare du Nord, then changing platforms for the overnight service, which leaves at 10.28pm and arrives early Saturday morning in Chambéry, Albertville, Moûtiers, Aime la Plagne, Landry and finally at 8.44am to Bourg St Maurice. It returns on Saturday evening arriving at London St Pancras on Sunday at 11.16am. For prices and reservations see Ⓦwww.raileurope.co.uk; ☏+44 (0) 844 848 4088.

A final option is to take the **Eurostar** to Paris (or Brussels) then switch to ordinary scheduled national trains to the Alps, though in Paris this usually involves a change of station across the city. For prices, reservations and connections see Ⓦwww.raileurope.co.uk or Ⓦwww.europeanrail.com. See also p.375 for more train resources.

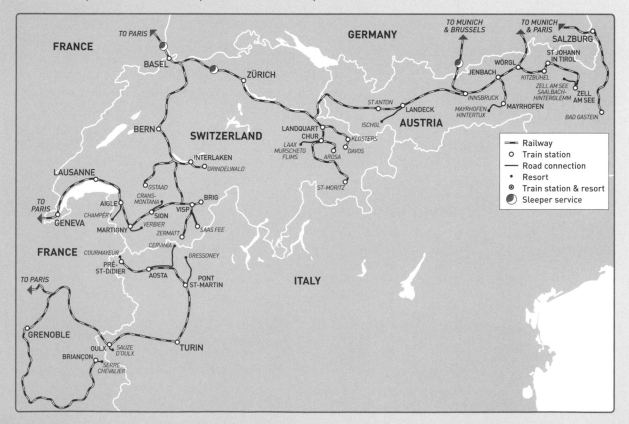

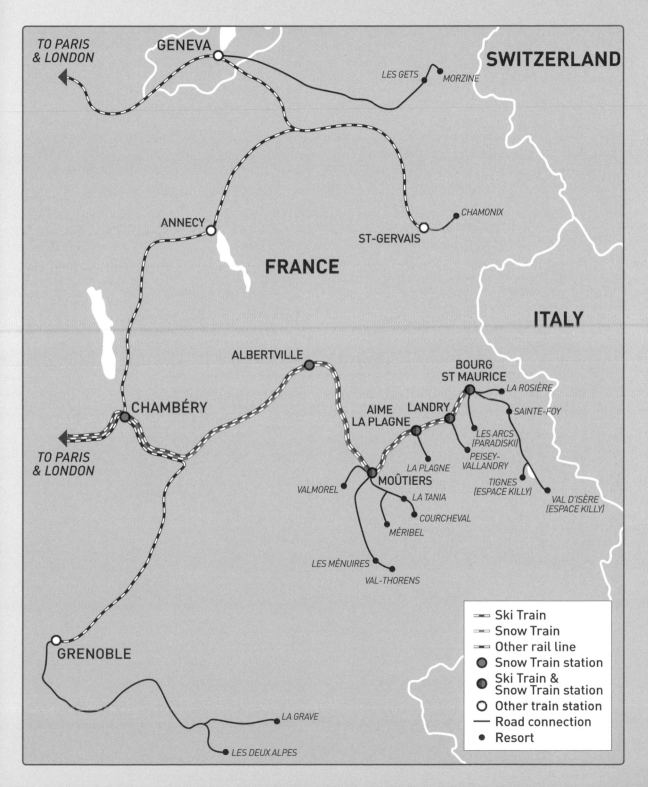

TO PARIS & LONDON

GENEVA

SWITZERLAND

LES GETS MORZINE

ANNECY

CHAMONIX

ST-GERVAIS

FRANCE

ITALY

ALBERTVILLE

BOURG ST MAURICE

LA ROSIÈRE

AIME LA PLAGNE   LANDRY

SAINTE-FOY

CHAMBÉRY

LES ARCS (PARADISKI)

LA PLAGNE

PEISEY-VALLANDRY

TO PARIS & LONDON

VALMOREL

MOÛTIERS

TIGNES (ESPACE KILLY)

LA TANIA

VAL D'ISÈRE (ESPACE KILLY)

COURCHEVAL

MÉRIBEL

LES MÉNUIRES

VAL-THORENS

GRENOBLE

LA GRAVE

LES DEUX ALPES

Ski Train
Snow Train
Other rail line
Snow Train station
Ski Train & Snow Train station
Other train station
Road connection
Resort

MEDITERRANEAN ISLANDS

FRANCE

SPAIN

CORSICA

100

103

096

MENORCA

101

IBIZA

099

098

097

104

FORMENTERA

MALLORCA

105

102

107

SARDINIA

096 Take the train to Vizzavona, Corsica
097 Chill out in Ibiza
098 Go on a Green Ibiza Tour
099 Stay on an organic farm in Ibiza
100 Monitor whales and dolphins in the Ligurian Sea
101 Discover the quieter side of Mallorca
102 Cycle across Sardinia
103 Walk across Corsica's Désert des Agriates
104 Cycle around the island of Formentera
105 Kayak around the Maddalena Archipelago, Sardinia

106 Walk in the Riserva dello Zingaro, Sicily
107 Lunch with shepherds in Sardinia
108 Under the volcano, Mount Etna National Park
109 Port side at the Petit Hotel, Sicily
110 Stay in a traditional Sicilian farmhouse
111 Help to save Europe's largest bird, Croatia
112 Head into the mountains of Crete
113 Sea kayaking along the Dalmatian Coast, Croatia
114 Stay at Milia Mountain Retreat in Crete
115 Eat in Crete

096 TAKE THE TRAIN TO VIZZAVONA, CORSICA

If you want to enjoy Corsica's spectacular mountain scenery without embarking on multi-day treks up from the coast or the gruelling sixteen-stage hiking route of the GR20, then a good option is to take the train into the heart of the island's massif.

The railway connects the ports of Calvi and Bastia with Ajaccio in the west and stops off halfway at Vizzavona, high up in the mountainous interior. Vizzavona is also a rest point midway along the GR20, so the handful of *gîtes d'étapes* (hikers' hostels) and restaurants near the station can get crowded with walkers in summer. Just ten minutes' drive from the village, though, is Hotel Monte D'Oro, a classy, family-run hotel that oozes antiquity without being ostentatious. Sepia pictures hang on the walls and the ivy-clad restaurant serves food from the owner's farm with a range of Corsican wines.

The hotel, as the name suggests, is at the foot of the Monte D'Oro mountain, which you can walk up from Vizzavona in about five hours to enjoy wonderful views of the island. From the hotel, you can also explore forests of beech and laricio pine, or swim by the waterfalls at Cascade des Anglais.

Need to know *ⓦwww.monte-oro.com; ☎ +33 (0) 495 472 106. Trains run from Ajaccio or Bastia to Vizzavona, where the owner can collect. There is also a gîte d'étape adjacent to the hotel, which costs €17 per person per night: ☎ +33 (0) 495 452 527. For train and bus connections in Corsica see ⓦwww.corsicabus.org.*

097 CHILL OUT IN IBIZA

If you're stuck for something to do with the family on a Sunday, spend a few hours at Casita Verde, Ibiza's ecology and education centre. Based at a farm a few kilometres northwest of San José, the centre has some unusual features – a house part-made with bottles, a toilet that looks like a giant sugar cube and a washing machine that runs off solar energy. The aim is to show how easy it is to have a greener lifestyle, particularly by incorporating solar and wind power in everyday use.

Children are looked after in a supervised play school, allowing you to stroll around the outdoor centre, learn how to cultivate plants and herbs, or try fresh smoothies and infusions at the juice bar. But if that sounds too much like hard work for a sleepy Sunday, you could just chill out with a massage at the natural therapy centre or sit with a drink looking out over the valley, knowing that the kids are in safe hands.

Need to know *Casita Verde is only open to the public on Sundays (2–6pm). Entrance is free (donations accepted) but visits are by telephone appointment only: ☎ +34 (0) 971 187 353. For directions and details of Casita Verde's work see ⓦwww.casitaverde.com.*

098 GO ON A GREEN IBIZA TOUR

Ibiza can surprise you: although it's best known as a clubbing capital, it also has many quiet coves and beaches where the locals go, particularly in the northeast, as well as lots of unspoilt areas in the interior where you can see a variety of wildlife.

During the summer solstice Green Ibiza Tours runs a guided walking tour to some of the island's hidden gems, organized by volunteers from Casita Verde (see above). You'll go on natural history walks inland, visit Las Salinas nature reserve where you can see storks, herons and flamingos, and explore some of the island's most remote coves. The base for the week is the Campsiteat Camping La Playa near Es Canar on the east coast, where you'll start the day with yoga, pilates or tai chi in the shade of the forest by the sea.

Need to know *Tours begin in Ibiza Town from where you'll be taken to Camping La Playa. For further details see ⓦwww.greenibizatours.com; ☎ +34 (0) 971 187 353. For general info on shops, cafés, green places to stay and low-impact activities in Ibiza and Formentera see ⓦwww.greenheart-guide.com.*

(Clockwise from top left) Santa Agnes Coastal path, northwestern Ibiza; the bottle house at Casita Verde; aloe vera crops at Casita Verde; foliage you might encounter on a walk around Platja d'en Bossa; Spectacular Ibizan coastal scenery at Punta de sa Galera

Pollination in action; Can Marti's stylish rooms are individually themed; tending the young plants in the garden permaculture; the Olivo cottage

099 STAY ON AN ORGANIC FARM IN IBIZA

If you've ever dreamt of escaping to the Med and buying a farmhouse, a stay at Can Marti will show you how it can be done successfully. Swiss owners Peter and Isabelle have spent over a decade transforming their traditional Ibizan finca into an idyllic country home and the island's first genuinely eco-friendly accommodation.

Couples can choose between three self-catering studio apartments (individually themed: Mexican, Indian and Spanish rustic) in the old stone farmhouse, while up to four can stay in a separate arabesque, clay-plastered stone house that overlooks the estate's sloping terraces of almond, carob, olive, pistachio and walnut trees.

For breakfast, there's home-made wholemeal bread, local jam and honey, and you can stock up on groceries and wine at the on-site organic shop. There's no shortage of sun on Ibiza, so Can Marti's electricity is run off solar panels, but since water is a precious resource there's no swimming pool and rainwater is harvested. Waste water is also reused in the estate's permaculture gardens.

If you're able to stir yourself away from this country idyll, there are plenty of swimming spots at the coves and beaches along the northeast coast. One of the best, close to Portinatx, is Cala d'en Serra – an arching sandy bay (with excellent snorkelling) where you can have drinks and grilled fish at a *chiringuito* among the pine trees behind the beach. After a few days at Can Marti, dipping in the clear-blue waters along this less-visited side of the island, you'll have to pinch yourself that this is the same island that thousands of the world's clubbers descend upon each summer. It's another world.

Need to know *A bus goes from Ibiza Town to Sant Joan (2km from Can Marti), where the owners will collect by arrangement. For directions, accommodation details, prices and booking see Ⓦwww.canmarti.com; ☎ +34 (0) 971 333 500. There are regular ferry services to Ibiza from the other Balearic Islands, as well as Barcelona (overnight), Valencia and Denia (both 4.5hr): Ⓦwww.balearia.com.*

100 MONITOR WHALES AND DOLPHINS IN THE LIGURIAN SEA

Here's your chance to see what it's like to be a marine biologist working in the warm waters of the eastern Mediterranean. In collaboration with Oceans Worldwide, The Whale and Dolphin Conservation Society (WDCS) lets volunteers help scientists monitor several species, including bottlenose dolphins and the enormous fin whale – the world's second-largest animal. You'll spend five days out in the Ligurian Sea between Italy and Corsica on board a motorized sail boat (which is also where you sleep), spending your time learning identification techniques. Regular "swim stops" at various islands are scheduled during the trip so you can relax and cool off. Chances are you'll come dangerously close to changing your career.

Need to know *Tours start and finish at Portosole harbour near San Remo on Italy's Ligurian coast. A percentage of proceeds from the trips goes towards supporting the conservation work of WDCS. For itinerary details and prices see Ⓦwww. oceansworldwide.co.uk/italy.htm; ☎ +44 (0) 845 290 3218.*

101 DISCOVER THE QUIETER SIDE OF MALLORCA

The resorts of the Bay of Palma may define mass tourism, but away from these concrete jungles, Mallorca is surprisingly wild and beautiful – a place where hilltop villages and monasteries look out over sweeping agricultural plains. The Tramuntana Mountains – which stretch from the western town of Andraitx to the island's northernmost cape – encapsulate this remoteness, and make for a great region to explore at a leisurely pace.

Based in the coastal town of Sóller in the heart of the Tramuntana Mountains, Tramuntanatours organizes day-trips into the mountains. Choose between walking tours, mountain biking, canyoning and sea kayaking around the coast. Groups are typically of four to eight people and tours include a guide, who will inform you about the native flora and fauna as well as the region's surprisingly rich cultural history. You're encouraged to find accommodation in and around Sóller; one of its recommended places to stay is Casa Bougainvillea, a small B&B in a traditional townhouse. The rooms are in simple Mediterranean style, there are potted plants everywhere and even an honesty bar for essentials. Magaluf it is not.

Need to know *For details and prices of tours see ⓦwww.tramuntanatours.com; ⓣ +34 (0) 971 632 423. Casa Bougainvillea: ⓦwww. casa-bouganvillea.com; ⓣ +34 (0) 971 633 104. There's a fast catamaran from Barcelona to Palma on most days of the week (3hr 45min) and an overnight ferry from Barcelona and Valencia: ⓦwww.trasmediterranea.es. For ferry services from the other Balearic Islands see ⓦwww.balearia.com.*

102 CYCLE ACROSS SARDINIA

Sardinia's flat coastal roads, gently undulating interior and forested mountains make it ideal for cycling. Choose your route carefully and you will enjoy long stretches of traffic-free asphalt roads that pass olive groves and vineyards, wind through valleys of oak or meander across sand dunes along the island's jagged coastline. For those that like to get some height, there are several steep mountainous routes, particularly in the north, where you can enjoy breathtaking scenery in Gallura's Limbara Mountains and the Supramonte before long descents towards the coast and a deserved swim in warm turquoise waters.

Need to know *Sardinia-based cycling specialists Dolcevita (ⓦwww.dolcevitabiketours.com; ⓣ +39 (0) 709 209 885), IchnusaBike (ⓦwww. ichnusabike.it; ⓣ +39 (0) 707 738 424) and Saddle Skedaddle (ⓦwww.skedaddle.co.uk; ⓣ +44 (0) 191 265 1110) organize guided and self-guided cycling throughout the island.*

Cycling along the coast of Sardinia

103 WALK ACROSS CORSICA'S DÉSERT DES AGRIATES

Most of Corsica's tourists go to the resorts in the south or to the umbrella-lined beaches of Ajaccio on the west coast. Yet some of the island's most idyllic beaches are in the north, in the unlikely setting of the Désert des Agriates – a remote, 50-square-kilometre protected area of dense scrubland east of Île Rousse.

The most easterly of these beaches, Plage de Loto, can be reached by any number of pleasure boats from the jetty at St Florent, or you can walk there from St Florent via a 40km trek along the desert's rugged coastal path – one of the longest stretches of protected coastline in the Mediterranean. The route west from St Florent to Plage de Loto is the most popular, so if you want to go it alone start from the west – at Ostriconi – and head east. A good place to stay the night before is the nearby Pietra Monetta, a *ferme-auberge* (farm inn) where you can feast on homegrown Corsican food – such as roast lamb sautéed in local herbs – on the vine-clad outdoor terrace or inside the eighteenth-century dining room.

The path into the desert leaves from behind the dunes of Plage de Ostriconi and you'll soon experience the waft of sweet-smelling

Walking along the Désert des Agriates coast path

shrub (maquis) – home to warblers, pipits and buntings. After a few hours walking inland, the path heads out to the coast, passing several small rocky coves and pockets of beaches and eventually leading to the welcome *gîte d'étape* at Plage de Ghignu.

The following day, it's just a few hours' walk to Plage de Saleccia, a kilometre-long sweep of soft sand with an impressive backdrop of high dunes. Plage de Loto is just a 40min walk east along the coast, but if you want to have these beaches to yourself (once the day-trippers have gone), you can pitch a tent in the shade of trees behind Saleccia's dunes at Camping U Paradisu.

The final stretch to St Florent is a much greener section and is popular with people walking the other way to Plage de Loto, so the trail cuts a more beaten path than the wilder stretch of the previous day. The desert can get intensely hot, especially as the dense scrub creates a very humid atmosphere, so take plenty of water. But if you walk in (instead of taking the boat cruises) and are well prepared, you'll come away feeling that you've seen the best of the desert, not just the famous beaches.

Need to know *Pietra Monetta: ⓦwww.location-agriates.com; ☏ +33 (0) 495 602 488. Camping U Paradisu (closed Nov–April; booking essential; €5 per pitch, meals €15): ☏ +33 (0) 495 378 251. A night at the gîte d'étape in Ghignu costs €9 per person; contact Syndicate Mixte Agriate (☏ +33 (0) 495 370 986). For details of ferme-auberges throughout Corsica see ⓦwww.bienvenuealaferme-corse.com (French only).*

104 CYCLE AROUND THE ISLAND OF FORMENTERA

In contrast to the hills of Ibiza, the small island of Formentera – 17km to the south – has a network of flat, quiet roads that are ideal for a day's cycling. You can cross the island's two plateaux in a few hours via a central isthmus, passing fields of wheat, carob

and fig trees among the arid countryside, but you'll never be far from uncrowded, dune-backed sandy beaches.

The only way to reach Formentera is by ferry from Ibiza. At the port of La Savina, you can pick up a *Green Routes* leaflet from the tourist office, which includes details of signposted cycling paths to some of the island's hotspots. Among these are archeological remains (such as the Bronze-age ruins at Barbària), the island's tiny capital Sant Francesc Xavier and the large beach at Platja de Mitjorn where you can have lunch by the sea.

In the early evening, cycle past the island's wetland habitat in the north (home to herons, egrets, warblers and the odd flamingo) and up to Platja de ses Illetes by the Ses Salines Natural Park, where you can watch the sun set over this beautiful, untouched corner of the island.

Need to know *The ferry from Ibiza to La Savina takes 30–65min: ⓦwww.balearia. com. There are several bike hire companies at La Savina, including Bicicletas/Moto Rent Mitjorn (ⓦwww.motorentmigjorn.com; ☏ +34 (0) 971 322 306). Eco Ibiza (ⓦwww.ecoibiza.com; ☏ +34 (0) 971 302 347) runs full-day guided cycling excursions on Formentera.*

Wooden gangway at Playa de ses Illetes beach, Formentera; *Flipper & Chiller* bar-café, Platja de Mitjorn

105 KAYAK AROUND THE MADDALENA ARCHIPELAGO, SARDINIA

Much has been written about the celebrity highlife of Sardinia's Costa Smeralda, as well as the island's traditional cuisine and its distinctive character and customs. Less well known is that Sardinia has some of the best-conserved coastline in the Mediterranean, thanks to government legislation that bans building property within 2km of the sea around the entire island.

One of the best ways to enjoy Sardinia's coastline is by sea kayak. Away from the hum of the pleasure boats, paddling under your own steam, you can reach some of the island's most unspoilt beaches. In particular, the protected islands of the Maddalena Archipelago in the Straits of Bonifacio between Corsica and northeastern Sardinia provide excellent conditions for an island-hopping kayaking

adventure. There are seven main islands (five are uninhabited) and over fifty islets around which you can paddle for days in warm, translucent water, searching for that ideal spot to land along the wind-blown granite coastline – home to gulls, cormorants and herons. The best time to go is outside of the main holiday season – either from early April to May, or better still in September and October when the sea is warmer and the water is clearest.

Need to know British-run Location Sardinia hires out kayaks for £30/€40 a day, and also organizes week-long kayaking trips around the archipelago, including accommodation and guide. For further info see ⓦwww.locationsardinia.com; ⓣ +39 (0) 328 6156 352. Ferries go to Olbia from Piombino (4.5hr), Civitavecchia (5hr), Livorno (6hr or overnight) or Genoa (9.5hr): ⓦwww.mobylines. com. For public transport and events on Maddalena see ⓦwww.lamaddalena.com.

Spargi Island, Maddalena Archipelago

106 WALK IN THE RISERVA DELLO ZINGARO, SICILY

The Riserva dello Zingaro in the northwest of Sicily (about an hour from Palermo) is the island's first nature reserve, established to protect a 7km stretch of coastline that's home to numerous endemic flora and fauna. Most people come to the reserve for the isolated beaches, but if you're feeling energetic there are lots of walks inland, including several strenuous routes in a mountainous section. It's also a birders' paradise: 39 species nest and mate here, including bunting, Greek partridge, blue rock thrush and one of the last remaining pairs of Bonelli's eagles.

There are two entrances – in the north at San Vito Lo Capo and in the south at Scopello. Vehicles (and dogs) are banned from the reserve so the only way in is on foot; there's a small entrance fee of €3 (pay in cash at the gates). Given the proximity to Palermo, it's a popular day-trip from the capital and is best avoided on summer weekends, but go mid-week or out of season and you'll have the place to yourself. Thankfully the reserve's protected status has kept the developers at bay and the reserve has become a life-saver for the local environment. That's good for the wildlife, of course, but it's also excellent value for anyone who enjoys a hearty walk to a pristine beach.

Need to know *An information hut at the Scopello entrance provides a free basic map showing the beaches and main walking routes. There is nowhere to fill up with water in the reserve so take plenty with you; the hut sells snacks and cold drinks. For details about the reserve's history, wildlife and walking itineraries see ⓦwww.riservazingaro.it (Italian only).*

107 LUNCH WITH SHEPHERDS IN SARDINIA

If you want to escape the heat of Sardinia's coast then head for the Supramonte Mountains, home

Agrituristica Guthiddai and the spectacular rock face of the Supramonte Plateau

to one of Europe's few remaining primary forests. From the natural spring at Sorgente Su Gologone you can walk into the Lanaittu Valley and up to a Bronze-Age Nuraghic village tucked into a cave near the top of Tiscali Mountain.

It's possible to find your way up to the top on your own, but you can get hopelessly lost among the maze of confusing pathways, so it's better to hire a guide through the Association for Tourist Services Culture and Environment in Orgosolo. These local guides can also take you to meet shepherds in the mountains, where you'll share in an al fresco lunch of boiled sheep with *patat'a perras,* roasted pork, bread, salami and their own cheese and local wine.

There are several good converted farmhouses on the slip road from Oliena to Su Gologone. Agrituristica Guthiddai is excellent value for money and is run by the English-speaking daughters of a farmer who still makes wine and olive oil on the estate. There are ten rooms with terraces where you can look out over the sheer rock face of the Supramonte plateau. Expect the kind of food that has won Sardinia many culinary admirers, including fresh ravioli, lamb pot roast and pork with fresh seasonal vegetables, all washed down with the owner's delicious red wine.

Need to know *For walking itineraries, tours, information on hiring a guide and having lunch with shepherds (spring and summer only; booking essential) see ⓦwww.supramonte.it. Agrituristica Guthiddai: ⓦwww.agriturismoguthiddai.com; ☎ +39 (0) 784 286 017. It is 7km east of Oliena, which has good public transport links. For details of travelling around Sardinia without a car see ⓦwww.getaroundsardinia.com.*

108 UNDER THE VOLCANO, MOUNT ETNA NATIONAL PARK

There's nothing quite like jumping out of bed and picking fresh fruit off a tree for breakfast. Especially when you're staying in the foothills of Mount Etna and in the distance you can see the mountain shimmering in the morning haze.

Etna Lodge, a renovated farmhouse on a former wine-producing estate beneath the mountain, is a great place to stay if you want to explore the national park. Sicilian owner Enrico and his Scandinavian partner Ingrid grow fruit and veg and make organic jams, wine, drinks and oil (all of which are for sale). You stay in the south and north wings of their nineteenth-century farmhouse, while dinner is served in the candlelit foyer of the main building.

There are any number of walks you can do around the foothills and outlying craters of Mount Etna as well as up to the summit. Tours leave from Catania or Taormina and usually include a full day of hiking through ash deserts and lava landscapes, and some offer a sunset trip. But if you'd prefer just to look at the mountain rather than walk up it, you can chill out back at the tranquil estate, read a book and pluck some fruit from the trees. No one will mind.

Need to know The lodge is open from April 1 to November 15; minimum stay is three nights. For directions, prices and booking see ⓦwww.etnalodge.it; ☎ +39 (0) 9564 8299. Mount Etna Experience (ⓦwww.etnaexperience.com) runs day-trips led by geologists fluent in English. For details on visiting the national park and guided nature tours (booking essential) see ⓦwww.parks.it/parco.etna.

109 PORT SIDE AT THE PETIT HOTEL, SICILY

Ports aren't known for their charm. Unless you're a boatyard junkie, most are chaotic, gritty places you can't wait to escape from. The port of Milazzo, however, on the north coast of Sicily, is popular with Italians as a destination in its own right, thanks to the beaches and well-equipped campsites at Capo Millazo, as well as being the main point of embarkation for ferries to the Aeolian Islands.

If you're worried about the air quality then stay at The Petit Hotel, a nineteenth-century building on the seafront overlooking the hydrofoil dock, which has an ionizing filter in every room to purify the air. The hotel was given a green makeover in 2002 using only natural materials (such as lime instead of concrete, and non-toxic paints). Breakfasts include organic yogurt, eggs and jams, and the restaurant serves traditional meals using organic and fair trade products.

Antonio, the owner, is also a paragliding pilot, so go easy on his organic wine, otherwise you might find the next day you've agreed to a spot of high-altitude soaring. It's marvellous for the head, though, so they say.

Need to know For directions and further details see www.petithotel.it; ☎ +39 (0) 909 286 784.

Volcanic terrain, Etna

110 STAY IN A TRADITIONAL SICILIAN FARMHOUSE

The success of *agriturismo* on the Italian mainland has prompted many owners of rural cottages in Sicily to transform their homes into country guesthouses. Some lose their character as a result, but at Il Roveto, a beautifully restored eighteenth-century farmhouse on the southeast coast (between Noto and Pachino), the timeless charm that epitomizes rural Sicily is still very much intact.

The road up to Il Roveto passes fields of olive groves and vineyards before turning off up a dusty track that leads to the farm. There's self-catering for up to six people in self-contained apartments, but if a prepared meal appeals there's a good restaurant in the main building that serves local meat cooked with produce grown on the farm, including lemons, potatoes, mandarins, oranges, prickly pears and olive oil.

The farm is just a few hundred metres from the Riserva Naturale di Vendicari, a World Heritage Site that's an important wetland habitat for migrating birds. You can walk down to the reserve from the farm, or if you have a car you can drive to other access points where there are well-maintained paths to several excellent beaches, such as Calamoshe. The southern part of the reserve is more protected, but there is one wide, sandy beach at Torre de Vendecari and several hides where you can watch the birds (some two hundred species have been recorded here).

Although it's not a large reserve, you can easily spend a day exploring the area, lounging on the beach and wandering around the marshes watching the birds before returning to the farmhouse for a meal produced entirely from the surrounding land. That's what people have been doing here for centuries.

Need to know *For prices and directions to the farmhouse see ⓦwww.roveto.it; ☎ +39 (0) 9316 6024. Minimum stay is three nights. The best time to see migratory birds in the Riserva Naturale di Vendicari is December and January.*

Eurasian griffon vulture

111 HELP TO SAVE EUROPE'S LARGEST BIRD, CROATIA

One of Croatia's most unspoilt islands, Cres, is home to the Caput Insulae Ecology Centre in the rustic village of Beli, where you can join a volunteer holiday to help protect the rare griffon vulture.

Now endangered in much of southern Europe, the griffon vulture – which has an awesome 2.5m wingspan that allows it to glide as far as 650km in a day – has historically fed on livestock carcasses on the rocky hills of Cres, but as traditional sheep-rearing has declined food sources have become scarce. The ecology centre exists to preserve the vulture population: it has a sanctuary where injured birds are rehabilitated for release, and the staff and volunteers also monitor feeding sites, collect data on bird behaviour and educate locals to leave dead animals out in the open.

There's also time to explore the island's many beaches, help to pick olives or develop the seven eco-trails in the area, or to spot the two hundred other bird species found on Cres. But there's no doubt that the ultimate thrill here is to be sitting in one of the Centre's hides as you hear the heavy flap of a vulture come to rest only metres away.

Need to know *Ferries go from both the Croatian and Italian mainland to Cres, from where there are two buses each weekday to Beli. Minimum visits are for one week. For prices, volunteer testimonials and details of the eco-trails see ⓦwww.supovi.hr; ☎ +385 (0) 913 357 124.*

112 HEAD INTO THE MOUNTAINS OF CRETE

Anna-Malai House is an elegant and simply furnished villa overlooking the White Mountains in western Crete. It is 4km from the white sands of Kiani Akti beach, where there's a small taverna that's popular with locals on Sundays. Come here on any other day of the week and you'll have the place to yourself.

Owned by a local – Stelios Botonakis – Anna-Malai is typical of an increasing number of old cottages and rural houses in Crete that have been restored and offered as holiday lets, in a backlash against economic migration from rural communities to coastal resorts. Stelios often runs trips to the nearby Taverna Lemonia, one of a handful of olive farms still using traditional olive presses, as well as to the nearby village of Malaxa, where a local has set up an organic food cooperative offering tasting evenings of organic dishes and local wine.

By staying in and visiting places like Anna-Malai – and there are several other similar places like it throughout Crete – you'll support rural economies and help to stem the exodus of people away from their homes, which will ultimately preserve their culture. And you'll be treated to something a little more authentic and appetizing than resort-style moussaka.

Need to know *British firm Pure Crete rents out a range of locally owned and restored houses and villas throughout Crete, including Anna-Malai House. In April and May, it runs wildflower-walking holidays ("Crete in Bloom") led by botanists and environmentalists. For more see ⓦwww.purecrete. com; ☎ +44 (0) 845 070 1571.*

113 SEA KAYAKING ALONG THE DALMATIAN COAST, CROATIA

A necklace of islands licked by glimmering waters, Croatia's Dalmatian Coast is one of Europe's most beautiful shorelines. And by far the best way to explore it is to get in a kayak and paddle out, meandering leisurely between the islands as you sit a few centimetres above the water, taking a dip in the glassy sea or soaking up the sun on empty, white-sand beaches. Adriatic Kayak Tours, an organization based in Dubrovnik, offers small-group trips lasting from a few hours to a whole week; they also run quirky themed tours such as "Cliffs and

Hvar town and outlying islands, Croatia

Caves" and a "Wine and Cheese Sunset Paddle". At the end of each salty, tiring but exhilarating day, knowledgeable guides direct weary canoeists to family-run restaurants where freshly caught seafood and local meats are dished up alongside liberal quantities of local wine. The bling may be returning to Dubrovnik, but Croatia's real jewels are still to be found out to sea.

Need to know *No previous experience is necessary as tours start with training. For more on the types of tours offered, reservations and frequently asked questions see Ⓦwww. adriatickayaktours.com; ☏ +385 (0) 2031 2770.*

114 STAY AT MILIA MOUNTAIN RETREAT IN CRETE

High above the Topolia gorge in the western foothills of Crete's White Mountains, a group of locals has breathed new life into an abandoned settlement and transformed it into one of the island's most innovative places to stay.

The success of Milia Mountain Retreat is due largely to its simplicity. Thirteen guesthouses have been restored from the foundations of derelict buildings, using traditional methods that incorporate local stone and chestnut wood. The furnishings have been bought in from the surrounding villages and at night the only light is provided by candles. Spring water is piped in, bread is baked in wood-fired ovens, and the farm produces most of the ingredients needed for the local dishes served up in Milia's restaurant, such as potato, chestnut and onion stew.

The retreat is surrounded by over a square kilometre of land, so there are plenty of footpaths that lead into the hills if you want to work up an appetite for dinner. Further afield there's a sandy beach at Elafonissi and Byzantine churches at Kandanos. Weather permitting, there's a small spring-fed pool to dip into when you return from your excursions – a reminder that the simple pleasures in life can be among the best.

Need to know *Bring a torch as the electricity supply isn't always reliable. For prices, accommodation details and directions to Milia from Chania see Ⓦwww.milia.gr; ☏ +30 (0) 282 104 6774.*

115 EAT IN CRETE

The villages of Crete's mountainous interior are far away, in lifestyle if not distance, from the resorts on the island's northern coast. Here the pace of life is determined by seasons and harvests, and traditions remain strong: potters still make clay jars in their workshops and farmers still use carts to transport produce. Life moves slowly.

If it's this side of Crete you want to explore, you may want to indulge in a gastronomic tour with Crete's Culinary Sanctuaries, which takes small groups of up to eight visitors to stay in remote rural villages, immersing them deep into local life. In spring guests might harvest artichokes or fennel; in summer you'll see beekeeping and winemaking techniques; in winter the olive harvest dominates island life. Tours of wineries, olive oil presses and traditional bakeries are usually included, plus on some of the tours there are cooking classes.

Guests stay in simple rural lodging, mingling with residents, talking to traditional farmers and fishermen, and exploring the rugged beauty of the countryside. It's an experience that aims to open a window onto a world that consciously chooses to reject some of the excesses of modern life and instead work to its own seasonal rhythm.

Cretan life: traditional clay jars are still made and used to store goods; local cheese; wine in waiting; baking the traditional way

Need to know *For details, dates and prices of itineraries, as well as sample recipes, see Ⓦwww. cookingincrete.com.*

Rail and sail to the Med

TO BORDEAUX · TO LIMOGES & PARIS

TOULOUSE

FRANCE

MONTPELLIER

NARBONNE

TO LYON & PARIS

MARSEILLE

TOULON

ANDORRA

GOLFE DU LION

5h 45

TO MADRID

SPAIN

BARCELONA

5h 45m

9h 30m

7h

3h 45m

BALEARIC SEA

TO MADRID

VALENCIA

11h

MALLORCA

Alcúdia

1h

Ciutadella
Mahon

MENORCA

Palma

IBIZA

Ibiza Town

30—65m

2—5h

5h 30m

La Savina

FORMENTERA

M E D I T E R R A N E A N   S E A

As fly-and-flop destinations go, the Mediterranean has everything: from the pearl-white beaches and turquoise waters around Corsica to the sumptuous food of Sicily and the enduringly popular clubs of Ibiza. Though the quickest route is to fly, it's surprisingly easy to reach many of the popular islands by taking the train to the coast and then catching a boat across the sea, especially in summer when many operators put on faster vessels. You can get to Corsica, for instance, in fewer than three hours from Nice, and Menorca can be under four hours from Barcelona.

Most of the main ports have conveniently fast rail connections so you can whizz down by train in a day or take an overnight sleeper and sail across to the islands the following day. You'll soon be basking in the balmy weather without having racked up a huge carbon footprint. This map indicates the most popular trans-Mediterranean routes from the south coasts of Spain, France and Italy.

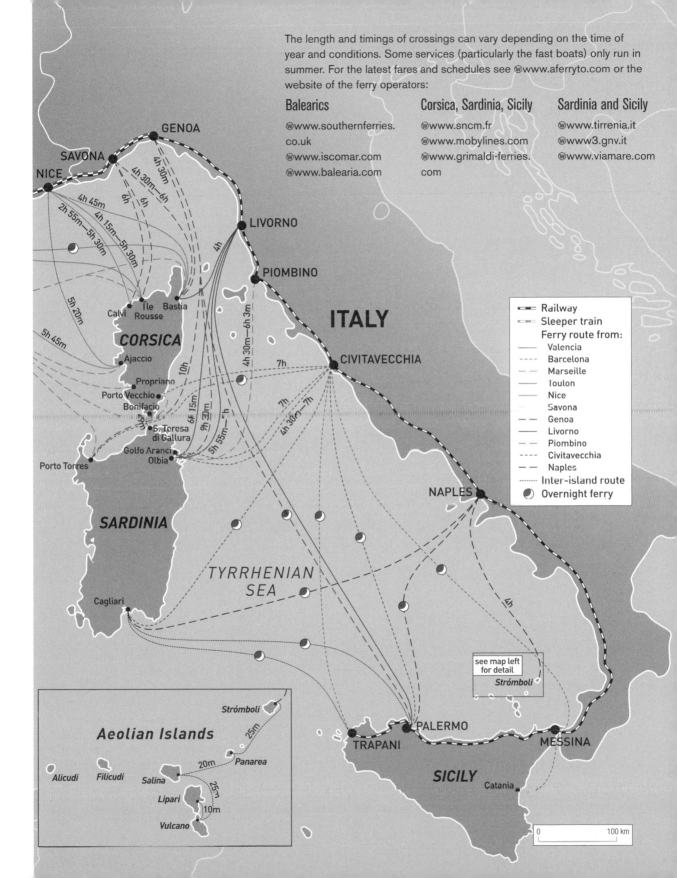

The length and timings of crossings can vary depending on the time of year and conditions. Some services (particularly the fast boats) only run in summer. For the latest fares and schedules see ⓦwww.aferryto.com or the website of the ferry operators:

Balearics
ⓦwww.southernferries.co.uk
ⓦwww.iscomar.com
ⓦwww.balearia.com

Corsica, Sardinia, Sicily
ⓦwww.sncm.fr
ⓦwww.mobylines.com
ⓦwww.grimaldi-ferries.com

Sardinia and Sicily
ⓦwww.tirrenia.it
ⓦwww3.gnv.it
ⓦwww.viamare.com

GENOA
SAVONA
NICE

4h 30m
4h 30m
4h 30m—6h
6h
6h
6h
2h 55m—5h 30m
4h 45m
4h 15m—5h 30m

LIVORNO

PIOMBINO

ITALY

5h 20m
5h 45m
Calvi
Île Rousse
Bastia
CORSICA
Ajaccio
Propriano
Porto Vecchio
Bonifacio
S. Teresa di Gallura
Golfo Aranci
Olbia
Porto Torres

4h
4h 30m—6h 3m
7h
CIVITAVECCHIA
7h
4h 30m—7h

10h
6h 15m
9h
5h 55m—7h
5h 55m

SARDINIA

NAPLES

TYRRHENIAN SEA

Cagliari

4h

see map left for detail
Strómboli

PALERMO
TRAPANI
MESSINA
SICILY
Catania

Legend:
- ▬▬ Railway
- ▬▭▬ Sleeper train
- Ferry route from:
  - Valencia
  - Barcelona
  - Marseille
  - Toulon
  - Nice
  - Savona
  - Genoa
  - Livorno
  - Piombino
  - Civitavecchia
  - Naples
  - Inter-island route
- ◗ Overnight ferry

Aeolian Islands

Strómboli
25m
20m
Panarea
Salina
25m
Alicudi *Filicudi*
Lipari
10m
Vulcano

0   100 km

ICELAND

130

128

NORWAY

120
119

131

123

134

SWEDEN

FINLAND

117

129

121

124

118

132

122

133

116

DENMARK

135

125 126 127

SCANDINAVIA

116 Take the no-fly route to Scandinavia
117 Stay under the turf at Gålå, Norway
118 Swim across Finland's lakes and rivers
119 Join the Sami Reindeer Migration, Norway
120 Group together at Ongajok, Norway
121 Rafting on the Klarälven, Sweden
122 Cycle along the Göta Canal, Sweden
123 Cross-country skiing in Kuusamo, Finland
124 Stay in a charcoal hut at Kolarbyn, Sweden
125 Get on your bike, Copenhagen

126 Fresh herring and hippy herbs, Copenhagen
127 Sleep somewhere green, Copenhagen
128 Go on a dog-sledding safari in Svalbard, Norway
129 Follow in Shackleton's footsteps at Finse, Norway
130 Whale-watching off the coast of Iceland
131 Paddle and pedal around the Lofoten Islands, Norway
132 Car-free on Koster, Sweden
133 Learn to ride a horse the natural way, Sweden
134 Track red foxes in Vålådalen nature reserve, Sweden
135 Become a light camper in Denmark

116 TAKE THE NO-FLY ROUTE TO SCANDINAVIA

Flying is the easy way in to the Nordic countries, but travelling there by boat or train is far more interesting and certainly better in terms of your carbon footprint. You can forget all about airport hassle and luggage reclaim and take it slow, enjoying the scenery as you go.

Trains go to Copenhagen from Hamburg (with connections from London via the Eurostar to Brussels and Cologne). Deutsche Bahn operates a comfortable sleeper train route, so you can catch a late-afternoon Eurostar train from London to Brussels, sleep overnight on the train to Hamburg and then connect to Copenhagen, arriving in the early afternoon. From Copenhagen you can take a ferry up to Oslo (16hr 30min) or cross into Sweden overland by train in 30min, from where you can whizz up the west coast or on to Stockholm.

Cruise ferries go from the east coast of England (Harwich) to Esbjerg in western Denmark (20hr), from where there's a train to Copenhagen (3hr 15min). Ferries also go from northern Germany to Trelleborg in Sweden, from Rostock (5hr 45min) and Sassnitz (4hr). Or you can catch a ferry from Rostock to Gedser in Denmark (1hr 45min), from where you can take a train or a bus to Copenhagen (both 2hr 30min).

If you're in a rush to get back to mainland Europe, the quickest way is usually by train from Copenhagen. You can take a return sleeper service, but it's also possible to get to London from Copenhagen in a day. There are three changes – but each just involves crossing platforms at Hamburg, Cologne and Brussels – and the latter joins the Eurostar direct to St Pancras. Leave Copenhagen at 7.42am and you'll be in London just after 10pm.

Need to know *For train times and advice on rail networks in Europe see Ⓦwww.seat61.com. For prices and ferry timetables from Harwich to Esbjerg and from Copenhagen to Oslo see Ⓦwww. dfdsseaways.co.uk. For ferries from Rostock and Sassnitz to Trelleborg and from Rostock to Gedser visit Ⓦwww.scandlines.de.*

117 STAY UNDER THE TURF AT GÅLÅ, NORWAY

The elevated vista is classic Norway: pine and birch forest surround the glistening blue waters of Lake Svintjern and in the distance loom the snowy peaks of the Jotunheimen Mountains. The silence at the small resort at Gålå, in the region of the same name, is addictive. Tucked up next to a wood-burning stove in a highland cabin, no-one need know you are here: the roofs of the cabins are turfed with grass, which is excellent for camouflage (as well as insulation).

If you want to venture out and explore the district of Gudbrandsdalen, local organization Summer Arena runs numerous activities, including pony-trekking, canoeing, white-water rafting on the River Sjoa, hiking, fishing and mountain biking (helpful route notes are provided in the cabins). Or you can go a little further afield to the Rondane National Park, home to the last wild reindeer herd in Norway. Here's a place where you feel a part of nature, not a lord of it.

Need to know *To get there from Oslo take the train to Vinstra (2hr 40min; Ⓦwww.nsb.no) where you'll be collected, by arrangement, for a 30min drive to Gålå. To book local activities with Summer Arena visit Ⓦwww.gala.no; ☏ +47 (0) 6129 7665. For further details of accommodation, prices and activities see Ⓦwww.inntravel.co.uk; ☏ +44 (0) 1653 617 920.*

118 SWIM ACROSS FINLAND'S LAKES AND RIVERS

It's the first dip of the day that's the hardest. Not because you're worried that the water will be cold – the lakes of southern Finland are shallow and the summer sun quickly heats the water. Rather, it's the thought of a whole day's exercise that makes you pause. But as soon as you take the plunge you've no time to reconsider. Off you go into the blue yonder, cutting a swan-

Taking the plunge at Lake Sakara

like trail across the clear water, immersed in the moment.

Your hosts for the trip are Finnish couple Maria and Petri, who open up their summer holiday home by Lake Sakara to swimming holiday company Swimtrek. Petri knows the local area well and – with the help of a professional swimming guide – he leads the way across the lakes and rivers. You swim approximately 5km a day (usually in two sessions) but you don't have to be a professional swimmer; so long as you can swim at a steady pace for this distance you'll be fine.

After each morning's swim, you stop for lunch (sausages over an open fire) then you've an hour or so to explore the area on foot or doze off, before beginning the afternoon's swim. After that you can walk or be driven back to the cabins; either way, when you get there Maria will have lit the wood-fired sauna and prepared the evening meal – expect moose lasagne followed by one of her "specials", such as raspberry sponge cake and pineapple.

Need to know *Trips run in July and August only. Swimtrek (⑩www.swimtrek.com) runs swimming holidays at other times of the year in various other destinations. A greener way to get there is to take the train to Rostock in northern Germany (⑩www.bahn.de) then the ferry to Helsinki (25hr approx; ⑩www.tallink.ee) followed by the train to Riihimäki (1hr 10min, buy ticket at train station for €30 return), where you'll be collected by the tour minibus.*

119 JOIN THE SAMI REINDEER MIGRATION, NORWAY

Travel like the Sami – with the Sami. Norwegian tour operator Turgleder offers a unique opportunity to join Scandinavia's indigenous people as they follow the annual migration of reindeer from their inland winter habitat in the far north of Norway to their costal grazing land. This is emphatically not a made-for-tourism experience: the Sami use one or two snowmobiles to carry their equipment but other than that this is how they've been herding reindeer for centuries. So expect to eat and sleep like them in their *lavvus* (Sami tipis), cook over an open fire and go ice-fishing.

The trip begins at Engholms Husky Lodge, 6km outside Karasjok, where guests spend the first two nights acclimatizing to the conditions and learning about the Sami; you'll also tour a Sami museum and the Sami parliament. You then join up with a Sami family and spend four days travelling with the reindeer, feeding and caring for the herd and protecting them from predators (wolves and lynx) as they move across the desolate landscape. Not only will you witness the spectacular migration of hundreds of animals, but you'll also be given a genuine – and privileged – insight into the life of the itinerant people of Scandinavia.

(From top) Sleighs and shiny noses; On the trail of Norway's great reindeer migration; A lavvu (Sami version of a tipi)

Need to know The trip lasts eight days and departs mid-April. To get there from Oslo take the train to Rena (2hr 15min; Ⓦwww.nsb.no), where you will be taken, by arrangement, to Engholms Husky Lodge (Ⓦwww.engholm.no). For prices and booking see Ⓦwww.turgleder.com; Ⓣ +47 (0) 9116 7303.

120 GROUP TOGETHER AT ONGAJOK, NORWAY

Often it's the hardest places to reach that are the most rewarding. It's certainly a schlep to get to Ongajok, a converted farm in Norway's Arctic Lapland, but the splendid isolation of this remote mountain farm is worth all the effort.

Ongajok is in the heart of Finnmark, land of the Sami people: the kind of place where the locals learn to ski before they can walk. Its focus is on communal living, offering a range of low-impact outdoor activities including cross-country skiing, ice-fishing, reindeer-sledding and snow-shoeing. Dinner is served around a large table in the main dining area where you'll be treated to regional specialities including reindeer, grouse, capercaillie, salmon, trout and local mushrooms and berries.

Alternatively you can spend an evening crowding round a fire in a nearby *lavvu*, listening to traditional chanting and hearing from local Sami about their way of life. Afterwards you can lie in a large outdoor bath tub heated by a firewood stove, gazing up at the clear Norwegian night sky. Group bonding, Sami-style.

Need to know The only way to get to Ongajok is to fly from Oslo to Alta (1hr 50min; Ⓦwww. sas.no), from where you can be collected in a minibus by arrangement – it's then a bumpy 25km journey to the farm. Prices depend on group size: approximately 1,790kr per person, half-board. For details of activities and accommodation see Ⓦwww.ongajok.no/omsetraeng.html; Ⓣ +47 (0) 7843 2600.

121 RAFTING ON THE KLARÄLVEN, SWEDEN

Tired of tailored tours? For the ultimate DIY travel experience, build your own timber raft with operator Vildmark I Värmland and float down the Klarälven, Sweden's longest river. The idea is to construct a floating raft big enough to carry five or six people using just a dozen ropes and logs. Your teamwork (and sense of humour) will be put to the test but if you're worried your clove hitches are more like granny knots, helpful instructors are on hand to give advice.

You can build a raft in a morning and take it out on the river for the afternoon, but to get the most out of your craft – and the river – it's best to go on a five- or eight-day trip to enjoy the tranquillity of Värmland (Sweden's most southerly wilderness) and have time inland to explore the villages along the Klarälven. You can choose to stay overnight under canvas on your moored craft or in a tent by the river. There are no guides on board to show you the way, but you'll be well briefed beforehand on how to navigate the river and you'll soon pick up how to handle your raft with pole and paddles while keeping an eye out for sandbanks and eddies.

There are periods of intense activity (crossing rapids and whirlpools) but much of the trip is a slow meander so you can keep an eye out for beaver and moose and even go fishing (permit required). But the best thing about the trip is the sense of achievement at having built your own raft and navigated yourself downstream.

Need to know *Minimum ten people for two rafts. For directions, accommodation details and booking see ⓦwww.vildmark.se; ☏ +46 (0) 5601 4040. The tour begins at Gunnerud, 95km north of Karlstad, from where you'll be taken to the raft-building site. There is a direct train service from Copenhagen to Karlstad (7hr 15min; ⓦwww.sj.se) with a local bus to Gunnerud from there (2hr).*

Teamwork is required for raft building; floating along the serene River Klarälven

122 CYCLE ALONG THE GÖTA CANAL, SWEDEN

Spend a gentle day's cycling in the fresh air and at the same time learn about a proud part of Sweden's heritage. The Göta Canal was one of the country's largest civil engineering projects: built between 1810 and 1832 to transport goods for export, it has a whopping 58 locks that link rivers and lakes for 190km, from Mem on the east coast to Sjötorp at Lake Vänern.

There are several long sections of the canal where you can cycle along a renovated towpath. The most popular attractions are the canal museum at Sjötorp (where there are classic boat motors and old naval maps) and the seven locks at Berg, where you can watch boats being lowered over 18m.

One of the greenest places to stay en route is the House of Nature at Tåtorp – just a few minutes' walk from the shore of Lake Viken (where there is one of the canal's two hand-operated locks) and a great base if you want to explore the west and east sides of the canal. The hotel, which is constructed entirely from timber using eco-friendly materials and paints. Organic breakfasts and dinner (usually local fresh fish) are served in an attractive garden café. Owners Jonas and Margareta Fallström hire out bikes, so why not spend a full day cycling along the towpath to the towns of Töreboda (Thursday is market day), Hajstorp and Norrkvarn (where there's a large canal-side restaurant). If you've the energy you may get as far as Sjötorp (10km from Norrkvarn) where you can treat yourself to the local speciality of smoked salmon.

If your limbs ache after a day's cycling, you could opt for a change of scene the next day, and either go kayaking or just relax at the water's edge and enjoy the calm of the canal.

Need to know *To get there from Stockholm, take the train to Strömstad (5hr 45min; ⓦwww.sj.se) and then local bus #505 to Töreboda (1hr), from where the owners will collect by arrangement. Nature Travel (ⓦwww.naturetravels.co.uk; ☏ +44 (0) 1929 463 774) organizes cycle tours along the Göta Canal based at the House of Nature. For more information about the history of the Göta Canal, events and other places to stay en route see ⓦwww.gotakanal.se.*

(From left) Cycling along the Göta canal; the timber-framed House of Nature at Tåtorp; pleasure boats cruise the canal

123 CROSS-COUNTRY SKIING IN KUUSAMO, FINLAND

The Alps may be the European capital of downhill skiing but the Nordic countries are the place to go for the cross-country alternative. A great place to develop the art of kicking and gliding across long flat terrain is the resort of Kuusamo in northeast Finland, which has over 500km of prepared tracks.

A small family-run company, Northtrek, organizes cross-country treks from its base in the resort, including a 17km overnight forested trail to the Kero Wilderness Camp in Oulanka National Park. At the camp you can learn how to read animal tracks and take part in survival-skills training, before relaxing in a sauna and eating dinner in the cosy cabin. Northtrek also arranges snow-shoe treks, cross-country horse-riding and ice-fishing. And don't think you'll miss out on the kind of nightlife you'd expect at a European ski resort: head into Kuusamo one evening and you'll see that the Finns take their après ski just as seriously.

Need to know *The most practical way to reach Kuusamo is to fly from Helsinki (1hr; www.finnair.com). For details of activities, prices and directions see www.northtrek.net; +358 (0) 404 182 832.*

124 STAY IN A CHARCOAL HUT AT KOLARBYN, SWEDEN

Fit for a hobbit, Kolarbyn's forest huts are modelled on the dwellings of the former charcoal workers in this forested region of Sweden, two hours from Stockholm. The huts are basic but cosy, with sleeping bags on hard beds, but it's just a 5min walk to the beautiful Lake Skärsjön where you can swim, canoe or enjoy messing around in a rowing boat.

The forest site is only part of the story, for if you sit still for a moment, Kolarbyn's enthusiastic manager Marcus Jonson will whisk you off on one of his adventurous moose-and-wolf safaris. You're guaranteed to see moose because the king owns the land and keeps it well stocked for hunting. Encounters with wolves aren't so likely, but Marcus knows the best places to go to hear them howl. Alternatively you can try tracking the wolves on horseback, staying out overnight in a traditional *lavvu* tent (Sami tipi). After a night out in the wild, the primitive charcoal huts will feel like a hotel.

Need to know *Trains run hourly from Stockholm Central Station to Köping, from where a bus connects to Skinnskatteberg – the owners will pick you up from here by arrangement. For prices plus details of accommodation and tours see www.kolarbyn.se; +46 (0) 704 007 053. Nature Travels (www.naturetravels.co.uk; +44 (0) 1929 463 774) organizes multi-activity tours throughout Sweden and includes all activities at Kolarbyn in its itineraries.*

(From top) Charcoal hut at Kolarbyn; the first brew of the day; A cosy home fit for a hobbit

GREEN COPENHAGEN

Copenhagen is regularly voted the best city in the world in which to live. Its high quality of life and proximity to such an attractive coast give it a headstart over other cities, but it is Copenhagen's enlightened urban development that is so impressive. Designed to maximize good living as well as safety and security, the city strikes a perfect balance between the old and the new: cutting-edge design juxtaposed with unspoilt medieval architecture, trendy cafés and gourmet dining, pedestrian streets packed with designer shops and an abundance of open green spaces. The city also takes its environmental responsibilities seriously. Top billing is the city's renowned cycling culture, but there are many other ways you can enjoy a green day out in the city. Here are our favourites.

125 Get on your bike

Let's face it, cyclists and car drivers aren't always the best of friends. In Copenhagen there are hundreds of thousands of cyclists (more than 1.1 million kilometres of cycling are clocked up every day) yet many other residents drive to work. To find a traffic system compatible with both, Copenhagen's authorities have run a successful pilot programme known as the Green Wave. The idea is that the traffic signals on cycling lanes are synchronized with cyclists' average speed (approximately 20km per hour), so you can cycle the length of the city without ever having to stop at the lights. Green Waves currently exist from Nørrebrogade to the lakes and Nørre Farimagsgade to the city centre, with more soon to be installed along Copenhagen's 40km of cycling lanes.

There are several places to hire a bike in the city, including an enlightened scheme at Baisikeli, a 5min walk from Nørreport station, where part of the hire cost goes towards delivering second-hand bikes to villages in Ghana, Sierra Leone and Tanzania.

Need to know *For bike hire prices, suggested itineraries and guided tours see ⓦwww.cph-bike-rental.dk; ☎+45 (0) 2670 0229. Ask for the excellent Copenhagen cycling map (also available from tourist offices), which includes details of cycling routes away from heavily trafficked streets. To hire a bike at the Central Station visit ⓦwww.copenhagen-bikes.dk, where you can join an excellent "Bike with Mike" guided tour to see the city's sights: ⓦwww.bikecopenhagenwithmike.dk; ☎+45 (0) 2639 5688.*

Mike and his bike on the bridge at Nyhavn

126 Fresh herring and hippy herbs

After a morning cycling around town, head to Nyhavn, the oldest part of Copenhagen's harbour. Though touristy, it is the place to go for fresh, local fish where you can sit looking out over the harbour. One of the best places to eat is Nyhavns Faergekro, which serves a large herring buffet with ten specialities and freshly made *smørrebrød* (open sandwiches) according to season. In the evening, cycle over to Morgen Stedet, an organic vegetarian restaurant in the fascinating quarter of Christiania – the part self-governing, part anarchic neighbourhood that's the heart of the city's hippy scene. The restaurant serves wholesome soups, noodle dishes and salads with fresh vegetables from a local farm (no alcohol is served but you can bring your own).

Need to know *For prices and menus at Nyhavns Faergekro (Danish only) see ⓦwww. nyhavnsfaergekro.dk; ☎ +45 (0) 3315 1588. For more on Morgen Stedet see ⓦwww.morgenstedet. dk.*

127 Sleep somewhere green

No points for style, but Copenhagen's greenest (and cheapest) youth hostel – conveniently located near the centre of town – has good intentions at its heart. Sleep-in Green is run by a youth development charity (its offices are upstairs), which aims to help reintroduce youngish offenders back into work. You sleep on bunk beds in dorms, there's just one large shower room and a small dining area where you can eat organic breakfasts and access free wi-fi. Don't be put off by the graffiti-covered stairwell outside reception; at 120DKK a night you get what you pay for, and your custom helps the staff hold down a job.

If you're looking for something more comfortable (or you are in town for business), there are three smart Scandic Hotels in the centre. Scandic is one of the few hotel chains that has genuinely tried to green up its act: it has committed to eliminate half its fossil CO_2 emissions by 2011 and all by 2025. The majority of its hotels have been awarded the Nordic Swan eco label and the group has announced it will no longer buy in bottled water, instead offering bottled filtered water from its own taps. So while their hotels might look like huge corporate beasts, they do have an impressive green underbelly.

Need to know *Sleep-in Green has a secure area for bikes. For prices and directions from the central train station see ⓦwww.sleep-in-green. dk; ☎ +45 (0) 3537 7777. For details of all Scandic Hotels see ⓦwww.scandichotels. com. For details of Scandic's environmental policies see ⓦwww.scandic-hotels.com/ betterworld.*

(From top) Feast on vegetarian food at Morgen Stedet in Christiania; A smørrebrød of fresh local produce; Nyhavn, the oldest part of Copenhagen's harbour

(From top) The pulling power of huskies; A six-dog sled charging across Svalbard's vast wilderness

128 GO ON A DOG-SLEDDING SAFARI IN SVALBARD, NORWAY

You're dressed in a snowsuit and sitting in a sled feeling a lot like Father Christmas. Six bright-eyed, frisky dogs are attached to the sled by harness; straining, barking and yelping with anticipation, their breath is visible in the crisp morning air. When the time is right, the main guide at the front gives the signal and without a moment's hesitation you're off, hurtling across the snow into the infinite white landscape.

In Arctic conditions it's difficult to get quickly from A to B without some form of assisted transport. Yet the noise and air pollution caused by snowmobiles (in addition to the disturbance they cause to wildlife) hardly does the fragile environment much of a favour. Dog-sledding is the only viable green alternative, which is why the Arctic tours run by Svalbard Villmarkssenter have passed the strict guidelines laid down by Ecotourism Norway (see p.249). It runs overnight tours as well as five-day dog-sledding trips from Longyearbyen southward through Spitsbergen's glaciers and fjords.

Svalbard Villmarkssenter also provides the option of a combined polar skiing and snow-kiting trip. En route, you'll have a good chance of spotting polar foxes, seals and polar bears as well as the northern lights. This low-impact tour is in sharp contrast to the increasing number of motorized trips out of Longyearbyen, from where as many as seventy snowmobiles depart every day. Opt for the dog-sledding alternative and you'll help to protect the Arctic wilderness and see more of the local fauna.

Need to know The only way to get to Longyearbyen is to fly from Oslo (4hr) or from Tromsø (1hr 40min) with SAS (Ⓦwww.sas.no). The average temperature on Norway's west coast in winter is minus 12°C, so be sure to pack warm clothes. For itineraries, prices and advice on what to bring see Ⓦwww.svalbardvillmarkssenter.no; ☎ +47 (0) 7902 1700. For general information about Svalbard see Ⓦwww.svalbard.net.

129 FOLLOW IN SHACKLETON'S FOOTSTEPS AT FINSE, NORWAY

At Finse, the highest stop on the Norwegian rail network, there is a ski resort with no lifts. No jostling queues; no pylons; no concrete silos housing noisy machinery. Just kilometres of cross-country tracks across a vast unspoilt landscape of frozen lakes, mountain chains and glaciers where the snow can last from early December until mid-June.

Finse Hotel is the life and soul of this small resort. It was built in 1909 and used by some of the great polar explorers such as Nansen, Amundsen and Shackleton to prepare for their Arctic adventures. You can also stay at Finsehytta, a large hostel run by the Norwegian Mountain Touring Association. Guided cross-country tours from Finse (which aren't suitable for beginners) include a demanding trek to Hallingskarvet (5–7hr), while a gentler option is the return trip to Klemsbu Cabin, 5km north of Finse (3–5hr). As well as cross-country skiing, you can try ski-sailing, dog-sledding and glacier-walking on Hardangerjøkulen Glacier (summer only). This is an extreme location so come here to find your inner explorer; who knows where it might lead.

Need to know The only way to travel to Finse is by train from Oslo (4hr 15min) or Bergen (2hr 15min); for prices and timetables see Ⓦwww.nsb.no. For details of the hotel (where you can pick up a ski map), activities and timings for trail marking in Finse see Ⓦwww.finse1222.no; ☎ +47 (0) 5652 7100. Finsehytta hostel: Ⓦwww.finsehytta.no (Norwegian only); ☎ +47 (0) 9085 2245.

130 WHALE-WATCHING OFF THE COAST OF ICELAND

Iceland's waters are blessed with large numbers of almost every kind of whale: blue, fin, humpback, sperm, sei, minke, killer and pilot whales, to name just a few. Not to mention the abundance of dolphins and other marine life.

The largest whale-watching operator in Iceland is North Sailing, which organizes three-hour trips on board a renovated oak fishing boat from Húsavík as well as a sailing trip on board a two-mast schooner, which visits a puffin island and all the traditional whale-watching sites. There's also a three-day sailing excursion, which includes a visit to a herring and whale museum plus a few hours on the small Arctic island of Grímsey, home to a variety of seabirds, including puffins and auks.

Whale-watching is big business in Iceland. Since the early 1990s the annual numbers of whale-watchers in Iceland have grown from a few hundred to around ninety thousand, contributing almost as much to Iceland's economy as whaling did in its peak between 1950 and 1980. Whatever your view on whaling, one of the best ways you can support the conservation of whales is to join a responsible tour like those offered by North Sailing– it will help show that a whale is worth more alive than dead.

Need to know *For itineraries, prices and reservations for North Sailing's whale-watching trips see* Ⓦ*www.northsailing.is;* ☎ *+354 (0) 464 7272.*

Up close to a breaching humpback whale

131 PADDLE AND PEDAL AROUND THE LOFOTEN ISLANDS, NORWAY

Dotted with pretty fishing villages, rugged landscapes and quiet bays warmed by the Gulf Stream, the Lofoten Islands are Norway's flagship eco-destination: an adventure playground for walkers, cyclists and kayakers.

Lofoten Kajakk is the first kayaking operator to be recognized by Ecotourism Norway (see p.248), the country's new responsible tourism certifier. It runs courses for kayaking as well as day-trips and multi-day adventures with overnight camping into the Trollfjord (a deep, narrow fjord surrounded by snow-covered mountains) and the Risvær/Svellingan archipelagos – home to white-tailed sea eagles, ptarmigans, seals and porpoises. As well as these, Lofoten Kajakk runs multi-sport trips (including hiking, mountain biking and rowing), taking care not to overuse the few marked trails and travelling instead on harder, more durable terrain so as to protect Lofoten's fragile ecology.

Kayaking around the Lofoten Islands is one of the best ways to view the fragile ecology of the area

Need to know *To get there from Oslo take the train (via Trondheim and Fauske) to Bodø (18hr; ⓦwww.nsb.no) then a local bus to Lofoten (ⓦwww.nor-way.no). For prices, booking and details of activities see ⓦwww.lofoten-aktiv.no; ☏ +47 (0) 7607 3000. Listings for accommodation and events in Lofoten are at ⓦwww.lofoten.info.*

132 CAR-FREE ON KOSTER, SWEDEN

The Koster Islands are one of Sweden's best-kept secrets. Close to the border with Norway on the west coast, this small archipelago is being turned into a 450-square-kilometre national park ("Kosterhavet") to protect the unique marine life around the islands as well as its sandy beaches and heath-clad moorland.

There are just three hundred inhabitants on the two main islands, which are linked by a small cable ferry. Cycling is the main mode of transport (you can hire a bike by the main pier), while kayaking is the best way to explore the outlying islands. Larger boats find it difficult to navigate around the tightly knitted islands, rocks and skerries, so you're likely to have the waters to yourself. As you paddle around, keep an eye out for arctic terns and skuas as well as one of Sweden's largest populations of harbour seals.

There are several places to stay on South Koster. Hotel Ekenäs is the main hotel (100m from the pier), close to a sandy beach and with rooms that look out over the Koster fjord. In summer, it opens a

specialist fish restaurant in an attractive garden among oak trees. For lunch, the café at Koster Gardens (a 10min cycle from the hotel) serves organic food supplied mostly from its own permacultural gardens. In the far north of North Koster, there's a small seaside campsite among pine trees where you can hire kayaks for the day and return for a barbecue as the sun sets over this remarkably unspoilt part of western Sweden.

Riding "bit-less" horses

Need to know To get there from Copenhagen take the train via Gothenburg to Strömstad (8hr 45min; Ⓦwww.sj.se), then catch the ferry from Strömstad North Harbour to Ekenäs on South Koster (45min; Ⓦwww.vasttrafik.se) from where it's a 5min walk to the hotel. Nature Travel (Ⓦwww.naturetravels. co.uk; ☎ +44 (0) 1929 463 774) organizes three-day kayaking tours around Koster. Hotel Ekenäs: Ⓦwww.sydkoster.se; ☎ +46 5262 0250.

133 LEARN TO RIDE A HORSE THE NATURAL WAY, SWEDEN

If you were inspired by *The Horse Whisperer*, you can try the real thing on a natural horsemanship tour, run under the expert eye of Olle Forsell – a maverick horse-trainer who has been pioneering this wild form of horse-riding in Sweden for more than a decade. At his remote Kalvefall farm, near Tranås in south-central Sweden, you'll learn how to handle a North Swedish horse that has been trained to carry riders without the bit between the teeth (you tug the lower part of the horse's head using a rope "side-pull" instead of a bridle).

It takes just a morning's tuition in the classroom and paddock to learn the theory behind the technique and to understand how to put it into practice; handling the horses with firm – but not aggressive – tugs of the rope (and the odd command), and you only progress from walking to trotting to cantering when you have mastered each with full control.

Once everyone feels secure, you'll trot out of the paddock along dirt roads, then canter (and occasionally gallop) over forested hills, across bubbling streams and through verdant pastures. You'll spend the entire day out in 300 square kilometres of riding ground before returning to the farm for a soak in an outdoor wooden tub where you can soothe those muscles you didn't know you had. A hearty evening meal is prepared by Olle's partner Anette, after which you can look forward to a deep sleep in the quiet of the old farmhouse's timber log cottage.

Need to know This trip has been certified by Nature's Best (see p.248). To get there from Stockholm take the train to Tranås (3hr approx; Ⓦwww.sj.se), from where the owner will collect, by arrangement. For accommodation, prices and booking see Ⓦwww.sagaadventures.se; ☎ +46 (0) 140 911 33. Nature Travel (Ⓦwww.naturetravels. co.uk ☎ +44 (0) 1929 463 774) organizes five- and seven-day riding tours at Kalvefall farm.

Red fox in the Swedish snow

134 TRACK RED FOXES IN VÅLÅDALEN NATURE RESERVE, SWEDEN

Speed isn't everything. Of course there's nothing like the exhilarating, spine-tingling sensation of hurtling down a mountain slope on a pair of skis or a snowboard, but that way you've little chance of coming across any of the shy wildlife that lives in the mountains. To do that, you're better off strapping on a pair of snow-shoes and going walkabout into the wintry beyond.

From the Vålådalen mountain station at the foot of Ottfjället Mountain in western Jämtland, two Swedish biologists, Annica and Torkel Ideström, run shoeing tours through the hilly, pristine forests of the Vålådalen nature reserve. Covering 6–10km a day and camping out at night, you'll investigate tracks of red fox, moose, reindeer, otter and mountain hare and learn about survival techniques in the wild. If you're lucky you may spot the tracks of lynx and wolverine, or hear the distant barking of an Arctic fox high above the tree line in the Syl Massif. And if you live a charmed existence, you might witness the Northern Lights.

The four-day round trip ends back at the mountain station where you can have a well-earned beer and sauna followed by a hearty dinner, with Arctic char, elk and reindeer on the menu. If you're not yet ready to return to civilization, you can book yourself in for a few days' dog-sledding, cross-country skiing or ice-fishing. Be warned: downhill skiing can seem a little one-dimensional after this.

Need to know *To get there from Stockholm take the night train to Undersåker (www. sj.se) and then a local bus to Vålådalen, from where the owners will collect by arrangement. A four-day snow-shoeing tour costs SEK4900 per person, including equipment, all meals and a guide (maximum 12 people). Tour departs end of February. For more info (in Swedish only) see www.mountainexperience.se; + 46 (0) 6473 5253. This trip has been certified by Nature's Best (see p.248).*

135 BECOME A LIGHT CAMPER IN DENMARK

Hike with a tent on your back and you're known in Denmark as a *lette campister* (light camper). Wild camping is not permitted in Denmark, but the majority of approved campsites put aside a dedicated area for light campers, so you're guaranteed a place to pitch your tent even if the site is otherwise full with baggage-laden cars.

The west coast of Jutland is particularly camping-friendly and has several long-distance footpaths, such as the 180km path from Bulbjerg to Nymindegab. En route, there are several campsites that have been certified by the Green Flag eco label, which identifies camping areas that limit their use of water and energy, use eco-friendly washing agents and provide recycling facilities.

If you want to travel around at a quicker pace, you can cycle along the 550km-long west-coast cycle path, which passes through cool dune plantations, sand heaths and lakes as well as the recently opened Thy National Park – Denmark's first national park – where millions of migratory birds visit in spring and autumn.

Need to know *For contact details of all Danish campsites (those certified by Green Key are marked) see www.campingraadet.dk. The Danish Ramblers' Association helps preserve long-distance routes; for information about their work and footpaths see dvl.dk/352/68. Ferries go from Harwich on England's west coast to Esbjerg (20hr; www.dfdsseaways.co.uk). Bike hire is available at the harbour (Esbjerg is on the west-coast cycle path).*

Going green

Flying is the quickest way from A to B, but once you factor in security and shuttling to and from airports, the time difference between flights and alternative transport can be relatively slight. Taking the train is often considered the most eco-friendly form of motorised transport, yet a car with passengers can be just as carbon efficient, as can a full coach. The graphs below shows the carbon emissions produced by seven popular trips from London to Europe by plane, train, car and coach and the length of time each takes, including check-in time, security and travel to the city centre.

Emissions of CO_2 per person vary depending on the type of vehicle used and how full it is. The emissions given are CO_2 equivalent ("CO_2e"), as they include a factor that takes into account that aviation has significant effects on the climate beyond CO_2 emissions alone. Emissions for cars are for two people per vehicle, while both car and coach trips assume a Dover to Calais ferry crossing.

The figures given on the chart show the minimum emissions per passenger journey likely for each type of transport, but it is important to note that older aircraft, diesel trains or larger cars may have twice these emissions or more. The calculations are based on data published by government and transport industry bodies and adjusted, where necessary, in line with certain assumptions about load and types of vehicle, and the impact of fuel production. The data is provided by the sustainability charity, Forum for the Future, as part of their Overland Heaven project: Ⓦwww.forumforthefuture.org

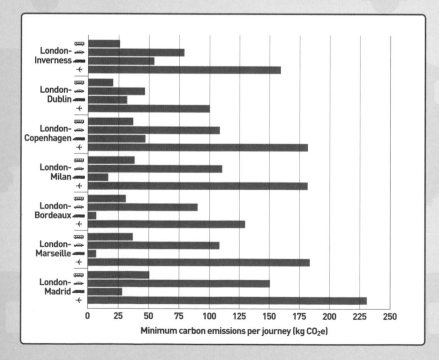

Minimum carbon emissions per journey (kg CO_2e)

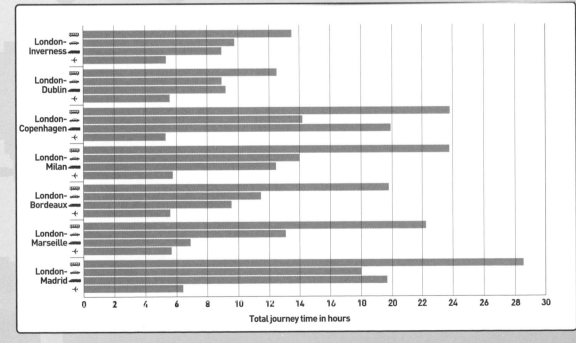

ESTONIA 137

LATVIA 136

LITHUANIA

POLAND

CZECH REP. 138

146 SLOVAKIA 149

AUSTRIA

HUNGARY

143

UKRAINE

MOLDOVA

142
148

147 ROMANIA 139

BULGARIA

GEORGIA 140

ARMENIA 144

145

GREECE

141

TURKEY

150

EASTERN EUROPE AND THE AEGEAN

136 Bog walking in Estonia

137 Sea kayaking the Baltic

138 Stay on an eco ranch in Bieszczady National Park, Poland

139 Canoe the Danube delta, Romania

140 Explore Borjomi-Kharagauli National Park, Georgia

141 Turtle power in Zakynthos, Greece

142 Wildflowers and Saxon villages, Romania

143 Stay in a Ukrainian village

144 Ride towards Mount Ararat, Armenia

145 Live among birds of prey at Dadia, Greece

146 Cycle the Heritage Trail in Bohemia

147 Hike in Retezat National Park, Romania

148 Be the guest of a count in Transylvania

149 Take to the waters at Aquacity, Slovakia

150 Hide away in a Turkish lighthouse

136 BOG WALKING IN ESTONIA

Estonia is said by its locals to have a fifth season – the flood season. Nowhere is this truer than in Soomaa National Park, situated in the southwest of the country between Viljandi and Pärnu. Soomaa, whose name means "land of bogs", is a vast complex of swampy marshes and wet alluvial forests that provides a home to bears, wolves and elk as well as nests for spotted eagles and black storks. Tour operator Karuskose offers two of the best means to explore the bogs: either by canoe or by wearing bog-shoes, which allow walkers to wade through the water without getting stuck.

(From top) Walkers negotiating the bogs of the Soomaa National Park; Männikjärve Bog Endla Nature Reserve

Towards the end of the Communist era almost no-one came to this park; now visitor numbers are finally growing. Karuskose – run by local environmentalist Alvir Ruukel – has played a large part in this boom, as it offers a host of unusual experiences, from nocturnal canoe safaris to kicksledding along frozen rivers. Whatever the activity, Alvir ensures that visitors leave with a deeper understanding of this sodden ecosystem.

Need to know For details of all activities and tours offered by Karuskose, as well as accommodation, dining options, location and booking see Ⓦwww.soomaa.com; ☎ +372 506 1896.

137 SEA KAYAKING THE BALTIC

Over fifty million migratory birds visit Estonia each year, with many rare species – like the velvet scoter and red-breasted merganser – settling on the country's northern islands to breed. These wildlife havens were the chance consequence of Soviet deportations in the 1950s to allow military tests to take place: when the locals were forced out, the birds began to move in.

You can explore this twitcher's paradise on guided kayak tours with Reimann Retked, an adventure-holiday specialist certified by the Estonian Ecotourism Association. You can paddle from island to island, approaching the birds without disturbing them, or leave the canoes onshore and hike over the flat scrubland. The

latter can be somewhat eerie, as these islands are still dotted with crumbling farmhouses and deserted Soviet watchtowers, half-rusted by the salty air. Covered in white gulls against a setting sun, though, they make for a great photograph.

Need to know *As well as sea kayaking, Reimann Retked offers rafting, snow-shoeing, bogwalking and kicksledding tours. Tours start at Valkla Beach, about one hour's drive from Tallinn. Accommodation on overnight trips is in restored farmhouses. For full details and prices, see Ⓦ www.retked.ee; Ⓣ +372 511 4099.*

138 STAY ON AN ECO RANCH IN BIESZCZADY NATIONAL PARK, POLAND

The view from the 12km-long ridge at Polonina Wetlinska in the Bieszczady National Park is an unbroken panorama of ancient forests of pine, beech and oak stretching across lush valleys and hills. The world here looks wild; untouched by man. Some sensitive development has been permitted here though, including the construction of the Eco-Frontiers Ranch, a great place to stay while exploring the area.

Designed by Andrezj Czech and his girlfriend Aga, the ranch combines traditional Carpathian building techniques with a modern environmental philosophy. Located between the villages of Michiniowiec and Lipie in an area of remote wetlands, it is entirely off-grid; power instead comes from wind turbines and solar panels. Inside the main house the timber rooms are cosily decorated, plus there's a lounge, kitchen and library; a real haven when you come in from the evening cold.

Beavers have been reintroduced to the land surrounding the ranch, and as dusk sets guests can walk out towards their dams, hoping for a rare glimpse of these shy creatures. More often you'll just get the chance to study their handiwork, while Andrezj explains how it affects the surrounding land (with a doctorate in beaver behaviour, he's a pretty good authority on the subject).

The beavers may be elusive, but you can't miss the Hutsul horses, a rare breed that the ranch is working to protect. One of the pleasures of staying here is the chance to ride out on them across the neighbouring woods and fields. This is the best way to get a glimpse of the wildlife that lies in the forests. You're unlikely to see more than tracks of the bears, wolves and lynx that live here, but there is a good chance of spotting European bison, roe deer and various birds of prey.

By the time you're back at the ranch you'll have worked up quite an appetite. Good news, then, that vegetarian meals rustled up by Aga, sourced from what's in the biodynamic garden, are rather tasty. And you can wash them down with ten different home-made beers and various fruit liqueurs. As you nod off – suitably full – in the total silence and darkness of the park, it's difficult not to be inspired by the way this lodge fits its environment so well.

Need to know *Details on how to get to Ustrzyki Doine (where the owners will collect you) from Kraków, Rzeszow and Sanok are on the website (Ⓦ www. ecofrontiers.net/index.php), which also has details of rooms and rates plus activities, wildlife in the region and volunteering opportunities.*

Modern eco design is combined with traditional Carpathian building techniques (top and middle) at the remote Eco Frontiers Ranch located in the heart of the Bieszczady National Park (bottom)

139 CANOE THE DANUBE DELTA, ROMANIA

Paddling through the vast Danube delta, almost 3000km from where the river began in Germany's Black Forest, offers the chance to combine some of the best birdwatching in Europe with visits to communities little touched by industrialization. Each spring hundreds of species ranging from spoonbills to warblers migrate here from the southern hemisphere, when the area's vast silence is broken by their songs and mating calls. In the autumn, huge flocks again gather here to prepare for the long journey south. On canoe trips with Barefoot Tours through this vast maze of channels, forests, sand dunes and reeds, you'll have the advantage of approaching on the water almost noiselessly, enabling you to get close to the birds without disturbing them or their habitat.

Tours last anything from a day to a week, with nights spent at homestays and lodges in the villages of Tulcea, Crisan and the curiously named Mila 23, all of which are accessible only by water; the main mode of transport in each is canoe. Staying here gives you plenty of opportunity to learn about the locals' work harvesting reeds and fishing. If you can, it's worth coming for at least a few days to allow yourself to drift into the gentle, age-old rhythm of the river and the lives of the people here.

Need to know *For details of tours, prices, availability and getting there see Ⓦ www.barefoot-tours.com;* Ⓣ *+40 07448 61828.*

140 EXPLORE BORJOMI-KHARAGAULI NATIONAL PARK, GEORGIA

It may be the same size as Ireland, but Georgia has more animal and bird species than any other country in Europe – and the best way to see them is on guided walks through the Borjomi-Kharagauli National Park, a vast wilderness of coniferous forest where bears, lynx and chamois dwell.

The family-run Marelisi guesthouse in the village of the same name at the park's northern edge provides an ideal base to plan walking routes, book guides and fill up on local food. Hikes from here pass along rhododendron-lined rivers and meadows whose subalpine grasses seem to shift colour as they waft in the mountain breeze. Marelisi village itself is almost totally self-sufficient: a place where people still grind their corn in communal watermills known as *tiskvili*. Before you set out, be sure to stock up on sweet *churchkela*, a snack made by boiling nuts in grape juice and a useful energy source while hiking.

More adventurous trekkers can spend the

Colony of pelicans on Uzlina Lake, Danube Delta, Dobrogea

night at one of the many shelters found along the nine official park trails, several of which lead out from Marelisi – there are no cooking facilities but each has a fireplace should it get cold. And you can always warm yourself a little further with a bottle of the local vintage: Georgia claims to be the oldest wine-producing region in the world (it's been made here since around 7000 BC) and there are plenty of excellent local varieties to sip on as you watch the sun sink over the pines at the end of the day.

Need to know *The train from Tbilisi to Poti/Batumi stops in Marelisi (2.5hr approx). The guesthouse has four double rooms (US$8 a night, dinner US$5). Trails are open from April to October and the rhododendrons flower in April and May. ⓦwww.borjomi-kharagauli-np.ge; ☎+995 (8) 99 233 449.*

141 TURTLE POWER IN ZAKYNTHOS, GREECE

There's no point getting up early to bag a deckchair on Gerakas beach in southern Zakynthos. No-one is allowed onto the beach before the sun rises. Also, there are no deckchairs.

Not a typical Greek beach then. The reason for this is that loggerhead turtles come here to lay their eggs: too many lights would disorientate their nocturnal arrival, so the beach is off-limits to tourists from dusk until dawn. And deckchairs would churn up the nesting sites, destroying the eggs – so they're banned.

With resort facilities absent, tourism here is designed to complement the natural beauty of the surroundings. Ionian Eco Holidays, run by Iannis Vardakastanis, one of the leading environmentalists in the area, encourages guests to learn more about the delicate environment of Zakynthos. Visitors can take catamaran trips to view the turtles or explore the countryside by jeep or on foot, with or without a guide. Both the island of Kephallonia and the site of Olympia are short ferry rides away.

Accommodation is in a range of locally owned traditional villas and apartments, refitted with solar panels. For a family there's Sula, a stone cottage with exposed beams that's a short walk from the beach. Those seeking a bit of isolation – and the chance to work off dinner – can hide away at Ziva, a thirty-minute walk from the beach atop a forested hill with great views. Olive groves and fruit trees line the gardens and provide ingredients for the meals.

Volunteering opportunities are also available throughout the summer, helping to clean up litter that threatens the turtles' welfare or monitor the beaches during the nights of nesting season – the only way you'll get to take a moonlit stroll along Gerakas's empty shore.

Beach at Gerakas; loggerhead turtle

Need to know *A bus goes every day from Athens to Kylini (4hr) where a ferry connects to Zakynthos (1hr; ⓦwww.ferries.gr). Accommodation is available from May to October for one- or two-week stays. For prices, booking and information on volunteering see ⓦwww.relaxing-holidays.com.*

142 WILDFLOWERS AND SAXON VILLAGES, ROMANIA

A little weary from a morning's hiking, you sit for a rest on the grass outside the shepherd's wooden hut, looking across the flower-covered fields that stretch back to the village below. Not a bad spot for a lunch stop.

Meanwhile your guide begins to unpack the picnic: slices of pork from local Durac pigs; *zacusca*, a tomato and pepper sauce made to your guide's mother's own recipe; wine from the grapes in her cobbled courtyard; and cheeses – salty *cas* and ricotta-like *urda* – recently made by the shepherd's wife. And of course strong *palinka* spirit, home-distilled from plums.

Meals like this on Discover Tarnava Mare's food and culture tours are a perfect example of how well many Romanians still live off the land. Visits through Saxon villages in this fertile region of southeastern Transylvania are tailored however you want them, whether you book far in advance or just turn up that morning. The idea is that they are opportunities to share in the villagers' lives for a day or more. Guests stay in local homes, breakfasting on bread, eggs, cheeses and whatever your host's speciality is.

It is in one of these villages – Viscri – that Charles, Prince of Wales has bought a house, so enamoured is he of their way of life. There are plenty of characters here he'd probably get along with, like Mr Pandrea, an octogenarian beekeeper who'll allow you to taste his honeys, or Rosalie, who makes teas with the fragrant herbs that hang in her wooden shed.

Since 1945, Europe has lost over 95 percent of its semi-natural grasslands due to the spread of intensive agriculture. In the meadows of Tarnava Mare, which have never seen an artificial spray, hundreds of different wildflowers create a kaleidoscope of colour in spring and summer. Were this way of life to stop, within three years the flowers would be gone. Every mouthful of traditional food you eat helps these meadows, and the people who live among them, to continue to flourish.

Need to know *Discover Tarnava Mare's office is in the village of Saschiz, under an hour's drive from Sighisoara. For more on activities and costs, see* Ⓦ *www.discovertarnavamare.org.*

143 STAY IN A UKRAINIAN VILLAGE

You have to go a long way east to get to the centre of Europe. In the Ukrainian village of Dilove, a stone placed by the Austro-Hungarian Empire in 1897 marks the spot. Trouble is, there's also a similar column in Lithuania, a sculpture in Hungary, and both Belarus and Poland have laid claim to it. Wherever that elusive point lies, though, it's likely to be further east than you might think.

Central Europe – if that's how we should think of the mountainous region of western Ukraine – is an area with few international visitors, but already a sustainable model of tourism is being developed in the area. The Rural Green Tourism Association (RGTA), set up in 1996, is a community-run volunteer organization that helps villagers earn extra income through hosting guests. For example you could stay in the wooden houses of the Hutsul people in villages like Vorokhta or Yavoriv.

Visitors can spend their time walking in the *polonyas*, the mountain meadows where cool breezes waft across the long grasses. After a day's hiking, expect to be liberally plied with food and drink, all made and prepared by the villagers, such as *banosh* (a mixture of sweetcorn, bacon and sour cream). Hospitality is unceasingly friendly and you'll probably get a chance to watch or join in traditional dances (typically accompanied by the alp-horn-like *trembita* and the *sopika*, a form of flute) or to listen to their plaintive folk songs. Whether it's officially the centre of Europe or not, life here is refreshingly traditional.

Need to know *There's an overnight train from either Kiev or Lviv to Ivano-Frankivsk, from where buses go to the various villages. For more information on the RGTA of Ivano-Frankivsk, nearby hiking trails, getting there and how the homestay scheme works, see* Ⓦ *members.aol.com/chornohora.*

(Clockwise from top left) Traditional Ukrainian embroidery; village herds; Mr. Pandrea's apiary; Local Romanian village transport; Ploughing the fields; Geese and ducks have the run of Malancrav in heart of Transylvanian Romania; Milking the sheep to make cheese.

Khor Virap Monastery with
Mount Ararat in the background,
Armenia

144 RIDE TOWARDS MOUNT ARARAT, ARMENIA

A horse trek with the Ayrudzi Riding Club is
a journey into the distant past. Trips on their
thoroughbred horses through the fruit groves
and meadows lining the mountain streams of
Armenia, which can last anything from a few
hours to several days, take in pagan sanctuaries,
a ninth-century church carved into a volcanic
cave and the mighty Mount Ararat, where Noah
is said to have finally found land. At night you
either camp under the stars, often beside ruined
castles or temples, or stay back at the cottages
that adjoin the riding club. At the latter, organic
meals are accompanied by Armenian shadow
theatre (an ancient form of shadow puppetry) or
folk songs to the tune of the Zourna flute – two of
the many traditional activities revitalized since
Ayrudzi started bringing visitors through these
remote areas.

Need to know *The riding club is in Ashtarak,
20km from Yerevan. All levels are catered for and
equipment is provided. The best time to visit is*
June to September. For further details of tours see
Ⓦ *www.ecotourismarmenia.com or* Ⓔ *v_hugous@
yahoo.com;* Ⓣ *+374 10 278 728.*

145 LIVE AMONG BIRDS OF PREY AT DADIA, GREECE

As you begin the hour-long walk from Dadia
village to the bird hide, griffon vultures circle
slowly overhead in the clear sky. According to
the local guides accompanying you, nine in the
morning is the best time to see the various birds
that live around this medieval settlement, 50km
from Alexandropolis in northern Greece. It's best
to leave for the hide well before eight though,
since as all but two of Europe's 38 raptor species
inhabit these woodlands, you're bound to get
waylaid trying to spot some of them – such as the
black vulture and the sea eagle – en route.

To make sure you get there on time you can
stay at the ecotourism centre in Dadia, which has
simple rooms in single-storey white stone buildings
surrounded by forest. It also means that when

your eyes aren't trained on the birds, there's plenty of time to soak up the gentle pace of life in the neighbouring villages and sample home-cooked meals made by the local women's co-operative.

Need to know *There are rail and bus connections from Alexandropolis to the town of Soufli, where a bus service connects to Dadia village. For more on ecotours and rates see ⓦwww.ecoclub.com/dadia; ☎+30 25540 32263.*

146 CYCLE THE HERITAGE TRAIL IN BOHEMIA

Many visitors to Vienna and Prague find plenty to keep them entertained in these two historic capitals, but for those who fancy exploring the medieval towns and villages that lie along the rivers and meadows in between, there's now a five-day bike route through the Bohemian countryside connecting the two.

The route is divided into sections of between 35km and 60km each day, though there's still ample time to dismount and explore the many World Heritage Sites along the way, such as Český Krumlov, a picturesque medieval settlement with a magnificent castle, the chateaux of Valtice and Lednice, and the Renaissance town of Telč. You can try wines produced in the Sobes vineyard near Znojmo, or sit back and watch birds flocking over the hundreds of fishponds that surround the historic town of Třeboň, while sampling the local specialities of carp and Regent beer, brewed here since 1700. Nights are spent in either rural or small town-centre guesthouses, and as Heritage Trails was set up by the founder of the European Centre for Ecological and Agricultural Tourism, visitors can be assured that bringing the benefits of tourism to rural areas is at the heart of everything it does.

Need to know *Tours can be taken in either direction. Spring or autumn is best, with many local wine festivals occurring in September. A support vehicle transfers luggage between guesthouses each day. For more on tours and accommodation see ⓦwww. heritage-trails.cz; ☎ +420 541 235 822.*

147 HIKE IN RETEZAT NATIONAL PARK, ROMANIA

Retezat in Romanian means "cut off", and the hikes between the peaks of this UNESCO Biosphere Reserve in the southwestern corner of Transylvania are about as far from civilization as you can get. Much of the park is covered by some of Europe's last remaining ancient forest, a wilderness where you're more likely to see bear or wolf tracks than hear a plane fly overhead. The park's beauty is perhaps best captured in the name the locals give it – "the land with blue eyes" – after the hundred alpine lakes that reflect the dramatic mountain scenery.

A good base for hiking routes is the award-winning Dora Mountain House, a timber lodge perched on a hill near Răuşor, 30km from Haţeg. It has a nearby ski piste and can arrange mountain guides on request, plus it's a welcoming place to return to at the end of a long day's trek or ski.

Need to know *Information on the park, sample excursions and how to get there is at ⓦwww. panparks.org. Dora Mansion House: ⓦwww. pensiuneadora.ro; ☎ +40 (0) 722 566 929.*

Mountain stream in Retezat Mountains

The drawing room at Count
Kálnoky's Castle, Transylvania

148 BE THE GUEST OF A COUNT IN TRANSYLVANIA

The roads from Brasov are unpaved and potholed, passing through sleepy one-street villages where horse-drawn carts are more noticeable than cars. You're deep in Transylvania and looking for a Count; if this didn't seem a bit Bram Stoker before then it certainly does now.

When you eventually arrive at the Count's residence, a restored sixteenth-century hunting manor at Miklósvár, the fantasy continues. A housekeeper ushers you in to a drawing room filled with antique furniture and pours a glass of local cherry brandy. The Count won't be long, she says, and then disappears. You wait a little nervously beside the crackling fire.

When Count Tibor Kálnoky arrives, though, he is amiable, talkative and not at all spooky. Inviting you to sit with him under the vines and share a lunch of local cheeses and meats, he tells his story with a gentle aristocratic grace. An exile in his early life, he returned to Romania after the death of Ceaușescu and has since worked – via his Kálnoky Trust – to restore parts of the country his family have called home since 1252.

The Trust, supported by tourist fees, works to preserve the region's architecture and culture: nature trails are being developed through forests to avoid them being cut down, while watermills are being restored so they continue to mill flour. When the Trust hears of delapidated buildings for sale, they can buy them and renovate buildings elsewhere using the original materials. Every bedroom of the guesthouse is testament to this, from the flagstone floors to the heavy wooden beds.

Most of the Count's guests spend their time here walking or horse-riding in the surrounding countryside, while dinners are served in the candlelit cellar, surrounded by racks of dusty wine bottles. After a few homely meals of goulash, pike perch and carraway dumplings, you may find yourself starting to become disarmingly cosy in this remote Transylvanian retreat.

Need to know *Staff can pick you up (for a fee) from Brasov train station. For details on prices, availability, tours and restoration projects see* Ⓦ *www. transylvaniancastle.com;* ☎ *+40 0742 202586.*

149 TAKE TO THE WATERS AT AQUACITY, SLOVAKIA

At minus 120°C, the cryotherapy centre at Aquacity in northern Slovakia is colder than any natural place on Earth. As you prepare to go in for the first time, wearing nothing but a pair of woollen shorts, mittens, socks, a headband to protect your ears and a small paper mask over your nose and mouth, you may well feel a little underdressed, to say nothing of foolish. The experience itself, which lasts the two coldest minutes of your life as you pace in a circle round a small chamber filled with freezing dry ice, might seem like a surreal Soviet cosmonaut experiment but is apparently good for your body in all sorts of ways.

This is probably the oddest of the various treatments on offer at this extensive water park, built over and almost entirely powered by a natural geothermal spring in Poprad, at the foot of the High Tatras mountain range. Along with the outdoor thermal pools there are water slides, a children's area, an Olympic-size pool, a floating bar and the Vital Zone, which takes sauna to a new level. In its several steam rooms you can be treated with everything from menthol scents to salt, flower essences or healing herbs. For cooling off there is an ice fountain, a chilly plunge pool and a snow cave where if you're brave (or just mad) you can throw snowballs at each other's bare skin – all while indoors on the second floor.

As the hordes of local people pouring in every day show, Aquacity is not an elite spa. It's designed to be fun for everyone and is a proud focal point of the community, almost two hundred of whom work here, either in the award-winning hotel or the restaurant where classic Slovakian dishes are served using organic local ingredients. And there's plenty to see nearby, from the hiking and skiing resorts in the Tatras to the tranquil medieval town of Levoča. Whether you take the cryotherapy course or simply whizz down the slides, Aquacity provides a unique base from which to discover one of the less-visited parts of Europe.

Need to know *The park is five minutes from the railway station at Poprad Tatry, easily accessible from both Budapest and Kraków. For more on accommodation, opening hours, treatments and prices see Ⓦwww.aquacity.sk; ☎ +44 (0) 158 274 8840 for booking from the UK.*

150 HIDE AWAY IN A TURKISH LIGHTHOUSE

Yediburunlar is Turkish for "seven noses" – an apt description of the shapes carved by the seven bays beneath the lighthouse of the same name, and the steep, verdant promontories that divide them. It's

View of the "seven noses" from Yediburunlar lighthouse

the perfect place to appreciate the beauty of this remote part of Turkey's south coast. Looking down over the 600m drop to the sea from each of the six bedrooms' private terraces, your vision is filled with the vast blue of the Aegean; your ears with the total silence that such isolation affords.

The solar-powered lighthouse is situated halfway along the Lycian Way, a 500km path that follows the coast from Fethiye to Antalya, considered one of the world's great walking routes. Each day there's an optional guided hike, perhaps stopping for lunch in remote fishing settlements or walking to the 2,500-year-old ruins of the Lycian settlement of Sidyma, where the village of Dodurga sits among the remains – its houses constructed using pillars and other pieces of ancient stone as building materials. If these hikes have built up an appetite, hostess Semra's dinners won't disappoint: expect five-course extravaganzas ranging from smoky roasted aubergine with local cheese and walnuts to a crisp broccoli salad with lemon dressing. It's a hard place to leave, but as Semra also offers vegetarian cooking classes, at the very least you'll have the chance to recreate her dinners when you get home.

Need to know *The lighthouse (open May–Oct only) is two hours' drive from Dalaman. For further info on rooms, activities, rates and booking see Ⓦwww.exclusiveescapes.co.uk/destinations/property/yedi/detail.*

Miscellany

▶▶ FIVE FACTS

- You can travel up to 1037km on a bicycle on the energy equivalent of a single litre of petrol.

- There are more tigers in private ownership in the US than wild in the rest of the world.

- Over eight percent of global jobs are in tourism.

- There are approximately 48,000 flights worldwide every day.

- There are now more boats on Britain's waterways than there were during the Industrial Revolution.

▶▶ FIVE GREAT BOOKS ON UNUSUAL (AND CLEAN) JOURNEYS

In the Empire of Genghis Khan by Stanley Stewart (Flamingo). A journey of a thousand miles across Mongolia on horseback, with sensitive and humorous insights into the prevalent nomadic culture.

The Cruellest Journey by Kira Salak (Bantam Books). One woman's solo journey by canoe down the Niger River to Timbuktu, in the shadow of British explorer Mungo Park.

The Kon-Tiki Expedition by Thor Heyerdahl (Flamingo). A travel classic: Heyerdahl's crossing of the Pacific Ocean on a balsa-wood raft in a bid to prove his hypothesis that Pacific Islanders originally came from South America.

Round Ireland in Low Gear by Eric Newby (Picador). A somewhat grumpy travelogue based on the acclaimed writer's journey around the Emerald Isle by bicycle with his wife in tow.

Stranger on a Train by Jenny Diski (Virago Press). Partly autobiographical, this meditation on solitude and friendship is drawn out via encounters with various memorable characters met on trains across the American wilderness.

▶▶ BUZZWORDS OF NEW TOURISM

Barefoot luxury Simple living with a bit of style.

Couchsurfing Sleeping in other people's houses for free, and letting them do the same at yours.

Glamping Glamorous camping; a night under canvas with a bit more than a sleeping bag.

Off-grid Self-sufficient lodging not connected to public utilities (eg electricity or mains gas) and providing its own supply of these.

Voluntourism Volunteering while on holiday.

▶▶ NOT CRICKET

◀ **Bog snorkelling** Competitors swim underwater for sixty yards in a murky bog, without using a recognized swimming stroke and instead propelling themselves by their flippers alone. The international championships are held every year in Wales.

Bol Chumann na hEireann (Irish Road Bowling) Competitors try to roll a 28oz (794g) iron ball along a road course averaging around 4km in as few rolls as possible. For more see ⓦwww. irishroadbowling.ie.

Buzkashi The national sport of Afghanistan and Kyrgyzstan. In essence, polo with a decapitated animal, involving several hundred horsemen trying to get a headless goat or calf into a target circle while opposing riders try to wrestle or whip it out of their hands.

Kabbadi Two teams face each other across a court. One leaps forward, holding his breath and tries to touch as many of the opposing team as possible before they have to take a breath. This Indian game was a display sport at the 1936 Olympics.

Sipa The national sport of Singapore, and popular under different names in other Southeast Asian countries, it's like volleyball but without the use of hands or arms. Competitors are staggeringly athletic, performing backflips, overhead kicks and some of the most elaborate gymnastic moves you'll ever see.

▶▶ PUBLIC TRANSPORT WORLDWIDE

Chicken buses, Guatemala (pictured, top). Former North American school buses typically decked out with religious memorabilia and an over-the-top speaker system. They only leave once they're full to bursting, normally with some chickens on board (hence the name).

Cycle rickshaws, London. If you're feeling nostalgic about Asia or just want to see the city at a slower pace, a ride on a rickshaw taxi is great fun. There are usually plenty around Covent Garden and the West End theatres, or you can book them direct via operators such as Ⓦwww.londonrickshaws.co.uk or Ⓦbugbugs.com.

Jeepneys, The Philippines. Lumbering, brightly painted jeep-buses often bearing reassuring slogans such as "If tomorrow never comes" on the hood. They'll let you off anywhere: just bang on the roof with a coin and shout "para!", then pass your money along the line until it reaches the driver.

Matatus, East Africa. White Nissan minibuses that ply the main routes; like chicken buses (see above) they leave once they're full of passengers, livestock and baggage. Speed rather than safety is the priority, so feel free to get out if your driver seems intent on dying today.

Tuk-tuks, Thailand (pictured, bottom). A motorized version of the rickshaw that can duck and weave through heavy city traffic. Be sure to negotiate the fare before you jump in.

▶▶ ONE NEW WAY TO SMELL THE WORLD

In most societies sight is the primary sense with which we negotiate and understand the world. People are "good-looking"; if we understand we say "I see"; and everything from advertising to politics relies on "being seen". Not so for the Ongee, a tribe living on the remote island of Andaman in the oceans between India and Thailand. For them, the primary sense is smell. When people refer to themselves they touch their nose (while we might touch our heart). The times of day and year are understood by the differing scents released by plants or as the dew settles, and although locals daub themselves in what appears to be elaborate natural make-up, its primary use is not to alter their appearance but their smell. Death is considered to be the final loss of smell.

▶▶ THE LONGEST UNBROKEN TRAIN JOURNEY...

...in the world is the bi-monthly Moscow–Pyongyang route. The 10,200km journey takes a week.
...in Europe is the bi-weekly Paris–Moscow sleeper, a 2500km journey that takes 48 hours.
...in Africa is on the Tazara railway, a 1870km route from Dar es Salaam to Zambia's Kapiri Mposhir, taking forty hours.
...in the US is the Sunset Limited Florida–LA train, the only transcontinental route in the US, taking 48 hours to cover 2350km.
...in Australia is the Indian Pacific from Sydney to Perth, a 4352km trip taking 66 hours.

▶▶ THE ARK OF TASTE

If you like trying new foods when on holiday, check out the Slow Food Foundation's Ark of Taste (Ⓦwww.slowfoodfoundation.org/eng/arca/lista.lasso), a collection of a thousand rare foods from around the world, from Tennessee fainting goats to Nagasaki cabbage and the Ischian cave rabbit. Seeking out and eating these unique local delicacies while on holiday helps keep them commercially viable. Only then will farmers be able to afford to keep planting and breeding them, thus saving them from possible extinction.

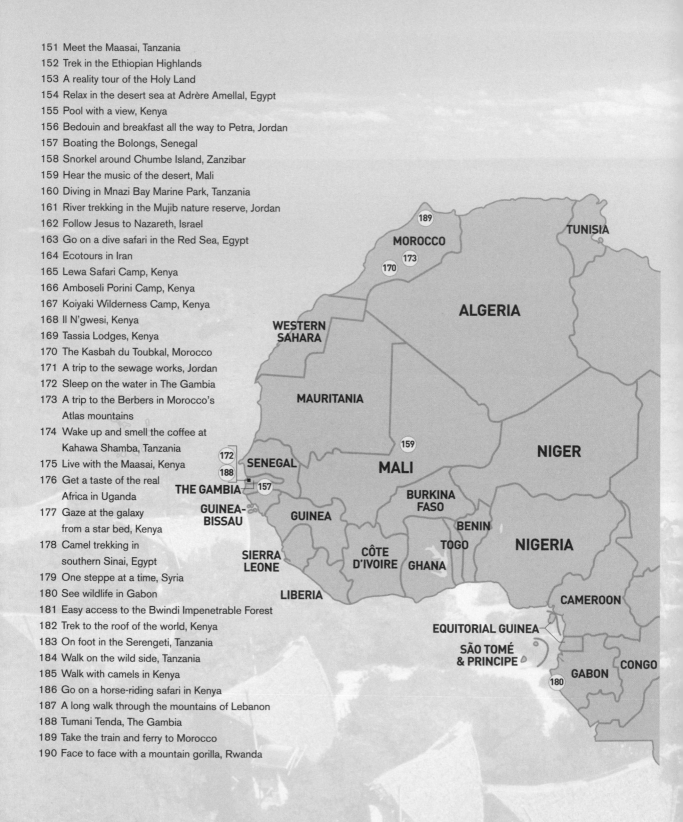

151 Meet the Maasai, Tanzania

152 Trek in the Ethiopian Highlands

153 A reality tour of the Holy Land

154 Relax in the desert sea at Adrère Amellal, Egypt

155 Pool with a view, Kenya

156 Bedouin and breakfast all the way to Petra, Jordan

157 Boating the Bolongs, Senegal

158 Snorkel around Chumbe Island, Zanzibar

159 Hear the music of the desert, Mali

160 Diving in Mnazi Bay Marine Park, Tanzania

161 River trekking in the Mujib nature reserve, Jordan

162 Follow Jesus to Nazareth, Israel

163 Go on a dive safari in the Red Sea, Egypt

164 Ecotours in Iran

165 Lewa Safari Camp, Kenya

166 Amboseli Porini Camp, Kenya

167 Koiyaki Wilderness Camp, Kenya

168 Il N'gwesi, Kenya

169 Tassia Lodges, Kenya

170 The Kasbah du Toubkal, Morocco

171 A trip to the sewage works, Jordan

172 Sleep on the water in The Gambia

173 A trip to the Berbers in Morocco's
    Atlas mountains

174 Wake up and smell the coffee at
    Kahawa Shamba, Tanzania

175 Live with the Maasai, Kenya

176 Get a taste of the real
    Africa in Uganda

177 Gaze at the galaxy
    from a star bed, Kenya

178 Camel trekking in
    southern Sinai, Egypt

179 One steppe at a time, Syria

180 See wildlife in Gabon

181 Easy access to the Bwindi Impenetrable Forest

182 Trek to the roof of the world, Kenya

183 On foot in the Serengeti, Tanzania

184 Walk on the wild side, Tanzania

185 Walk with camels in Kenya

186 Go on a horse-riding safari in Kenya

187 A long walk through the mountains of Lebanon

188 Tumani Tenda, The Gambia

189 Take the train and ferry to Morocco

190 Face to face with a mountain gorilla, Rwanda

NORTHERN AFRICA & THE MIDDLE EAST

LIBYA

EGYPT

154

SYRIA
179

LEBANON 187

ISRAEL 162

153 161

156 JORDAN

178 171

163

IRAQ

IRAN

164

KUWAIT

BAHRAIN

QATAR

U.A.E.

OMAN

SAUDI
ARABIA

YEMEN

CHAD

SUDAN

ERITREA

DJIBOUTI

152

ETHIOPIA

SOMALIA

CENTRAL
AFRICAN REP.

UGANDA
176

182 185 186

155

177

165

168

169

RWANDA 181

190

184 167 KENYA

183

151 174

175

166

D.R. CONGO

BURUNDI

TANZANIA

158

160

A Maasai tribesmen in Ngorongoro, Tanzania

151 MEET THE MAASAI, TANZANIA

On a walk with the village's herbalist, the parched plains of northeastern Tanzania soon appear less bare than when you first looked across their expanse of wiry plants. Every few minutes he bends a different branch down from a tree, offering a leaf to rub between your fingers to smell. Or he crouches down to the ground, digs away with his fingers and pulls up a gnarled root. For every such root or leaf he explains, by motioning to a part of his body, what ailment the particular plant is used against, such as the pepper bark tree, whose rough, black bark is used to treat malaria.

People2People's cultural safaris are made up of countless intimate experiences like these. Accompanied by a translator, guests embark on customizable tours to visit and stay with members of four different tribal groups in Tanzania. You might join a Maasai warrior bringing his cattle in at dusk, help gather the harvest on a Bantu farm, or hunt for spring hares and grapple with the curious clicking languages of the Khoisan.

No specifics are guaranteed, however, as these aren't displays put on for your benefit but a rare chance to interact with local villagers, observing and taking part in whatever they're doing. In rural Africa time is fluid, and you may well spend several hours simply sitting under some welcome shade chatting with the elders. Then again, you may be lucky enough to be there for a special occasion such as a wedding, where distant family members will assemble from across the region and beyond, gathering for days of celebration and feasting. Whatever you see, it will be a different Africa from the one seen through binoculars from the back of a jeep.

Need to know *People2People will customize a safari to suit your needs, which can also include more traditional activities such as wildlife-watching and trekking. In general allow a little over US$100 a day per person. Most safaris start in Arusha, which is well connected by bus with Dar Es Salaam, Dodoma and Nairobi. For typical itineraries and reservations see ⓦwww.p2psafaris.com; ☎+255 272 503 849.*

152 TREK IN THE ETHIOPIAN HIGHLANDS

After a day of trekking across stony fields worked with ox-drawn ploughs, you get the feeling that the scenery in this part of northern Ethiopia hasn't changed for centuries. Mountains trail off into the horizon and below there's a patchwork of fields dotted with thatched dwellings. A small troop of baboons feed among the cliffs while birds of prey soar in the thermals. Watching the pale sunset with your English-speaking local guides feels like a privileged way to experience the hospitality and beauty of the ancient Ethiopian Highlands.

The emphasis on trips organized by TESFA (Tourism in Ethiopia for Sustainable Future Alternatives) – an NGO in Addis Ababa – is on seeing village life and experiencing the ancient culture of the Amhara people. TESFA first ran trips to the remote parish of Mequat Mariam, though it has since developed itineraries to other villages as well as treks to the Abuna Yoseph mountain.

TESFA arranges a walking route between the villages according to your schedule and fitness (some routes are suitable for children), which is very much a no-frills experience: you may be invited to drink beer with village elders, or invited into a home for a coffee ceremony. Children abandon the family animals and rush to talk to you, wildly excited and very polite. You can also arrange to visit a school (donations of books or other supplies are welcome).

Each community has built a village camp, sleeping up to six in traditional thatched huts called *tukuls*, which are clean and simply furnished with comfortable mattresses and heavy blankets. Local food or simple Western dishes is served in the dining *tukul* or outside in the sunshine. Much of the income from TESFA's trips goes directly to the villagers, who then decide collectively how to spend it, which in many cases means supplementing their incomes as subsistence farmers. At Mequat Mariam, the villagers have set up a "grain bank" to buy cheaper grain after the harvest, to safeguard against price rises later in the season. Others have put the money into savings, which could be their only hope if the rain fails. TESFA's treks make that much difference.

Need to know *For directions, prices, itineraries and reservations see Ⓦwww.community tourism-ethiopia.com; ☎+251 (0) 11 122 5024. For details of local tour operators and travel agents in Ethiopia see Ⓦwww.tourismethiopia.org.*

Women carry water containers on their heads on their way back from Lake Tana to their village

153 A REALITY TOUR OF THE HOLY LAND

The Sea of Galilee, the Mount of Olives, Solomon's Pools...these famous names are so well-documented in the pages of history that they sound almost mythical. Nowadays we tend to hear their names portrayed only in terms of war and attrition, yet here remains a land of beautiful alleyways and bazaars, age-old art, ancient ruins and mountain wilderness.

On the trail from Tiberias to Nazareth; Ruins at Galilee

Despite the occupation, it's possible to visit many of the most historic places in the region on a "spiritual" or "political" tour arranged by the Alternative Tourism Group, a Palestinian NGO that takes guests into the heart of the region.

Guests walking the "Nativity Trail", an eleven-day, 160km-long journey from Nazareth to Bethlehem, are taken to meet Franciscan priests on Mount Tabor and Muslim clerics at village mosques, while staying in an assortment of locally owned accommodation, including villagers' homes, local B&Bs and monasteries. Other trips run by ATG include a visit to the Dead Sea to float in its buoyant waters and a trip to the first Palestinian brewery. By visiting the region's small-scale enterprises, you'll not only help contribute to their local economies, but you'll gain a balanced insight into the culture and varied landscape of this ancient land that has endured for thousands of years.

Need to know *Arrangements for each tour differ. Groups meet at Jerusalem's Old City gates or East Jerusalem's Ambassador Hotel (Ⓦwww. jerusalemambassador.com). Visitors coming from Israel are escorted by a guide to checkpoints where they are met by a Palestinian guide; those coming from Jordan will be met at the border crossing. For more details see Ⓦwww.atg.ps; ☎+972 2277 2151.*

154 RELAX IN THE DESERT SEA AT ADRÈRE AMELLAL, EGYPT

After a sweaty ten-hour ride from Cairo – for the most part spent gazing out at the undulating sands the Egyptians call "the grand sand sea" – the taxi stops deep in the Sahara desert, not far from the border with Libya, on the edge of the Qattara Depression. There's no doubt about it – Siwa *is* an oasis town.

It's always been an arduous journey – locals like to remind visitors that the Persian army lost fifty thousand men when they attempted to cross the Sahara in 500 BC – but Siwa now has a treasure that's worth the effort. The Adrère Amellal ecolodge is enchanting, especially when it's awash with the golden light of dusk. A mini-medina, its traditional mud houses huddle cosily around the base of the colossal chalk- and apricot-coloured rock that gives the boutique

property its name, meaning "white mountain".

Before the sun sets you are shown directly to your candlelit room (there's no reception or electricity here). The rustic cave-like interiors are simply furnished with fixtures crafted from olive wood or – curiously – salt, including salt bedsteads and side tables.

The brainchild of Dr Mounir Neamatalla, Adrère Amellal is just one element in a grander plan to safeguard Siwa's heritage and culture, with an eye on environmental conservation. Dr Neamatalla has also invested in projects and provided micro-financing to the Siwans to develop organic farming and renewable energy sources, to preserve traditional local crafts and to start small businesses, such as an olive-processing factory.

Simply prepared meals made from local produce are served on a terrace, by a pool or on the sand. In between you can explore Siwa or relax with a good book in the nooks and crannies about the property, each boasting sweeping views of the town. If you tire of the panorama, you could take a dip in the Roman pool, have a stroll through the palm-shaded gardens (yes, Siwa really is an oasis), visit the Temple of the Oracle of Amun, or ride the smooth waves of the grand sand sea by 4WD on a desert excursion.

Need to know *You can reach Siwa from Cairo by taxi or private car with driver (US$170 each way) or take an air-conditioned bus (US$10 each way). Details of rooms, excursions and cuisine are at ⓦadrereamellal.net; ☎+202 2736 7879. Rooms start from US$660, not including meals. For further info about Siwa see ⓦwww.siwa.com. Cheaper eco-friendly accommodation at Siwa includes Albabenshal Hotel and Shali Lodge (doubles around US$120; see ⓦwww.siwa.com for details of both).*

155 POOL WITH A VIEW, KENYA

Surely this is the best pool view in Africa. When you take a dip in the spring-fed natural pool at Sarara Camp in northern Kenya, you look out onto an arc of forested peaks on the remote

The infinity pool at Sarara Camp is filled with natural spring water and overlooks an elephant watering hole

northern side of the Mathews Mountains. That would be majestic enough for any setting, but there's more – the infinity pool overflows down to a watering hole where many animals come to drink. So you may find yourself enjoying the view and the ambience with an elephant or two.

Sarara Camp is in the 300 square kilometres of land protected by the Namunyak Wildlife Conservation Trust, the largest community-owned conservancy in Africa and one of the best places to see leopards and wild dogs. The focus of the camp is on walking safaris led by game scouts from the Namunyak community, and if the opportunity arises, take the chance to experience the local herdsmen singing when they ceremoniously pull up water from the wells.

Need to know *Fly from Nairobi (Wilson Airport) to Lewa (ⓦwww.safarilink-kenya.com; ☎+254 720 888 111), from where staff will collect you. For prices and bookings see ⓦwww.sararakenya.com.*

(Clockwise from top left) The view of the Treasury facade from the Siq at Petra; Feynan Ecolodge; The Bedouin are renowned for their generous hospitality: a local Bedouin shares coffee in a traditional Bedouin tent; Hiking in Dana Nature Reserve; Ancient rocks at Petra; A camel takes a rest at Petra

156 BEDOUIN AND BREAKFAST ALL THE WAY TO PETRA, JORDAN

The ancient Nabataean city of Petra is one of the world's top attractions, yet this magical place can be hard to appreciate when you have to battle through crowds of tourists and souvenir stalls to reach the site's main entrance. For a closer connection to the history and wilderness of this archeologically rich region, Walks Worldwide offers a guided week-long desert adventure extending from the top of Jordan's southern Rift Valley to the desert lowlands of Wadi Araba, staying in ecolodges and camping with the Bedouin before arriving early morning at Petra via an alternative entrance.

Accommodation at the start of the trek is provided by Wild Jordan, which uses income from its lodges and campsites to maintain the reserve. Your first night is at the Rummana campsite, based in a dramatic setting on a small plateau overlooking an escarpment of the valley below. The camp has all the necessary facilities for a comfortable night before the trek, including an outdoor dining-room area, kitchens and showers; each of the twenty tents has mattresses, pillows and blankets.

In the morning you go on the easy three-hour "Steppe Trail" across to Dana village, where you begin the descent to Wadi Araba (if you'd prefer not to camp, you could stay the first night in Wild Jordan's Dana Guesthouse in the village). The trail to Wadi Araba takes about five hours, through the spectacularly steep-sided Dana Valley, passing red-and-white sandstone cliffs, home to nearly six hundred kinds of plants as well as vultures, eagles and kestrels.

At the foot of the reserve is the Feynan Wilderness Lodge. Here, the long, black flapping tents of the old Bedouin camp have been replaced by a modern adobe-walled, solar-powered Arabesque building. The lodge is staffed by Bedouin – it's a cool place to escape to during the heat of the day, and at night the inward-looking lodge has a monastic feel, with the soft glow of over 250 goatskin-covered candles illuminating the atrium against the starry night sky. Around a hundred archeological sites have been identified in the region around Feynan, in particular copper mines a short distance from the lodge that are over two thousand years old and considered the most important archeological complex in southern Jordan outside Petra.

For the next three days you criss-cross the arid plains and herb-scented hillsides of the Rift Valley, following Bedouin routes that pass streams and springs, trekking up basalt and sandstone escarpments and negotiating your way though a maze of rock pinnacles until you reach the mountains of Petra. During this stage of the trek guests camp out in bivouacs under the stars in remote locations, feasting on hummus, barbecued lamb, olives and rice around hillside campfires. The final day's trek begins early in the morning from the Ammarin campsite (Ⓦwww.bedouincamp.net) to Little Petra and then a little-used trail to the Monastery above Petra, before heading down to the rose-red city to see the famous sights, such as the vast facade of the Treasury and the theatre chiselled from sandstone. This is no easy route in, but at this time of the day, before the crowds appear, you have this fascinating place to yourself.

Need to know *The best time to trek is from April to November (Rummana campsite is open March–Oct). Jordan-based Adventure Jordan (Ⓦwww.adventurejordan.com), Via Jordan Travel and Tours (Ⓦwww.viajordan.com; ☏+962 3201 2299) and Petra Moon (Ⓦwww.petramoon.com; ☏+962 3215 6665) run locally led wilderness treks throughout the region. UK-based Tribes Travel (Ⓦwww.tribes.co.uk; ☏+44 (0) 1728 685 971) and Walks Worldwide (Ⓦwww.walksworldwide.com; ☏+44 (0) 1524 242 000) also organize walking treks from Rummana campsite to Petra. For more information on Wild Jordan see Ⓦwww.rscn.org.jo*

157 BOATING THE BOLONGS, SENEGAL

For many years civil war kept outsiders from visiting Basse Casamance, a fertile strip of southwestern Senegal. It's a shame, as despite its recent troubles, and the ongoing presence of the army for reasons of security, the region is a tropical idyll unspoiled by mass tourism. One of the big draws is the bolongs – river tributaries with mangroves growing on small islands, which create a network of green tunnels. Birds build their nests in the mangroves' branches, oysters grow in their roots and fish flourish in this submarine ecosystem.

On the week-long "Villages, Bolongs and Beaches" trip through the region with Help Travel, your journey starts in Ziguinchor, a multicultural harbour town where you can watch stevedores hauling crates of mangoes and bananas onto boats in the port. You'll then head east along the river on a handcrafted canoe, piloted by a local guide, past flocks of flamingos and stands of purple jacaranda. On occasions you'll stop for a visit to rural villages where, thanks to the many community development programmes that Help Travel undertakes, you and your local guides will be greeted like friends.

Towards the end of the trip guests get involved in these programmes themselves and spend a day working alongside some of the villagers – perhaps constructing a well, working in a school or assisting a handicrafts group. Whatever you choose to do, you'll find yourself the guest of honour at a village feast once the task is done. And like so many other days on this trip, you'll be dancing with the villagers to the rhythms of their drums long after the sun has set.

Need to know *Minibuses depart daily from Tambacounda to Ziguinchor – most leaving early – or you can catch a twice-weekly ferry from Dakar. Accommodation is in local guesthouses and family homes. For details of itineraries, lodging and rates, and to customize your own itinerary, visit ⓦwww.helptravel.org; ☎+221 775 160 653.*

158 SNORKEL AROUND CHUMBE ISLAND, ZANZIBAR

In the turquoise waters around Chumbe Island Coral Park, 6km off the west coast of Zanzibar, there are around four hundred species of fish and two hundred species of stone coral. Quite simply, this tropical island nature reserve is home to one of the world's richest coral gardens.

On day-trips to the reserve from Zanzibar, you can follow snorkelling trails along Chumbe Island's shallow reef (fishing and scuba diving are prohibited in the reserve's waters, though you can dive neighbouring reefs). On land several nature trails comb through the island's protected coral-rag forest (home to pied kingfishers, fish eagles and peregrine falcons) and you can climb to the top of Chumbe Lighthouse. Though there are no beaches as such, it's possible to walk all around it at low tide, when you can poke around rock pools for crabs and starfish.

But the best thing about Chumbe is that you can stay the night on the island in beautifully designed bandas (two-tiered bungalows) with thatched palm roofs. Rainwater is collected and stored in cisterns under the floors of the bandas, where it's heated by solar power to feed the showers and basins. The clever design of the roofs ensures that there's plenty of ventilation – though you can detach a removable side-wall

The Bolongs – river tributaries with mangroves growing on small islands – are unspoiled by mass tourism

to allow natural sea breezes to waft in. With just seven bandas available, there are never more than fourteen guests on the island in the evening. Candlelit dinner is served in the former lighthouse keeper's home.

Despite its luxury, Chumbe somehow manages to pull off being an environmental educational establishment too. It runs a comprehensive school programme with courses in marine biology, forest ecology and environmental protection. But while the commitment to conservation is impressive, it is not forced upon you; the work goes on in the background while you enjoy the tropical idyll. In the privacy of your banda you can lie back in your hammock, watch the palm trees sway and listen to the water lap against the shore. The only disturbance might be the school kids as they run past chatting excitedly about what they've discovered in the rock pools and along the reef.

Need to know There are eight to ten crossings a day from Dar Es Salaam to Stone Town, Zanzibar (1.5–2hr, around US$35 one-way) and you can buy tickets on arrival at the port. Ferries to Chumbe depart from Mbweni Ruins Hotel, 7km south of Stone Town, at 10am daily (45min, around US$75, including lunch and activities). Transfers are free if you stay on Chumbe. For prices and bookings see www.chumbeisland.com; ☎+255 (0) 242 231 040.

Chumbe Island is home to one of the world's richest coral gardens; At low tide it is possible to walk all the way around Chumbe Island

159 HEAR THE MUSIC OF THE DESERT, MALI

Few journeys to a music festival can build up the sense of excitement like driving in a 4WD for days through the red dust of the Sahara. And unless you ride a camel like the local Tuaregs, that's the only way to get to the "Festival of the Desert", a showcase for Malian music that takes place so far into the sands of West Africa that when you reach Timbuktu you've still got 65km to go. Taking place each January in the oasis town of Essakane, the three-day festival attracts thousands of musicians and music lovers from around the world, who join the throngs of camels and their riders crossing the dunes, all lured by the flutes, guitars and drums that mark the Malian sound.

On the festival's website you can find many locally run 4WD tours that take you there, some starting in Timbuktu, others in Bamako or Mopti. Alternatively, overland specialist Dragoman Adventures will take you to the festival as part of its 21-night "Sounds of the Sahara" trip, which includes a three-day trek between villages inhabited by the Dogon, an animist people whose harsh lives are patterned with masked dances and rituals. Your group will also spend a few days in Timbuktu itself, a town built mostly of mud that was once a seat of great learning and whose buildings are said to have inspired the Spanish architect Gaudí. By the end of this three-week musical tour, after you've taken in nightclubs, drumming workshops and countless impromptu performances around the campfire each night, your memories of these lonely sands will be filled with sounds.

Need to know *The festival's website (ⓦwww. festival-au-desert.org) contains clips from former years, along with details on how to get there. The Dragoman trip starts and ends in Bamako, with tents, food and transport included. For further details see ⓦwww.dragoman.com; ☎+44 (0) 1728 861 133.*

The Tuareg band Igbayen at the Festival in the Desert, Mali; Sankore Mosque, Timbuktu, Mali

160 DIVING IN MNAZI BAY MARINE PARK, TANZANIA

Southern Tanzania is the place to go if you're looking for unspoilt reefs. Marine biologist and conservationist Martin Guard runs a PADI centre in the quiet fishing village of Mikindani in Mtwara, from where he takes divers to the 200-square-kilometre Mnazi Bay Marine Park – a little-visited protected area full of coral and fish species. You're likely to see large turtles and giant groupers as well as channel and patch reefs, spectacular drop-offs and extensive spur and groove formations.

Accommodation is next door to the centre at Ten Degrees South – an English-owned rustic retreat with a bar and seafood restaurant staffed by locals. The dive centre also doubles as a marine research and environmental education centre. A levy of US$1 from every dive goes to a fund for the local Naida community, while US$10 is taken from each diver's daily fee to help the marine park authorities keep this untouched area pristine and ensure the diving remains world-class.

Need to know *Mikindani is approximately 500km (8hr) from Dar Es Salaam by road. For prices, reservations and details of the research volunteer programme see ⓦwww.eco2.com; ☎+255 (0) 784 855 833. Further info on Ten Degrees South is at ⓦwww.tendegreessouth.com.*

161 RIVER TREKKING IN THE MUJIB NATURE RESERVE, JORDAN

Desert and drought define much of the wild areas of the Middle East, but there are nonetheless pockets of fertile, wildlife-rich areas if you know where to look. One particularly biodiverse region is the Mujib Nature Reserve in the west of Jordan, where the waters that flow from the highlands to the Dead Sea provide ideal conditions for river trekking in the wet season.

The only place to stay in the reserve is at the fifteen-room "Chalet Village" on the shores of the Dead Sea's Madash peninsula. The chalets are a short walk to the visitor centre and the entrance to the stunning Mujib canyon, where you can hike through deep gorges of red sandstone lined with palm trees. The "Siq Trail" (2hr) follows the main gorge of the Mujib River to a waterfall where you can swim in a large pool, while the more challenging "Malaqi Trail" (6–8hr) takes you up into the surrounding mountains, where you can picnic by natural pools and then follow the river trail on an exhilarating trek down the Mujib gorge (wearing buoyancy aids and sometimes holding onto ropes), before abseiling down a 20m waterfall and returning to camp.

The Wadi Mujib Reserve is the lowest nature reserve in the world and is home to a diversity of wildlife, including red foxes, mongooses, Arabian leopards and the beautiful Nubian ibex – the subject of a captive breeding programme managed by Jordan's Royal Society for the Conservation of Nature (RSCN), which uses tourism profits to fund its valuable work. Tramping along a river rollercoaster of torrents and pools might not be the classic way to spend time in a nature reserve, but this adrenaline-charged adventure is just as beneficial to wildlife conservation as are the guided birdwatching and hiking tours, albeit somewhat wetter.

Need to know *The Siq and Malaqi trails are open April–Oct. The only way to reach the reserve is by car (90min from Amman). Independent hiking or camping is not allowed in the reserve and as the gorge is prone to flash flooding it's essential to go with a local guide. Numbers of guided tours are strictly limited to only those run by RSCN-approved operators. For entrance fees to the reserve, guiding charges, trail opening times, directions and reservations see ⓦwww.rscn.org.jo; ☎+962 6533 7931.*

Wadi Mujib canyon

162 FOLLOW JESUS TO NAZARETH, ISRAEL

Secreted away in the souk quarter behind the Basilica of the Annunciation, in a maze of streets too narrow for cars, lies the Fauzi Azar Inn – a 200-year-old mansion that has been converted into the most welcoming place to stay in Nazareth. Centred on an arched courtyard, its ten adjoining rooms are decked out with heavy drapes and cushions that soften the heavy sandstone walls and high painted ceilings, making this an oasis of calm beside the daily hubbub of the markets.

But the Inn's owner, Maoz Inon, has bigger dreams for Fauzi Azar, and has designed it to be more than just a relaxing hideaway. He has developed a "Jesus Trail" – a 65km walking route that traces a path between some of the most significant points in the story of the

Chill out at the 200-year-old mansion, the Fauzi Azar Inn

Gospels, from the fields and forests that surround Nazareth, along the Sea of Galilee to the place where Christ gave the Sermon on the Mount. With the help of volunteers (who get free lodging in Nauzi Azar for four weeks or more in return) he has worked with various other guesthouses to mark out the route with accommodation stops along the way. So rather fittingly, the Jesus Trail ensures that in one of the world's most divided countries, there is always a welcome at the inn.

Need to know *For directions, rates, reservations and volunteering info see ⓦwww.fauziazarinn.com; ☎+972 4602 0469. Further info on the Jesus Trail is at ⓦwww.jesustrail.com.*

163 GO ON A DIVE SAFARI IN THE RED SEA, EGYPT

Packed with coral reefs, abundant tropical fish and an assortment of World War II wrecks, there is something for every diver in the Red Sea. Yet if you go to many of the popular offshore sites you can find them swamped with dive boats, while below water there can often be more divers than fish. Thankfully, there's far more to the Red Sea than Hurghada and Sharm El-Sheikh. Join a dive and camel-trekking trip organized by Sinai-based Embah Safari and you'll be taken to some of the less well-known areas along the coast, such as the Nabq Managed Resource Protected Area, which has excellent diving and can easily be reached from the shore.

At the small coastal village of Dahab you spend the first day getting back into the swing of diving; an easy shore dive to Eel Gardens and then a more technical dive to the Blue Hole. After that you'll head to Ras Mohammed National Park – Egypt's only national park, which hosts Napolean wrasse, butterfly fish and turtles. Early the following morning, the real dive safari begins: you pack your belongings onto a camel and trek north for four days along the coast of Nabq towards Dahab, camping overnight with Bedouin in the desert. You'll dive two to three times a day at various rarely visited locations – including reef tables and walls, mangroves and seagrass beds – under the experienced eye of local dive masters. Along the way you're likely to see rays, sea horses and a huge variety of coral and brilliantly coloured fish. But best of all, there will hardly be another dive boat in sight.

Need to know *Dahab is close to Sharm El-Sheikh (1hr) and Taba (2hr). Taxi transfers can be arranged when you book. For itineraries, prices and reservations see ⓦwww.embah.com; ☎+20 69 3641 690. Tours can also be booked through UK-based Baobab Travel (ⓦwww.baobabtravel.com; ☎+44 (0) 121 314 6011). Because of the desert trekking, it's best to avoid July and August. Group sizes are limited to twelve divers maximum and no more than six divers can be in the water at the same time. You will also undergo proper buoyancy checks to avoid overweighted divers damaging the reefs.*

164 ECOTOURS IN IRAN

As you tramp through dense forests of oak, elm and cypress, the sweet aroma from the cherry and mulberry orchards in the village below mixes with the fresh mountain air. In your backpack there's some flatbread and jam made from those very mulberries – which will make for a handy energy replenisher as you hike through the highlands of Telash in the Alborz Range, above the Caspian Sea in northern Iran.

When you think of holidaying in Iran you probably imagine yourself haggling for carpets in the grand bazaars, gazing at the splendid mosques of Esfahan or traipsing around the spectacular ruins of Persepolis. You probably don't picture yourself trekking through an array of landscapes beside the dramatic snow-topped mountains and glacial valleys of Mount Alam Kuh, or through the thick forests and velvet green slopes of the Caspian Sea's coast.

But that's exactly the kind of trip Ecotour Iran offers on its award-winning tours, from nature photography to birdwatching. On the latter you might spot some of the rarer of Iran's five hundred bird species, such as the Caspian snowcock or the Iraq babbler, while on the wildlife-watching tours it's possible to spot endangered animals such as the Persian fallow deer, which was thought to be extinct, or the Asian cheetah, of which around a hundred survive in Iran.

Horses grazing on the banks of the Caspian Sea

Need to know *For details of tours, quotes and reservations visit ⓦwww.ecotour-iran.com; ☎+9821 8831 5366. Ecotour Iran can also organize visas, transport, accommodation, meals, specialist guides and permits to visit national parks. Accommodation varies depending on the tour but ranges from city hotels to camping on mountain treks.*

SAFARI LODGES IN KENYA

Kenya is the safari capital of East Africa. Elephants, buffalo and wildebeest roam across vast plains, flamingos in their thousands wade in lake shallows, lions doze on sun-baked savannahs and herds of hippos graze by river banks. Yet in the scramble to see the country's wildlife, local culture often gets overlooked and tribal people have been marginalized from the financial benefits of their land's natural riches. Happily, there is now a new breed of lodges where the local tribes manage the camp, train as guides and receive a share of the profits, which go towards environmental and wildlife conservation. Below are five of these progressive lodges where local guides will take you on some of the best safaris in Africa.

Relax among the branches at the secluded Lewa Safari camp; Guests at Lewa can go on a Maasai-led camel-trekking safari

165 Lewa Safari Camp

Chances are you'll tick off the Big Five while on safari in the 250-square-kilometre Lewa Conservancy in the foothills of Mount Kenya. Primarily a sanctuary for endangered animals, Lewa is home to all the big game, including about ten percent of Kenya's black rhinos (about 45), twenty percent of its white rhinos (about 35) and 25 percent of the world's Grévy's zebras (about 500). As well as the usual game drives, there are bush walks and camel-trekking safaris led by local Maasai. All profits from Lewa Safari Camp go to the Lewa Wildlife Conservancy (Ⓦwww.lewa.org), which funds education and medical clinics in the communities adjacent to the conservancy.

Need to know *The camp is closed in April and November. Lewa is approximately five hours' drive from Nairobi. For directions and more information about the camp see Ⓦwww. lewasafaricamp.com. Prices and bookings are administered by Nairobi-based travel company Bush and Beyond: Ⓦwww. bush-and-beyond.com.*

166 Amboseli Porini Camp

Come to Amboseli Porini for some of the best birdwatching in Africa, to see elephants, lions, leopards, wildebeest and giraffes, and for spectacular views of Mount Kilimanjaro. The camp is in the Selenkay Conservation Area, a 60-square-kilometre private game reserve bordering the northern boundary of Amboseli National Park. It is co-owned by the local Maasai and Gamewatcher Safaris – a Nairobi-based travel company which organizes Maasai-guided walks as well as day and night safaris into the conservancy and the national park. Track game with the Maasai and you'll learn a trick or two from the people who have lived here for centuries.

Need to know *Gamewatcher Safaris also operates Maasai-guided safaris at Porini Rhino Camp in the Ol Pejeta Conservancy, Mara Porini Camp in the Ol Kinyei Conservancy and Porini Lion Camp in the Olare Orok Conservancy. For prices and reservations at each camp see ⓦwww.porini.com; ☎+44 (0) 207 100 4595.*

167 Koiyaki Wilderness Camp

Superbly positioned for a close view of the migration of wildebeest and zebra along the northern plains of the Maasai Mara, Koiyaki Wilderness Camp is the first community-owned lodge in the Mara. It also funds the adjacent Koiyaki Guiding School, where up to 25 Maasai school-leavers a year are trained to become professional safari guides. Part of their work experience is to help run the camp, while the more experienced Maasai guides take you on walking safaris, 4WD safaris and night drives. The game here is as good as anywhere else in the park – with all those wildebeest running around there are lots of predators about.

Need to know *Fly from Nairobi to Siana (ⓦwww.airkenya.com; ☎+254 2060 5745), from where you will be collected by arrangement. The wildebeest migration is from mid-June to the end of October. Wilderness Journeys runs safaris based at Koiyaki Wilderness Camp; for prices and bookings see ⓦwww.wildernessjourneys.com; ☎+44 (0) 131 625 6635. For more information about the guiding school see ⓦwww.koiyaki.com.*

168 Il N'gwesi and 169 Tassia Lodges

Both these luxury lodges lie among the wild scrubland and ancient migratory routes of northern Kenya. Il N'gwesi is on a rocky outcrop by the Ngare Ndare River on the edge of the dramatic Mukogodo Hills. There are six double thatched *bandas*

Il N'gwesi lodge is perched on a rocky outcrop on the edge of the Mukogodo Hills

and an infinity pool with wonderful views of the Samburu Game Reserve and the Mathews Range. Tassia Lodge is perched on the edge of a rocky bluff, looking out over the Northern Frontier District towards Samburu, Shaba and the Lolokwe Mountain. The lodge has six rooms (including a children's bunkhouse which sleeps six) and is a four-hour walk or a morning's game drive from Il N'gwesi.

Both Tassia and Il N'gwesi are owned and run by local Maasai, who lead guided safaris and birdwatching tours in the Ngare Ndare River Valley – where you'll have a good chance of seeing elephants, buffalo, lions, wild dogs, hyenas, cheetahs and leopards. This is community-owned pastoral land, so while you're out on safari expect to come across herders and their cattle – and the real Africa.

Need to know *Il N'gwesi is approximately two hours' drive from Lewa (see opposite). For more information about the camp see ⓦwww.lewa.org/ilngwesi_lodge. You can book both camps through Nairobi-based travel company Let's Go Safaris (ⓦwww.lets-go-travel.net; ☎+254 204 447 151).*

The terrace at Kasbah du Toubkal in the heart of the Atlas Mountains

170 THE KASBAH DU TOUBKAL, MOROCCO

On the drive up through the Imlil Valley into the foothills of the Atlas Mountains, you have a sense that you're going somewhere special. The road passes rose-coloured adobe villages and fields terraced with ancient irrigation channels that nourish apple, cherry and walnut orchards. Mules trot along the road carrying children, women return from the fields with sacks of wheat, and men congregate in small groups by the roadside. As you swing around steep-sided bends, you get glimpses of the looming massif at the head of the valley, and by the time you reach the mountain village of Imlil – just 65km from Marrakesh – you know you're in another world. The light is brighter, the air thinner, the streets empty and the jagged peaks resplendent against the sky.

No wonder Martin Scorsese chose this setting for *Kundun*, his film about the life of the Dalai Lama. The grandeur and remoteness of the Atlas Mountains is every bit as magnificent as the Himalayas. Here, the Kasbah du Toubkal, the former summer home of local ruler Caid Souktani, is perched at 1800m in the shadow of Morocco's highest peak, Mount Toubkal.

Run and staffed by Berbers, the Kasbah calls itself a "hospitality centre", so expect pots of mint tea on your arrival, and *jellabahs* (long-sleeved robes) and leather *babouches* (traditional leather slippers) to slip into. The rooms have been furnished by Berber craftsmen using local materials and range from basic communal salons (often used by school groups) to comfortable private double rooms and one lavish, three-bedroom apartment.

Guests come on day-trips from the capital to dine on tagines on the large rooftop terrace, from where there are sweeping views of the valley. But you'll need to stay here for a few days to make the most of the spectacular setting. You can hire a guide and climb Mount Toubkal in a day, then return to the *hammam* (steam bath) and dine in the Kasbah's restaurant. Or try a four-hour trek to Toubkal Lodge in the Berber village of Idissa. Its three double rooms are similar in style to the plush apartment at the Kasbah, and are designed for just a handful of guests to use as a base for day-hikes in the mountains or as part of an overnight circular walking route from the Kasbah du Toubkal. And if you don't fancy the four-hour trek over the mountain pass from the Kasbah to the village, you can ride in on horseback or go by mountain bike.

Need to know *Take a shared taxi or local bus from Marrakesh to Asni then a local taxi from Asni to Imli (about 2hr in total). Alternatively, book a 90min transfer with the Kasbah (€85 per car). From Imlil it's a steep 15min walk (a mule will carry your bags). The Kasbah does not stock alcohol, though you can bring your own. For prices, room reservations and booking transfers at both the Kasbah and Toubkal Lodge see ⓦwww. kasbahdutoubkal.com; ☏+33 (0) 545 715 204. A five percent tax on hotel invoices goes to the Imlilillage Association, which funds local community projects.*

171 A TRIP TO THE SEWAGE WORKS, JORDAN

Jordan is a birder's paradise. Bang in the middle of the migratory route of millions of birds from Europe, northwest Asia and Africa, you can tick off pages of elusive species by heading to Aqaba, and in particular, to the home of a favourite avian stopover: the Aqaba sewage works. This marshy habitat is proving to be so reliably good for birdwatching that an observatory is being established overlooking the works' large lagoons; though by exploring on foot around the pools, bushes and trees you will also come across a huge variety of species, including common cranes pausing on migration, pipits, gulls and sedge-warblers...we could go on but you get the drift. Hold your nose and get ticking.

Need to know *The lodge is open all year, though the best time to see birds at the reserve is outside high summer. For details of activities and trails, directions, prices and reservations see ⓦwww. naturetrek.co.uk; ☎+44 (0) 1962 733051.*

172 SLEEP ON THE WATER IN THE GAMBIA

Mandina River Lodge, situated over the banks of the Mandina Bolon tributary on the northern edge of the Makasutu Culture Forest, is the remarkable vision of two Englishmen, who have created one of The Gambia's first luxury bush lodges run by locals and based on ecologically sound principles. Each of the floating and stilted handcrafted thatched cabins has its own jetty, is solar-powered and is reached by an elevated wooden walkway across matted mangroves. Local guides run day-trips along the river in dug-out canoes to show you kingfishers, monitor lizards and troops of migrating baboons. It's a morning well spent, but make sure you're back in time for lunch at the nearby Baobab Cultural Area, where you can feast on fish caught that

day, sample palm wine and meet some of the local people who live in this thriving, protected part of West Africa.

Need to know *The Makasutu Culture Forest is 5km from Brikama. For prices and reservations see ⓦwww.makasutu.com.*

Traditional music and dance at the Baobab Cultural Area; the luxury floating handcrafted thatched cabins at Mandina River lodge; wildlife spotting on trek through the mangroves

173 A TRIP TO THE BERBERS IN MOROCCO'S ATLAS MOUNTAINS

Hidden away in the middle of an amphitheatre of barren 4000m-high peaks in Morocco's High Atlas mountains, the fertile valley of Ait Bougmez is a lush patchwork of fruit orchards, barley fields and scattered mud-brick villages. It was only as recently as 2001 that the first asphalted road was laid in this valley. Even now, if there is a particularly heavy snowfall the route in can be blocked for several days.

This remoteness has enabled the valley's inhabitants – most of whom are Berbers, the indigenous people of Morocco – to continue their farming lifestyle relatively undisturbed by changes elsewhere. An excellent place to stay is at Dar Itrane, a lodge built of stone, wood and adobe using traditional techniques, and run by local Berbers who are committed both to preserving their culture and sharing it with guests, from the communal meals they serve (and will teach you how to cook if you wish) to the library stocked with Berber literature and

The Berber-run Dar Itrane Lodge is built of stone, wood and adobe using traditional techniques

music, or the many excursions available in the surrounding valley and hills. Whether you want to trek or ride a horse, they will be your guides to nearby villages where you can soak up the slow pace of life in these parts. Back at the lodge – lit by candles at night – there's a *hammam* (steam room) to relax in, and a roof terrace for gazing at the stars.

Need to know *From Marrakesh take a shared taxi to Azilal, and then another to Tabant/Bougmez Valley. Dar Itrane lodge is open all year round, though expect snow on the mountains in January and February. For rates, reservations and further info see ⓦwww.origins-lodge.com; ☎+33 (0) 472 537 219.*

174 WAKE UP AND SMELL THE COFFEE AT KAHAWA SHAMBA, TANZANIA

The sunny slopes and fertile volcanic soils of the foothills of Kilimanjaro provide excellent scenery as well as excellent conditions for growing coffee. At Kahawa Shamba ("coffee farm" in Swahili), small-time coffee growers have started inviting guests to stay in their village to help supplement their income as part of the Kilimanjaro Native Cooperation Union, whose members supply coffee to the Fairtrade company Cafédirect.

At the village of Lyamungu, the local Chagga tribe has built four traditional huts – made of vines from the nearby forest and thatched with dried banana-leaf – which they

now own and run. Each hut has twin wrought-iron beds plus showers, with breakfast served in a communal dining hut among breadfruit, papaya and coffee bushes overlooking the forested Weruweru gorge down to the river below.

The villagers will take you along lush forest trails to some of the local sights, including a farm where you can see how coffee is processed, from harvesting the beans to drying them on parchment, followed by a tasting of the final product – Bourbon and Kent arabica coffee. If there's a caffeine-fuelled spring in your step afterwards you can go on a variety of guided walks in the area, from strolls along the Weruweru Valley, where there are several waterfalls, to long treks to nearby caves once used by the Chagga to shelter from Maasai raiders.

Mount Kilimanjaro is of course the magnet in this part of Tanzania, but if you want to pause for a few days and experience more of the local culture then come to Kahawa Shamba. You'll learn about the rural way of life in Tanzania, perhaps even a bit of Swahili, and, in future, whenever you smell fresh coffee, you'll be instantly transported back to this beautiful, tranquil place. That's a fair trade.

Need to know *Kahawa Shamba is 20km (a 1hr drive) from Moshi. For prices and reservations visit Ⓦwww.tribes.co.uk; ☎+44 (0) 1728 685 971.*

175 LIVE WITH THE MAASAI, KENYA

As you sit back on the dusty ground after dinner, your stomach stretched contentedly after one too many balls of *irio* – the staple food formed by mixing green corn with beans, potatoes and greens – your Maasai host challenges you to a game of *bao*, said by some to be the oldest board game in the world. Like many such games, it appears a simple matter of getting your pieces from one end to the other – until you start playing and discover the endless rules that govern your moves.

Over a week spent living with a Maasai family in the village of Olturuto, in the Kajiado district 30km from Nairobi, you'll have plenty of time to grapple with *bao*'s intricacies. You'll also become immersed in other aspects of daily life of the herders and their families. Helping with the chores may not seem like a holiday, but a few days grinding maize to make flour, milking the cows or collecting water from the borehole is the best way to learn what life's really like in an African village. The reality is that most of your day is spent not working as we know it, but slowly passing time – catching up on local gossip, making arrows, weaving baskets or simply taking some time to contemplate the vastness of your surroundings.

Crafts being made by a Maasai in the Maasai Mara

Assisted at all times by a translator, you'll also get the chance to talk with elders and medicine men and spend two days on a more traditional tourist activity on safari in nearby Amboseli National Park, home to elephants, lions and giraffes. And while the chance to see a lion from the back of a jeep is what brings most tourists to Kenya, very few get the chance to experience the simple rhythms of life as a Maasai.

Need to know *GSE Ecotours organizes homestays (lasting four to fourteen days) in five villages in the Great Rift Valley and Central and Eastern provinces. Prices start from around KES6200 (US$80) per person per night, which includes accommodation, meals and ground transportation from Nairobi. For further enquiries see Ⓦwww.gse-ecotours.com or ☎+44 (0) 870 766 9891.*

176 GET A TASTE OF THE REAL AFRICA IN UGANDA

Fried grasshoppers don't sound wildly appetizing, but when your host, Tinka, has just offered you some as a welcome-to-my-home snack, it would be rude to refuse. Actually they're better than they look: crunchy, a bit like pork crackling, and a good accompaniment to the local homebrew.

Tinka and his wife Betty, who live in the west of Uganda right by the Bigodi wetlands, offer homestays in association with the Uganda Community Tourism Association (UCTA), which has spent the last decade working to develop holidays that enable tourists to mix closely with communities. Walking along the tree-lined paths through the wetlands, you stand a good chance of spotting great blue touracoes, yellow-backed weavers and woodland kingfishers. All the while the branches above rustle as colobus and vervet monkeys dart among the canopy.

Alternatively, if you stay in UCTA accommodation elsewhere in the country, you could kayak on Lake Bunyoni and dine with the fishermen on freshly caught crayfish, or base yourself in a community-run lodge by the entrance to Bwindi National Park, one of the best (and last) places in the world to see mountain gorillas. Or follow the Kabaka's Trail to see the fourteenth-century Kasubi Royal Tombs from the Baganda people's royal lineage.

On all of the activities, there'll be plenty of time to chat with the villagers, play games with the children, listen to folk stories and songs, and dance to the drums as the sun goes down. And whether you're discovering forgotten monarchies or sampling surprisingly appetizing bugs, these community trips connect you to a part of Africa far from the usual tourist trails.

Need to know *The UCTA is based in Kampala. For details of all the programmes organized by the UCTA, as well as directions and prices, see ⓦwww.ucota.or.ug.*

177 GAZE AT THE GALAXY FROM A STAR BED, KENYA

Ask anyone on safari what they love about the African bush and many mention the mesmerizing night sky – and one of the best ways to view it is from the comfort of a "star bed" at Loisaba Lodge in northern Kenya. If the weather is fair, you can wheel these handcrafted wooden four-posters out onto the deck of your cabin and sleep under the stars. The beds have mosquito nets and are on a raised platform (fitted with a bathroom, a thatched dining area and a fire pit) and are available in two locations: the first is a 20min drive from the main lodge in one of the eastern valleys overlooking the "Kiboko" waterhole; the second a 40min drive from the lodge on the banks of the Ewaso N'giro River, where guests are hosted by members of the local Koija community.

Loisaba Lodge itself is on a 250-square-kilometre private ranch and wildlife conservancy on the edge of the Laikipia plateau. The game here is excellent – there are elephants, giraffes, antelopes, buffalo, Grévy's zebra, kudus, dik-diks, wild dogs and some big cats. Guests who stay at the star beds have access to all the facilities at the main camp – so after a day in the bush, you can return for a dip in the cliff-top pool, followed by dinner in the shady garden and then a doze under a thousand stars.

Need to know *All profits from the Loisaba Lodge go towards conservation of the Loisaba Wilderness area and to fund community health and education projects with the neighbouring Maasai tribes. For prices, activities and bookings see ⓦwww.loisaba. com; ☏+254 (0) 623 1072.*

178 CAMEL TREKKING IN SOUTHERN SINAI, EGYPT

As a region to lure trekking enthusiasts, Egypt's southern Sinai has all the right ingredients.

An endlessly photogenic vista of mountain passes and shimmering desert, it also has some of the oldest human settlements in the world – as the meeting point of Europe and Africa it is scattered with ruins from the Pharaohs onward. Among these expanses of rock and sand lie fertile valleys where Bedouin nomads and traders have gathered for as long as anyone can remember.

Excluded by by the development of urban life, the Bedouin are one of the poorest groups in Arab society. But if, like them, you'd rather escape the chaos of Cairo, their unparalleled knowledge of the desert makes them the perfect guides. Sheikh Sina, a Bedouin-run operator that works with eight Bedouin communities, offers treks to remote areas of the South Sinai Mountains. The eight treks on offer vary between three levels of difficulty and can include visits to tribes, snorkelling, exploring canyons and much more; camels carry your equipment and food so you need only be burdened by your daypack.

Some nights you'll pitch camp along the way, in sand dunes or lush oases; at other times you'll stay with Bedouin groups in their tents. And if you plan on seeing St Katherine's Monastery while here, it's worth including a stay at the El Karm Ecolodge, located in Wadi Gharba about three hours' walk along the old pilgrims' route to the monastery. Solar powered and constructed from the rocks that surround it, few places feel as much a part of their environment as this peaceful stone lodge.

Sheikh Sina was founded to equip Bedouin guides with hospitality and language skills, and to secure their livelihoods, install amenities such as wells and compost toilets, and promote small businesses. Its success shines through in the welcome the Bedouin provide. *Diyafa* (the code of hospitality) is for the Bedouin the highest of virtues, and there is no more important practice than to honour your guests.

Need to know *Sheik Sina's offices are located in the town of St Katherine, accessible by bus from all over Egypt (for details see Ⓦst-katherine.net). Treks last about six hours each day, with camps set up by your guides each night. For further info on treks, itineraries, ecolodges and the southern Sinai region see Ⓦwww.sheikhsina.com; ☏+20 693 470 880.*

Camel trekking among the vast expanse of rock and sand in southern Sinai

Arabian Oryx

179 ONE STEPPE AT A TIME, SYRIA

Palmyra – Queen Zenobia's ruined ancient city – is a fixture on the itineraries of most travellers to Syria, who set aside a few days to explore the spectacular temples, visit the seventeenth-century castle and kick back in the easy-going oasis town nearby. But the vast majority of visitors overlook Talila Nature Reserve, just 20km away and in many ways equally remarkable.

The local Bedouin call the stony semi-arid area around Palmyra "Al Badia", meaning "the steppe", but as desolate as the landscape looks, it's actually home to a wealth of wildlife, including 260 bird species. First established in 1996 to protect the area's rich biodiversity and reverse desertification caused by overgrazing, Talila consists of 1300 square kilometres of nature reserve and strictly managed rangeland, entrusted to three Bedouin communities who work with environmental specialists.

Talila's main achievement has been the reintroduction and breeding of two endangered animals, the sand gazelle and Arabian oryx – much to the excitement and disbelief of local families whose grandparents would tell them how they once roamed the area like flocks of sheep. Since their reintroduction, the original eight oryx have increased to 38 and the original thirty gazelles to three hundred. The ultimate goal is to release them into the wild again.

Talila will also be the home of the odd-looking northern bald ibis (famous for its punk haircut), thought to be extinct for seventy years until it was rediscovered near Palmyra in 2002 by Italian biologist Gianluca Serra and a team of Bedouin hunters. The reserve will house an enormous aviary to breed these critically endangered birds.

Simple accommodation and decent restaurants are plentiful in Palmyra, the closest town to Talila. The best budget option is the Ishtar Hotel, which has welcoming staff and a casual eatery dishing up home-cooked Syrian food. The renovated Zenobia Hotel has the most atmospheric location, with traditionally decorated rooms and Palmyra's finest restaurant with a terrace overlooking the ruins.

To get the most out of a trip to Talila, organize your visit through Gianluca Serra of Ecotourism Syria and BirdLife International, Syria's most respected eco-tour operator, who can connect you with local guides to drive you around the reserve and point out wildlife. Don't forget to pack the binoculars.

Need to know *Buses depart Damascus frequently for Palmyra (3hr); from there you'll need to arrange a driver or taxi to take you to the reserve. Alternatively, hire a car in Damascus and drive yourself. For more info see* Ⓦ*www.ecotourismsyria. com. Ishtar Hotel:* Ⓦ*www.ishtarhotel.net;* ☏*+963 315 913 073. To contact Zenobia Hotel* Ⓔ*cham-resa@net.sy.*

180 SEE WILDLIFE IN GABON

Gabon is Africa's wildlife destination of the future. Some seventy percent of the country is covered in forest, yet only recently has it been given any kind of conservation status. Thankfully it now has thirteen national parks, protecting a huge range of animals including western lowland gorillas, forest elephants and chimpanzees.

The jungles in Gabon have the highest diversity of tree and bird species anywhere in Africa (over 670 bird species have been recorded). It's also a place where the wildlife of the equatorial rainforests tumbles out onto its Atlantic beaches: you're just as likely to see hippos playing in the surf as you are elephants and buffalo roaming along the beach or humpback whales cavorting offshore.

Although Gabon is one of the most stable countries in the region, transportation and infrastructure are still developing and not all the parks are easily accessible yet, so you'll need to do your homework before you go. Only three national parks – Loango, Lope and Ivindo – are currently geared up for tourism and realistically accessible, but others are bound to follow.

An innovative pilot project known as Operation Loango has helped to establish ecotourism in the Loango National Park, a diverse ecosystem of forest, savannah, rivers, lagoons and beaches. The success of the project has led to the foundation of the travel company Africa's Eden, which leads guided tours into the forest to see lowland gorillas, as well as operating humpback whale-watching trips from July to October. Trips into the forest are based from several lodges, such as Tassi Savannah Camp, a small tented camp by the beach, from where you can see green, olive ridley and leatherback turtles. The choice, then, is yours: hippos, lowland gorillas, elephants, turtles or the best birdlife in Africa.

Need to know *For prices and itineraries of Africa's Eden's trips see ⓦwww.africas-eden. com. UK-based Wildlife Worldwide also organizes trips to Loango, Lope and Ivindo national parks; for rates, bookings and itineraries see ⓦwww. wildlifeworldwide.com; ☏+44 (0) 1962 737 630.*

181 EASY ACCESS TO THE BWINDI IMPENETRABLE FOREST

Bwindi Impenetrable Forest National Park in western Uganda lives up to its name. Unless any of the three groups of habituated gorillas have ventured near to where most of the accommodation is near Bohoma, you usually have to jump in a jeep and endure a ride of several bumpy hours to the trailhead. But in the south of the park (home to one habituated group), guests staying at the new Clouds Mountain Gorilla Lodge need only walk a few hundred metres from their private cottage to the Ugandan Wildlife Service hut – the starting point of the trail that leads into the park.

The lodge is a partnership between The Uganda Safari Company, the Africa Wildlife Foundation (ⓦwww.awf.org), the International Gorilla Conservation Programme (ⓦwww. mountaingorillas.org) and the local Nkuringo community, who receive a share of the lodge's income to fund community projects. The lodge caters for the luxury traveller – there are ten en-suite cottages with private verandas as well as a dining room and a lush botanical garden. But don't expect the trek into the forest to be quite as cushy; it can take up to three hours of strenuous uphill climbing – sometimes through slippery terrain – to reach the gorillas in the dense jungle. But then that's all part of the appeal.

Need to know *The drive from Kampala to Clouds Mountain Gorilla Lodge is an arduous eleven hours; alternatively drive to Lake Mburo National Park (4–5hr), from where it's a 6hr drive to Bwindi. Clouds Mountain Gorilla Lodge can only be booked through The Uganda Safari Company; for prices and reservations see ⓦwww.safariuganda. com; ☏+256 414 251 182. For more information on gorillas in Uganda see ⓦwww.uwa.or.ug.*

SAFARIS IN THE SLOW LANE

Go on safari in a 4WD and you have the best of both worlds: a safe, secure vantage point from which to spot wildlife, and the mobility to whizz off as soon as the news comes over the radio of where to go for the best action. Go on walking or horse-riding safaris and the pace is much slower, but you are able to follow tracks off-road, catch the scent of animals, hear birdsong more clearly and get a closer connection to the bush. And if you're lucky, you may just have that once-in-a-lifetime close encounter with an elephant or a lion. Below are our five favourite slow safaris.

182 Trek to the roof of the world, Kenya

Follow an ancient game trail on foot up to the Losiolo escarpment to one of the best viewpoints of the Great Rift Valley, then tackle a 3000m descent to a riverside camp in the beautiful Lerachi gorge. And that's just day one. Donkeys will carry all the equipment as you follow a guide from one of the Ndorobo tribes – accompanied by ten Samburu warriors – among the isolated mountain ranges of Samburu that are home to leopards, hyenas and mountain reedbucks. Choose between a five-day trip or a more strenuous eight-day trek into the Rift Valley, including three days in the private wildlife reserve of Mugie. En route you'll explore several flat-topped peaks with views of the arid plains below, swim in natural pools and visit traditional Samburu villages in this ancient, volcanic land.

Need to know For further details, info about the Samburu region, prices and reservations see Ⓦ*www.samburutrails.com;* ☎*+44 (0) 131 625 6635.*

183 On foot in the Serengeti, Tanzania

It's back to basics on this walking safari in the Serengeti National Park. Walking in the mornings only and in small groups of two to eight people, the three-day to five-day treks begin in the Longossa Hills and then follow ancient riverbeds to the Orangi River, where you're likely to see elephants, buffalo and hyenas. You'll camp in the bush in canvas-dome tents, before returning on the final day to Serengeti Wilderness Camp, where there are several permanent water sources that attract lots of game. This seasonal camp has eight tents and a large dining area, but no permanent structures (lighting is solar and there are compost toilets) so that it can be transported easily to follow wildlife.

Need to know The operators are one of only a few granted a permit to lead treks in the Serengeti. The walking and camp teams have radios, mobile phones and a GPS, and you are accompanied throughout by an armed Tanzania National Parks guide. For dates, prices and reservations see Ⓦwww.rainbowtours.co.uk; ☎+44 (0) 20 7226 1004.

On safari in the northern Maasai Mara

184 Walk on the wild side, Tanzania

Watching the annual mass migration of wildebeest and zebra as they move from the Serengeti back to the Maasai Mara is impressive enough on any game drive, but on a walking safari you feel even closer to the action. On this unique trip, walking no more than 15km per day, Maasai guides will lead you to safe vantage points on rocky mounds where you'll feel the ground tremble as thousands of animals roam across the plains. Each night, you'll camp out next to waterholes or small tributaries in lightweight fly camps, and you'll eat dinner around a camp fire wondering if there are as many wildebeest in the Serengeti as there are stars in the African night.

Need to know *Trips depart January to March. For itineraries, prices and bookings see ⓦwww. wildernessjourneys.com; ☎+44 (0) 131 625 6635.*

185 Walk with camels in Kenya

Don't want to carry your bags on a walking safari? Then let the camels do it. On a tour with Karisia Walking Safaris you'll follow game tracks with Maasai warriors across the Laikipia Plateau in northern Kenya. Walking itineraries vary from a few days to a seven-night hike along the Ewaso River. En route you'll camp at various spots along the river, pass a nesting site for a pair of Verreaux eagles, and see elephants and hippos at the water's edge. The trip ends at Ol Malo, a luxury lodge on the edge of the Laikipia Plateau where you can swim in a pool and enjoy wonderful views of Mount Kenya.

Need to know *For prices, itineraries and reservations see ⓦwww.karisia.com; ☎+254 (0) 2089 1065 or UK-based Tribes Travel: ⓦwww. tribes.co.uk; ☎+44 (0) 1728 685 971.*

186 Go on a horse-riding safari in Kenya

At Borana Lodge, a working ranch with two thousand cattle at the edge of the Samangua Valley in Kenya's remote Laikipia region, guests can combine the thrill of horse-riding with game viewing. Choose between rides over grassland among giraffes, hartebeest and impala, or explore the forest at the foot of Mount Kenya. You'll spend between four and seven hours in the saddle every day, camping out overnight in the bush if you wish. The lodge is luxurious yet was built using only local building materials and dead wood from the ranch. Each of the eight cottages has its own veranda and shares the wonderfully well-sited pool that overlooks a watering hole popular with elephants. This is safari tourism made easy.

Following game tracks on a camel walking safari

Need to know *The ranch caters for all riding abilities and there are a few smaller bush ponies for children. For more information about Borana Lodge see ⓦwww.borana.co.ke; ☎+254 722 464 413. For prices and bookings of horse-riding trips based at Borana see ⓦwww.aardvarksafaris.co.uk; ☎+44 (0) 1980 849 160.*

A walking safari with a Samburu warrior in Kenya's Rift Valley

(Clockwise from top) The Qadisha Valley; Horses along the route from Qannoubine to Ehden; Trekking from Hasbaiya to Marjaayoun; Your local guides on the Qbaiyat to Tachea walk; Breathtaking views on the route between Ehden and Qannoubine

187 A LONG WALK THROUGH THE MOUNTAINS OF LEBANON

The Lebanon Mountain Trail, launched in 2007, is the country's first long-distance hiking route. Running from Qbaiyat in the north to Marjaayoun in the south along the Mount Lebanon range, it makes use of ancient trade routes and rural tracks to connect national parks and nature reserves with 75 villages at altitudes of 1000–1800m. The 440km circuit is divided into 26 sections, each walkable in a day.

Intended to bring additional income to neglected mountain areas, while safeguarding Lebanon's environmental and cultural heritage, the trail has united religious and political groups – previously in conflict during the Lebanese civil war – towards a common national project. While it was the brainchild of Lebanese-

American expatriates, it was only through the co-operation of local families, community groups and Lebanese NGOs that it was able to happen.

Along the way you might stop at historic Ehden, home to some of Lebanon's oldest churches (one dating to 749 AD) and spectacular natural springs; Hasroun, in the Qadisha Valley, which boasts lush orchards and gardens, stone houses with red-tiled roofs and traditional coffeehouses; and Niha on the peak of Niha Mountain, with a medieval fort, an important religious site for the Druze community called Nabi Ayoub Shrine, and dense forests of pine, cypress and oak.

Accommodation is in B&Bs in renovated stone houses, decorated with rustic wooden furniture and bold Bedouin *kilims* (tapestry-woven rugs). You can hire local guides, trek independently or go with specialized tour operators which also offer mountain biking, rafting, caving, snow-shoeing, birdwatching and star-gazing. And when you're done? Well, you can do as the Lebanese do and head to the slopes for some skiing – then down to the coast for a swim.

Need to know *For a map of the trail and information on transport, tour operators and guides, plus accommodation, villages and facilities on the route see ⓦwww.lebanontrail.org; ☎+961 5955 302. To hike the southern Lebanon sections of the trail you'll need a security clearance from the Lebanese Ministry of Defence, and a guide is recommended. Spring and autumn are the most vibrant seasons, summer sees consistent blue skies but sweltering heat, while in winter you'll be walking through snow.*

188 TUMANI TENDA, THE GAMBIA

If you'd prefer to escape the resort beaches and get an insight into traditional Gambian village life, head to Tumani Tenda ("Tumani" is the name of a local peanut picker, "Tenda" means riverbank), a Jola village 25km east of Brikama on a tributary of the Gambia River. It's a place laden with fields of maize, millet, peanuts and watermelons, where you can spend the day with the local fishermen or help women to collect oysters.

You can stay in a collection of mud huts built by the villagers; they're rustic but comfortable and are decorated with local handicrafts, with meals served around a wooden table in a large hut. Guests have a variety of cultural tours to choose from, though birdwatching is the main draw – Tumani Tenda is one of the few places where you can see the brown-necked parrot (qualified guides will take you in a dug-out canoe to the best places on the river to see it). But if you really want to sample local culture, go on a farming tour and learn how the villagers process salt from the river and harvest groundnuts and rice. The money raised from tourism goes towards a village development fund, which has helped build a school and provide medicine.

Tumani Tenda is a member of ASSET-Gambia

– a pioneering association of small tourism businesses, including craft vendors, guesthouses and local tour operators. The association provides a voice for these small players, helping them to get a share of the income from the mainly foreign-owned tourism industry. The Gambia is the smallest mainland country in Africa, yet it has a thriving tourism industry dominated by large package-holiday firms. A stay at Tumani Tenda helps benefit directly the people who actually live here.

Need to know *Maximum ten guests at a time; avoid the rainy season between May and October. For information on Tumani Tenda village, directions, transfers, activities, and bookings see ⓦwww.tumanitenda.co.uk; ☎+220 984 5823. For more about ASSET-Gambia see ⓦwww.asset-gambia.com.*

189 TAKE THE TRAIN AND FERRY TO MOROCCO

On the early-morning ferry, it takes just one hour to cross the Straits of Gibraltar from the southern Spanish port of Algeciras to Tangier in Morocco. Just enough time to wipe the sleep from your eyes and pinch yourself. You're in Africa.

Once you emerge from customs at Tangier, it's a quick stroll into town and then a 30min walk (or a 10–15min ride in a petit taxi for about 20 dirhams) to the Tangier Ville train station, from where there are modern, air-conditioned trains to Fes (4hr 20min), Casablanca (5hr 45min) and Marrakesh (10hr 30min, via Casablanca). Leave mainland Spain in the early morning and you can be sipping mint tea in Marrakesh's Djemaa El Fna square in the evening.

Need to know *From Paris, take the overnight sleeper to Madrid (see p.55) and then the train to Algeciras (ⓦwww.renfe.es). For prices and timetables of ferries to Tangier see ⓦwww.trasmediterranea.es or ⓦwww.nautas-almaghreb.com. Information for trains in Morocco is at ⓦwww.oncf.ma.*

Adult Silverback Mountain Gorilla of the Shinda group, Volcanoes National Park, Rwanda

190 FACE TO FACE WITH A MOUNTAIN GORILLA, RWANDA

No matter how many wildlife documentaries you've seen, nothing can prepare you for the moment you first see a mountain gorilla in the wild. The trackers tell you over the walkie-talkie radio that you're close, but it isn't until you hear a muffled sound among the dense foliage that your senses spring to red alert. The adrenaline flows faster as your guide points to a small clearing in the undergrowth. There, just a few metres away, the bulky black figure of an adult silverback mountain gorilla squats calmly among a nest of vegetation in the dappled morning sunlight. Weighing some 200kg and not far off 2m tall (when standing upright), with deep-set eyes, a mass of coarse fur and bulging muscles, it is a fearsome sight.

Yet once you've reeled from the terror of being so close to this huge wild animal, you become mesmerized by it. The shock turns to awe. At first you are encouraged to make a low grunting sound to let him know you are there – and to stifle your giggles at the release of "gorilla gas" (a consequence of their diet). Then after a good deal of posturing and staring, you are accepted into the fold and it reverts back to eating, grooming, playing in its natural home and letting rip with the occasional whopper. Most people spend the full allotted time (usually one hour) transfixed.

Finding a mountain gorilla in the wild takes patience and skill. There are only about 680 left in the world in just two dense forest regions of Central Africa – in the Virunga Volcanoes region (which straddles Uganda, Rwanda and eastern Democratic Republic of Congo) and the Bwindi Impenetrable National Park in southwest Uganda.

One of the best places to see the gorillas is in the Parc National des Volcans in the far northwest of Rwanda, which is home to half of the entire population of mountain gorillas. Rwanda Ecotours runs trips to see seven groups of gorillas that are habituated to humans. Tours range from a one-day trek (based at the Mountain Gorillas Nest hotel, 2km from the Kinigi park headquarters at the base of the Virunga Mountains) to a six-day hike that includes a visit to the Dian Fossey Research Station where you can hear about the programme's Mountain Gorilla Conservation work (Ⓦwww.gorillafund.org). The pick of the bunch is a ten-day "Best of Rwanda" tour where you'll see mountain gorillas and also visit local villages, Lake Kivu and Nyungwe National Park – the only place in the world where you can see more than five primate species in a single location, including chimpanzees, mountain monkeys and Angolan black-and-white colobus monkeys.

Rwanda Ecotours is co-run by Edwin Sabuhoro, a Rwandan who was awarded a young conservationist prize for his work in turning gorilla poachers into tourism guides. Edwin helped local communities establish the Iby'Iwacu Cultural Village in the Musanze district, where you can practise drumming with the villagers, taste local food and beers, and meet a traditional healer. Visits to the cultural village have become integral to Rwanda Ecotours' itineraries en route to seeing the gorillas, and as a fifth of the income from these trips goes directly to the villagers, Edwin's tours have convinced many to turn their back on poaching.

Need to know *Tours begin from Kigali International Airport, where guests are transferred to Mountain Gorillas Nest in Ruhengeri. For itineraries, reservations and more about gorilla conservation see Ⓦwww.rwandaecotours.com; ☏+250 500 331. Edwin is the Rwanda contact for Your Safe Planet (see p.378). For more information on places to stay, other tour operators and contact details for permits to visit the gorillas (issued by The Rwanda Tourism Board in Kigali or Ruhengeri) visit Ⓦwww.rwandatourism.com; ☏+250 576 514. Tours vary depending on levels of participants' fitness; porters are recommended.*

The New Travellers

More and more people are questioning the way they travel and exploring alternatives, whether by avoiding flying or staying with locals rather than paying for hotels. While you may not be able to follow exactly in the footsteps of the following five pioneers, their experiences are instructive for anyone searching for a new way to see the world.

THE TRAVEL NETWORKER

In 2008, Vicky Baker travelled through Central and South America, staying with locals – from apartments in Colombia to the thatched huts of the Kuna tribe of Panama's San Blas Islands. She was able to do this through the rise of travel networking websites such as couchsurfing.com (see p.377), where members offer one another accommodation in their homes for free. She also used networking sites to get to know local people, who showed her the cities, towns and villages she visited, enabling her to discover the sort of things no tourist normally finds, from a village of descendants of Laotian refugees in French Guiana to the coolest underground music spots in Quito – courtesy of an Ecuadorian musician.

Vicky's blog and a wealth of information on hospitality exchanges can be found at ⓦgoinglocaltravel. com.

THE ADVENTURER

Jonny Bealby's first book, *Running with the Moon*, details the ten-month solo motorbike trip he took down the west side of Africa from Cairo to Cape Town in 1994. He's also ridden along the Silk Route on a horse, just as Marco Polo did some seven hundred years before, and travelled through the remotest parts of Afghanistan and Pakistan. His love of adventure led him to set up a travel company called Wild Frontiers (see p.286), whose aim is to entice more people to get off the beaten track and out of their comfort zone while on holiday. Needless to say, as a man with such wanderlust in his soul, Jonny still personally guides many of the trips his company offers.

THE NO-FLYERS

In 2007, Ed Gillespie and his girlfriend Fiona King took a sabbatical and headed off on a round-the-world trip. But rather than select the seven airports their plane tickets would let them stop at, they declined to fly and went instead by as many other forms of transport as they could, from coaches through Eastern Europe to camels in the Mongolian desert. Along the way they were battered by a severe storm in the Bay of Biscay, drank with fellow travellers on the Trans-Siberian Express, rode mopeds through the hills of Vietnam and watched whales from the deck of a cargo boat while passing the Great Barrier Reef.

To read about Ed and Fiona's trip, as well as the travel blogs Ed's written since coming home, go to ⓦwww.lowcarbontravel.com.

THE CYCLISTS

When Amy and Wim Meussen got married, they didn't opt for two weeks in the sun for their honeymoon. Instead, they took ten months off and cycled first from Belgium to Turkey, then through the deserts of North Africa, and finally from Singapore up through Southeast Asia into China, pedalling over 10,000km along the way. Averaging about four hours on the road each day, they had plenty of time to learn how to distill schnapps in Germany, dive Mediterranean coral reefs in Turkey and enjoy water fights with the locals in Laos on New Year's Eve. Along the way they camped in Europe and stayed in cheap hotels in Asia, with their whole trip costing them less than €10,000. To read a blog of their travels visit ⓦ*amyandwim.travellerspoint.com*.

THE CARAVANNERS

One cold winter's day in 2007, John and Thea Verhoeckx, a couple of middle-aged Dutch social workers living in the North Sea town of Breda, decided to chuck it all in. They sold their house and made that legendary mid-life investment – a horse-drawn cart. Over the following year, accompanied by their dog and two horses, they travelled 3200km across Europe in the slowest way imaginable, wending their way through the Netherlands, Germany, Slovakia and the Czech Republic. So intent were they on freeing themselves from all cares that they didn't even take a map, choosing to simply go where fortune took them. Along the way they were interviewed by various newspapers and TV stations and, as a result, were inundated with offers of places to stay or meals to share by people fascinated by their courage and perhaps a little envious of their freedom. You can read their story at ⓦ*www.slow-express-journey.com*.

THE TRAIN TRAVELLER

Mark Smith, better known as The Man in Seat 61 (after his favourite seat on Eurostar) is a lifelong train enthusiast who has travelled all over the world by rail. His website (ⓦwww.seat61.com) is a labour of love and the first port of call for anyone looking to travel by train. Combining knowledge gained from his own experiences with those from the legions of fans who send information garnered from their own trips, this marvellous resource provides details on just about every rail route in Europe as well as extensive information on worldwide train travel, from advice on how to get visas and where to buy the best tickets for your journey, to photographs of carriage interiors from Almaty to Zambia. If your eyes tire from squinting online for too long, you can buy his book on travelling to Europe – *The Man in Seat 61* (Bantam Press) – whose clear, unfussy layout will help you browse, dream and plan.

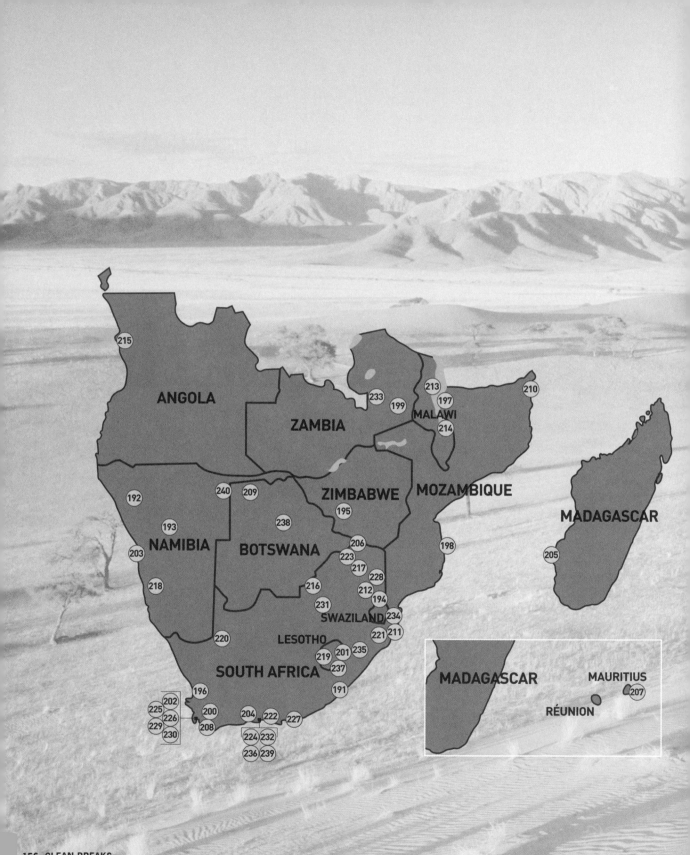

ANGOLA

215

ZAMBIA

233

199

MALAWI

213

197

214

210

ZIMBABWE

195

MOZAMBIQUE

198

MADAGASCAR

205

NAMIBIA

192

193

203

218

BOTSWANA

240

209

238

206

223

217

216

231

228

212

194

234

SWAZILAND

220

219

201

235

237

221

211

LESOTHO

SOUTH AFRICA

191

196

202

225

200

226

229

208

230

204

222

227

224

232

236

239

MADAGASCAR

MAURITIUS

207

RÉUNION

SOUTHERN AFRICA

191 Go local on the Wild Coast, South Africa

192 Stay at a community-run camp in Namibia

193 Track cheetahs on foot, Namibia

194 Become a game ranger at Kwa Madwala, South Africa

195 Camp Amalinda, Zimbabwe

196 Ride the Cederberg Heritage Route, South Africa

197 Relax by the Lake of Stars, Mozambique

198 Arrange a trip on a dhow, Mozambique

199 Stay in an African village, Zambia

200 Take an eco wine-tour, South Africa

201 Ride to the top of Lesotho

202 Walk with the Chacma baboons, South Africa

203 Kayaking with seals at Walvis Bay, Namibia

204 Wake up with meerkats, South Africa

205 Voluntary services underseas, Madagascar

206 Track wild dogs in the Limpopo, South Africa

207 See the pink pigeons of Mauritius

208 Visit the world's richest floral kingdom, South Africa

209 Take a mekoro through the Okavango Delta, Botswana

210 Have the reef to yourself at Guludo, Mozambique

211 Natural heritage at Isimangaliso Wetland Park, South Africa

212 Help save the chimpanzee from extinction, South Africa

213 Plant trees with Ripple Africa in Malawi

214 Kayak on Lake Malawi

215 Be one of the first to visit Kissama National Park, Angola

216 Take the kids to Madikwe, South Africa

217 Go birding in ancient forest, South Africa

218 See the fairy circles in the Namib Rand, Namibia

219 Pony-trekking in the mountains, Lesotho

220 Stay the night in one of South Africa's National Parks

221 Conservation in action at Phinda, South Africa

222 Whizz through the forest at Storms River

223 Walk with rhinos at Leshiba

224 Kayak with whales in Plettenberg Bay

225 Ride a bike in a township

226 Taste fine Cape wines at Spier

227 Drink with locals in a township

228 Fair game at Umlani

229 A night on Long Street, Cape Town

230 See hippos near Cape Town

231 Stay in Soweto

232 Walk with rastas in Knysna forest, South Africa

233 See the rare sitatunga deer, Zambia

234 Tembe Elephant Park, South Africa

235 The Midlands Meander, South Africa

236 Live the high life at Tsala Treetops, South Africa

237 Trek the Drakensberg, South Africa

238 Watch the zebra migration, Botswana

239 Hide away in the treetops of Knysna forest, South Africa

240 Meet the Bushmen at Nhoma, Namibia

191 GO LOCAL ON THE WILD COAST, SOUTH AFRICA

(From top) Canoeing with a local guide on the Khora River; Child in calamine face mask; The view down to Bulungula's huts and beach

So clear are the skies above Bulungula Lodge that if you lie out at night and haven't seen a shooting star within thirty minutes, you're compensated with a free night's accommodation. It's a pretty safe gamble on the owners' part: when the sun goes down, the depth of the surrounding darkness makes you realize why this remote region is called the Wild Coast.

There's no road to the lodge, so the staff collect you from Mthatha, three hours' drive away. When you finally get to the brightly coloured huts of Bulungula, perched high above the beach from which it takes its name, the sense of isolation is total. The only man-made sound at Bulungula is the whirr of the small wind turbine which, along with the solar panels, provides power. Equipped with compost toilets and paraffin-fuelled showers, in one day the lodge uses the same amount of electricity as a toaster operating for one hour.

You could spend all your time here on the wide white-sand beach, but for those seeking a little more, the members of Nqileni village – whose huts are scattered across the hills behind the lodge – also run various activities. You can watch malachite kingfishers on a leisurely canoe trip along the Xhora River, learn about traditional medicine on a forest walk with a herbalist, or spend a few hours grinding flour and building mud-bricks with one of the local women. The Nqileni community owns forty percent of the lodge, and several families have members who work for it. The plan is that the villagers will eventually own and manage it all.

A stay at Bulungula makes one think about what is possible. This may be crime-ridden South Africa, but there are no locks on any of the doors and no thefts to report: the lodge and its guests are treated as a part of the surrounding village. And if you don't just visit as a guest, but arrange to work in the garden or offer other skills that will make a meaningful contribution to this community's development, then your accommodation is free for as long as you stay and help.

Need to know *A shuttle bus to Bulungula Lodge (ZAR60) collects from the Mthatha Shell Ultra City petrol station at 3pm daily. You must call to book your seat the day before. For more info on getting to Mthatha, accommodation rates and details of community projects see* Ⓦ*www.bulungula.com;* ☏*+27 (0) 475 778 900.*

192 STAY AT A COMMUNITY-RUN CAMP IN NAMIBIA

Scattered throughout Namibia's vast wilderness are over thirty lodges, camps and homesteads supported by NACOBTA, a not-for-profit organization that develops community-based tourism. Many are simple campsites with basic facilities, but there are also several joint ventures between communities and private operators that offer more sophisticated accommodation as well as trips to see wildlife and sites of cultural heritage. NACOBTA has two great benefits for these communities: it's a source of much-needed income and also provides business training in how to run the camp.

Two of the best-run camps are Damaraland and Doro !Nawas, both of which are partnerships between communities and Wilderness Safaris, a long-established operator in southern Africa. Damaraland is a small camp of just ten en-suite, adobe-style thatched lodges by the Huab River Valley, where you can go on game drives to see elephants, gemsboks and greater kudu, springboks. Doro !Nawas Lodge is a slightly larger camp at the edge of the dry Aba-Huab River and is a good base to go on guided trips to the ancient Twyfelfontein rock cavings, Namibia's first World Heritage Site.

Need to know For contact details, prices and activities see ⊛www.nacobta.com.na/joint_ventures.php; ☎+264 (0) 6125 0558. Expert Africa (⊛www.expertafrica.com; ☎+44 (0) 208 232 9777) can organize trips to all of NACOBTA's lodges and camps. Wilderness Safaris: ⊛www.wilderness-safaris.com.

193 TRACK CHEETAHS ON FOOT, NAMIBIA

Few people ever see a cheetah in the wild. As well as being one of the shyest of the big cats, it's also one of the most endangered: perhaps only ten thousand remain, around a quarter of those in the barren expanses of Namibia.

If you're keen to see one then the Africat Foundation, the world's most successful cheetah and leopard rescue-and-release programme, offers the best cheetah-spotting odds anywhere outside a zoo. Based on the 223-square-kilometre Okonjima guest farm near Otjiwarongo, where guests stay in luxurious thatched chalets, Africat funds a programme to rescue cheetahs captured by farmers, thus saving them from the gun. It then cares for the animals with a view to their

possible reintroduction to the wild (around 85 percent are ultimately released). The hundred or so cheetah on site live in enclosures ranging in size depending upon the state of their rehabilitation.

Thanks to the radio collars used to monitor them, the cheetahs are far easier to find than would normally be the case. In some places, the guides will take you to around ten metres from a pair of cheetahs to watch them devour a kill, or you'll follow them on foot as they track impala through the bush. Sometimes they'll run off, but generally they accept your presence. It's a great opportunity to see how the animals are honing their hunting skills and becoming ready to fend for themselves again. Some argue that the cheetahs here aren't truly wild, but Africat is doing more to help this animal survive than almost anyone else, and a visit here is a chance to see it happening close up.

(From top) The speed signs are for you rather than them; A cheetah looks on

Need to know Okonjima is three hours' drive north of Windhoek by car or bus, halfway to Etosha National Park. As well as cheetah-watching programmes, there are also opportunities to view leopards and wild dogs. For details of rates, activities and the lodge see ⊛www.okonjima.com; ☎+264 6768 7032/3/4.

194 BECOME A GAME RANGER AT KWA MADWALA, SOUTH AFRICA

Few jobs have as romantic an image as being a game ranger. At Kwa Madwala Game Reserve, near to Kruger National Park, you can find out if you've got what it takes to track lions and hyenas on foot, tag and release birds of prey, or count antelope populations from a microlight. Over the last few years the owners of the estate have been turning a former trophy-hunting lodge back to the pristine wilderness it once was. One of the ways they fund this enterprise is by inviting guests to assist the rangers in their work. If you've got a few weeks or more to spare, then you can stay at a former farmhouse looking out over a small lake with resident hippos and crocodiles, and try out most aspects of a ranger's work – from darting lions and rhinos to sleeping out in the bush under the stars.

Need to know *Info on project opportunities, prices and how to apply at ⓦwww.kwamadwala.net/gap-year-experiences; ☎+27 (0) 216 837 826.*

(From top) A ranger with tortoise, one of the smaller inhabitants of the bush; White rhino; a hawk looks on; Sidney the ranger pointing out animal tracks in the earth

195 CAMP AMALINDA, ZIMBABWE

For anyone interested in the origins of Africa, the Matobo Hills in Zimbabwe contain a higher concentration of San Bushmen art than anywhere else on the continent. These vast, smooth granite boulders also provide the resting place of Cecil Rhodes, the founder of diamond company De Beers and one of the most notorious British colonialists. From Camp Amalinda – a luxury safari lodge built among these hills some 50km outside the city of Bulawayo – you can explore all these landmarks, or just relax in the outdoor spa overlooking the hills.

Camp Amalinda is also a partner in the Mother Africa Project, which is committed to ensuring tourism benefits the communities and wildlife of Zimbabwe. When guests at the lodge aren't marvelling at snake eagles or trying to spot elusive leopards amid the rocks, they can visit projects the organization funds with Camp Amalinda's support, such as a primary school and clinic. Alternatively, people with more time can volunteer on either of Mother Africa's conservation or community programmes, during which a part of their thirty-day experience will be based at the lodge. Either way, a stay at Amalinda will make you feel a part of Zimbabwe's efforts to build itself a better future.

Need to know For more on accommodation and activities at Camp Amalinda, as well as details of the Mother Africa project, see Ⓦwww.campamalinda. com; ☎+263 (9) 243 954. Camp Amalinda charges a fully inclusive rate of US$220 per day. Thirty-day volunteer programmes cost around US$2500.

196 RIDE THE CEDERBERG HERITAGE ROUTE, SOUTH AFRICA

Looking out from the cart across the red-rocked panorama of the Cederberg Mountains, the mark of modern man is barely visible. Here, just

Matobo Hills Lodge, Bulawayo & Matobo Hills, Zimbabwe

200km north of Cape Town, folded peaks and limestone formations rise over the vast, stark landscape of the Cederberg Wilderness Area. Despite the challenges such terrain imposes, man has been here for millennia (as the 6000-year-old cave art attests) and wildlife still abounds: leopards, bat-eared foxes and grey mongooses can occasionally be spotted foraging around the rocks.

The Heuningvlei Donkey Cart Adventure, organized by Cederberg African Travel, is a languorous three-night journey across the rugged wilderness, punctuated by stays with local communities in this little-visited region. Whether you are riding in the cart or hiking beside it, villagers will act as your guides, pointing out wildlife and explaining customs before you head home for a simple meal accompanied by the area's best-known product – rooibos tea, produced organically for generations by farmers whose livelihoods are greatly aided by tourist visits.

Need to know The Cederberg Mountains are approximately 2.5 hours' drive north of Cape Town. Trails start from Clanwilliam. For bookings see Ⓦwww.cedheroute.co.za; ☎+27 (0) 274 822 444.

(Clockwise from top left) Nkwichi lodge at night; The luxury bamboo huts; A dip in the river; A place to relax at the lodge; Canoeing on the lake

197 RELAX BY THE LAKE OF STARS, MOZAMBIQUE

It feels like a tropical island: soft sand between your toes and the water extending to the horizon, as if you were looking out to sea. In fact you're gazing out over Lake Niassa – what Livingstone romantically dubbed "The Lake of Stars" – and the water is saltless, crystal clear and contains a greater variety of indigenous fish species than any other lake in the world.

Behind you is thick forest, shielding the seven luxury huts of Nkwichi Lodge, each designed from local wood and stone so as to be harmonious with their surroundings. All are solar-powered and more luxurious than your average jungle hut, with four-poster beds and private outdoor showers hidden among the trees.

This is pristine wilderness – so remote that the last 10km to the lodge has to be travelled by boat. But it is also home to one of Africa's most successful community projects, which thanks to funding from tourist fees has involved twenty thousand Nyanja people in schemes ranging from building schools and a clinic to improving productivity of local farmers (many of whom supply the lodge with organic food).

Whatever you choose to do during your stay, the Nyanja are here to be your guides. You can camp for a night in the vast reserve amid the birds, deer and even the odd elephant. Or you may want to explore the lake in a kayak and stop for a picnic on an empty beach. Or just lie back on *Miss Nkwichi* (she's a boat) and let the wind decide which way you go.

Need to know *Details on how to get to the lodge (by ferry, yacht or car) as well as booking info, rates and activities are at ⓦwww.mandawilderness. org.*

198 ARRANGE A TRIP ON A DHOW, MOZAMBIQUE

Dhow sailing is hard work. It takes a huge effort just to hoist the sail, and as soon as it's up the ropes have to be quickly fastened so that it keeps its place in the wind. A plank of wood nailed across the hull is where you sit, while the captain tills the wooden rudder. Yet despite their simplicity, when the breeze fills the sail they cross the ocean as gracefully as any yacht.

The dhows are still used by fishermen along the coast of Mozambique from Ponto D'Ouro to Pemba, and while there are few organized trips, by asking around you should be able to arrange a ride. It's a good idea to be guided by the fishermen – they will probably know of uninhabited islands, secluded bays and mangrove-lined inlets where they can take you. You'll get the freedom of being on the open water, knowing that your fee is helping the fishing communities, which are struggling to compete against industrialized fishing and motorized launches. You may not be strong enough to raise the dhow's sail on your own, but as tourism

develops in Mozambique, you can at least help steer it in the right direction.

Need to know *You can probably persuade a fisherman to take you on a dhow anywhere along Mozambique's coast, especially around Pemba, Maputo or Vilanculos, where they are more used to tourists. You'll need to bring all your food and water, though. In the main resorts more organized trips are springing up, such as Mapapay Dhow Trips in Vilanculos (ⓦwww.dhowtrips.com; ☎+25 882 973 7160).*

199 STAY IN AN AFRICAN VILLAGE, ZAMBIA

To understand what daily life is really like in an African rural community, a stay in Kawaza village, on the edge of Zambia's South Luangwa National Park, offers an authentic introduction to its rigours and rhythms. Guests can drop in for the day or stay as long as they like; on arrival, you'll have a chat with your guides to plan a programme that suits. Visitors are encouraged to get as involved as they can, whether it's learning about traditional herbal medicine, fishing in wooden dugout canoes or simply helping to prepare traditional meals.

This is no show village, however. The Kunda people, former hunters who now mostly survive through subsistence farming, have seen how low-impact tourism can protect them against the vagaries of farming in extreme conditions. Villagers who provide services to guests are given a monthly salary and the remaining profit is ploughed back into the community, improving facilities at the school and helping those most in need. And at Kawaza visitors don't just get the chance to see the school their money has helped fund – they are encouraged to help with some teaching too.

Need to know *The village welcomes visitors from April to November. For directions and rates see ⓦwww.kawazavillage.co.uk.*

Grapes thrive in the Cape's climate; Walks wind around the green mountain

200 TAKE AN ECO WINE-TOUR, SOUTH AFRICA

Many of South Africa's legendary wine routes offer a glimpse into the country's past, from their old Cape Dutch houses to stories of slave labour or bottles quaffed at Napoleon's court. But take a walk or cycle around Groenland Mountain – just an hour from Cape Town – and you'll discover a new route, one that is looking forward rather than back.

On the Green Mountain Eco Route you'll travel to organic vineyards and gardens along old ox-cart trails through the mountain-fringed coastal scenery of the Cape Floral Kingdom, rich with scented heather and proteas. As you stop off to meet the vineyards' owners and sample their wines, you'll sense why they're working so hard to protect the diverse plant kingdom in which their estates lie. Along the way you can easily pick up some picnic food from a farm stall and lunch by one of the many rivers flowing down from the Overberg. One bit of advice: at the end of the day you may find that cycling in a straight line has become considerably more tricky.

Need to know *Accommodation is offered at many of the estates or in locally run guesthouses. Full information on tours, trails, farm stalls and accommodation availability is at* Ⓦ*www. greenmountain.co.za;* ☎*+27 (0) 218 440 975.*

201 RIDE TO THE TOP OF LESOTHO

For those who like their holidays laden with superlatives, a four-day horse-riding trip into Lesotho with Drakensberg Adventures will give you three. Your first starts the moment you leave the company's lodge, situated beneath the Sani Pass in eastern Kwazulu Natal. The rubble-strewn track, a former mule path for traders now only accessible by 4WD, is the highest pass in southern Africa.

Passing the border crossing at its top (three men in a hut), it's time to stop at superlative number two – The Sani Top Chalet, where a sign lets you know that at 3482m you are now sitting in the highest bar in Africa. It's more mountain refuge than country pub, but looking out at the pass winding sinuously down below, it's hard to think of a beer garden with a better view.

With the first two under your belt in no time at all, the real journey begins, towards your third. Your guide helps you saddle up on Basotho ponies, whose stocky frames make them ideal for what lies ahead – two days' riding, sleeping in a community-run lodge one night and a shepherd's hut the next, in order to reach Thabana Ntlenyana. Here, at the highest point south of Kilimanjaro, you stop for a well-earned lunch and a fabulous view. Along the way you'll be picking up supplies in remote farming villages, bringing much-needed income to families who would otherwise see almost none.

When you finally get back to Sani Lodge on day four, aching from the saddle, you can even squeeze in a fourth (of sorts). No bed will feel more comfortable than the one you lie in that night.

Need to know *Tours include transport, guide, food and accommodation. For more details, as well as info on getting to the lodge, rates and other activities, see* Ⓦ*www.sanilodge.co.za;* ☎*+27 (0) 33 702 033 027.*

202 WALK WITH THE CHACMA BABOONS, SOUTH AFRICA

Most of us would imagine that going for a stroll among baboons would be about as sane as going for a swim with crocodiles – their vicious teeth and ear-piercing shrieks hardly make them ideal rambling companions. Yet the team of guides at the charity Baboon Matters propose exactly this, and they're not mad; they believe that if people develop a better understanding of the much-maligned baboons that live in the hills around Cape Town, then they will be less likely to consider them as pests.

To further their aim of getting people to learn to live alongside primates, Baboon Matters uses tourist fees to fund educational visits to schools and houses in the areas where the baboons are common. They also employ community members as monitors who work to keep the baboons out of human settlements; so far this has proved an effective strategy in keeping intrusion levels low.

Tourists are taken up into the hills and walk for around two hours to the baboons' territory, where they can observe around thirty individuals from a distance of a few metres. Far from displaying aggression, though, the baboons regard their visitors with curiosity, or more often just carry on as if you weren't there. One prods around under some stones with a stick, hoping for something to eat. A mother strides on all fours across the ground, her baby riding on her back. Two young males posture and mouth off in front of a bored-looking female. As you spend time among these fascinating creatures, apprehension is soon replaced by hushed wonder as the complexity of their relationships begins to unfold.

Need to know *Information on tour booking, times and costs are at* ⓦ*www.baboonmatters.org.za;* ☏*+ 27 (0) 217 822 015.*

203 KAYAKING WITH SEALS AT WALVIS BAY, NAMIBIA

Most people come to Swakopmund, a Bavarian-style town surreally out of place on the edge of the Namib Desert, to explore the vast dunes. Few who visit know that the sandy Atlantic shallows of nearby Walvis Bay are also home to 2500 cape fur seals – one of the country's last remaining colonies – as well as a resident population of diminutive benguela dolphins.

Namyak Namibia, a tour operator based in a community crafts shop in the centre of Swakopmund, offers kayak trips in the bay. Canoeing among the seals in the early morning is a joyous experience: the seals surround the canoes and leap across the bows, while the pups look up at you like labradors waiting for a stick to be thrown. The dolphins are a little more circumspect, but will swim alongside, weaving this way and that only so long as you paddle furiously enough to keep up with them.

But all this activity serves a serious purpose. Namibia's seal cull is the second largest in the world after Canada's. Thanks in part to the popularity of the Walvis Bay colony with tourists, the seals here have so far escaped such a fate. The more people who come to Swakopmund and show interest in the seals, the better the chance that they will remain safe from culling, and that the tourism-minded Namibian government will rethink its approach to seals elsewhere along the coast.

Need to know *Swakopmund is about five hours' drive by car or bus from Windhoek, or you can take the Desert Express train (*ⓦ*www.desertexpress. com.na) between the two cities. No previous kayaking experience required. For details of excursions and rates see* ⓦ*www.nam-c-yak.com;* ☏*+264 6420 3665.*

Kayaking among the hundreds of seals in Walvis Bay

WILDLIFE WATCHING

Top of the wish list of the majority of safari tourists is the iconic Big Five (lion, elephant, buffalo, rhino and leopard), yet southern Africa is home to far more animals of interest as well as hundreds of species of birds. Below are four responsibly managed experiences where you'll get up close to some of Africa's lesser-known animals without unduly disturbing them. These trips help raise awareness about their plight and provide much-needed income that contributes to their survival.

204 Wake up with meerkats, South Africa

The jeep stops at 5.30am outside dusty Oudsthoorn, a small town in the Western Cape. Everyone in the group gets out and walks a short distance away, tired but excited, binoculars trained on the holes in the bare ground nearby. A few minutes pass. Then, without warning, a furry head pops up like a jack-in-the-box. And another. Suddenly a group of sleepy meerkats are bobbing up and down, sunning themselves, foraging for food and playfighting.

Meerkats sunning themselves in the early morning light

Meerkats are normally shy creatures, and it's thanks to Grant Mcilrath (known hereabouts as "Meerkat Man") that this insight into their world is possible: they are used to him, and he knows how to find out which burrows in the 10km-wide conservation area they will have moved to overnight. As the sun rises higher and the urge to giggle at their antics subsides, the meerkats approach to within a few metres, seemingly unfazed. Before your stomach has even rumbled for breakfast, you've witnessed up close an animal society that few get the chance to see even from a distance.

Need to know *The Meerkat Magic Conservation Project, from where tours start, is in Oudsthoorn, accessible via Routes 62 or 328. Tours cost ZAR600, to be paid in cash. For more info on tours and booking see* Ⓦ*www.meerkatmagic.com;* ☎*+27 (0) 82 413 6895.*

205 Voluntary services underseas, Madagascar

Some of the best diving in the Indian Ocean is off the west coast of Madagascar, where you can put your skills to good use on a voluntary conservation expedition with Blue Ventures, a marine conservation organization. Participants learn to identify the coral and fish species in the lagoons of the Grand Récif de Tuléar – one of the largest coral reefs in the world – and gather data for scientists that will help establish a management plan for preserving the reef systems. Expeditions last between six and twelve weeks; on average there are fourteen volunteers at the camp and never more than two volunteers per staff member. If you're in any doubt about whether it's for you, Blue Ventures helps put you in touch with previous volunteers – so you can find out exactly what the local rum punch is like.

Need to know *Expeditions run throughout the year. For more on research programmes and costs see* Ⓦ*www.blueventures.org;* ☎*+44 (0) 20 8341 9819.*

206 Track wild dogs in the Limpopo, South Africa

The Endangered Wildlife Trust is a non-profit organization in the Limpopo region that has worked to ensure wild dogs' survival for over three decades. One of their successes has been to show farmers that wild dog-tracking is a viable form of ecotourism that can protect the dogs while benefiting local communities. Spending nights at the thatched Little Muck Lodge in Mapungubwe, guests are led by a trained conservationist on 4WD tours that allow them to observe the dogs roaming in their natural habitat – hunting, if you're lucky – and the fees from this are used to manage fenced reserves that keep the animals away from local farmers' stock. So far it's proving an effective strategy: the wild dog population in Limpopo is finally rising after a long decline.

Need to know *Mapungubwe is about three hours' drive north of Makhado. Booking and rates for Little Muck Lodge and wild dog-tracking are at Ⓦwww. soutpansberg-tourism.co.za/tourism_cd/html/little_ muck_lodge.html; ☏+27 (0) 15 534 2986.*

207 See the pink pigeons of Mauritius

As well as its five-star hotels and idyllic sandy beaches, Mauritius is best known for once being the home of the dodo. The extinct flightless bird has bought the island international recognition, but ironically, some of the island's other endemic species have meanwhile been sliding towards the brink of eradication. Much of the island's vegetation has been replaced by sugar-cane plantations and sprawling development, and what wildlife remains is under threat.

The Mauritian Wildlife Foundation (MWF) has for the last twenty years championed the conservation of the island's flora and fauna. To help raise funds for its work, it organizes guided trips to the small islet reserve of Ile aux Aigrettes, which is home to giant tortoises and the pink pigeon, one of the organization's success stories. Numbers of this endemic bird

have recovered from only ten individuals in the early 1990s to over 360 today, about 75 of which live on Ile aux Aigrettes. Visitors tour the reserve by boat and then go on a guided walk around the island to see the native wildlife, the diversity of which gives an insight into how Mauritius once was.

Need to know *The two-hour tour (Ⓦwww.ile-aux-aigrettes.com) costs MUR800 per person and departs six times a day from the Old Sand Jetty at Pointe Jerome on the southeast coast. MWF also takes on conservation volunteers; see Ⓦwww. mauritian-wildlife.org/ volunteer.php.*

(From top) Coral off Madagascar; African wild dog; one of Mauritius' rare pink pigeons (each one is tagged and monitored)

208 VISIT THE WORLD'S RICHEST FLORAL KINGDOM, SOUTH AFRICA

Perched on a slope overlooking one of the Cape's most spectacular bays, Grootbos Nature Reserve defies easy categorization. Its five-star eco-hotel is so luxurious that King Hussein of Jordan once stayed here, yet the reserve is also home to over six thousand endemic plant species. And if botany isn't your thing, you can go birding, explore nearby prehistoric caves or watch humpback whales just 30m from shore. So what is Grootbos all about?

The first clue comes with the food. Ask where your meal's ingredients were sourced and the response is likely to be a finger pointed a little into the distance. Hidden among the trees beneath the terrace is Green Futures, the first gardening college in southern Africa. Set up by the hotel, it trains young people from the local townships – where over half are unemployed – to be organic gardeners. Much of the fresh produce eaten at the hotel comes from their work.

It is for the cultivation of something other than fruit and veg, though, that Grootbos is best known. An area of degraded farmland surrounding the hotel has been cleared of invasive species and replanted with indigenous fynbos, the most diverse floral system on earth. (You can explore the fynbos on foot, or the hotel hires horses to cover the ground a bit quicker.) From a distance the conservancy appears like a heavily heathered moor, but up close its variety becomes bewildering, as butterflies flit about in all directions, drawn by the scents from the yeasty proteas, fresh-smelling ericas and distinctive wild herbs.

This scene fills the floor-to-ceiling windows that look out from each of its suites, built from locally sourced stone and wood, towards the sea below. From the moment you wake up to when you watch the sun set over the bay, you feel an intimate part of this remarkable blend of restoration and natural harmony. And that, in the end, is what makes a stay at Grootbos special.

Need to know *Grootbos is two hours' drive from Cape Town along the N2. Information on rates, booking, activities and conservation projects is at* Ⓦ*www.grootbos.com;* ☏*+27 (0) 28 384 8000.*

209 TAKE A MEKORO THROUGH THE OKAVANGO DELTA, BOTSWANA

The best way to experience the maze of islands and rivers that makes up the Okavango Delta is in a *mekoro*, the traditional dugout canoe used on these waterways for centuries. While your poler stands at the back and guides it through the lilies and reeds, he's also watching out for crocodiles and hippos. His vigilance means you can keep your binoculars trained on the bathing elephants and herds of antelope, which have fled the barren Kalahari that surrounds the delta to mass on these shores.

While many operators offer these trips, the community-run Okavango Polers' Trust also gives you the chance to connect with some of the folk who live among this vast network of channels. Based at Mbiroba bushcamp at the northern end of the delta, the trust employs around 75 people from the nearby village of Seronga as guides, cooks and administrators. Trips last up to three days, using locally made fibreglass canoes – since the hardwoods traditionally used are being logged indiscriminately – and camping on different islands each night, making sure you leave no mark of your visit behind. But though your presence may leave little trace, it's likely that the sound of a distant hippo's roar while you glide through the water at sunset will be with you for ever.

Need to know *Mbiroba camp can be reached in a few hours by car or ferry from Maun. The mekoro fits two adults plus luggage, as well as the poler/ guide. Further info on getting to the camp, as well as prices for accommodation, meals and tours is at* Ⓦ*www.okavangodelta.co.bw;* ☏*+267 687 6861.*

(Clockwise from top) African elephant herd crossing swampland in the Okavango Delta; African hippo yawning; The rare pincushion protea at Grootbos; The best way to see Botswana's Okavango Delta is in a mekoro with a local guide

210 HAVE THE REEF TO YOURSELF AT GULUDO, MOZAMBIQUE

Traditional fishing boats on the deserted shores at Guludo; Local women make extra income weaving baskets and jewellery from palm leaves

The reefs of the Quirimbas National Park, off the coast of northern Mozambique, are among the most pristine in the world – it's such a new diving destination that much of it remains unexplored. And thanks to a partnership between the Mozambican government, WWF and local communities to limit development while providing local jobs, the signs are that tourism here will help to preserve the environment and traditional lifestyles rather than despoil them.

Guludo is a small, British-owned luxury lodge in the national park, named after the coastal fishing community that permitted development on its otherwise deserted beach. In return, the lodge is committed to help improve the villagers' lot. The cool, adobe-style eco cottages were all built by Guludo villagers and filled with locally produced furniture and crafts. The lodge's restaurant, which serves fresh fish and great vegetarian food, is staffed entirely from the village. Tourist fees have helped to build a new school, run anti-malaria programmes and enable a women's co-operative to sell bags, necklaces and hats from palm leaves. Guests are encouraged to visit all these projects, and even to have a go weaving the palms themselves.

Ultimately, though, you clatter the four hours north up the only road from Pemba to spend your time on or under the water. Visitors can help the resident marine biologists monitor the humpback whales who come here every year from July to September, or sail across to nearby Rolas island to see the giant coconut crabs that scuttle across its deserted beaches. Yet getting most out of the Quirimbas reefs requires nothing more complicated than swimming through the tranquil coral gardens with just the fish, turtles and rays for company.

Need to know *Guludo will collect guests from Pemba. For more on accommodation, activities and rates see ⓦwww.guludo.com; ☏+44 (0) 207 127 4727.*

211 NATURAL HERITAGE AT ISIMANGALISO WETLAND PARK, SOUTH AFRICA

KwaZulu Natal is blessed with hundreds of kilometres of Indian Ocean coastline – from Port Edward to Manguzi – but if you like your beaches uncrowded then Isimangaliso Wetland Park in the north is the place to go.

Kosi Bay – a reserve in the park close to Mozambique – comprises four lakes, surrounded by forest and connected by narrow channels that open into the sea at Kosi Mouth. Hippos and crocodiles inhabit the brackish lakes, and the area is home to giant leatherback and loggerhead turtles, and over 250 species of birds. Jet-skis, quad bikes and self-launching boats are banned, and the only road access is along a sandy path, so a 4WD is essential. Admission to the reserve's car park is limited to fifteen vehicles a day (permits must be booked one day in advance from the reception gate).

Just outside the entrance to Kosi Bay is a fifteen-pitch public campsite with basic amenities, though if you're looking for comfort, the best place to stay is Amangwane Camp, a community-run initiative where you stay in reed chalets with en-suite bucket showers. Amangwane is co-run by Elmon Mkhonto – a local Thongan – and a former ranger from Natal, Anton Roberts. Elmon will show you how to spear-fish the Thongan way, while Anton runs fly-fishing and kayaking trips in Kosi Bay's lagoon.

For those with deeper pockets, Kosi Forest Lodge lies among the raffia forests. Its safari tents are shaded by forest canopy and open out on to a deck overlooking the lake. Local guides will take you to see the turtles nesting at night (from November 15 to January 15) and there are early-morning kayak trips with the lodge's guides on which you'll glide along reed-lined rivers, keeping an eye out for hippos, watching the banks for monitor lizards and scanning the skies for fish eagles.

Further south along the Isimangaliso coast is its sister camp, Thonga Beach Lodge, tucked between Lake Sibaya, the largest freshwater lake in South Africa, and a vast empty beach from where you can dive tropical reefs. Camouflaged

within the dune forest, the camp is almost invisible from the shore: the lights in its twelve thatched rooms are deliberately concealed so as not to disturb the turtles that nest on the beach. The owners have entrusted 68 percent ownership to the local Thonga community, and money from guests' visits has helped to build a new school and develop agriculture projects. Staying at the the concealed lodge, you can spend the evenings watching turtles crawling up the beach to lay their eggs – all the while knowing that your presence helps keep the poachers away.

Compared to Cape Town, Thonga's beach is gloriously empty; A loggerhead turtle

Need to know *Kosi Bay is seven hours' drive from Johannesburg or four from Durban. Kosi Forest Lodge and Thonga Beach Lodge: www.isibindiafrica.co.za; +27 (0) 35 474 1473. Beach permits are included when you stay at Amangwane Camp (www.kosibay.net; +27 (0) 35 590 1233), which costs ZAR850 per person per night, including accommodation, meals and activities. Rainbow Tours (www.rainbowtours.co.uk) organizes combined tours to a selection of these lodges plus Tembe Elephant Park (see p.181) and Hluhluwe-Imfolozi Park.*

212 HELP SAVE THE CHIMPANZEE FROM EXTINCTION, SOUTH AFRICA

Amadeus likes to pick flowers and stare at women. Zeena won't let anyone hold her, but from time to time enjoys a tickle. Abu is fond of peanut butter and spends most of his time letting the rest of the group know who's boss.

It's 11.30am, feeding time, and over the last few minutes they and the other fourteen chimps living in the Jane Goodall Chimpanzee Eden have been gathering in hungry expectation. As you sit watching them from the safety of the viewing platforms, the guide tells you their names and their stories. All share a similar history: they were caught by bushmeat hunters and sold illegally to zoos, circuses and medical research facilities, until they were rescued and brought here.

Situated just 12km from the South African city of Nelspruit on the Umhloti Nature Reserve, the Chimpanzee Eden is developing rehabilitation techniques so that as many chimps as possible can be released into the wild. For those too traumatized by their experiences, it provides a place similar to their natural habitat to live out their lives peacefully. You can drop in for an hour-long tour or stay for a week or more, helping to monitor behaviour or record the sounds they make when communicating, although no handling by guests is allowed. Experts reckon our closest relative will be extinct within their natural habitats in as little as a decade. Time (and money) spent watching the likes of Amadeus and Abu helps the sanctuary prevent this from happening.

Need to know *Prices for the volunteer courses range from US$441 a week, including meals and budget accommodation, to US$1431 a week in a luxury suite at Umhloti lodge. For more on accommodation rates and tours see Ⓦwww.janegoodall.co.za; Ⓣ+27 13 7457406..*

Zeena, one of the chimps living at Chimpanzee Eden

213 PLANT TREES WITH RIPPLE AFRICA IN MALAWI

A volunteer holiday with Ripple Africa involves you in a vital project to establish four hundred community nurseries in Malawi, a country with severe deforestation problems. Three thousand local people are already involved in the scheme, which has established over 150 nurseries and in 2008 planted over 1.25 million trees (the aim is eventually to grow four million new trees annually). The renewal of the forests has practical benefits beyond carbon offsetting: fruits trees are planted for food, other trees to provide sources of sustainable timber or to prevent soil erosion.

Ripple Africa is acutely aware of the dangers

of misplaced aid and ensures guests' help is given where it's most useful, and where it won't stop locals from working. Accommodation is at Mwaya beach on the shores of Lake Malawi, in eco-friendly huts with private verandas overlooking the water, where swimming, diving and kayaking are among the best ways to relax.

Need to know *The minimum stay is one week, although volunteers are encouraged to stay longer. Food costs are not included; reckon on no more than US$2 a day. For more on volunteering projects available, costs and testimonials see ⓦwww.rippleafrica.org; ☎+44 (0) 1525 216346.*

214 KAYAK ON LAKE MALAWI

Exhilarating as paddling across Lake Malawi is, it's important from time to time just to sit still and allow the waters around you to become calm. When that happens, it's like peering down into a giant aquarium, filled with fish of every conceivable colour. The cichlids alone, of which Lake Malawi has six hundred species, are so dazzlingly various that they are sometimes given the name peacock fish.

Kayak Africa, based in laid-back Cape Maclear, employs fishermen from the nearby village of Chembe as guides, to share their lifetime's understanding of the lake and the many islets and caves that line its shore. Accommodation is at exclusive bushcamps on either Mumbo or Domwe, otherwise deserted tropical islands so picture-perfect that the urge is to play Robinson Crusoe and not come home. Spend a few evenings on the empty beach, enjoying your freshly caught dinner and watching the lights from the fishermen's boats flicker on the darkening horizon, and that feeling will only get stronger.

Need to know *Cape Maclear is a bumpy 115km bus ride from the capital Lilongwe. As well as kayak trips lasting anything from a few hours to several days, snorkelling, PADI-certified scuba-diving and spear-fishing are also available. For tour details and rates see ⓦwww.kayakafrica.co.za; ☎+27 (0) 21 783 1955.*

215 BE ONE OF THE FIRST TO VISIT KISSAMA NATIONAL PARK, ANGOLA

Angola, ravaged by 27 years of civil war until 2002, is just beginning to get back on its feet. Virtually no tourists come here, so if you want to experience its vast national parks and enjoy white-sand beaches with hardly anyone else around, now is the time to visit.

One of the shining lights in the slow birth of Angolan tourism is Kissama National Park, some 70km from the capital Luanda. Bordering the Atlantic coast, this 12,000-square-kilometre reserve once rivalled the great parks of Africa in terms of its animal population. Unfortunately much of the reserve's wildlife was lost as people hunted for food during the war, although the birdlife is incredibly diverse. Endemic species abound, including the grey striped francolin and red-crested turaco.

Other than the birds, Kissama's current appeal is more for its sense of solitude than its fauna. All this may change, however, if visitor numbers improve and bring in fees that can be used for conservation. Over the past few years an ambitious restocking scheme – called Project Noah's Ark – has already brought back elephants, giraffes and other big game from Zambian and South African parks that are presently overstocked.

There's a long way to go, especially as the park is not just committed to restocking wildlife but also finding sustainable livelihoods for the eight thousand people living within its boundaries. In the meantime, though, there are few places further from mass tourism than this, southern Africa's last frontier.

Need to know *To get to Kissama from Luanda, take the coastal road south for 72km and then cross the Kwanza River. Follow the dirt road for 3km and then turn left at the sign for Kawa; this turning leads for 37km to the camp. Entry fees are US$10 per car. You can stay in Pousada Càua, thatched chalets overlooking the floodplain of the Cuanza River, for around $180 a night, including breakfast. For more on Operation Noah's Ark and contact details see ⓦwww.kissama.org.*

216 TAKE THE KIDS TO MADIKWE, SOUTH AFRICA

The sprawling bushveld at Madikwe Game Reserve on the border with Botswana is home to some of Africa's most elusive animals – black and white rhino, leopard and cheetah – as well as over three hundred bird species and popular game like elephant, zebra and giraffe. As one of the few reserves in South Africa that's malaria-free, it's also a great place to go on a family safari.

There are over thirty lodges here, but choose either Thakadu River Camp or Buffalo Ridge Safari Lodge and your stay will directly benefit some of the people who live around the reserve. Both are run as a collaboration between North-West Parks, a South African tour operator, and the local Molatedi and Balete Ba Lekgophung communities. Camp staff and rangers are from nearby villages, including Patience Bogatsu (at Thakadu), one of the first black women in South Africa to become a certified safari guide.

And just because there's a local connection, don't expect mud huts and cross-legged dining. Thakadu is luxury camping – there are double beds with cotton sheets, an en-suite bath and sliding doors onto a private outdoor deck, plus a swimming pool overlooking the Marico River. Buffalo Ridge Safari Lodge is another notch up, with king-sized beds and en-suite walk-in showers. Meals are taken in the main building – across a wooden bridge over a ravine – where you can feast on barbecued bushbuck meat while enjoying spectacular views over the reserve's northern plains.

Need to know *At Thakadu, there's also an eight-bed camp (Little Thakadu) which caters for small groups and large families. For details of each lodge, rates and how to get there see* Ⓦ*www.madikwecollection.co.za;* ☎*+22 (0) 11 805 9995. Rainbow Tours (*Ⓦ*www.rainbowtours.co.uk) organizes package trips to both camps.*

217 GO BIRDING IN ANCIENT FOREST, SOUTH AFRICA

As he passes through the forest, David Setsaolo hardly makes a sound. "Over there," he whispers, "A Knysna touraco." As you stare forlornly into the thick forest he picks up another call. "And there, on the low branch – a black-fronted bush shrike." Two of the rarest birds in South Africa, and you've only been in the forest five minutes.

David is an award-winning bird guide, and when he's not showing guests around the forest surrounding the ecolodges that together make up Kurisa Moya (meaning "tranquil spirit") he's training other aspiring guides. His knowledge isn't confined to birds either: following animal tracks through thick grass, he smells dung for freshness to know when the tracks were made. He identifies toadstools and tiny orchids breaking through the ground cover.

To really appreciate Kurisa Moya you need to stay for a few days, cut off from the rest of the world. There are four separate self-contained houses, each unique in their design – from the quirky wooden furnishings of family houses to the romantic forest lodges with their balconied beds; each secluded in their own clearings or perched upon the Schnelkop hill looking over the valley. Built with sustainable materials, they're filled with crafts by local artists. There's no electricity, but solar power provides your light and log-burning fires keep you warm.

As the sun sets each night there's nothing but

Patience Bogatsu, one of the first black women in South Africa to become a certified guide

the dark forest and light of the stars. At dawn, you wake with the birds. You may never see the fabled touraco in the dense canopy, but with David as your guide, at least you'll know when you hear it.

Need to know *Kurisa Moya is 45 minutes' drive from the city of Polokwane. For more on directions, activities, accommodation and rates see Ⓦwww. krm.co.za; ☎+27 (0) 82 200 4596.*

218 SEE THE FAIRY CIRCLES IN THE NAMIB RAND, NAMIBIA

Namibia's Namib Rand is southern Africa's largest private nature reserve – a vast 1800 square kilometres of shimmering mountains and red-hued desert. Its wonder is typified by the so-called fairy circles, unexplained halos of metre-high grass standing out from the semi-desert scrub around them. Found only here, they have been the subject of much study and speculation. Some people say they are caused by termites, others radioactivity; the bushmen say this is where their ancestors' spirits reside and that at

night they rise up to dance, trampling the ground below.

The best base from which to see the circles is at one of the luxurious solar-powered camps run by Wolwedans, which has committed to protect ten square kilometres of the Namib Rand for every bed it makes available. Most of the staff here come from desperately poor local communities and have been trained up on-site in the Wolwedans Desert Academy.

Wolwedans also runs safari-style trips into the park, where the attraction is as much the desolate and otherworldly landscape as it is the animals. A haven for photographers, the colours and shapes of the hills shift slowly as the day unfolds. Standing atop a million-year-old dune, watching the sun set in one direction as the moon rises in the other, feels as far from anywhere as one can possibly be.

Need to know *Wolwedans is around six hours' drive from Windhoek or Swakopmund; you'll need a 4WD vehicle. Accommodation is for a minimum of two nights. Further info on rates, reservations, activities and the Desert Academy at Ⓦwww. wolwedans-namibia.com; ☎+264 61 230616.*

The otherworldly scenery at Wolwedans

Basotho ponies provide a sure-footed ride through Lesotho's mountains

in isolated hamlets, where ragged flags above the houses indicate what's on sale within: yellow for sorghum beer (an acquired taste), white for maize beer, blue for fruit or vegetables. These aren't shops but householders, doing their best to make a vital bit of extra money through local enterprise.

All the treks are managed by locals and all the ponies are community-owned. A large proportion of the lodge fees are used to fund a trust whose projects have created a new orchard, a small earth dam to help collect water and a local school. It's a form of slow travel that's rapidly making a difference to these remote communities.

Need to know *Malealea is around two hours' drive from the capital Maseru. For details of activities and costs see Ⓦ www.malealea.com; Ⓣ +27 (0) 82 552 4215.*

219 PONY-TREKKING IN THE MOUNTAINS, LESOTHO

It might not be the quickest means of transport, but if you want to really get a sense of the pace of life and raw beauty of Western Lesotho, then opt for a pony. From Malealea mountain lodge, high in the remote Malealea Valley, you can spend from a few hours to several days riding over the misty valleys, the smell of peach blossom thick in the air as your sure-footed steed negotiates the precipitous inclines.

Accommodation is in tents or simple mud huts

220 STAY THE NIGHT IN ONE OF SOUTH AFRICA'S NATIONAL PARKS

South Africa's twenty national parks contain a range of terrain like nothing else on earth, from the empty deserts of the Karoo to the sandstone cliffs of Golden Gate and the dense Tsitsikamma indigenous forest. Yet despite this diversity, each contains one thing that unites South Africans – a proper place to barbecue. At every accommodation or picnic spot there are wonderfully located braai sites for you to cook whatever you fancy, while watching zebra graze, waves crash against the shore or eagles soar overhead. Each day, camp staff clean out your braai and often then light it for you in the afternoon, so it's ready when you return from a day of watching game or trekking in the hills.

Apart from the chance for a dramatic backdrop to your burger, it's well worth coming for a night or two, as accommodation is generally of a superb standard, ranging from low-impact log cabins to tented camps. And staying the night in the parks means that once the day-visitors clear away (and it's not like the parks ever feel crowded) it's just you, the click of fruit bats or whoop of hyenas, and the crackle of burning coals under starry skies.

Need to know *The San Parks website (ⓦwww. sanparks.org) has accommodation and booking facilities, information on conservation initiatives, and even webcams showing what's going on at your favourite waterhole. ☎+27 (0) 12 428 9111.*

elephants, rhinos, cheetahs, caracals or leopards. These projects have raised local awareness of game conservation and recently led to an amendment to South Africa's hunting laws, thereby saving the lives of many animals.

Need to know *Phinda is six hours' drive from Johannesburg or three from Durban. For details of lodges, rates, activities and local attractions see ⓦwww.phinda.com; ☎+27 (0) 11 809 4314. For volunteer programmes see ⓦwww. conservationafrica.net; ☎+44 (0) 870 241 5816.*

221 CONSERVATION IN ACTION AT PHINDA, SOUTH AFRICA

At the seven different lodges in Kwazulu-Natal's Phinda Resource Reserve, no attention to detail is missed – from the private infinity pools to personal butlers. These hideaways of opulence are not ecolodges in the strict sense: towels are changed daily and the lightbulbs aren't even low energy. Yet their environmental benefits are nevertheless impressive, since profits from the lodges have been used to create one of the most successful nature reserves in South Africa.

It's hard to believe that twenty years ago Phinda was degraded farmland with just a handful of people scratching a living from it. Today the 160-square-kilometre park is a potent symbol of regeneration: it's an excellent place to spot cheetah (the reserve was the first to successfully reintroduce the cat and now supplies young animals born here to other parks); the critically endangered black rhino has also been reintroduced; and some 4500 local people benefit from the new clinic, schools and employment the lodges have created.

Phinda's accommodation may be as exclusive as it gets, but the reserve runs several research projects in partnership with African Conservation Experience, which enables volunteers to stay in a simple farmhouse and enjoy the reserve at less expense. Twice a day, volunteers head out in safari vehicles to monitor

(Clockwise from top left) Giraffe and young; The pool at Phinda's Mountain Lodge; There are more than enough bugs and beasties to excite most kids

FAIR TRADE HOLIDAYS

South Africa has the world's first fair trade tourism scheme, with a growing range of places involved. The following ten experiences offer much of the best South Africa has to offer – from wildlife-watching to townships to wine tasting – plus you'll know that the local communities benefited from your visit. For details of all the participants in the scheme see ⓦwww.fairtourismsa.org.za.

The high wire through the Tsitsikamma Forest

222 Whizz through the forest at Storms River

If you've ever watched monkeys swinging through the trees and wondered how it feels, try the Storms River canopy tour in the Tsitsikamma Forest. Twenty metres up in the treetops, you slide in a breathless rush on steel cables between wooden platforms, learning from your guide about forest ecology at each stop. Over a thousand local children (including AIDS orphans) get a free ride each year – but it's hard even for grown-ups not to feel like a kid as you zip through the trees, then wait for another go.

Need to know *Storms River is just off the N2 motorway, 65km from Plettenberg Bay. For prices and bookings see ⓦwww.stormsriver.com; ☏+27 (0) 422 811 836.*

223 Walk with rhinos at Leshiba

Because there are no lions or elephants on the plateau that surrounds Leshiba lodge, you're encouraged to go out on unguided walks. The leopards are too shy to bother you and the rhinos don't see or hear well – and so long as you're upwind, won't smell you either. If one approaches, stay still and let it pass; if that doesn't work, make lots of noise; if all else fails, get up a tree.

Leshiba's luxury lodge is a synthesis of traditional Venda mud-brick building techniques and modern design. It runs community programmes revitalizing traditional skills to ensure the Venda people don't lose touch with their heritage. This is also the philosophy behind the unguided walks – it's about experiencing the bush as the Venda's ancestors always have.

Need to know *Leshiba is an hour's drive west of Louis Trichardt on the N1, five hours' north of Johannesburg. Further info on rates and activities at ⓦwww.leshiba.co.za; ☏+27 (0) 155 930 076.*

224 Kayak with whales in Plettenberg Bay

In the waters around Plettenberg Bay, the whales come so close to the shore on their annual migration that you can paddle out to see them. The best whale-watching operator in the area is Ocean Blue – and thanks to its conservation work you can approach to within 50m of the whales (the usual limit is 300m). Lolling gently in the waves, you'll hear them clear their blowholes, and feel rocked by the thwack of their tails against the water.

Need to know November is the best month to see humpback and southern right whales. A two-hour sea kayak (min 2 people) costs ZAR250. For details of tours and courses see Ⓦ www.oceanadventures.co.za; Ⓣ: +27 (0) 445 334 897.

225 Ride a bike in a township

AWOL (Adventure Without Limits) offers bike tours round Masiphumelele township, visiting the crèche, crafts shops and healer before finishing with lunch in one of the women's homes. You'll feel part of the vibrant life on the streets, probably with a group of children in tow. With the money from these tours, members of the township run a bicycle workshop, repairing, selling and renting old bikes to the community. Far from making you feel out of place, a ride with AWOL helps bring two worlds a little closer.

Need to know AWOL will pick you up from anywhere in Cape Town. Tours cost ZAR600 per person, for group sizes between four and twenty. Ⓦ www.withoutlimits.co.za; Ⓣ +27 (0) 217 881 256.

226 Taste fine Cape wines at Spier

The environs of Cape Town are filled with wineries, but Spier is unique for its luxury hotel, spa and connection with Stellenbosch University, which pioneers sustainable development. You can also play golf, go horse-riding or get up close to cheetahs at the on-site cheetah rehabilitation project. Ⓦ www.spier.co.za; Ⓣ +27 (0) 218 091 100.

227 Drink with locals in a township

On a tour of the townships of Nelson Mandela Bay with Calabash, it's a great idea to visit some of your guide's favourite watering holes (shebeens). Here you can drink with the locals and shake your stuff to the marimba bands who often play outside the bars. Ⓦ www.calabashtours.co.za; Ⓣ +27 (0) 415 856 162.

228 Fair game at Umlani

Deep in the Timbavati Nature Reserve, Umlani Bushcamp uses no electricity, which lends it a feel of old-world safari adventure. Activities on offer include microlight flights, balloon safaris, white-water rafting and excursions to local villages. Ⓦ www.umlani.com; Ⓣ +27 (0) 217 855 547.

229 A night on Long Street, Cape Town

Don't fancy a hostel in Cape Town, but can't really stretch to a boutique hotel? Then the self-catering apartments run by Daddy Longlegs may be perfect. Located on Long Street, the most buzzing road in the centre, the apartments have much of the style of the latter at a price not too far off the former. Ⓦ www.daddylonglegs.co.za, Ⓣ +27 (0) 214 223 074.

230 See hippos near Cape Town

It's still possible to see big game if you are staying in Cape Town. At nearby Rondevlei Nature Reserve, you can take a boat trip out to see the Cape's only resident hippo population, training your binoculars on the plentiful birdlife on the way. Ⓦ www.imvubu.co.za; Ⓣ +27 (0) 217 060 842.

231 Stay in Soweto

At Lebo's Soweto Backpackers you can go one further than visiting a township for a few hours, as this is a chance to stay in the most famous one of all. Being there at night also means you can visit the bars and music clubs when they really get going. Ⓦ www.sowetobackpackers.com; Ⓣ +27 (0) 119 363 444.

Lions at Umlani; The view from the terrace at Leshiba; Local marimba band playing in the shebeen on the Calabash tour

Exploring the fynbos with a Rastafarian guide

232 WALK WITH RASTAS IN KNYSNA FOREST, SOUTH AFRICA

From the moment your dreadlocked host greets you with a gentle knock of his clenched fist against yours and an exclamation of "Irie" (roughly meaning "respect"), you know this isn't going to be your typical township tour. While the representatives of the House of Judah, the local church, come and introduce themselves, you notice that all the houses are painted in striking tones of crimson, yellow and emerald. One thing's for sure: you're in Rasta territory.

In 2003, tired of being perceived as dope-smoking outcasts, the Rastafarian community in Khayalethu – a township between the outskirts of Knysna and the surrounding forest – went to the local tourism board with a proposal. They wanted to show tourists what their life was really like, and to protect to the richness of their local forest. It worked. Guests now make visits to people's homes and are led on guided nature tours through the surrounding fynbos ecosystem, a complex ground-level array of succulents and heathers, most seen nowhere else in the world. Those keen to hang around a little longer than a few hours can stay in one of the families' homes.

For most people in Khayalethu, the forest represents an easy – and unfortunately rapidly depleting – source of firewood and building materials. One of the aims of the tourist trail is to show that the forest can be a long-term source of income if preserved in its natural state. And while guiding guests on these walks, it also gives the Rastas the chance to explain about the arcane roots of their religious beliefs, leaving you assured that there's far more to their culture than dope and reggae.

Need to know Knysna is on the N2, the main road along South Africa's Southern Cape, about six hours' drive from Cape Town. For more info and contact details see Ⓦwww.openafrica.org/participant/house-of-judah-rastafarian-community; ☎Brother Paul +27 (0) 73 117 6103 or Brother Maxi +27 (0) 84 205 8305.

233 SEE THE RARE SITATUNGA DEER, ZAMBIA

The best time and place to spot a sitatunga, Africa's elusive swamp-dwelling deer, is at dawn and up a tree. Eighteen metres up a mahogany, to be exact, since the Fibwe tree hide in Zambia's Kasanka Park offers an unbeatable vantage point, from where you might also see the equally endangered roan and sable deer. As the morning mists clear across the papyrus swamps below the hide, sitatunga take to the water to avoid leopards and other predators, though the water also has its dangers: visitors to the hide can occasionally spot the snouts of crocodiles floating loglike amid the reeds.

The park is privately owned by the UK/Zambian charity the Kasanka Trust, which spends its profits from tourist fees on conservation and community projects, from controlled timber production to local vegetable gardens, as well as providing employment as guides on walking safaris and canoe trips. Accommodation is in two solar-powered lodges and three campsites.

All of these efforts have greatly reduced poaching in the area, making your prospects of seeing sitatunga all the better. And for those with more than a few weeks to spare, they're always after volunteers keen to help this flagship scheme in its efforts.

Need to know Kasanka Park is around five hours' drive from Lusaka. The best time to come is June to September, although in November the park witnesses the nightly spectacle of five million bats taking to the sky to feed. For more info see Ⓦwww.kasanka.com; ☎+873 76 206 7957.

234 TEMBE ELEPHANT PARK, SOUTH AFRICA

When you are eyeball to eyeball with an enormous bull elephant, the chances are you will be the first to blink. Just don't run. The trick is to stay calm, control the surge of adrenaline and wait for your safari guide to interpret the tell-tale signs of the elephant's mood. The brief from the guide is simple: the elephant is the boss. It will let you know when you can move on.

Close encounters with elephants are common at Tembe Elephant Park – home to the Big Five game and a huge range of colourful birds – in the north of South Africa's KwaZulu Natal province. For centuries the ancestors of these elephants roamed freely across the sand forests of Maputuland, the region that straddles the border of South Africa and Mozambique, but their numbers collapsed during the Mozambiquan civil war due to poachers and land mines. In 1989 a fence was erected across the border to protect those elephants that remained on the South African side and now, after twenty years of successful rehabilitation, their numbers are again thriving.

The only camp in the park is Tembe Elephant Lodge, a joint collaboration between a Durban businessman and the local Thongan community, the historic custodians of Maputuland. There are luxurious tented pavilions with large double beds and outdoor showers, while meals are prepared by women from the village and served in a boma (eating area) under a thatched canopy. The safari camp's facilities are standard for South Africa, but what sets Tembe apart are the thrilling game drives in the experienced hands of local guides. When you're close up to one of these enormous bulls, you'll appreciate having them around.

Need to know *Tembe is around four hours from Durban and eight hours from Johannesburg. For more on getting there, excursions, accommodation and rates see ⓦwww.tembe.co.za; ☎+27 (0) 31 267 0144.*

Elephant at Tembe; Local guide Tom Mahamba always has a tale to tell about the birds you can see at Tembe

235 THE MIDLANDS MEANDER, SOUTH AFRICA

Weaving its way through the rolling farmland and small villages dotting the foothills of the Drakensberg Mountains, the Midlands Meander arts and crafts route offers a taster of the Zulu Kingdom's great diversity. Pick up a map from shops and cafés along the way – or download one from the website – for details and directions to over a hundred places to eat, shop, drink or stay, all scattered along the picturesque 80km circuit that skirts the uKhahlamba-Drakensberg Park between Pietermaritzburg and Mooi River. The project, started in 1983 by local craftspeople aiming to get more visitors into their galleries and workshops, now includes tea rooms, potters' and weavers' outlets, treehouses with spas and sustainably managed bushcamps.

There are plenty of activities on offer too: you can walk or cycle on mountain trails through nature conservancies, follow birding routes to see the endangered Cape parrot or orange ground thrush; explore one of a thousand caves painted with ancient San rock art; or abseil

At work in the Ardmore Ceramics Studio on the Midlands Meander

down a 54m-high waterfall in the Karkloof forest. This woodland is the only habitat of the rare Karkloof blue butterfly, now protected with funds drawn from tourist fees.

But it's not just craftspeople and local wildlife that benefit from the scheme – it also supports disadvantaged schools and helps to develop permaculture food gardens. Simply by guiding people through this plethora of local opportunities, the Midlands Meander project reveals a hidden world and enables it to prosper.

Need to know *For further info see* Ⓦ*www. midlandsmeander.co.za;* ☏*+27 (0) 33 330 8195.*

236 LIVE THE HIGH LIFE AT TSALA TREETOPS, SOUTH AFRICA

As you look round at the balconies and elevated platforms jutting out across the forest, you'd be forgiven for thinking you've stumbled upon a palace of a forgotten civilization. Monkeys squabble among the trees or scurry across the raised walkways that connect the ten individual suites to the central lodge. Hidden high in the dense canopy of the Tsitsikamma forest outside Knysna, Tsala Treetops – an architectural extravaganza of rough stone, exposed wood and floor-to-ceiling glass – appears modern yet feels somehow ancient.

So total is the attention to luxury – your suite's drinks cabinet has its own cocktail shaker, for example – that it's surprising to discover that Tsala Treetops is also one of the most sustainable hotels on the Cape. Waste water is reused in the vegetable garden, while all the organic waste is composted and every cleaning product is biodegradable. Hardly any indigenous trees were removed to create this treetop paradise built from sustainably harvested forests. Hotel staff continually clear non-indigenous species and reintroduce native ones, returning the area of forest that it owns and protects ever closer to how it once was.

Need to know *Tsala Treetops is 24km from Knysna, signed 1.5km off the N2. For more on accommodation, dining, booking and rates see* ⓦ*www.hunterhotels.com;* ☏ *+27 (0) 44 501 1111.*

Giants Castle Peak, Ukhahlamba Drakensberg Park, KwaZulu Natal, South Africa

237 TREK THE DRAKENSBERG, SOUTH AFRICA

The responsible trekker's aim is usually to leave no trace. But anyone who sets off from Matatiele on the five-day hike with the Mehloding Community Trust will be going one better, by having a beneficial impact on the remote rural communities their journey passes through. This is a route of extremes: while the Sisonke district of KwaZulu- Natal Province has some of South Africa's most stunning scenery, including the indigenous forests and towering sandstone escarpments of the southern Drakensberg region, it is also a journey into a region of great poverty, where sustainable tourism is helping to keep local economies afloat.

Over the last few years the trust has developed a trekking programme that now employs four hundred locals as guides or chalet staff. Much of the food served on the way is grown in community farming schemes, while activities available en route are also guided by villagers, from horse-riding and bird watching to visits to the village shebeens (bars), or meetings with craftspeople and sangomas (traditional healers). The fee includes a levy that goes towards projects such as building creches, clinics and schools. For trekkers it means genuinely warm welcomes from whomever they encounter, passionate guides and the assurance that this is one hike leaving a positive footprint.

Need to know *Matatiele is 70km from the town of Kokstad. For more on accommodation, trail details, bookings and rates see* ⓦ*www.mehloding.co.za;* ☏*+27 (39) 737 3289.*

A herd of Burchell's zebras in the dry riverbed of the Boteti River, Botswana

238 WATCH THE ZEBRA MIGRATION, BOTSWANA

Every year as the floods recede, the saltpans of Botswana become too dry to support life, forcing the wildlife there to return to the Boteti River for water. For millennia this has been one of the largest migrations in Southern Africa, but because of drought the river has not run since 1991; the last pool dried up in 1995.

To combat this, Meno a Kwena (a camp based on the river whose name means "crocodile's teeth") has built pumps that fill three water holes in the river bed. Its elevated position means that guests can watch as thousands of animals come to drink from the pools. The camp acts as a buffer zone between the farmers and wildlife, preventing poaching, and by employing locals also offers a financial incentive not to kill the animals.

There's no electricity at the camp, cooking is over an open fire, and you sleep at night in tents looking onto the bush. Each morning you can study the tracks in the sand to see what passed by in the night. Depending on the time of year,

it could be up to 25,000 zebra, in which case you probably heard them anyway.

The camp also offers excursions out onto the saltpans, five hours' drive away. It's an unworldly place; in every direction the land is dry and white, and so uninterruptedly flat that you can see the horizon follow the earth's curvature. Sometimes the surface is peeled up like tiny waves (formed of dried algae), while elsewhere the land is covered with an assortment of what seem to be bleached pebbles. In fact they are fossilized pieces of vegetation and animal bones, all in various stages of calcification.

Sleeping out on a rug on these pans is magical. The stars fill the sky and it is so quiet you can hear a footstep up to a 1km away. Driving back to camp the following day, you pass the occasional lone zebra or wildebeest, following migration patterns that Meno a Kwena, and you as a guest, are helping to keep alive.

Need to know *Meno a Kwena is 1.5 hour's drive from Maun; transfers from Maun airport are included in the price. June to October is the best time to visit. For rates and further info see Ⓦwww. kalaharikavango.com; ☎+267 686 0981.*

239 HIDE AWAY IN THE TREETOPS OF KNYSNA FOREST, SOUTH AFRICA

It's dusk. You lie back in the outdoor bath with a glass of wine, looking at the stars. The smell of the coals from the barbecue lingers in the air. Vervet monkeys chatter in the distance. Other than that, darkness, and the serenity of another night in the indigenous forest, deep in the hills facing the Outeniqua Mountains. Staying in a treehouse was never this snug.

The eight lodges at Teniqua Treetops were adapted to the space available among the trees, so they all have a different design. During their construction only non-indigenous species were removed, whose wood, along with reclaimed glass and old army tents, was then used to build the lodges. Each is self-catering – including one with full disabled access – and has a deck for lingering sundowners.

As you'd expect in a set of treehouses, children are encouraged (they won't disturb the neighbours, since the lodges are so secluded from each other) and well catered for, with a swimming pool, table-tennis set and forest trail. There's a fun walk for grown-ups too: a steep path through the dense tangle of vines and trees to the remote Karatara River, stained brown by leaf tannins.

A word of warning, though: Teniqua Treetops is set in pristine indigenous forest, which means you're more likely to meet an oversized insect than another person. But if you're content with isolation and the occasional spider or moth, it's a great escape from urban life, and a vital project in returning rare woodland ever closer to its original state.

Need to know *Teniqua Treetops is 23km from Sedgefield, which is eight hours from Cape Town by coach. Staff will fill your fridge with local food and wine (for a charge) if given a week's notice. More info on accommodation, tariffs and local places of interest at ⓦwww.teniquatreetops.co.za; ☏+27 (0) 44 356 2868.*

240 MEET THE BUSHMEN AT NHOMA, NAMIBIA

Nhoma, a simple tented camp owned and run in partnership with the nearby Bushman village of Nhoq'ma, on the border of Khaudum National Park, offers guests a chance to get back to their primeval roots. Always wanted to know how to start a fire or make an arrow? Immersed in a hunter-gatherer society, you will here.

After a morning spent hunting spring hares or porcupines with the Bushmen, learning how to make small traps from twigs and animal sinews, there's usually time in the afternoon to join in their games and perhaps buy a few souvenir ostrich-shell necklaces.

At night, after dinner back at camp, guests can trek back through the dark dunes to sit and watch the Bushmen gather to dance and sing, with their shaman often falling into a trance which, they say, enables him to communicate with their ancestors. They've been doing this for tens of thousands of years. Staying at Nhoma is one of the best ways of ensuring these traditions continue.

Alone in the trees at Teniqua Treetops; Hunting spring hares with Bushmen at Nhoma

Need to know *Nhoma is over 200km from the nearest petrol station in Grootfontein, along sandy tracks (some only traversible by 4WD) and visitors should bring spare fuel. For rates, details of activities and further info on getting there see ⓦwww.toumkwei.iway.na/ NhomaCamp.htm.*

Carbon offsetting

The idea of offsetting schemes is to calculate the emissions of carbon dioxide and other greenhouse gases produced by activities that burn fossil fuel, and then finance projects (usually renewable energy and reforestation programmes) that are supposed to reduce the equivalent amount of climate-altering pollution. Increasingly you see offsetting schemes claim that this work renders those activities "carbon neutral". This last term is extremely debatable, and probably best forgotten about. Yes, offsetting does finance projects that reduce pollution, but it's not the same pollution, occurring at the same time or in the same place as those original harmful emissions. Critics of carbon offsetting say that it only delays meaningful action, and accuse many of the schemes of mismanagement.

The most effective way to reduce carbon emissions directly is to emit less in the first place. Yet perhaps offsetting shouldn't be dismissed entirely: paying a reputable company to invest in work that improves the environment is surely a worthwhile endeavour. Some schemes focus just on emissions caused by flights – the fastest-growing contributor to global warming – while others work out emissions from specific train, car and ferry journeys. Below is a guide to how offsetting works and which schemes to trust.

THE MAIN METHODS OF CARBON OFFSETTING

Tree planting

Most of the early carbon-offset schemes used their income to plant trees, which over the course of their life cycle were intended to absorb the same amount of carbon dioxide as emitted on a journey. However, critics object that climate change is too immediate a problem for us to have the luxury of waiting until a tree has fully grown to clean up what we have caused today.

There are also other problems with planting trees as a means of offsetting carbon emissions. Some organizations planted fast-growing species such as eucalyptus, but these put undue amounts of pressure on another scarce resource, water. Some tree-plantation projects have also resulted in the removal of poor communities from their lands. Finally, there has been a regular problem with mismanagement, with trees being neglected and failing to grow to maturity, as famously happened in the case of the so-called Coldplay forest, where a plantation bought to offset the climate costs associated with the tour was soon neglected.

Keeping the trees in the ground

Deforestation accounts for twenty percent of human-induced climate change. To try to slow this, certain organizations buy up areas of mature forest and protect them from loggers. The land should then be returned to some form of community ownership, so local people can benefit from secondary forest crops that they often rely upon for their livelihoods. For example, Cool Earth works with the Awacachi Indians of Ecuador to protect a 3500-square-kilometre corridor of rainforest in the country. Much of this area is at threat from palm-oil plantations and other logging activities. Working with local Indians and other partners, Cool Earth is supporting the development of alternative sustainable enterprises, such as native bamboo production and cacao growing.

Keeping the carbon underground

The third option – investing in technologies that don't rely on fossil fuels and so don't produce the CO_2 in the first place – is seen by many as the most attractive. The idea is to develop and provide cleaner alternatives to fossil-fuel based methods of generating power and heat. This could be anything from cleaner stoves for rural villages to wind turbines or small hydropower schemes. Many of these also have added community benefits, such as reducing the amount of coal smoke people have to breathe, or providing meaningful, sustainable employment.

WHICH CARBON OFFSETTING PROGRAMMES ARE WORTH USING?

With ever more organizations offering offsets, it can be increasingly hard to know where to turn. Carbon Catalog (@www.carboncatalog.org) rates over a hundred different organizations and provides detailed information on how they operate, including how much a tonne of CO_2 nominally costs to offset with them, and what percentage of your money actually goes to the projects they invest in. We can recommend the following four schemes:

ANTI-DEFORESTATION ORGANIZATIONS

Cool Earth (@www.coolearth.org)

The most high-profile of the organizations, with a list of supporters that ranges from James Lovelock, the scientist behind the Gaia theory, to Rough Guides founder Mark Ellingham. It's not a traditional offset scheme in that you can't pay for a specific flight to be offset; instead you donate as much as you wish to help protect areas of rainforest in Ecuador and Peru and support local communities.

The World Land Trust (@www.carbonbalanced.org)

Over the last 25 years the trust, whose patron is David Attenborough, has protected and returned to community ownership several thousand square kilometres of threatened forest. As well as flights, you can offset journeys by motorbike, car, bus, tram and train.

RENEWABLE ENERGY SCHEMES

Atmosfair (@www.atmosfair.de)

Developed by a German environmental NGO and a coalition of German tour companies, Atmosfair provides impressively detailed information on the schemes it invests in and is refreshingly honest about the limitations of carbon offsetting. Schemes funded vary from developing a hydropower plant in Honduras to providing efficient wood-burning stoves in Nigeria, thus helping to alleviate deforestation. Its carbon calculator even allows you to select which aircraft you are flying in.

The Pure Trust (@www.puretrust.org.uk)

A UK-based not-for-profit organization, The Pure Trust invests your donations in clean energy projects around the world, typically generating electricity through hydropower and biomass. The scheme is not just for flights, and you can offset for all aspects of your lifestyle.

ALASKA

267
268

CANADA

274

249

272 241
265 242
      248

258 273

250

244

247 246

257

253 254
255 256

251

UNITED STATES

275

266

264

279
245

269

270
276

280 243
271

259
261 260
263 262

HAWAII

277

278

252

NORTH AMERICA

241 Skoki Lodge, Alberta

242 Shadow Lake Lodge, Alberta

243 Slow ski at Lake Placid

244 Moonlit meanders in Oregon

245 Cross-country skiing in Québec

246 Ski-touring in Jackson Hole, Wyoming

247 Stay in your own private Idaho

248 Dog-sledding in the Canadian Rockies

249 The bear necessities of life on Vancouver Island, British Columbia

250 Canopy life at Cedar Creek Treehouse, Washington

251 Off-grid at Treebones, California

252 Take a walk on the wet side, Florida

253 Follow the trail to anywhere, Yosemite

254 Ski cross-country, Yosemite

255 Meander along the Merced, Yosemite

256 A dip in a natural pool, Yosemite

257 Eat your way round California

258 Surround sound in a Free Spirit Sphere, Canada

259 Get a bird's-eye view from the harbour, New York

260 Bite around the Big Apple

261 Discover the roots of hip-hop, jazz, gospel or salsa, New York

262 Sweet dreams in Sugar Hill, New York

263 To shop, or not to shop? New York

264 Eco chic in the mountains of Québec

265 Log off in a log cabin, Canada

266 Party with a purpose at Rothbury Festival, Michigan

267 Room with a view at Camp Denali, Alaska

268 Away from the trail in Alaska

269 Fresh air in Nova Scotia

270 Visit Montréal's Biodôme

271 Stock up on food at St Lawrence market, Toronto

272 Stretch your legs in Jasper National Park

273 Go green in Vancouver

274 Visit the totem poles of Gwaii Haanas, Canada

275 Follow in the footsteps of Sitting Bull

276 Mountain biking along the Kingdom Trails, Vermont

277 Humpbacks off Hawaii

278 Watch lava become land in Hawaii

279 Whale-watching in Québec

280 Meet a moose in Algonquin, Canada

241 SKOKI LODGE, ALBERTA

Skoki Lodge, in the heart of
Banff National Park

Tucked away in a dense spruce-and-pine forest
in the heart of Banff National Park, Skoki Lodge

is so remote that it can only be accessed via an
18km ski or hike from Lake Louise, due west.
The lodge's isolation, situated high up at 2164m
and surrounded by five deep valleys trimmed
with beautiful mountain ridges and dotted with
alpine lakes, is a major part of its appeal; guests
come here to get away from busy downhill ski
resorts with their packed ski slopes, and frenetic
bars and restaurants.

The first place in Canada to cater for ski-
tourists, the lodge was built in 1931, and today
exudes a cosy, antiquated feel. The main timber
lodge, supported by huge wooden beams on the
walls and ceiling, has two warming woodstoves
and a small library full of historical photographs
and 1930s ski equipment. There's little in
the way of mod cons: no electricity, phones or
televisions – just candlelight and kerosene
lamps, and water fetched from a nearby creek.
To energize guests for a full day's cross-country
skiing and touring the valleys, the lodge lays
on generous quantities of wholesome food: fresh
bread is served every morning, while there's
also hot bacon, cheese, cakes, fresh fruit and
vegetables on offer throughout the day.

With such basic facilities and excellent ski
conditions, Skoki Lodge – and others like it
(see opposite) – is fast becoming a popular
alternative skiing experience. It's a trend that's
in common with the widely held view that if the
ski industry is to deal with the charges levelled
at it by environmentalists, it has to diversify
and provide low-impact options other than the
resource-hungry downhill resorts. Ironically, it
seems that the future for skiing may lie in this
kind of basic, back-to-nature retreat that's firmly
rooted in the past.

Need to know *Skoki Lodge is 60km west of
Banff (and 185km west of Calgary). For prices and
reservations* Ⓦ*www.skoki.com;* ☎*+1 877 822 7669.
The trek from Lake Louise to Skoki Valley is both
uphill and downhill, so bring backcountry skis with
skins rather than ordinary cross-country skis. Wilson
Mountain Sports hires skis at Lake Louise (*Ⓦ*www.
lakelouisewilsons.com;* ☎*+1 866 929 3636).*

242 SHADOW LAKE LODGE, ALBERTA

Another equally remote ski lodge is Brewster's Shadow Lake Lodge, also in Banff National Park. From the trailhead of the Trans-Canada Highway, guests will need to cross-country ski or snow-shoe the 14km trail to the lodge, where you'll be welcomed with a much-needed afternoon tea of home-made bread, scones and cakes.

Shadow Lake Lodge is a collection of cosy cabins nestled in the pine trees; each cabin is equipped with solar panelling, washbasins and comfortable beds, and has panoramic views across the mountains and forest. Evenings are snug and relaxed, with roaring fires and enormous, home-cooked meals – stoking guests up for a full day in the snow the next day.

And you'll need the energy: there are four main cross-country skiing routes from Shadow Lake Lodge into the mountains, ranging from the easy 1.9km hike to Shadow Lake to the tougher day-trip to Ball Pass, on the divide between Alberta and British Columbia. The surrounding scenery is splendid – glassy lakes, sheer mountain ridges and snow-covered forests – and there's the chance to spot Bighorn sheep, black bear and hoary marmots, as well as a variety of pretty alpine plants.

(From top) View from the lodge; Cosy winter cabins at Shadow Lake Lodge

Need to know *For directions, prices, all-inclusive packages and reservations at Shadow Lake Lodge see ⓦwww.shadowlakelodge.com; ☎+1 403 762 0116. For avalanche conditions in Banff National Park and an equipment checklist for backcountry travel see ⓦwww.parkscanada.ca. You are also strongly advised to check with the information centre in Banff (☎+1 403 762 1550) for the latest weather and trail conditions before departing.*

THE NEW WORLD OF SNOW

North America's ski resorts are the envy of the world. The service is reliably slick, the lift queues move quickly and there's huge versatility, from the mellowness of Québec's Mont Tremblant to the sophistication of Aspen, the rawness of Jackson Hole and the steep slopes of BC's Fernie. But ploughing down perfectly groomed pistes all day long can feel restrictive, and while you'll often find fresh powder in-bounds, there will always be the temptation to go out of bounds into the real wilderness. There are risks (so consider going with an experienced guide) but as long as you follow the correct etiquette, are fully trained and have the right equipment, you'll discover a whole new world of snow. Here are six of our favourite ways to enjoy the backcountry bliss.

243 Slow ski at Lake Placid

In upstate New York, just a few hours' drive from Albany, Syracuse, Montréal and Ottawa, Lake Placid's Adirondack Park is a convenient place to discover off-piste adventure. Nordic (cross-country) skiing specialist High Peaks Mountain Adventures runs several guided backcountry tours in the park, from a couple of hours' introduction to snow-shoeing (and navigational skills) to a full-day's Nordic skiing, ski touring or telemarking (free-heel skiing) in the rolling hills of the High Peaks region. There's also a one-day course on ice-climbing, where you'll climb up frozen waterfalls and learn the basics of tool placement and crampon footwork. Ⓦ www.highpeakscyclery.com; ☎ +1 518 523 3764.

244 Moonlit meanders in Oregon

Snow-shoeing at night through hidden forest trails can be a magical, eerie experience: the snow glistens under the light of the moon and the crunch of powder underfoot is all you can hear among the hush of the trees. For a few nights over the full moon from December to April, Wanderlust Tours runs several moonlit snow-shoe tours in the High Cascade Mountains of central Oregon. En route through the snowy forest, you'll be shown how to look for signs of nocturnal animals as well as how to understand the different constellations of the night sky, before reaching a bonfire in the middle of an amphitheatre, hand-carved into the snow, where you can sit and enjoy hot chocolate and marshmallows amid the solitude of the forest. Ⓦ www.wanderlusttours. com; ☎ +1 800 962 2862.

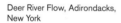

Deer River Flow, Adirondacks, New York

245 Cross-country skiing in Québec

Cross-country skiing is to the Québecois what rambling is to the rest of the world, and with over 4000km of trails across the province there are hundreds of ski areas and opportunities to go off-piste. The largest ski centre is at Mont-Sainte-Anne (Ⓦwww.mont-sainte-anne.com), which features 208km of trails, though to escape the crowds head to the Gaspé National Park (Ⓦwww.sepaq.com), where you can go cross-country skiing across the Chic Chocs mountain range.

246 Ski-touring in Jackson Hole, Wyoming

The rugged terrain around Jackson Hole Mountain Resort is an excellent place to learn the art of backcountry ski-touring. The resort's Backcountry Touring Clinic is a four-day programme for telemark skiers, snowboarders and alpine skiers, which focuses on avalanche awareness, safety and how to tour efficiently in the backcountry, including the rigours of Teton Pass. Ⓦ*www.jacksonhole.com;* ☎*+1 307 739 2686.*

247 Stay in your own private Idaho

The best way to get to know the backcountry is to stay overnight in the wilds, such as in the Tenth Mountain Division Huts in Colorado (Ⓦwww.hutski.com) and the cabins run by the Alpine Club of Canada (Ⓦwww.alpineclubofcanada.ca). A more novel way to do it is along the network of yurt-to-yurt trails in the mountainous backcountry of southeast Idaho, which is known for its wide powder slopes that are perfect for snow-shoeing and cross-country skiing. The yurts along the Portneuf Range Yurt System are spaced so you can reach each one in a day, or you could just make one your base from which to do day-trips into the backcountry. The lower-altitude yurts are accessible to beginners and families, while the higher yurts are designed for more experienced skiers. Each is basic but comfortable, fitted with a wood stove, gas cooker and lantern, pots, axe and bunk beds. Ⓦ*www.isu.edu/outdoor/yurt.html;* ☎*+1 208 282 2945.*

248 Dog-sledding in the Canadian Rockies

If pounding your way through the wintry beyond on a pair of snow-shoes or skis sounds too much like hard work, then why not be pulled along on a sledge by a group of husky dogs? Snowy Owl Tours, a family business based in Banff, runs circular dog-sledding tours along the mountain trails of the Spray Lakes Valley in the Canadian Rockies. The dogs are highly trained and exceptionally well-treated (the owners are working on standard criteria for the ethical treatment of working dogs in Canada). The tours begin with a lesson on safety, commands and the history of dog-sledding, and last from two hours to two days (staying overnight in a Sioux Indian tipi), beginning on soft powder trails and progressing to more advanced carving techniques through the spectacular mountain wilderness. Go mush! Ⓦ*www.snowyowltours.com;* ☎*+1 403 678 4369.*

Snowshoeing and dog-sledding in the Canadian Rockies

249 THE BEAR NECESSITIES OF LIFE ON VANCOUVER ISLAND, BRITISH COLUMBIA

Hunched up in a small hide by the fast-flowing river, you're metres away from a hulking 300kg grizzly bear, its shaggy coat dripping with water as it ambles along the shallows. Suddenly, its deep-set eyes focus upstream and it charges through the rushing torrent. Within moments it has trapped its prey under huge claws, and, snatching the flapping, silvery salmon from the water, the bear wastes no time in tearing it to shreds, devouring every last bit of bony flesh with its powerful jaws.

You might think that observing such raw animal behaviour would be the privilege of patient wildlife film-makers or local fishermen, yet on a Great Bear Nature Tour in a remote northern corner of Vancouver Island you'll have an excellent chance of witnessing this natural feeding frenzy. The tours are based at Great Bear Lodge, a small floating cabin in Smith Inlet, one of the many fjords in the heart of the Great Bear Rainforest. The only way in is by a 45min seaplane flight from Port Hardy, and as it's the only place to stay in this region, guests have exclusive access to this protected wilderness.

From late August to October, bears are drawn to the salmon-spawning streams that flow into the Nekite River. Guests are led by a guide along the riverbank to a hide, where you'll look for bears hunting for the fish that will see them through the long winter hibernation, which can last up to seven months. There can be as many as thirty bears down by the river at any one time, and this is also the best time of the year to see the beguilingly cute cubs.

At other times of the year, you'll be taken out on a small boat to glide gently along the estuaries: in late spring, you might see bears by the side of the river grazing on sedge, while in summer you have to work harder to find the bears, following them as they move looking for berries, protein-rich barnacles, crabs and even some early salmon. Summer is also a good time to see harbour seals and merganser ducks, while in August and September you may hear wolves howling.

The Bear Tours have been developed by Tom Rivest, an expert on the natural history of this isolated part of the island; he is the president of the Commercial Bear Viewing Association and a certified guide trainer. He uses his low-impact trips to help build up a better understanding of bear behaviour (all sightings are recorded by his guides). The floating lodge is powered by wind and solar power; there are only five rooms, so groups are limited to ten guests at a time; and his boats use a four-stroke engine, which is more fuel-efficient and less polluting than the more commonly used two-stroke version.

In between each bear trip (two daily), other organized activities include sea kayaking in the nearby Johnstone Strait, and a rainforest hike to see some of the wildlife living amidst the trees: as well as attracting grizzly bears, the salmon run also brings in bald eagles, gulls and ravens to the riverbanks, while the forest is home to grey wolves, otters, black bears and mink. To help you identify some of the wildlife you've seen during the day, there's a small nature library in the lodge, and in the evenings the guides often give slide shows and video presentations of the local natural history. This place will immerse you in the natural world, in all its wild beauty.

Need to know *Three nights costs Can$2140 (May 7–June 30), Can$1805 (July 1–Aug 19) or Can$2975 (Aug 20–Oct 31), including transfers, accommodation, meals, presentations and guided bear-viewing trips, hiking and kayaking. For directions from Vancouver Island and Seattle to Port Hardy and bookings of Great Bear Tours see ⓦwww.greatbeartours.com; ☎+1 250 949 9496.*

Grizzly Bears, North Vancouver

250 CANOPY LIFE AT CEDAR CREEK TREEHOUSE, WASHINGTON

If you don't have a head for heights then it may be best to skip this one. As lofty lodgings go, Cedar Creek Treehouse is vertiginously high. Perched 15m above ground, it is wrapped around the trunk of an enormous 200-year-old red cedar oak, clear above the tops of the pine trees below.

The treehouse is the brainchild of Bill Compher, who has created this stellar abode by a forested creek at the border between Mount Rainier National Park and the Gifford Pinchot National Forest in Washington. Access is along a 25m-long suspension footbridge, through a rainforest of cedars, sword ferns and evergreens, then up a five-storey stairway whose fourth floor is a glass-enclosed observation area, where you can swing in a hammock and enjoy the mountain views. On the fifth floor, the treehouse is split into two levels: from the entrance there's a surprisingly spacious living room, kitchen, bathroom and sun room, while upstairs the loft has two double beds and skylights so you can take in the night sky.

But if this isn't enough of a bird's-eye view, you can climb up a separate 30m "stairway to heaven", walk across another suspension bridge to a glass observatory and admire the 360-degree views of the dense forest, craggy Sawtooth Ridge and icy peaks of Mount Rainier. But the faint of heart should take note that the owner posts a warning on his website: "Climbing an 85-foot spiral staircase, walking a 45-foot-long suspension footbridge to a treehouse observatory 100 feet in the sky and viewing mountain goats through a spotting scope ... that takes a special kind of person." If you are that kind of person, you'll love this place.

Need to know *The treehouse is 15km by car from the Nisqually River entrance to Mount Rainier National Park. For prices, photos, details of activities and reservations see ⓦwww. cedarcreektreehouse.com; ☎+1 360 569 2991.*

251 OFF-GRID AT TREEBONES, CALIFORNIA

If you like the idea of watching whales but can't stomach the boat journey out to sea for a closer view, then Treebones' yurt camp could be just the ticket. The camp – named after an old lumber mill – is high up on a hill overlooking the sea at the southern end of the Big Sur, the 145km stretch of rugged Californian coastline flanked by the majestic Santa Lucía Mountains and the rocky Pacific coast.

Seven of Treebones' sixteen yurts face the ocean, where several species of whales can be seen throughout the year: grey whales from December to April as they pass through on their annual migration between Alaska and Baja California; blue whales from June to October and humpback whales from late April to early December.

The yurts here have polished pine floors, wood-burning stoves and clear-domed roofs that allow sunlight to flood in, and which are perfect for stargazing at night. Other than telephone lines, the resort is entirely off-grid: it has its own well, and everything is powered by propane-fuelled turbines; the heat produced in the process is used to warm the water, swimming pool and hot tubs.

Inside a yurt at Treebones, California

The swamp waters of the Everglades

Recycling facilities are comprehensive, restaurant scraps are used as compost and, according to the owners, "the vegetables grown in the garden are incorporated into our menu to help move us towards being ever more 'locavore'".

Day-trips are organized to Julia Pfeiffer-Burns State Park and Limekiln State Park, but if you want to get out into the big blue, you can go ocean-kayaking at the southern end of the Monterey Bay National Marine Sanctuary, the largest protected marine area in the US – home to sea otters, harbour seals and dolphins.

Afterwards you can kick back at the camp and relax in a wooden "nest" – a small cradle up among evergreen trees overlooking the sea. It was created by local artist Jason Fann of the Big Sur Spirit Garden (a creative and musical community centre an hour north of the camp; ⓦwww.bigsurspiritgarden. com; ☎+1 831 667 1300). The idea of the nest, insist the owners, is that it's either for an overnight "extreme eco sleep" or for spending an afternoon of quality "alone time", where you can "ponder, meditate or pray". Though this is only available 3–6pm daily, "weather permitting". Only in California.

Need to know *For directions, prices and reservations see ⓦwww.treebonesresort.com; ☎+1 877 424 4787. If yurt camping is your thing, check out these other yurt camps in North America: ⓦwww. yurts.com/how/yurt-vacations.aspx. For prices and reservations of the full-day hiking see ⓦwww. centralcoastoutdoors.com; ☎+1 888 873 5610. For ocean kayaking see ⓦwww.kayakcambria.com; ☎+1 800 717 5225.*

252 TAKE A WALK ON THE WET SIDE, FLORIDA

Spotting an alligator basking a few metres away on the banks of the swamp might make you wonder what you're doing, standing in your wellies almost waist-deep in water. But this is an Everglades "wet hike" and you're here to appreciate the wilderness, alligators and all.

Considered one of the most important wetlands in the world, the Everglades is a vast sodden expanse at the southernmost tip of Florida. Dragonfly Expeditions runs three-hour guided tours through its swamps, around the complex tangles of mangroves, sawgrasses and cypress trees that rise up out of the watery quagmire. To stop your feet getting wet, you'll wear snug neoprene aquasocks and water-shoes, and be given a walking stick to help you stay upright on the slippery undergrowth as you search for river otters, wading birds and of course those 'gators. Many coloured orchids – including, occasionally, the endangered ghost orchid – and bromeliads hang from boughs overhead, while frogs croak loudly and butterflies dance above the surface of the water.

You'll be convinced grasses in the water are snakes as they wrap around your leg, and you'll probably jump the first time your foot hits a branch underwater. But you'll soon get used to the sensation, by which time the magnificent wildlife will probably have monopolized your attention – plus there's a great slap-up lunch of fresh seafood and locally grown salad in a gourmet restaurant overlooking the Barron River to look forward to once you return to dry land.

Need to know *The best time to visit is mid-September to mid-May. A percentage of every tour goes towards conservation efforts in the Everglades. Dragonfly also offers kayaking trips and the chance to see manatees up close. For prices and more information visit ⓦwww. dragonflyexpeditions.com; ☎+1 305 774 9019.*

YOSEMITE NATIONAL PARK

The founding father of modern conservation, John Muir spent many years living in California's Yosemite Valley, and his campaign to safeguard its wild beauty convinced Congress in 1890 to establish Yosemite National Park. Today visitors pay a fee to enter the park, and if you want to stay overnight in the backcountry (only one in a hundred visitors do) you also have to obtain one of the limited "wilderness permits" (one per person, approximately 10–40 per trail; available from the Tuolomne Meadows Wilderness Center on ☎+1 209 372 0740). This quota system acts to reduce the impact of tourism on the park's ecology while helping to fulfil its mandate to provide "outstanding opportunities for solitude". Those who venture forth discover a landscape still as beautiful as the one that inspired Muir: magnificent mountain vistas, huge granite domes, wildflower meadows, meandering rivers and towering waterfalls. Here are our favourite ways to enjoy this specially protected area.

253 Follow the trail to anywhere

With around 1300km of hiking trails snaking their way across the park – of which 95 percent is designated as wilderness – you can walk for days and only see a handful of people. In the backcountry you are free to camp wherever you wish, subject to a few safety limitations, though in some of the more visited areas you can pitch on primitive campgrounds. There are several popular trails (such as the John Muir Trail) but one of the least trodden paths – with no less magnificent scenery – is along the north rim of Yosemite Valley, a 50km, 2–3 day hike that links the summit of El Capitán with Eagle Peak, the top of Upper Yosemite Fall (with lots of good places to camp) and North Dome.

Ranger-led snow-shoe walk in the Bader Pass Ski Area, Yosemite

Need to know *For bus information in Yosemite National Park see ⓦwww.yosemitepark.com. For a list of trail quotas see ⓦwww.yosemite.org.*

254 Ski cross-country

With visitor numbers a fraction of what they're like in the summer, winter is an excellent time to visit Yosemite – especially for cross-country skiers, who have virtually the entire park at their disposal. Whole books have been written about cross-country skiing here so the options are endless, but if you're looking for lessons or a skiing spot near rental facilities then head to the Badger Pass Ski Area, where there are a couple of restaurants, ski-hire facilities, a school and 560km of skiable trails (ninety of them marked).

From here you can ski 17km (4–5hr) to Glacier Point, stay overnight at the rustic Glacier Hut –where you'll dine on a wholesome, carbohydrate-rich dinner – then return the following day; the more adventurous can join a guided ski tour at Glacier Point and stay out for several days.

Need to know *For prices of equipment hire, lessons and trips to Glacier Hut see ⓦwww.badgerpass.com; ☎+1 209 372 8444.*

255 Meander along the Merced

The emphasis in Yosemite is on taking it slow. White-water rafting is banned in the park, but at Curry Village Recreation Center you can rent a small inflatable raft and float downstream along the relatively calm waters of the Merced River and enjoy wonderful views of the park's forested riverbanks and towering cliffs, including Half Dome and Yosemite Falls. Though it's possible to paddle your way along the 5km route in little more than two hours, it's best to make a day of it, pulling up at a sandy beach for a picnic. Give yourself a healthy dose of life in the slow lane.

Need to know *Rafts (for 4–6 people) cost from US$20.50 per person per run or US$13.50 for under-13s, including return shuttle bus to the Curry Village Recreation Center (☏+1 209 372 8319).*

256 A dip in a natural pool

There's nothing quite like a swim in a natural pool to cool off after a long day hiking. Yosemite is not short of places to swim, and though the water is generally cold, from mid-July to September (when there's no longer the early season snowmelt and the days are hot) the water temperature rises sufficiently for a nice dip. The two most popular areas for swimming are the Merced River in Yosemite Valley and the south fork of the Merced River in Wawona, but for a quiet spot head to Sentinel Beach or Swinging Bridge, with superb views of the jagged mountain range that lines the U-shaped glacial valley.

GO CAR-FREE

Help to reduce traffic congestion in and around Yosemite by taking public transport into the heart of the park (⊛www. amtrak.com; ☏+1 800 872 7245). Trains go from San Francisco (3.5hr; US$34) and Los Angeles (6hr; US$38) to Merced, 130km southwest of Yosemite Valley. From Merced you can take a YARTS bus (Yosemite Area Regional Transportation System) that goes all the way to Yosemite Valley for US$25, which includes the park's US$20 entrance fee (3hr; ⊛www.yarts.com; ☏+1 877 989 2787).

Cooling off in one of Yosemite's many rivers; Taft Point, Yosemite

Springtime mustard in Meridian's vineyard, Edna Valley; Feast on organic slow food at Chez Panisse

If you've got the appetite, you can carry on your gastronomic odyssey across the whole state. Slow Food Groups (Ⓦwww.slowfoodusa. org) host regular events showcasing their favourite recipes. Plenty of restaurants espouse the joys of Slow Food too, from Central Market in Petaluma (Ⓦwww.centralmarketpetaluma. com) to San Diego's Market Del Mar (Ⓦwww. marketdelmar.com), which serves up exquisitely presented sushi each day, alongside the finest fish and meat from nearby farms. Best of all for seafood lovers is a trip to Monterey, where a project between the town's aquarium and local restaurants ensures that diners can choose establishments serving fish from sustainably harvested stocks (Ⓦwww.montereybayaquarium. org).

Perhaps even more than its food, California is famous for its wine. Environmentally friendly wine growers are easy to find via the California Wine Institute (Ⓦwww.discovercaliforniawine. com), which has a "green" section highlighting tours and tastings. If you're in Santa Barbara County, meanwhile, where the oenophile film *Sideways* was set, then you can join dedicated sustainable wine tours (Ⓦwww.sustainablevine. com) showcasing the best the country has to offer.

For a probably short-lived souvenir of your visit, you can buy (and if necessary have shipped home) a few of your favourite wines at many of the vineyards. And if you'd also like to take home a few Californian recipes and cooking tricks then stop off in Santa Barbara, where Laurence Hauben runs the Market Forays cooking course (Ⓦwww.marketforays.com), where she guides visitors around the local markets before returning to her home to teach them how to cook with the ingredients. As she was born and raised in France before moving to California in 1983, you can assume Big Macs won't be on the menu.

Need to know *California has several farmers' markets (Ⓦwww.farmernet.com) and you can visit various farms to pick your own or get involved in the harvest (Ⓦwww.calagtour.org).*

257 EAT YOUR WAY ROUND CALIFORNIA

The arty town of Berkeley, and particularly Alice Waters' legendary Chez Panisse restaurant (Ⓦwww. chezpanisse.com), can lay claim to being the birthplace of Californian cuisine, whose emphasis on fresh ingredients and fusion of elements from the state's many gastronomic cultures has influenced restaurant menus the world over. And there are plenty more gastronomic delights to be discovered in the Bay Area: join a culinary walking tour of San Francisco (Ⓦwww.localtastesofthecitytours. com), for example, and you'll have the chance to explore the backstreet markets and restaurants of Little Italy or Chinatown.

258 SURROUND SOUND IN A FREE SPIRIT SPHERE, CANADA

Nestled in your cocoon of comfort, suspended among the canopy of giant Douglas firs, all you can hear is the wind whistling through the leaves and the chatter of forest birds. The only exit is across a suspension bridge to a spiral staircase that winds around the trunk of a tree down to the ground. Here, in a private forest near Qualicum Bay on Vancouver Island, is the latest treehouse incarnation: Free Spirit Spheres.

Two wooden capsules, hanging like pendants on a web of ropes attached to three trees, are much cosier than their minimalist exterior might suggest. They are heavily insulated, include a small electric heater, and have been wired for lights, telephone and built-in speakers, so you can exchange the sounds of the forest outside with the surround sound of your iPod and DVDs. The larger of the two spheres, "Eryn" (made from light sitka spruce), has a double bed, table, cupboard space, couch, sink, microwave and refrigerator, while the smaller pod, "Eve" (fashioned out of yellow cedar) is more spartan, with just a double bed and a few cupboards. Back on terra firma, a short walk from the spheres and on the other side of a pond, are all the other necessary amenities, including showers, a sauna, a kitchen and a covered deck for barbecues.

What started as an experiment in home design has grown into a flourishing treehouse business for owner Tom Chudleigh; he's planning to install up to fifteen spheres in the forest. If you'd like to know how to build one then he'll happily talk shop over the phone – but the best way to see what they're all about is to go and spend a few days up in the trees.

Need to know Ferries run from Vancouver to Nanaimo, Vancouver Island (ⓦwww.bcferries.bc.ca; ☎+1 250 386 3431), after which you'll need to catch a bus to Qualicum Beach (50min; Can$19; ⓦwww.islandlinkbus.com; ☎+1 250 954 8257)

– ask for Horne Lake Road, from where it is a 1km uphill walk to the camp. Alternatively, take the train from Nanaimo to Dunsmuir, from where it's an 8min walk to the camp. Eve costs Can$100 a night; Eryn is $150 a night. For reservations see ⓦwww.freespiritspheres.com; ☎+1 250 757 9445.

Top: Tree life in a Free Spirit Sphere; bottom: The larger of the two spheres – "Eryn" – is fitted with several mod cons, including a microwave and small refrigerator

THE NEW NEW YORK

Restaurants are celebrating farmers' produce; taxis and buses are running on hybrid fuels; community-run tours take visitors to see places they might have once avoided, run by people they'd never normally meet. Whether visiting for the first time or a regular who's done with downtown, the following will help you see New York with fresh eyes.

259 Get a bird's-eye view from the harbour

The iconic view of Manhattan is best appreciated from the water. On a 90min eco-cruise with The Audubon Society, one of the world's oldest conservation organizations, you'll also get close to a lesser-seen side of the harbour – its wildlife. Each summer three thousand herons – protected by Audubon's Harbour Heron's Project – roost on the islands, along with flocks of egrets and ibis; in the winter the waters are teeming with brants, cormorants and mergansers, kept company by a few barking seals. Guided by an Audubon naturalist, this trip is a reminder that this urban jungle is full of wildlife – and not just the human kind.

Need to know *For birdwatching trips in New York, go to ⓦwww.citybirder.blogspot.com. For more on the harbour's wildlife refuges see ⓦwww.nyharborparks.org. If you want to do it alone, ⓦwww.downtownboathouse.org/links.html has an extensive list of places to hire a kayak.*

260 Bite around the Big Apple

Restaurants come and go in New York, making the "Farm Chef Express scheme" a wholesome serving of stability. The programme connects quality farmers from the state of New York with city chefs, guaranteeing one a market and the other the best local ingredients. For a sweet treat, head to the Birdbath Neighborhood Green Bakery; it has walls made of wheat and serves the best cookies in the city. And for a taste of the city's Latin influences, Café Habana's two buzzy outlets serve delicious, authentic Cuban and Mexican food to a vibrant backdrop of regular burlesque and live music.

Need to know *Find a Farm Chef Express restaurant at ⓦwww.farmtochefexpress.org. For more on Birdbath, see ⓦwww.birdbathbakery.com, and for Café Habana go to ⓦwww.ecoeatery.com.*

261 Discover the roots of hip-hop, jazz, gospel or salsa

Music-lovers: head for Harlem. Whichever genre you're into, Harlem Heritage Tours will cater for you. On a jazz tour, expert local guides take guests to see the sights – houses, clubs and restaurants – associated with greats such as Lena Horne, Duke Ellington and Coleman Hawkins, finishing up in one of

Hudson River, New York

Harlem's legendary nightclubs to listen to some contemporary jazz. Gospel tours take in a gospel church service and a walk to see various places of worship. Harlem's fiery Spanish heritage is explored on the busy salsa tour: patriotic murals in the El Bairro district, tasty tacos, and then some rhythmic salsa. If you're after a bit of hip-hop, look no further than Hush Tours, whose bus and walking tours, led by rap kings like Grandmaster Flash and Kurtis Blow, unearth the roots of the genre.

Need to know *For more on Harlem tours, see Ⓦwww.harlemheritage.com. Hush Tours are at Ⓦwww.hushtours.com. For a complete set of walking and cycle routes, along with public transport maps, go to Ⓦwww.transalt.org/resources/maps or see p.374.*

262 Sweet dreams in Sugar Hill

Located in the Sugar Hill area of Harlem, the Sugar Hill Inn is an abiding tribute to some of New York's greatest jazz musicians. Each room in the beautifully restored 1906 townhouse is named after celebrated performers such as Ella Fitzgerald, Louis Armstrong and Miles Davis, and thoughtfully decorated in a style corresponding to the personality: warm, soft colours in Ella's room, a slick, large room for Louis and an earthy space with a fireplace and antique lamps for Miles. Guests at this solar-powered B&B will enjoy genteel hospitality, a leafy back garden and delicious organic breakfasts, as well as a trip down memory lane.

Need to know *Ⓦwww.sugarhillharleminn.com; ☎+1 212 234 5432.*

263 To shop, or not to shop?

While New York has countless eco-boutiques, thrift shops and vintage markets, perhaps no shop has better credentials than Sustainable NYC: the East Village store not only sells eco-friendly clothes and gifts, ranging from recycled handbags to T-shirts and chocolate, it's built from 300-year-old reclaimed wood. Alternatively, check out Reverend Billy and his "Church of Stop Shopping": dressed like a Baptist minister in a white tuxedo, Billy and his choir sing the gospel of anti-consumerism in exuberant shows, often around Times Square, sometimes in the middle of various big-brand stores, and occasionally in community spaces and church halls across the city.

Need to know *Sustainable NYC (Ⓦwww.sustainable-nyc.com) is open daily from 11am to 8pm. For thrift and vintage markets go to Ⓦwww.ny.com/shopping/flea. The Church of Stop Shopping's upcoming events can be found at Ⓦwww.revbilly.com/events.*

Duke Ellington and Ella Fitzgerald

A flea market in Chelsea, New York

Guests staying at Chic Chocs Mountain Lodge can explore the Matane Wildlife Reserve on skis

264 ECO CHIC IN THE MOUNTAINS OF QUÉBEC

When you strap on your snow-shoes just outside the changing rooms and see in the distance that a 50m-high waterfall has frozen solid you know you're in for a chilly day. Temperatures in the Matane Wildlife Reserve can fall to below minus 20°C, but the upside of enduring these extreme winter conditions is snowfall that can reach up to 8m a year. And there can be few more stylish places from which to get the most out of the snow than Chic Chocs Mountain Lodge, just outside the Chic Chocs mountain range in the east of Québec.

The lodge is perched discreetly on a hillside overlooking the reserve, and offers direct ski-in ski-out access to this 60-square-kilometre adventure playground. And the great bonus is that guests of the lodge have exclusive use of the reserve, so the only contact you're likely to have is glimpses of moose, caribou and white-tailed deer. Although snow-shoes are the most convenient way of getting around, the more adventurous can take to alpine skis or even try telemark skis with in-built skins that allow you to trek uphill and ski (albeit slowly) downhill – perfect if you want to enjoy the downhill forest tracks at a gentle pace.

The lodge and reserve are run by the Société des Etablissements de Plein Air (Sepaq), the government-backed organization that manages most of Québec's national parks and wildlife reserves. There are any number of off-piste tracks to explore, including one that links the summit of Mont 780 with L'Epaule trail, which opens out at a breathtaking spot overlooking the Cap-Chat river valley and Frère-de-Nicol-Albert mountain.

In the summer, the reserve is open for hiking and mountain biking – with over 100km of forest roads leading into the heart of the park you've a good chance of seeing bald eagles, hawks and falcons. If you go in winter, make sure you take appropriate clothing. It's also a good idea to check the conditions before you go (see website details below): if the snow bulletin says it's going to be cold, expect it to be *very* cold.

Need to know *The coach from Montréal to Cap Chat costs Can$138 return, not including local taxes (*ⓦ*www.orleansexpress.com), from where you are collected for a three-hour journey by snowcat along the forest track to the lodge. For prices and reservations see *ⓦ*www.sepaq.com; *☏*+1 800 665 3091.*

265 LOG OFF IN A LOG CABIN, CANADA

If you like the idea of hiding away in the mountains but would like a few creature comforts while you're there, Nipika's log cabins have pretty much all you could wish for. Situated in the south of the Rockies 260km from Calgary and 110km from Banff, Nipika has a main lodge, which sleeps thirteen, or a set of smaller cabins, sleeping between two and six. Private and snug with deep sofas and cosy wooden beds, all the accommodation has huge fireplaces, barbecues for summer dining and of course sweeping views of the mountainous backdrop.

The owners also run a sustainable timber-felling operation in the forests that cover much of Nipika's estate, and so the cabins, and much of the furniture inside them, is made from wood that they own. The continuous supply of logs also keeps the fires burning, and the cabins are well-stocked with board games in case the weather sets in. There are no televisions, and without reception, your mobile phone won't be much use. Internet is available for those desperate for contact with the outside world.

Of course, not many people come to the Canadian Rockies to stay indoors, surf the net or play Scrabble. From the cabins, numerous hiking and mountain-biking tracks branch out into the hills, and in neighbouring Kootenay National Park you can walk for hours through vast stands of pine forest, or kayak on the glassy blue lakes, and not see a soul.

Winter means snow, and lots of it, with nearly 2m falling on average each season. Nipika maintains 50km of cross-country skiing trails straight from its doorstep, and also offers snow-shoeing treks – guided, if you wish, by their resident naturalist. Afterwards you can take a dip in the hot springs a short drive away, or even try out the lodge's own wood-fired hot tub and sauna. With so much on offer at Nipika, the life of a lumberjack here seems more than just OK.

Need to know *Nipika also runs several courses throughout the year, such as a week of cross-country skiing in the winter, or combined hiking and kayaking in the summer. For directions to Nipika, accommodation details, prices and bookings see Ⓦwww.nipika.com; ☎+1 877 647 4525.*

266 PARTY WITH A PURPOSE AT ROTHBURY FESTIVAL, MICHIGAN

Despite only starting in 2008, Michigan's Rothbury Festival has got all the component parts right. Location? A ranch around three hours' drive from Chicago, with entry discounts for people who buy a "green ticket" that comes with public transport included. A lake to cool off in with a diving platform to bask under the July

sun. A forest to hook up a hammock and swing in by day, and to walk through at night between the many psychedelic displays hung from the branches.

Line-up? A diverse mix of seventy or so bands combining rarely seen legends like bluesman Taj Mahal and Frank Zappa's son Dweezil, with cutting-edge hip-hop from the likes of Diplo, blissed-out electronica from the Thievery Corporation and Disco Biscuits, or a bluegrass jam with Railroad Earth. Circus acts appear from nowhere. Then there's the vaudeville cabaret, fireworks at night and a fancy-dress stall so that you can look as odd as you choose, whenever you want.

Add an organic farmers' market, a zero-waste policy and an innovative approach to offsetting the bands' transport to the site (which essentially involves buying and installing a solar-panel system for a nearby school) and you'd imagine that all boxes would be ticked for a successful, environmentally responsible festival. But rather than rest on their laurels, Rothbury also saw the gathering of over forty thousand people as a chance for a constructive meeting of minds, and it now runs a think-tank looking at solutions to climate change. It's a progressive approach that should hopefully see this festival lasting long into the future.

Need to know *Rothbury Festival takes place in July. As well as campsites there are log cabins in the woods for hire that are within easy walk of the lake's beach. For details of the festival and to buy tickets visit Ⓦwww.rothburyfestival.com.*

Taj Mahal at the Rothbury Festival, Michigan

The view across to Mount McKinley from Camp Denali

267 ROOM WITH A VIEW AT CAMP DENALI, ALASKA

Looking out from the cosy wood-fired cabin across the still waters of Nugget Pond and the rolling green tundra of Denali National Park, you can see all the way to the ice-capped peaks of Alaska's iconic Mount McKinley (6193m), the highest peak in North America. Whereas many of the tallest mountains in the world protrude from a high plateau of other towering peaks, Mount McKinley looms all the way up from the tundra at just 610m above sea level, so from base to peak it is a clear 5583m. As vertical rises go, this is as impressive as it gets.

All seventeen cabins at Camp Denali, in the heart of the park by Nugget Pond, are spaced out over a sweeping ridgeline so that every guest has this view. The camp, which in 1951 became the first lodge in Denali National Park, has a strong ecological ethos, from the home-grown salad, vegetables and bread served in the restaurant to naturalist tours with trained guides (sometimes led by visiting experts) to see the park's animals, such as grizzly bears, caribou and moose. The emphasis of the walking, cycling and canoeing tours is on observing rather than just spotting wildlife, which is reinforced by fireside evening lectures on natural and cultural history.

While there are several other lodges in the park, Camp Denali is the only one with views of the mountain, though you do have to pay for the privilege (a minimum three nights costs Can$1425, including transfers, meals, guided outings and park entry fee). Though you might argue that views like this are priceless.

Need to know *Camp Denali is open from early June to early September. The "Denali Star" train from Anchorage to Denali Park station takes 7hr 40min (⊛www.alaskarailroad.com; ☎+1 907 265 2494). Staff will collect you by minibus at the station and take you to the camp (approximately 7hr, including a stop for a picnic dinner). For details of accommodation, prices and reservations see ⊛www.campdenali.com; ☎+1 907 683 2290.*

268 AWAY FROM THE TRAIL IN ALASKA

The whole point of walking in the designated wilderness area of Alaska's Denali National Park is that you can make it up as you go along. Unlike the smooth, well-managed paths around the park's entrance area, the backcountry has no managed trails, so you have to rely on good old-fashioned navigation and nous.

Occasionally you'll come across "social trails" of footprints where others have gone before you, but to limit your impact on the fragile ecosystem it's best to avoid these and forge your own route; negotiating the boggy tundra, traversing ridgelines and following the many rivers in this spectacular heartland of Alaska – home to wolves, Dall sheep, moose, caribou and bears. Anyone intending to spend the night in the wilderness must watch a 25min video at the Backcountry Visitor Center, which teaches you how to avoid contact with the bears, and what to do if you do happen to come across one. For safety tips in advance visit ⓦdnr.alaska.gov/parks/safety/bears.htm.

Within the wilderness area there are 41 "units" (backcountry access zones) that have a daily quota of between two and twelve campers. There are no established campsites in the backcountry – that's one of its most inviting features – so it's up to you where you pitch for the night, so long as you camp more than half a mile from the Park Road and out of sight of it.

The challenge of negotiating your way across the trackless tundra, camping out in the wild and pitting your wits against Alaska's elements requires determination, flexibility and ingenuity, but your reward is hiking in true wilderness with only wild animals and wildflowers for company.

Need to know *Reservations (only available one day in advance) are made at the Backcountry Information Center at the park's Riley Creek entrance area. Once you have made a backcountry reservation, you will be handed a free bear-resistant food container for your trip. For a checklist of equipment and advice on low-impact hiking in Denali see* ⓦ*alaska.org/denali/advice-denali-backcountry.htm. For a detailed description of the backcountry units see National Geographic's 1:200,000 Denali National Park and Preserve Trails Illustrated Map (Can$10).*

A wild iris; Fang Mountain, Denali National Park and Reserve

CANADA BY TRAIN

Flying may be the fastest way to cross Canada, but travelling by train is the scenic way to explore this enormous country, from the rugged coastline on the eastern seaboard to the wilderness of the prairies in the central provinces and the magnificent Rocky Mountains in the west. The country's national rail network, VIA Rail (ⓦwww.viarail.ca) runs three main services that enable you to cross all of Canada by train: the "Ocean", an overnight service between Halifax and Montréal (19hr); the modern inter-city service between Montréal and Toronto (4hr 40 min); and the transcontinental service known as the "Canadian" between Toronto and Vancouver (a whopping three days and three nights). Below are some suggestions on the best things to do along the way.

269 Fresh air in Nova Scotia

Before boarding the train to Montréal, it's worth spending a couple of days in Halifax – home to one of the world's finest waterfronts. At Point Pleasant Park, there are plenty of walking trails and a small sandy beach, and if you'd like to fill your lungs with salty air, Four Winds Charters runs a 2.5hr boat tour of the harbour. Highlights of the province of Nova Scotia include the highest tides in the world at the Bay of Fundy and the Cape Breton Highlands National Park, where there are 25 hiking circuits.

Need to know *For attractions, accommodation and visitor info on Nova Scotia see ⓦwww. novascotia.com. Four Winds Charters: ⓦwww. fourwindscharters.com; ☎+1 877 274 8421.*

270 Visit Montréal's Biodôme

Montréal's train station is in the heart of the city, from where it's just a few minutes' walk to the Biodôme, so before you make the trip to Toronto take time to visit this huge environmental museum, which replicates four types of ecosystem under glass: a tropical forest, an estuary, a Laurentian mixed forest and the polar regions. Over 750 plant species and 230 animal species inhabit these areas, which you can tour on walkways. A great choice for kids.

Need to know *For information on the latest exhibitions and virtual tours see ⓦwww.biodome. qc.ca; ☎+1 514 868 3065. As well as VIA Rail's overnight train from Halifax to Montréal, a daily train (the "Adirondack") runs from New York to Montréal (10hr 50min); for prices and departures see ⓦwww.amtrak.com; ☎+1 800 872 7245.*

271 Stock up on food at St Lawrence market, Toronto

With a three-day train ride ahead of you, it's a good idea to make a stop at Toronto's St Lawrence market – the city's best food and drink emporium – to stock up on essentials. In the heart of Toronto's old town, the market is packed with fresh fruit, vegetables, meats and craft stalls. The North Market building is home to the farmers' market (Sat only), while the South Market building (Tues–Sat) is home to over fifty permanent vendors.

Need to know *For opening times and details of stalls visit ⓦwww.stlawrencemarket.com. As well as VIA Rail's services, a daily train (the "Maple Leaf") runs from New York to Toronto in 12hr 20min; for prices and departures see ⓦwww.amtrak.com; ☎+1 800 872 7245.*

Hide and peek, Biodôme Parc Olympique, Montréal

272 Stretch your legs in Jasper National Park

The "Canadian" train is timetabled to reach the Rockies in daylight, and there's no better place to break up the journey to Vancouver than at Jasper National Park. En route, don't miss the chance to get a seat in one of the two dome cars – glass-roofed observation carriages from which you can admire panoramic views of the countryside. At Jasper, go for a stroll around Maligne Lake, the largest in the Rockies (ⓦwww.malignelake.com) or if you're more of a thrill-seeker you can go white-water rafting down the Athabasca River (ⓦwww.jasperrafttours.com).

Need to know The "Canadian" goes from Toronto via Winnipeg and Edmonton to Jasper and takes 2 days 17hr. "Comfort Class" is the economy option and features a reclining seat, while in "Silver and Blue" class you'll have a private bedroom and meals in the dining carriage are included. For timetables, prices and reservations visit ⓦwww.viarail.ca; ☎+1 888 842 7245.

273 Go green in Vancouver

To stretch your legs after the long train ride, cycle out to Stanley Park, the largest urban park in North America. Or if you're in search of a green space, take the excellent Blue Bus network (ⓦwww.westvancouver.ca) that runs from downtown Vancouver to the beaches along Marine Drive. For somewhere to eat in Vancouver, go to C restaurant (ⓦwww.crestaurant.com; ☎+1 604 681 1164) for delicious and sustainably sourced fish, or try Fuel (ⓦwww.fuelrestaurant.ca; ☎+1 604 288 7905) for regional, seasonal menus.

Need to know For bike hire see ⓦwww.bayshorebikerentals.ca or ⓦwww.stanleyparkcycle.com. The "Canadian" takes 20hr 25min to get from Jasper to Vancouver.

Lion's Gate Bridge, Stanley Park, Vancouver

Spirit Island, Maligne Lake, Jasper National Park

274 VISIT THE TOTEM POLES OF GWAII HAANAS, CANADA

Even when you reach the remote port of Prince Rupert on the west coast of Canada, there is still another day of travel by ferry and then two days of kayaking before you arrive at the islands of Gwaii Haanas, home to the Haida people. It's a long, slow journey across the treacherous waters of the Hecate Strait, but the reward for your perseverance is a true wilderness of rainforest-covered islands, sheltered coves, sandy beaches, hot thermal springs, unique wildlife and the largest collection of still-standing totem poles in North America.

The 138 islands of Gwaii Haanas are in the southern part of Haida Gwaii (Queen Charlotte Islands), 640km north of Vancouver and 130km off the British Columbia coast. In 1988 they were made a national park reserve, which is co-managed by the Canadian government and the council of the Haida nation. Before setting off into the park, you are required to attend a 90min orientation session on safety issues, the park's "leave no trace" camping etiquette, and the history and culture of the Haida, who have lived on the islands for more than ten thousand years. This orientation takes

Poles apart: the totem poles in Gwaii Haanas National Park Reserve; Bald Eagle

place at the Haida Heritage Centre (ⓦwww.haidaheritagecentre.com), which also features a museum of Haida crafts and artefacts.

Once you've arrived on the Queen Charlotte Islands, the main access to Gwaii Haanas is from Moresby Camp on Moresby Island, from where it takes about two days to kayak to the Tangil Peninsula. A popular (but more expensive) alternative is to charter one of the licensed motorboat tour operators, who will drop you and your kayak anywhere you wish in the park. There are over 1700km of shoreline to explore, though most kayakers keep to the east coast, which has a much gentler landscape than the rugged, steep west coast exposed to the Pacific.

Within the park you can visit three Haida sites that are looked after by Haida Gwaii Watchmen (a traditional role of camp guardian): Hlk'yah GaawGa (Windy Bay), Gandll K'in Gwaayaay (Hot Spring Island) and SGang Gwaay (Anthony Island). All three sites have the remains of ancient settlements, including house pits, longhouse posts and beams, fallen poles and in some cases, standing poles – intricately carved from a single red cedar with animal symbols (such as beaver, dogfish, frog, hummingbird, shark and killer whale) woven together to represent the different clans. At Gandll K'in Gwaayaay you can relax in geothermally heated pools or walk up a trail to a cliff-side pool that looks out over the Juan Pérez Strait.

The islands of Gwaii Haanas are thought to have escaped glaciation during the last ice age; subsequently the flora and fauna have evolved differently to those on the mainland, which has led the archipelago to be dubbed the "Canadian Galápagos". It is home to at least seven distinct animals, including the world's largest black bear. From May to August, 750,000 seabirds nest along the shoreline, including rhinoceros auklets, storm petrels and bald eagles, and the marine life is just as impressive: at the southern tip of the archipelago there's a large colony of Steller sea lions and twenty species of whales and dolphins have been spotted.

Access to Gwaii Haanas is controlled via a quota system – anyone visiting the park independently has to apply for a permit and those that go as part of a group (whose maximum size has to be twelve) can only do so with licensed operators. A visitor fee of Can$19.50 per person applies, which supports the orientation programme, the Haida Gwaii Watchmen and the maintenance of village sites. Thankfully, with such strict conservation measures, if you're prepared to make the long journey here you'll visit a unique wilderness that has barely changed in thousands of years.

Need to know *Trains run from Jasper, Edmonton and Vancouver to Prince Rupert (ⓦwww.viarail. ca), from where ferries go to Skidegate (7hr) and then across to Alliford Bay (20min), after which it's a short drive to Moresby Camp. Ferries also run from Port Hardy on Vancouver Island to Prince Rupert (20hr). For prices and timetables of all ferry services see ⓦwww.bcferries.com; ☎+1 250 386 3431. For more info download the "Trip Planner" from ⓦwww.pc.gc.ca/gwaiihaanas; for help in organizing a trip ☎+1 250 559 8818; to make a reservation ☎+1 250 387 1642.*

275 FOLLOW IN THE FOOTSTEPS OF SITTING BULL

If you want to understand the history of the Lakota, the Native American people whose most famous leader was Sitting Bull, then it's doubtful there's anyone better to ask than his great grandson, Ernie LaPointe. Ernie is one of the many indigenous guides working for Go Native America, whose tours give guests an unparalleled opportunity to learn about the many different histories and customs of the Indian tribes of the Great Plains. While many claim ancestry from the legendary holy man, only Ernie has the papers to prove it. When he talks of the battle of Little Bighorn, or of his experiences as a Sun Dancer (a religious role

Hopi Indian dancers and musicians

that Sitting Bull also held), he speaks from the heart.

Go Native America offers several small-group tours that get under the skin of Native American communities. You could spend a week trying to understand the complex cosmology of the Hopi, staying on the mesas with them in the deserts of Arizona. Or spend the weekend with modern Apaches touring the canyons and plains that their ancestors fought so hard to defend in what is now New Mexico.

The aim of the tours is not to romanticize the past but to present honestly the history and present-day experience of the USA's indigenous peoples. So while many of the tours involve a night in a tipi, guests also meet people living in mobile homes on the reservations, many of whose lives are blighted by alcoholism and depression. It's not always easy but it is always genuine, and Go Native America's respect for its peoples ensures there is no more authentic encounter with the descendants of Geronimo and Crazy Horse.

Need to know *Go Native America runs trips in Wyoming, South Dakota, Arizona, Montana, Nebraska and New Mexico. For further information, including details of tours, visit ⓦwww. gonativeamerica.com; ☎+1 888 800 1876.*

Cyclist in Vermont

276 MOUNTAIN BIKING ALONG THE KINGDOM TRAILS, VERMONT

Whether you get your kicks out of cycling over gentle, rolling slopes or steeper, twisting climbs, there's something for every level of experience at the Kingdom Trails in the hills of northeast Vermont. Around 160km of trails run across the west and east side of Darling Hill and over Burke Mountain, with the most popular including Dead Moose Alley, Fenceline, Pines, Pastore Point, Pound Cake and Sidewinder. The trail system is managed by a non-profit conservation organization called Kingdom Trails, which has developed smooth tracks along disused cart paths and scenic country lanes. The tracks are built using a comprehensive drainage system, which works to curb the effect that any build-up of water can inflict in terms of eroding soil and vegetation.

The trails are open from mid-May to the end of October (depending on conditions), but the best time to go is in the autumn, when the crisp air keeps you cool and you can admire the glorious autumnal colours of Vermont's broadleaf trees. When the season draws to a close (usually in late autumn), the tracks become a retreat for non-motorized winter sports, such as cross-country skiing and snow-shoeing – similarly low-impact activities that help keep this special place a year-round adventure playground.

Need to know *Trail passes (US$10 per day or US$35 per season, including map) are sold at the Kingdom Trails Welcome Center in East Burke Village on Route 114. For directions from Southern Vermont, Connecticut, Boston and Québec, as well as a list of bike shops and accommodation, see* Ⓦ*www.kingdomtrails.org;* ☎*+1 802 626 0737.*

277 HUMPBACKS OFF HAWAII

There are few more incredible sights than watching a 37-tonne humpback whale breaching completely out of the sea. And few better places to see this powerful display than Hawaii: between November and April each year, up to ten thousand whales migrate here to mate, give birth and nurse their young.

Several operators offer trips out to view the endangered humpbacks and the 21 other species of whale and dolphin here, though Wild Side Eco-Adventures, based about an hour from Waikki on Oahu Island, comes highly recommended. With groups kept to a maximum of twelve people (and sometimes as little as six), the company offers several whale- and dolphin-watching trips led by expert marine biologists, as well as the chance to charter a boat for some leisurely island-hopping.

But Wild Side isn't there just for entertainment: aware that whale-watching is fast becoming a popular activity, their staff are mindful of keeping a respectful distance from the mammals, while the company's marine biologists are constantly monitoring the whale behaviour and collecting data. In autumn, the company's Ocean Trekker Expeditions introduces small groups to the basics of whale and dolphin research; you'll learn about breaching, the whale's song and pectoral slaps, all the while recording their actions. Being a part of their conservation is the best way of getting closer to the mighty humpback whale.

Need to know *On the Ocean Trekker Expedition guests stay at the Makaha Golf Resort Hotel. It's also possible to volunteer for longer periods with* both Wild Side and the Wild Dolphin Foundation. For prices, itineraries, booking and more information on other cruises, see Ⓦwww.sailhawaii. com; ☎+1 808 306 7273.

278 WATCH LAVA BECOME LAND IN HAWAII

The best place to really appreciate Hawaii's volcanoes is Big Island, thirteen percent of which is given over to the Hawaii Volcanoes National Park. This World Heritage Site offers surreal trekking opportunities around Kilauea, one of the most active volcanoes on Earth, where you can watch lava flow from the fissures in the ground and form new landmass before your eyes as it cools and hardens when it makes contact with the sea. Alternatively you can hike to the top of the dormant and regularly snow-capped Mauna Kea (at 13,677m above sea level, actually taller than Mount Everest given that two-thirds of it lies beneath the Pacific). Some of the world's most powerful astronomical telescopes sit on its summit, one of the best places on Earth to view the night sky.

Big Island has some great eco-friendly accommodation too. Situated in the aptly named village of Volcano right on the border of the national park, Volcano Guest House's cottages are solar powered (including the hot tub), while a permaculture garden provides much of its food. It's a very family-friendly place, too, with a couple of cows, several dogs and ducks scurrying all over, and a forested garden of ponds and small waterfalls to explore. For a wackier alternative, the off-grid and solar-powered Lava Lova offers accommodation in funkily decorated yurts and two old (and non-operational) campervans situated 1.5km up the face of Mauna Loa.

Both places are closely connected to their local communities, and are happy to recommend and arrange hikes through the national park or the bird-filled rainforests that cover much of the rest of the island. The waters around the shores

Daisy the Daydream bus; Lava flowing into the sea, Hawaii Volcanoes National Park

are also teeming with life – you can stand on a black-sand beach and watch humpback whales breaching a few hundred metres out to sea, or go diving at night with shoals of manta rays. But the most unforgettable experience on Big Island is watching the sun set from the summit of Mauna Kea, as the mountain forms a perfect triangle of shadow across the clouds and ocean that stretch out beneath you, pointing the way back to the US mainland 2500km away.

Need to know There are no passenger boats from the US mainland to Hawaii, although it is possible to go by cargo boat (see p.344 for details). The Hele-On bus (Ⓦwww.hawaii-county.com) offers free transport around Big Island. Volcano Guest House: Ⓦwww.volcanoguesthouse.com; ☎+1 866 886 5226. Lava Lova: Ⓦwww.gladtravel.com/ lovalavaland/oceanviewbigisland.aspx.

Orca whales off the Mingan
Islands, Québec

279 WHALE-WATCHING IN QUÉBEC

Québec City is the proud, French-speaking capital of Québec province. It's also one of the prettiest cities in Canada, complete with a romantic old quarter of cobbled streets and inviting nooks and crannies. Little known to most visitors is that the city is the gateway to one of the world's greatest places for whale-watching.

Québec sits at the narrowing of the St Lawrence River (the word Québec means "narrowing" in the Algonquin language), which opens out to the estuary and gulf of St Lawrence where, just a few hours from the city centre – and from mid-May to mid-October – it's possible to see thirteen species of whale, among them the blue, fin, humpback, killer and minke.

The variety of whales is impressive, but it's the respectful manner in which you are taken to see them that marks Québec's whale-watching operators as world leaders. Aboard a cruise boat, inflatable or kayak, knowledgeable guides will give guests an insight into the behaviour

of the whales, their habitat and the ecology of the surrounding region. The operators have to apply for a permit and follow strict regulations that ensure they not only deliver memorable encounters with the whales but they do so without unduly disturbing the animals: boats aren't allowed closer than 100m to the whales, swimming within 200m is prohibited, and the maximum speed in an observation zone is ten knots. As a result, the gulf of St Lawrence continues to be a safe sanctuary and bountiful feeding ground for these beautiful creatures – and a sure bet for viewings.

Need to know *The best places to see whales are the Saguenay-St Lawrence Marine Park (with numerous departures from Tadoussac, Baie-Sainte-Catherine, Rivière-du-Loup and Trois-Pistoles), the Mingan Archipelago National Park Reserve of Canada and the Forillon National Park of Canada in the Gaspésie. For a list of whale-watching operators see* Ⓦ*www.quebecmaritime.ca and* Ⓦ*www.aventure-ecotourisme.qc.ca.*

280 MEET A MOOSE IN ALGONQUIN, CANADA

Few areas of wilderness as vast as Ontario's Algonquin Provincial Park are as accessible from a major city. Just four hours by direct train from Toronto and you're in 7600 square kilometres of maple hills, deciduous and coniferous forests, rocky ridges, spruce bogs, and thousands of lakes and streams. In the winter, this pristine park is the domain of dog-sledding expeditions, snow-shoeing and cross-country skiing, while in the summer thousands come for hiking, wild camping and canoe trips. Algonquin is one of the best places in the world to hear a wolf howling, or see moose and beavers, especially from the comfort of a canoe (there are an amazing 16,000km of canoe routes in the park).

To help you find your way around, Northern Edge runs guided canoe tours, including a three-day "Morning Tea with Moose" adventure where you'll learn about the park's ecology and be taken to some of the remote places where moose roam. It also runs wilderness survival courses and a four-day wolf-tracking trip. En route on all its trips you'll stop off to swim in clear lakes, eat around a camp fire and sleep in tents under the stars. The city lights of downtown Toronto will feel a million miles away.

Need to know *The Ontario Northland train runs from Union Station, Toronto to South River, Algonquin Park (4hr); for timetable see ⓦwww.ontarionorthland.ca; ☏+1 866 472 3865. The canoeing season is from early May to October. Park permits for backcountry camping cost Can$11 a night (ⓦwww.ontarioparks.com) but are usually included in the price of guided tours. For prices and itineraries of all trips at Northern Edge see ⓦwww.northernedgealgonquin.com; ☏+1 705 386 1595.*

The main attraction in Algonquin Park

Mapping your world

Editable media applications let people share information in ways never before possible. All sorts of map variants are emerging that allow independent travellers access to local knowledge of places they are visiting, from the official to the unusual. At the same time GPS technologies are making it easier to find your way back should you have decided to wander off on a path less travelled. More and more, these developments are creating new ways for us to navigate the world; here are some of our favourites:

MAP MASHUPS

Many people use Google Maps but not many know about the mashups of them (ⓦgooglemapsmania. blogspot.com). First created through hacking, then legitimized when Google released the necessary codes, the mashups work in a similar way to Green Maps (see opposite), in that people customize existing maps by adding icons of their own to express a certain theme or topic. They range from the extremely useful – such as where all the UNESCO World Heritage Sites are (with clicks through to information about them) or where to find a wi-fi hotspot in the US – to the more zany, such as a map of reported ghost sightings or America's drunkest cities. Mashups may be added to the basic Google Map, allowing you to create a multi-layered map, with all the information you could ever need.

A screengrab from ⓦwww.england-rocks.co.uk/index2.php, a Google mashup depicting locations of notorious musical heritage in the UK

GLOBAL POSITIONING SYSTEMS (GPS)

Developed by the US Defense Department (and managed by the US Airforce 50th Space Wing), GPS uses a network of between 24 and 32 orbital satellites to enable people to find their exact location in the world and then navigate to where they want to go. Already there are GPS-based tours of many cities around the world, while other companies – such as loopt.com – offer social-networking facilities so that you can know where your friends are in real time (and they you). Geocaching (see p.19) is basically a combination of treasure hunting and time capsules for the GPS generation, and is one of many new activities that have sprung up as a result of the technology.

GREEN MAPS

Open-source websites like Wikipedia have encouraged web users to pool their knowledge for the common good, and Green Maps is a cartographic offshoot of this trend: a project that allows people to share their knowledge of their local area's environmentally friendly facilities and attractions with the world. Users contribute information via a set of icons, as shown below, making it easy to read any map, whatever the nationality of those who produced it (at present there are over five hundred map projects being developed in 54 countries). The project's slogan is "think global, map local" and it is exactly that – a wonderful way of getting access to the sort of information normally only gained by living in a place.

It's not specifically targeted at travellers, although with the maps highlighting everything from where farmers' markets and volunteering sites can be found to good places to go birdwatching or watch the sun rise, it offers a great deal not normally found on a typical map. Not all maps are online, and it may be necessary on occasion to contact the producers via the Green Maps website (ⓦwww.greenmap.org).

Some of the symbols used in green maps

Wetlands

Farmers' market

Community garden

Volunteer site

Sunrise

Birdwatching

Autumn leaves

Traditional way of life

281 Birdwatching at Celestún Biosphere Reserve, Mexico

282 Discover Mayan ruins at Lago de Petexbatún, Guatemala

283 Shore Dive off Bonaire

284 Follow the coffee route to Finca Esperanza Verde, Nicaragua

285 Great Huts, Jamaica

286 Contribute to the Earthdive log in Tobago

287 Hideaway in the hills at Kido, Grenada

288 In the wake of the Maya, Mexico

289 Island-hopping in the Caribbean

290 Get an "overstanding" of Rasta, Jamaica

291 Root veg and culture, Jamaica

292 Find the soul of Trinidad

293 Get back to the roots, Grenada

294 Get under Cuba's skin

295 La Ruta Moskitia, Honduras

296 Las Terrazas, Cuba

297 Live with the Maya, Belize

298 Marvel at birds in Trinidad

299 A different Caribbean experience, Dominica

300 Lapa Rios, Costa Rica

301 Pacuare Lodge, Costa Rica

302 Luna Nueva Lodge, Costa Rica

303 La Cusinga Lodge, Costa Rica

304 Finca Rosa Blanca Country Inn, Costa Rica

305 Bosque del Cabo, Costa Rica

306 Danta Corcovado Lodge, Costa Rica

307 Costa Rica Treehouse Lodge, Costa Rica

308 Cerro Escondido, Costa Rica

309 Rara Avis Rainforest Lodge and Reserve, Costa Rica

310 Day-trips with a difference at Puerta Verde, Mexico

311 Pueblos Mancomunados, Mexico

312 Discover Saba

313 Meet the Kuna, Panama

314 The beginnings of tourism in El Salvador

315 In tune with the moon in Dominica

316 Monitor whales off the Bahamas

317 Learn Spanish in Nicaragua

318 Praslin Island, St Lucia

319 Rosalie Bay, Dominica

320 Treasure Beach, Jamaica

321 Eco-chic at Morgan's Rock, Nicaragua

322 Watch the clouds at Rancho de Caldera, Panama

323 Meet the Maya at Cotton Tree Lodge, Belize

324 Sail and dive in the Grenadines, Grenada

325 See the bioluminescence at Mosquito Bay, Puerto Rico

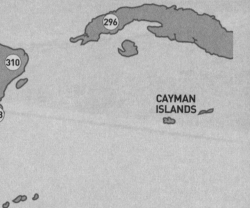

MEXICO, CENTRAL AMERICA AND THE CARIBBEAN

316

BAHAMAS

289

CUBA

294

HAITI

PUERTO RICO

325

DOMINICAN REPUBLIC

291   285
320   290

JAMAICA

312

ANTIGUA

ST KITTS & NEVIS

GUADELOUPE

DOMINICA

319
299
315

MARTINIQUE

ST LUCIA   318

ST VINCENT

BARBADOS

324
287

293   **GRENADA**

TRINIDAD & TOBAGO   286

292

298

ARUBA

283

CURAÇAO   **BONAIRE**

313

281 BIRDWATCHING AT CELESTÚN BIOSPHERE RESERVE, MEXICO

Bird Island (Isla de Pájaros) in the Yucatán's Celestún Biosphere Reserve is the venue for one of Mexico's best-attended bird parties. It rocks the most in winter, when flocks of the main host – the impressive pink American flamingo – come in their droves to this protected wetland. They are joined by numerous other guests – warblers and sandpipers, along with herons, cormorants, great egrets and pelicans.

You're very welcome to join in the party, though only from a distance. Local boatmen (*lancheros*) run boat tours from the dock at Celestún through the mangroves to the island (for an English-speaking guide, ask for a member of the Peregrinos, an association of young guides). While the boat engine is still running, you have to keep 60–80m from the flamingos, and even when it's switched off and the boatmen are poling along, you should never get within 50m. There can be as many as eighteen thousand flamingos congregating at once, but if they're disturbed then there's a risk that they will leave this area in search of quieter places.

Just 10km north of Celestún, on the coastal road towards Sisal, is Eco Paraíso Xixim, a small hotel nestled among a vast plantation of coconut palms on a private reserve overlooking the Gulf of Mexico. The resort is made up of fifteen spacious, thatched *cabañas* set behind the dunes, complete with fans, double beds and hammocks. Waste is recycled, solar power is used to heat the swimming pool and there's an engaging little natural history museum full of plant and animal specimens and skeletons. For a first-class fish supper try *La Playita*, a wonderful seafood restaurant in Celestún.

Back at Eco Paraíso, there's plenty to do: from April to July, you might see turtles nesting on the nearby beach; you can hire bikes or kayaks and explore the swampy waters of Cholul salt flats; or there are trips to see flamingos in the Celestún reserve at dawn, just before their party really gets going.

Need to know *Buses to Celestún leave from the bus station in Mérida hourly from 5am (2hr). The 90min boat tours (about US$30) generally stop at a freshwater spring where you can go for a swim – you're advised to cover up before swimming rather than applying chemical-based suntan lotion. Longer tours are also available. For prices, reservations and directions to Eco Paraíso see* Ⓦ *www.ecoparaiso.com;* ☏ *+52 988 916 2100.*

Pink flamingos at Celestún

282 DISCOVER MAYAN RUINS AT LAGO DE PETEXBATÚN, GUATEMALA

If you like your Mayan ruins a little less grandiose than Tikal but all to yourself, then try those in and around Lago de Petexbatún, a spectacular expanse of water ringed by dense forest to the south of Sayaxché. The region is home to several ruins, including Dos Pilas, Ceibal and Yaxchilán, though the most impressive is the partially restored Aguateca – a fortified city perched on a high escarpment overlooking the lake.

The best base for checking out these atmospheric ruins is Chiminos Island Lodge on Punta de Chiminos, a peninsula that juts into the lake. It was here that the last of the Petexbatún Maya sought refuge as the region descended into warfare at the beginning of the ninth century. Although little of their citadel remains today, the lodge was set up by two archeologists who wanted to preserve the site and also protect the surrounding wildlife and jungle.

The lodge's six thatched jungle bungalows (all set well apart from each other) are built on stilts from fallen hardwood. Each can sleep up to five people and has a bathroom and its own water-treatment system. The closest archeological attractions can all be reached from the lodge by boat, walking and on horseback in a day. While the crowds are bustling around the more well-known Maya sites in Guatemala, you'll have had a day's unhurried adventure in the jungle, enjoying these ancient sites in splendid isolation.

Need to know Aguateca is a short boat ride from the lodge then 20min walk, while Dos Pilas involves a short boat cruise then a 2.5hr walk. The lodge also organizes three-day trips to Yaxchilán, staying overnight in a jungle lodge. Buses go from Guatemala City to the town of Sayaxché (8hr); alternatively you can drive from Flores to Sayaxché, from where there's a river cruise (1.5hr) to Lake Petexbatún. For prices, reservations and links to archeological articles related to the Petexbatún area see ⓦwww.chiminosisland.com; ☎+502 2471 0855.

(Clockwise from top) Stelae in Aguateca; Indigenous girls from San Mateo wearing traditional costume; The view from the Royal Palace, Aguateca

Divers embarking on their journey into the clear blue waters off Bonaire

283 SHORE DIVE OFF BONAIRE

Off the coast of Venezuela in the Netherlands Antilles, the tiny boomerang-shaped island of Bonaire has some of the best diving in the world: calm, clear waters, healthy coral reefs and an abundance of tropical fish.

The reefs typically start at the water's edge and shelve off to a depth of about 10m, enabling you to see some of the best sites as shore dives without the expense of chartering a boat. In these shallow waters, you'll see multicoloured reef fish – parrotfish, butterfly and angelfish – flitting through the coral. Further out at the drop-off zone (usually between 10–12m) and beyond, there are vivid sponges, moray eels and groupers, and if you're lucky you may also see turtles, seahorses and dolphins – perhaps even nurse or whale sharks.

Despite its popularity and heavy tourist traffic, Bonaire is still one of the best-protected marine habitats in the world: Bonaire's shoreline (and the offshore island of Klein Bonaire) is under the careful management of the Bonaire National Marine Park. As the reefs are so fragile the park authority insists you carry out an orientation dive to assess your buoyancy control. There's an annual diving fee of US$25 (or a one-day pass of US$10), which goes towards the conservation of

the park; divers are encouraged to provide data on any turtle sightings by logging details on the website Ⓦwww.bonairenature.com. Spear-fishing is prohibited, as is anchoring boats on the reef – all of Bonaire's dive sites are marked with yellow buoys to which boats must tie a line.

While many of the world's popular coral reefs are suffering from damage caused by overcrowded dive sites and boat pollution, the Bonaire reefs are thriving. If there is such a thing as a model for sustainable diving, this is it: an unspoilt island where divers enjoy the dazzling underwater world, and at the same time help keep it that way.

Need to know *There is no ferry service between Bonaire and Aruba, Venezuela or Curaçao, so the only way to get there is by chartering a yacht or by air (see Ⓦwww.infobonaire.com for details plus a list of accommodation and dive operators). For more information on Bonaire's National Marine Park see Ⓦwww.stinapa.org, or for an overview of the island's dive sites visit Ⓦwww.bmp.org. Expect to pay around US$15–20 for a shore dive plus equipment rentals (US$8/day for regulators; US$10/day for snorkel, fin and mask; and US$12/ day for tanks, including weights).*

284 FOLLOW THE COFFEE ROUTE TO FINCA ESPERANZA VERDE, NICARAGUA

From the mountain city of Matagalpa in Nicaragua's northern highlands, the bus takes the unpaved road east to San Ramón, up to the cool, clear air of the cloud forest. At the village of Yúcul, you collect your belongings from the bus and walk uphill for an hour until you reach an organic farm, home to Nicaragua's trailblazing ecolodge.

At an altitude of 1220m and far from Nicaragua's tourism hotspots of Granada, León and San Juan, Finca Esperanza Verde (FEV) is a remarkable initiative. In 1998 a group of volunteers from North Carolina, with the help

of local farmers, transformed an abandoned farm into a thriving organic coffee co-operative. They replanted arabica beans, built an ecological coffee-processing facility and fashioned the muddy approach into a road. The coffee was sold back home in the US and with the profits they built a 26-bed ecolodge with double rooms and six-bed dorms, designed to showcase coffee production and provide an alternative income for local farmers. The lodge is built of handmade brick and other local materials, electricity is provided by solar panels and the water is spring-fed.

Guests can learn about coffee production and help pick and process the beans; if you wish you can then accompany the transportation of the coffee to Matagalpa, where it is sun-dried, graded, cupped and exported. The co-operative is now one of the farms on the tourist "coffee route" (Ⓦwww.vianica.com/visit/matagalpa) from Matagalpa, which also visits other coffee co-operatives in the region.

Coffee may be the main attraction at FEV, but you could easily just come here to relax at the lodge, enjoy the views and explore the area, home to a variety of wildlife including hundreds of species of birds, butterflies, mammals, trees and orchids (see FEV's website for the full list of species). The lodge organizes locally guided jungle treks to see howler monkeys, plus visits to waterfalls and a butterfly farm. However you choose to spend your time here, you'll be impressed by the difference this remote, rural coffee farm and ecolodge has made to the lives of the local farmers.

Need to know *FEV is 160km from the capital, Managua, and is open all year, though Nov–Feb is the best time to see coffee production. Week-long tour packages include four days at FEV and three days at a homestay in San Ramón. For further info including prices, reservations and directions from Managua see Ⓦwww.fincaesperanzaverde. org; ☎+505 772 5003. Ten percent of the lodge's income is invested in rural water projects and local schools.*

(From top) The main lodge at Finca Esperanza Verde; Coffee cherries; The view over the farm at Finca Esperanza Verde

Akan Tower, one of Jamaica's Great Huts; The view of Boston Beach; Interior of the Almond Tree hut

285 GREAT HUTS, JAMAICA

Stumbling through the thick vegetation that hides Great Huts' scattered thatched cabins and treehouses – some built of bamboo, some of mud – you might imagine that this was Africa rather than Jamaica. And that's very much the idea. Owner Paul Rhodes calls his unique accommodation "unvillas", to make the point that the Mediterranean townhouses found in many parts of Jamaica have little to do with its Afrocentric cultures. The huts are painted with African geometric designs and decorated with sculptures and paintings by local artists. The whole place is linked with its community, with twenty percent of all profits funding local projects such as supporting the homeless and elderly of nearby Port Antonio.

The family-friendly huts occupy an idyllic clifftop setting overlooking one of Jamaica's most unspoilt shores, Boston Beach. A favourite with locals, it's also the birthplace of jerk chicken, which sizzles enticingly on the grill at several stalls at the beach's edge. If you've had one drumstick too many, there's plenty of ways to work it off such as surfing and scuba diving, or you can horse-ride or hike to nearby waterfalls in the surrounding hills. Or, if you're really full, let a local guide paddle you slowly on a bamboo raft down the Rio Grande River.

Need to know Volunteers get to stay for just US$10 a night. For more on accommodation, activities, prices and reservations see Ⓦwww.greathuts.com; ☎+1 876 353 3388.

286 CONTRIBUTE TO THE EARTHDIVE LOG IN TOBAGO

Given that our knowledge about the effect of climate change on the oceans is still evolving, wouldn't it be great if divers made a note of what marine species they had seen on their dives, so we could develop a better picture of what is going on?

Thankfully this is already happening in the guise of Earthdive – a unique "citizen science" research project. The idea is that you put your dive to good use by recording sightings of what you see underwater, helping to build up a global snapshot of the world's marine species and providing valuable data for conservation organizations. If you want to participate, you can do so on Tobago, whose warm waters are home to manta rays (especially in April and May), south Atlantic coral (including one of the largest brain corals in the world at Keliston Drain dive site) and a variety of multicoloured tropical fish.

Tobago Dive Experience is a member of Earthdive and runs dives chiefly off the northeast coast of the island where there are forty dive sites, all within a 5–20min boat ride from the jetty in the fishing village of Speyside. It's based at Manta Lodge, a colonial-style beachside hotel with a training pool and dive shop, a 5min truck ride from Speyside Bay. After a day's diving, you can feast on salted fish in the lodge's restaurant then move to the bar for several varieties of local rum.

Divers in 119 countries have already joined Earthdive. The recording process on its website (Wwww.earthdive.com) is very simple: once you've registered, choose where you dived and tick off the fish and coral that you saw from the list provided. It's especially useful to record the key "indicator species" at the dive site, whose absence can alert scientists to any environmental pressures these species may be suffering, such as pollution and overfishing. And next time you dive, as well as following that well-known diving adage "plan the dive and dive the plan", add "see it, log it, map it".

Need to know *For info on dive courses, prices and bookings see Wwww.tobagodiveexperience. com; T+868 660 4888. For activities, prices and room reservations at Manta Lodge see Wwww. mantalodge.com; T+868 660 5268.*

287 HIDEAWAY IN THE HILLS AT KIDO, GRENADA

If you're willing to make the trek, Kido Ecological Research Station, lost in the dense forest of the island of Carriacou, is an escapist retreat like few others. From Grenada itself it takes two hours on the daily ferry, and when you disembark at Hillsborough, a one-street town that must rank as one of the world's smallest and most laid-back capitals, you've still got a 30min bus ride to reach Kido. But it's worth it: once there you're treated to a panoramic view from your elevated balcony out over the sea towards the atolls and reefs of Tobago Cays, with animal cries and birdsong the only noises. Accommodation-wise you have three options at Kido. The Octopus House sleeps four and has views out across the bay with a private set of steps down to the sea. Alternatively the Villa, tucked away amongst the foliage on a hill, is ideal for a family looking to get even further away from it all. Perhaps the most fun is the Pagoda, which sleeps up to ten and is popular with volunteers – with its trellised walls open to the elements your nights are cooled by the breezes coming up off the sea. Both the Pagoda and the Villa have their own kitchens, though guests are welcome to take advantage of the onsite restaurant serving vegetarian Italian and West Indian food.

Kido is a working wildlife research station and rescue sanctuary, and during the turtle-nesting season volunteers help the researchers between March and October, by tagging newborns, marking nests or patrolling the beaches by night. The station also makes a great base to explore the island's interior by foot or on mountain bike, on the lookout for such creatures as the red-legged tortoise or tree boa. Some of the best fauna and flora is underwater however, and Kido has its own catamaran to explore the waters around Carriacou, which are frequented by humpback whales from December to April and dolphins throughout the year.

Need to know *The Osprey ferry (Wwww. ospreylines.com) travels from St George in Grenada to Carriacou twice daily (and once a day at the weekend). For details of guided ecotours, rates and bookings see Wwww.kido-projects.com; T+473 443 7936.*

A red mangrove island with Magnificent Frigatebird nests, Sian Ka'an

288 IN THE WAKE OF THE MAYA, MEXICO

Mexico is awash with "Mayan experiences" of dubious authenticity. To escape the commercialization head to the 5000-square-kilometre Sian Ka'an Biosphere Reserve, the largest protected area in the Mexican Caribbean – home to 23 known archeological sites and a haven for pelicans, herons and white ibis.

The reserve's visitor centre, or Centro Ecológico Sian Ka'an – deep in mangrove and orchid forest near the Mayan ruins of Tulum, south of Cancún – is the main base for exploring the lagoons and mangrove channels the Maya once used as trading routes. An entrance fee of US$4 per person per day applies; additional revenue generated is used to fund conservation and education programmes.

The centre is run by an NGO and the staff are Maya, many of whom are trained as naturalist guides. You stay in simple wooden huts in the palm forest that are raised above the ground to allow ventilation, so no air-conditioning

is needed. The adjoining restaurant in a thatched dining area serves reasonably priced food, including *huevos motuleños* (fried eggs and tortillas with refried beans, salsa, cheese and peas). Solar and wind energy powers the complex, which also employs a waste-management system to ensure the wetland ecosystem isn't polluted.

The centre organizes several boat or kayak tours into the reserve on which you can visit unexcavated Mayan ruins and learn about the reserve's natural and Mayan history from experienced guides. If you've got time to spare, then the nine-day kayaking tour with Ecocolours Mexico, which includes camping for two nights on an island and two nights in a ranch, is highly recommended. On the fifth day the tour leaves the reserve so that you can go snorkelling at Gran Cenote near Tulum, visit the ancient pyramid at Chichén Itzá and then go to see the pink flamingos at Holbox Island in the Yum Balam Biosphere Reserve, staying the night in beachfront *cabañas* before returning to Cancún.

Need to know The Centro Ecológico Sian Ka'an is 17km south of Tulum. For details of activities, accommodation prices and reservations at the visitor centre see Ⓦwww.cesiak.org; ☎+52 984 104 0522. Kayaking tours with Ecocolors begin at Cancún airport, from where you are collected. For prices, trip dates and reservations see Ⓦwww.ecotravelmexico.com; ☎+52 998 884 3667.

289 ISLAND-HOPPING IN THE CARIBBEAN

Flying is the quickest way to travel between the Caribbean islands, but travelling by boat is usually much cheaper, is certainly better in terms of your carbon footprint and enables you to make the most of the warm waters and sunshine. If you don't have the luxury of your own sailing boat, you can hire a yacht from any number of chartering companies (eg Ⓦwww.sunsail.co.uk or Ⓦwww.caribbeansail.com) – either with a crew or by yourself ("bareboat"). If you're on a budget but have plenty of time, you can work on a yacht for free passage (see p.376 for a list of resources). For some of the smaller uninhabited islands, yacht charters are the only way to reach them.

Alternatively, there are plenty of ways to travel by ferry, water taxi or mailboat between the islands. While there is not one single ferry service that covers the entire Caribbean, there are lots of inter-island ferry services – particularly around the Virgin Islands (see Ⓦwww.vinow.com/general_usvi/interisland_ferry), St Vincent and the Grenadines (see Ⓦwww.scubasvg.com/travel/ferryschedules.html) and the Bahamas. Discovery Cruise Line (Ⓦwww.discoverycruiseline.com) sails every day from Fort Lauderdale in Florida to Freeport on Grand Bahama Island (5hr 15min); and Bahamas Ferries (Ⓦwww.bahamasferries.com) operates a daily high-speed service from Nassau to North Eleuthera,

Harbour Island and Governers Harbour. Bahamas Ferries also offers a slower passenger-vehicle ferry service to Eleuthera, Exuma, Andros and Abaco. Additionally the Bahamas government operates about twenty mailboats, which carry cargo and passengers from Nassau to all the Out Islands – trips can vary from a few hours to several days (for up-to-date details and schedules ☎+242 323 2166).

Other excellent inter-island ferry services include two high-speed services between St Lucia, Martinique, Dominica and Guadeloupe (Ⓦwww.express-des-iles.com and Ⓦwww.brudey-freres.fr [both French only]); two services between St Barts, Saba and St Maarten (The Edge: ☎+599 544 2640 and The Voyager: Ⓦwww.voyager-st-barths.com); between Grenada, Carriacou and Petite Martinique (Ⓦwww.ospreylines.com); and between Trinidad and Tobago (see Ⓦwww.patnt.com/ferry_schedule.shtml).

Need to know For more information on ferry connections throughout the Caribbean see Ⓦwww.travellerspoint.com/guide/Caribbean_ferries.

One of the many inter-island ferry services; Grenadines coastline

MIX IT UP WITH THE LOCALS IN THE CARIBBEAN

Away from its sun-drenched beaches, palm-adorned resorts and colourful reefs, the real pulse of the Caribbean is found in the homes of the locals, and on the sometimes sleepy, sometimes vibrant streets. The following five experiences will give you a little taster of Caribbean life.

290 Get an "overstanding" of Rasta, Jamaica

One of the most common phrases you'll hear a Rasta say is "I and I". Often used in place of "You" or "I", it refers to the union of man and Jah (the Rasta word for God), and expresses their belief in the importance of community. A great place to learn about the Rasta way of life is at the mellow Riverside Cool Cottages, run by Ras Solomon Jackson (known as Mokko), Doret and their four children. You'll enjoy delicious vegetarian food – what the Rastas call *ital* – go walking into the surrounding forests, or hang out with the family and their friends. Staying in the rural community of Sunning Hill gives you the chance to move from a limited understanding of Rastafarian culture to an "overstanding" – their particular term for an enlightenment that raises one's consciousness.

Need to know *Sunning Hill is a 1hr drive east of Kingston. Mokko will happily arrange a cab for you. For more information, and to find out about other homestays, see* Ⓦ*www.worldstogethertravel.com.*

291 Root veg and culture, Jamaica

There are carnivals and festivals of all shapes and sizes all across the Caribbean, but few so wholly local as Jamaica's week-long Trelawny Yam Festival. First held in Albert Town in 1997, it's a celebration of all things to do with Jamaica's favourite vegetable – the unprepossessing, potato-like yam. The festival aims to promote the consumption of the vegetable and to thereby boost the local economy. Along with singing and dancing recitals by eager schoolchildren, there's the obligatory "biggest yam" competition, and the more unusual "most congenial man" – all played out against a constant backdrop of dub and reggae.

Need to know *Albert Town is 100km northwest of Kingston. There's no public bus but private minibuses leave from the bus station. For information about the festival and nature tours in the area see* Ⓦ*www.stea.net;* ☏*+876 610 0818.*

Jamaican rastafarian sporting typical headwear; Yams are the central attraction at the week-long Trelawny Yam Festival

292 Find the soul of Trinidad

Home to the largest carnival in the world outside Rio, Port of Spain is the heart and capital of Trinidad. But the island's soul remains in the countryside – in sleepy agricultural communities like Brasso Seco. Paria Springs Eco Community runs homestays here with local families, and offers tours around the surrounding rainforest. They will also take you up to Grand Rivière in the north of the island, a wind-battered beach beloved by surfers and visited once a year by leatherback turtles, who come ashore in their hundreds to lay their eggs. For those few nights everyone in the little village is on high alert, rescuing hatchlings that have taken a wrong turn away from the shore and fending off greedy predators.

Need to know *The village of Brasso Seco is 2hr east from Port of Spain. Few taxis will know where it is, so make sure you arrange with your hosts how to get there first. Homestays costs US$50 per person per night. For further info see* ⓦ*www. pariasprings.com;* ☎*+868 622 8826.*

293 Get back to the roots, Grenada

Impromptu parties are a regular occurrence in the Caribbean: often kicking off in the middle of the street, with heavy bass beats booming out of huge speakers, accompanied by dancing and liberal doses of local rum. Trouble is, you never know when and where they're happening – unless you're staying with a local. Homestays Grenada organizes stays with families all across Grenada – from the picturesque harbour of St George and the long Grande Anse beach to the remote northern village of Sauteurs. Closely involved in the daily life of the home and the community, guests will be treated like a member of the family. Homestays Grenada also runs a variety of "Roots Tours", which range from a traditional Rastafarian picnic and a visit to local artists to demonstrations of herbal medicine. You could even learn how to play the steel drums – your own noisy contribution to those spontaneous shindigs.

Need to know *Homestays cost between US$30 and US$120 per person per night. Most of the homes are on the main island of Grenada although there's also one on Petite Martiniquc. For details see* ⓦ*www. homestaysgrenada.com;* ☎*+473 444 5845.*

294 Get under Cuba's skin

Cuban families have been allowed to host tourists in their homes since 1997, and there are now several thousand such residences all over the island. Known as *casas particulares*, they vary from elegant suites in grandiose apartments redolent of the crumbling grandeur of Havana to a sparse and simple room in a modest bungalow deep in the countryside. Wherever you stay, this is the way to get to meet Cubans on their terms, away from the tourist hubs and the accompanying touts. When you're in the country, these touts will constantly try to persuade you to stay in various *casas* so you're better off booking ahead – try the Cuba Casa website (ⓦwww. cubacasas.net), an extensive directory of the best *casas particulares*.

Squash for sale at a street market in Havana; Leatherback turtle hatchlings making their way into the sea for the first time at Grand Rivière, Trinidad

Need to know *The website also features detailed information on travelling around Cuba, including bus and train timetables.*

295 LA RUTA MOSKITIA, HONDURAS

The hardest thing about visiting the Rio Plátano Biosphere Reserve in northeastern Honduras is choosing where to spend your time: by the coast, inland on wide-open savannah or in the heart of the rainforest. Each setting is home to indigenous communities who have joined together to form a collective enterprise known as La Ruta Moskitia, which provides board and lodging and a range of activities in the reserve – the first place in Central America to be designated a World Heritage Site.

At the Yamari Savannah Cabañas you can go horse-riding across the plains of the Great Pine Savannah, meet Miskito guides who will teach you how to fish with nets, or explore creeks and lagoons from the comfort of a sit-on-top kayak. Jungle junkies, however, should head to Las Marías in the heart of the rainforest highlands (along the River Plátano), home to the Pech Indian community which organizes a variety of rainforest treks (from a couple of hours to a couple of days) to see monkeys, tapirs, birds and thousand-year-old petroglyphs carved into the rocks.

If you'd prefer cooler conditions, head to Belén on the Miskito Coast, where you stay just behind the beach at the Pawanka Cabañas (palm-thatched cabins) or at the Raista ecolodge near the country's first butterfly farm on the shores of the Ibans lagoon. Alternatively at Plaplaya and Batalla (both on the Garifuna Coast) you can see the hypnotic Garifuna drum-and-dance groups and the Plaplaya Sea Turtle Conservation Project.

Need to know For prices, reservations and details on how to reach the various destinations and communities see Ⓦwww.larutamoskitia.com; ☏+504 406 6782. Ten percent of revenues goes towards conservation projects in the reserve.

296 LAS TERRAZAS, CUBA

If you want a taste of life in the real Cuba (away from the all-inclusive resorts and state-of-the-art hotels) it's fairly easy to achieve by staying in private rooms (casas particulares – see p.229) and dining in local homes (paladares). Alternatively, one of the most harmonious and well-organized locally run places to stay is in the Sierra del Rosario reserve in the Guaniguanico range. Here, the Las Terrazas co-operative – a village established as a social project in 1971 and still with around a thousand residents – offers lodging, cafés, restaurants and trips into the surrounding reserve, where you can go swimming in natural pools, kayak on two lakes or go horse-riding and mountain-biking to visit coffee plantations.

The main place to stay at Las Terrazas is Hotel Moka, built in the Spanish colonial style around an ancient lime tree that climbs through two floors and up through the roof via a skylight. You can also stay in any of five villas comunitarias (casas particulares run by the hotel) in the heart of the village (where there are several cafés and restaurants that are part of a village cooperative), in two campsites near the natural pools, or in huts 13km away, which are convenient if you're trekking to San Claudio's waterfalls, where you can swim in natural pools at the foot of 20m cascades.

Need to know Las Terrazas is an hour's drive from Havana, 8km beyond the turn-off at Km 51 of the autopista. Unless you're staying at the hotel, there's a $4CUC charge to enter Las Terrazas, payable at a tollbooth at the entrance. For prices and reservations of Hotel Moka, community rooms and campsites, as well as opening times of cafés and restaurants and trips into Las Terrazas see Ⓦwww.lasterrazas.cu (Spanish only); ☏+53 7204 3739.

297 LIVE WITH THE MAYA, BELIZE

The world of the ancient Maya is an enduring draw for travellers, who flock to sites such as Tikal, Caracol and Chichén Itzá to marvel at the pyramidal temples, ball courts and glyphs. But the modern Maya, the descendants of those mighty jungle civilizations, are for the most part a people forgotten: in the Toledo district of Belize, for example, they comprise over half the population but four-fifths of them lie below the poverty line.

One programme in particular has sought to encourage tourism to the Mayan villages of southern Belize, giving them a chance to bolster their livelihoods. The Toledo Ecotourism Association (TEA) is managed by the participating Mayan communities – who elect their own chairman, treasurer and secretary every two years – and enables visitors to live in a purpose-built wooden lodge with eight bunk beds in the heart of each village. Guests take each of their meals in a villager's house, usually squatting around the *comal* (heated iron plate) with the kids, while mum cooks up a mix of tortillas, black beans, okra, avocado or chicken in *caldo* (a type of stew). Many of the Maya here speak English and are often happy to chat about their lives while you eat.

During the day there are plenty of guided activities to choose from, all led by villagers: tours of the village itself, of *milpas* (crop plots), of the jungle or of nearby ruins and caves; canoe trips; horse-riding excursions; birdwatching trips or craft-making demonstrations. It's a win-win situation: your guides know the area and culture intimately and eighty percent of your fees go direct to the village, with some retained for admin and to finance a communal fund for healthcare and education projects.

A five-star experience this is not – facilities in the villages are basic and you'll probably encounter a scorpion or spider – but this is tourism with the tour operator stripped out: you can spend your time with the Maya how you like. And as you swing in the hammock while the sun recedes over the village, and two excited children scamper up to you to tell you that dinner's ready for you, jungle life can feel pretty good.

Need to know *The TEA office is in the BTIA Information Center on Front Street in Punta Gorda, where you'll be advised on which village to visit (they host by rotation); all are accessible by public bus from the town. Accommodation plus three meals should cost around US$23 per day; activities are extra. It's a good idea to bring a torch, toilet roll, mosquito repellent and hiking boots. For further info and to arrange an itinerary see ⓦwww.southernbelize.com/tea.html or ⓦwww.plenty.org/mayan-ecotours/index.html; Ⓔteabelize@yahoo.com; Ⓣ+501 722 2531.*

(Clockwise from top left) Picking coconuts for an afternoon thirst-quencher; Villager cutting sugar cane in his milpa; Santa Elena village

298 MARVEL AT BIRDS IN TRINIDAD

Bananaquits and chachalacas might sound like trendy cocktails you'd order at a beach resort, but in fact they're just two of the hundreds of exotic birds native to Trinidad, the most biodiverse of the Caribbean islands. The best place to view the birdlife is from the Asa Wright Nature Centre, a reserve dedicated to wildlife conservation perched in the heights of the spectacular Northern Range. The centre's graceful terrace, hung with countless feeders, is a regular stop for squirrel cuckoos, toucans and parrots – and the vervain plant by reception attracts a plethora of hummingbirds. Various engaging bird trails have been cut into the surrounding dense rainforest, which you can follow accompanied by naturalist guides.

But it's not just birders who flock to see what wildlife can be found here. As Trinidad is the southernmost of the West Indies – at its nearest point it is just 11km from Venezuela – its flora and fauna is more typical of South America than the Caribbean. Despite being just 80km long, the island is home to more than two thousand species of flowering plant and over six hundred different butterflies. To really appreciate this diversity it's worth spending a night or two either in the main house or in one of the simple but comfortable cottages hidden away in the grounds. As you walk along the paths around Asa Wright, your senses are bombarded by a riot of smell and colour more overpowering than even the most potent of tropical cocktails. Little paper umbrellas are, admittedly, somewhat harder to find.

Need to know *The centre is 28km from Port of Spain. For directions, opening hours, admission rates, details of accommodation and birding packages visit Ⓦwww.asawright.org; ☎+1 868 667 5162.*

Bananaquits on coffee branch, Tobago

299 A DIFFERENT CARIBBEAN EXPERIENCE, DOMINICA

Dominica represents the alternative side to the Caribbean. No pearl-white beaches here: instead, mountain peaks dominate a landscape that is alive with bubbling volcanic fumaroles and towering waterfalls in dense rainforest. Dominica is a place where the absence of direct transatlantic flights has kept mass tourism away (other than day-visitors on cruise ships) and where the roads contain potholes that could swallow a whole banana tree.

Access to many of Dominica's natural attractions (such as Middleham Falls and the Emerald Pool) is being improved as part of the government's strategy to develop ecotourism on the island. For example, the formerly arduous trek up to the Boiling Lake is now much less of a slog thanks to the upgrading of the path en route to the lake through the sulphurous, moss- and lichen-covered Valley of Desolation.

Guided walks into the jungle are organized from Papillote, a locally run guesthouse in the south of the island, high up in the forest-covered Roseau Valley. Papillote was the first eco-inn on the island and is known throughout the Caribbean for its tropical garden nurtured by the owner, Anne Jno Baptiste, who over the past 25 years has developed an impressive collection of tree ferns, tropical fruits and orchids. The food is local and fresh, and there is the genuinely friendly touch that defines Dominica. The rooms range from simple doubles to much larger suites with private verandas overlooking the valley. There are also great views of the rainforest from the dining-room terrace, where the menu includes fruits from the organic garden, Creole chicken and home-made rum punch.

Fifteen minutes' walk away are the twin waterfalls of Trafalgar Falls, below which there's a natural bathing pool. And across the valley at Ti Kwen Glo Cho, an organic farm, there are hot-water tubs fed by bamboo pipes and sulphur-mud pools. But for post-adventure pampering to soothe the muscles, look no further than Papillotte's own four hot pools fed by a constant stream of volcanic mineral water from nearby springs. After a full day's hiking in the rainforest followed by a soak surrounded by lichen-covered statues of dragons and fish, it's hard to make any kind of comparison with the traditional Caribbean beach holiday, but it's easy not to worry too much about it.

Need to know *For further info including directions, rates and reservations see* Ⓦ*www. papillote.dm;* ☏*+1 767 448 2287.*

Trafalgar Falls, Dominica

ECOLODGES OF COSTA RICA

Almost a quarter of Costa Rica's land is protected in a well-organized network of national parks, private parks and reserves. Despite the large growth in tourism in recent years, by protecting its mountains, cloud forests, lakes, beaches and abundance of wildlife, Costa Rica remains Central America's premier ecotourism destination. The government's commitment to sustainable tourism (including its pioneering Certificate of Sustainable Tourism eco label, see p.248) has also helped develop dozens of genuine ecolodges that not only use low-carbon technologies but help to conserve biodiversity, promote low-impact activities and contribute to the economies of local communities. Here are our ten favourites.

300 Lapa Rios

Costa Rica's best-known luxury ecolodge has the maximum five stars in the government's Certificate of Sustainable Tourism, principally for its low-impact presence and protection of lowland tropical rainforest packed with rivers and waterfalls. The lodge has sixteen bungalows with sensational views of the forest and Pacific. Ⓦ*www.laparios.com*; ☏*+506 2735 5130.*

301 Pacuare Lodge

The most thrilling way to arrive at this lodge is by rafting the Pacuare River – one of the best white-water rivers in Central America. The lodge consists of thirteen cat-tail-thatched

wooden cabins (made by local Cabécar Indians) in the heart of the Talamanca Mountain Range, where you can explore the rainforest on foot or on horseback. Pacuare supports primary-school programmes and has helped to reintroduce howler monkeys to the forest. Ⓦ*www.junglelodgecostarica.com*; ☏*+506 2225 3939.*

302 Luna Nueva Lodge

Just 16km from the Arenal Volcano, this good-value ecolodge on an organic herbal farm is at the edge of a 200-square-kilometre conservation area of primary rainforest. Climb up an observation tower for views of the volcano, then join guided walking and horse-riding tours into the rainforest (including day-tours outside of the Arenal volcano area). Afterwards return for a soak in the natural spring-fed swimming pool or solar-heated hot tub before an authentic Costa Rican dinner looking out over the lush tropical gardens. Ⓦ*www.fincalunanuevalodge.com*; ☏*+506 2468 4006.*

303 La Cusinga Lodge

La Cusinga offers eleven simple, elegant cabins bordering 2.5 square kilometres of private rainforest reserve and the Ballena Marine National Park, established to protect humpback whales. There are locally guided trips into the forest while at the coast you can go snorkelling, surfing, kayaking, scuba diving or dolphin- and whale-watching. Ⓦ*www.lacusingalodge.com*; ☏*+506 2770 2549.*

In the lap of luxury at Lapa Rios ecolodge

304 Finca Rosa Blanca Country Inn

Sustainability and conservation go hand-in-hand at this luxury inn above the forests of the Central Valley, just half an hour from San José. The nine artistically decorated rooms, including two villas, have views of the coffee plantations and spring-fed swimming pool below. The Finca's certified guide, Manolo, runs naturalist walking tours; other activities include horse-riding and white-water rafting. Ⓦ*www.finca-rblanca.co.cr;* Ⓣ*+506 2269 9392.*

305 Bosque del Cabo

A great pick for wildlife enthusiasts. On the lodge's doorstep – where the rainforest meets the Pacific – is the Osa Peninsula, home to flocks of macaws, parrots, monkeys, coatis and sloths. Choose between ten solar-powered thatched bungalows or two houses along the bluff of Cabo Matapalo. Jungle cats (including pumas and jaguars) have been spotted on the property, so keep your eyes peeled. Ⓦ*www.bosquedelcabo. com;* Ⓣ*+506 735 5206.*

306 Danta Corcovado Lodge

The highlights here include the the Osa Peninsula rainforest and the Golfo Dulce (a tropical fjord). Run by a local family, this simple lodge is sited within a farm in Guadalupe, just 8km from the Los Patos sector of Corcovado National Park, and the closest place to the Guaymi Indigenous Reserve. Activities include kayaking through the mangroves and jungle walks by night. Ⓦ*www.dantacorcovado.net;* Ⓣ*+ 506 2735 1111.*

307 Costa Rica Treehouse Lodge

An intricately designed treehouse – built for up to six people – in and around a sangrillo tree behind Punta Uva beach, just south of Puerto Viejo in the province of Limón. Guests can explore the wilderness of the Gandoca-Manzanillo wildlife refuge by dugout canoe with indigenous guides or just lie in a hammock perched among the trees and admire the ocean views, deep in nature. Ⓦ*www.costaricatreehouse.com;* Ⓣ*+506 2750 0706.*

308 Cerro Escondido

The best way to arrive here is to arrange a horseback ride from Montaña Grande. Deep in the Karen Mogensen Reserve on the Nicoya Peninsula, this lodge has four simple teak *cabañas* from where guests can try guided birdwatching tours and excursions to the spectacular waterfall at Velo de Novia ("Bride's Veil"). *For further info see* Ⓦ*www. eco-indextourism. org; for reservations visit* Ⓦ*www. acluarcostarica.com;* Ⓣ*+506 2248 9470.*

309 Rara Avis Rainforest Lodge and Reserve

The only way to reach this remote lodge (other than to walk in 15km) is to ride for three hours on a tractor-pulled cart from Las Horquetas de Sarapiquí, a 90min drive from San José. Guests choose between a two-room riverside cabin or an eight-room lodge, in rustic rooms (each with a hot-water bathtub and balcony), a 5min walk from a waterfall in the heart of a thousand-square-kilometre tract of virgin rainforest. The reserve is home to bitterns, snowcaps, umbrella birds, great green macaws, parrots and toucans. Ⓦ*www.rara-avis.com;* Ⓣ*+506 2764 1111.*

Waterfall at Rara Avis in the heart of a private reserve; Rara Avis ecolodge

310 DAY-TRIPS WITH A DIFFERENCE AT PUERTA VERDE, MEXICO

Mountain biking through the jungle, swimming with whale sharks, kayaking in lagoons, trekking to Mayan ruins: these are the kinds of activities you'd probably expect to find in the Yucatán, but the day-trips organized by Kanché take you away from the crowds of a typical Cancún resort package and into the more remote parts of the peninsula.

Kanché works with fourteen co-operatives from rural communities in the north of Yucatán: twelve in the municipality of Lázaro Cárdenas (Quintana Roo) and two in the municipality of Valladolid (Yucatán). Four types of excursions are offered, though you can combine the itineraries and do them all in one go, staying out for three nights in cabins and with local families.

Kayaking and caving are just some of the activities Kanché offer that take you to less touristy parts of the Yucatán peninsula

On the first day you'll be taken to the caves of Nuevo Durango, where you will first visit a spider-monkey sanctuary and a Mayan music festival at Campamento Hidalgo. Day two includes climbing into the caves (with helmets, lamps, harnesses and rope), followed by mountain biking through the jungle, while on the third and fourth days you'll kayak in lagoons, take boat trips out to Isla Pájaros and camp out in the jungle, including a night expedition to see crocodiles.

The term "kanché" is used by the Maya to describe a wooden seed germinator that protects buds from insects and animals; as such the name suggests that the association will help to sow the seeds of sustainable development in these poor rural communities. By taking part in their tours, you'll help this enterprising initiative to make a genuine difference to the lives of the people they support.

Need to know *Tours include transportation, meals and bilingual guides. For itineraries, prices and reservations see ⓦwww.kanche.org; ☎+52 998 892 7767.*

311 PUEBLOS MANCOMUNADOS, MEXICO

Pine forests, wild mushrooms and a sunrise above clouds: not what you might associate with Mexico, better known for beaches, colonial cities and Aztec ruins. The mountains of the Sierra Norte, two hours' bus journey north of Oaxaca, are home to a cluster of villages, a semi-autonomous community known as "Pueblos Mancomunados" (meaning "united villages"), where you can stay in simple adobe *cabañas* called "tourist yu'u" (pronounced "you"). This tourist accommodation is a community business venture that has provided an alternative to logging and helped develop schools, roads and health posts in the region.

Here, at nearly 3000m altitude, it is cool but often sunny and, if abundant growth of lichen is proof, the air is exceptionally clean. After resting in a hammock, admiring the alpine scenery, you'll probably want to head off for an adventure. A guide from one of the villages will lead you through dappled groves on mountain bikes, horses or on foot, across kilometres of trails through pine forests, villages and valleys up to rocky viewpoints. The flora and fauna ranges by altitude and includes several endangered mammals, such as jaguar, spider monkey and tapir. In summer, you can pick baskets of wild shiitake or cep mushrooms.

Afterwards, sweat it out in a herb-scented *temazcal* – a Mexican sauna – before heading off to a kitchen-café in a villager's home. While donkeys bray and smoke curls into the crisp mountain air, you can tuck into soft tortillas, peppers stuffed with goat's cheese and refried beans, all washed down with herb and orange-peel liqueur.

Need to know *You can get to the Sierra Norte by bus from Oaxaca City (2hr). For details of excursions and rates see Ⓦwww.sierranorte.org. mx; ☏+52 951 514 8271. Cabañas cost M$479 (US$33) a night and sleep up to two adults and two children.*

312 DISCOVER SABA

A world away from the all-inclusive beach resorts, Saba is one of the unspoilt gems in the Caribbean. It's at the top of the Eastern Caribbean chain, northwest of St Kitts, and though only 13 square kilometres, there's a good mix of accommodation, a surprising number of places to eat, and several walking trails.

One of the best hikes, the aptly named Mount Scenery Trail, threads through thick rainforest up to the top of the island, where there are fabulous views. Ecolodge Rendez-Vous, a small, family-run resort, is just a short way up the trail: eleven individually themed solar-powered cottages (without phones or TV) scatter abandoned farmland, while the restaurant serves up great meals, which could include jerk chicken, papaya salad or the owner's home-made apple pie.

Saba is perhaps best known, however, for its exhilarating diving (you can book dive packages through Ecolodge Rendez-Vous). Like Bonaire (see p.222), a marine park extends around the entire island, administered by the Saba Conservation Foundation (Ⓦwww.sabapark. org). The charge to dive is US$3 per person, and there are 29 permanent dive moorings, all reachable in 5–20min by boat from Fort Bay, the main port in the southwest of the island. Lurking beneath the clear waters is a whole host of spiny, coloured or spongy creatures – lobsters, yellowtail snappers and stingrays,

along with majestic turtles and sharks.

The Saba Conservation Foundation also welcomes volunteers to help with conservation of both the island and its marine life. On land, jobs may include maintaining hiking trails, building footpaths and helping staff in the trail shop, while in the water, you can help out with maintenance of the moorings, monitor the status of the reefs, and conduct environmental education sessions for local schools and the community.

Need to know *The Edge ferry (Ⓦwww.stmaarten-activities.com; ☏+599 544 2640) runs Wed–Sun to and from Simpson Bay, St Maarten to Fort Bay, Saba (75–90min) or Dawn I' ferry (Ⓦwww.sabactransport. com; ☏+599 416 2299) runs Tues, Thurs and Sat from Fort Bay/Philipsburg to St Maarten. For prices and bookings at Ecolodge Rendez-Vous see Ⓦwww.ecolodge-saba.com; ☏+599 416 3888. Dive packages with PADI-recognized operators can be arranged from the lodge.*

Sunrise Cottage; View of the valley from the Mount Scenery Trail path on the Eastern Caribbean island of Saba

A Kuna woman, Panama

up programmes of labour for the community: cleaning the islands' footpaths (there are no cars on the three hundred or so islands) and maintaining the fresh water supply from the mainland. Visitors – who will need to book in advance as casual, unplanned arrivals are not encouraged – can stay at one of several breezy, beachside lodges and learn about village life. Guides will also paddle you in a dugout canoe to nearby islands and to the mainland to see where the men dig vegetable gardens.

The Kuna have protected their land from deforestation and overdevelopment and do not allow foreigners to buy it, hence all the island lodges are Kuna-owned. Some are on tiny palm-fringed specks with just one or two simple cabins, while others, such as Uaguinega, have accommodation (in wood and palm-leaf chalets with toilets and showers) for more than twenty visitors. Most are on privately owned islands, a short distance from the nearest island village. After a day's exploring in dugout canoe and by foot, visiting villages, learning about the animist religion, community history, handicrafts, fishing and agriculture, you may be lucky enough to hear the poet-historians recounting the myths of the Kuna as the evening draws in.

Need to know *The most practical way to access the San Blas archipelago is by air (Ⓦwww. aeroperlas.com). For info on the Kuna, tours, prices and reservations see Ⓦwww.uaguinega.com. Another accommodation option worth seeking out is Akwadup Lodge (Ⓦwww.sanblaslodge.com; ☎+507 263 7780).*

313 MEET THE KUNA, PANAMA

On Panama's Caribbean coast, the palm-fringed San Blas islands, more correctly known as Kuna Yala, are home to the indigenous Kuna people. Here the women wear gold nose-rings and colourful bangles, decorating their dresses with sewn layers of cloth, known as *molas*, for which they have become justly famous.

The Kuna are a strong, independent people who live quite separately from the rest of Panama. Chiefs lay down the laws from their hammocks in thatched meeting-houses, drawing

314 THE BEGINNINGS OF TOURISM IN EL SALVADOR

It's easy to miss El Salvador. The smallest country in Central America (and the only one without a Caribbean coastline), it's squeezed between Guatemala and Honduras on the south side of the pan-continental isthmus. The country's gruelling civil war in the 1980s has by and large deterred tourism, and its poorly developed infrastructure has made it a destination largely for the adventurous traveller. Those that do visit, however, are treated to lush lowlands, rugged mountain chains, cloud forests, towering volcanoes and 320km of uncrowded Pacific Coast coastline – with beaches, coves and bays as fine as anywhere in Central America.

Tours arranged by EcoExperiencias El Salvador are led by local guides in the departments of Sonsonate and Ahuachapán in the west of the country, and are designed to take visitors to see the best of El Salvador's cultural and natural heritage, from colonial markets and indigenous villages to birdwatching and hiking up to the summit of volcanoes. Itineraries include a 2hr walking tour of the streets of Nahuizalco (US$3), a 3hr jungle trek to the 40m-high Golondrinera waterfall (US$15) and a 2hr interpretative trip to the beaches of Los Cóbanos Protected Area, where you'll learn how to identify the shore's marine life – its crabs, shellfish, coral and seashells (US$7).

EcoExperiencias El Salvador is run by an informal group of travel agencies and businesses and was initially supported by USAID, though the aim is to hand it over to a local host to develop the network of trips throughout the country. It represents the green shoots of the kind of tourism that will benefit this struggling country: experiences focused on its plentiful natural assets and its people.

Need to know *The best time to visit is the dry season from November to March. There are regular buses from other Central American countries to El Salvador, such as Guatemala (18 daily; 5hr) and Honduras (5 daily; 6hr); for prices and timetables see* Ⓦ*www.ticabus.com. For prices, duration of tours, information on how to reach tour sites by bus and local contact details for EcoExperiencias El Salvador see* Ⓦ*www.elsalvadorexperience.com. A useful resource for information on travelling around El Salvador is* Ⓦ*www.elsalvador.travel.*

(From top) Pituba Beach, El Salvador; Eating frijoles in San Miguel; Volcan de Izalco

(From top left) The Dominican jungle; Handcrafted double bed at Crescent Moon Cabins; The wooden huts look out over the lush rainforest towards the sea

originally from Pennsylvania and fell in love with Dominica while teaching on the island. Ron – a former chef – learned many of the simple technologies you see at Crescent Moon from the locals: he discovered how to cook with the island's tropical fruits and vegetables, such as dasheen and tania; how to make cocoa by harvesting pods and drying them; and how to make charcoal from local wood. If you see Ron in the morning, expect him to be busy grinding and roasting fresh coffee; in the afternoon he'll be in his wellies wandering around the gardens plucking produce for the evening meal; later on he'll be in the kitchen preparing his latest dish, which might be peanut stew or home-made goat's-milk ice cream.

From the entrance, it's a short drive to take a dip at the Emerald Pool (a deep natural water basin beneath a waterfall), and the more adventurous can go on a four-hour hike through Morne Trois Pitons National Park's rainforest, taking in a 60m waterfall and even hiking with a local guide up to Boiling Lake, a natural cauldron of boiling water shrouded in mist. Back at Crescent Moon Cabins, a stone footpath leads into the forest or down to the river where you can have a dip; in the late evening it's refreshing to soak in the stone plunge-pool among the mango, pawpaw and almond trees.

And why Crescent Moon? Because Ron and Jean plant and harvest their garden according to the phases of the moon, just as the Dominicans do. Yet nothing they do is overly technical; they just do the simple green things well in a truly exceptional setting.

Need to know *There are infrequent buses from Roseau's New Market towards Emerald Pool – 20min uphill from Canefield ask the driver to drop you at the turn-off to Crescent Moon Cabins. Taxis from Roseau cost EC$50 (US$20). For further info including prices and bookings see ⓦwww.crescentmooncabins.com; ☎+1 767 449 3449. Guides can be hired for the walk up to Boiling Lake for about US$40 for the day from the trailhead, just past Titou Gorge.*

315 IN TUNE WITH THE MOON IN DOMINICA

Crescent Moon Cabins, a secluded and beautiful place to stay high in the Sylvania rainforest near Morne Trois Pitons National Park, is a lesson in self-sufficiency. Rainwater is used to fill the pools; juices come fresh from the fruits of the garden; and electricity is provided courtesy of hydro, wind and solar power. The four cosy wooden cabins are tucked into the side of the forested mountain, each with hammocks strung out on a balcony with panoramic views of the rainforest and distant sea.

The owners, Ron and Jean Viveralli, are

316 MONITOR WHALES OFF THE BAHAMAS

Ten metres away from where the whale surfaced less than a minute earlier your dinghy comes to a stop and lolls on the waves. Ahead of you a shiny sliver of grey slides through the waves – it doesn't look like much, but you know that it's a sperm whale, the world's largest carnivore, a creature that eats giant squids for breakfast. After a while it raises its head to breathe and seems to fix you with an eye the size of a melon. For the next quarter of an hour you sit transfixed, a kilometre from shore, until the whale flicks its massive tail and dives.

On an eleven-day Earthwatch volunteer trip to stay with marine biologist Diane Claridge on Abaco Island, you spend every other day out on the boat recording the behaviour of whales and dolphins that gather in the waters of the Bahama Banks to feed. Schools of dolphins often follow you, jumping into the air or across the boat's wake. Sometimes you'll spot reef sharks in the shallows. And if there are none of them around and a bit of time to kill, you can leap off and swim around the reefs.

On the days not tracking whales and dolphins you are back at the research station on the beach at Sandy Point, entering your data into the log and identifying animals by matching photos taken out at sea with ones stored in the files. It's an amazing insight into the life of a marine scientist, and will provide many more intimate encounters with cetaceans than any brief whale-watching trip can give you. An experience like this might change how you feel about volunteering, or even what you are doing with the rest of your life.

Need to know *The programme is available Jan–Feb and June–July. All meals are included, with cooking and cleaning done on a rota between the volunteers and members of Diane's team. For details and itineraries see Ⓦwww.earthwatch.org/ expeditions/claridge.html; ☎+44 (0) 1865 318 838.*

317 LEARN SPANISH IN NICARAGUA

Learning the lingo goes a long way when you're travelling in rural parts of Central and South America, so a Spanish language course makes for a great way to kick off your travels. You could, of course, learn Spanish in the laid-back quarters of downtown Quito, but come to La Mariposa Hotel, nestled in the tropical hills south of Nicaragua's capital Managua, and you'll also gain a glimpse of a different way of life in this little-visited country.

The hotel is based at an organic farm with simple but comfortable rooms that have a range of eco features, such as solar power for the lights and waste water to irrigate the garden. Courses cost US$300 full-board per person a week, including twenty hours of lessons, while extra individual tuition is US$8 per hour. There's no single-person supplement and you can request to stay in local homes if you wish.

You can stay for just a week, but you're encouraged to remain for longer to gain a better grasp of the language and see some of the local sights. Outside of lessons, students can try out guided walks, horse-riding or trips to Masaya Volcano – a live volcano where you can stroll around the crater or hire a guide and explore some of the 20km of trails and caves in the park. You can even trek to the volcano at night, when the lava glows in the moonlight like thick red treacle.

The two best cities to take in at the weekends are nearby Masaya – home to one of the country's best craft markets – and Granada, one of Nicaragua's most relaxing cities, with plenty of bars and restaurants. You'll return with a better knowledge of this off-the-beaten-track and often misunderstood country, and with your new-found language skills, the Spanish-speaking world will be your oyster.

Need to know *For directions, details of course programmes, activities, prices and bookings see Ⓦwww.mariposaspanishschool.com; ☎+505 418 4638.*

ALTERNATIVE CARIBBEAN BEACHES

The Caribbean idyll of a sandy beach backed by coconut palms is not hard to find: great swathes of spectacular beaches are commonplace throughout the islands, from Aruba to the Virgin Islands. Finding desert-island solitude, however, is trickier. Most of the best stretches of coastline on the popular islands have been developed to some degree with hotels, bars and motorized watersports. But there are places – still – where you can find yourself alone; you just have to know where to look. Here are three of our favourite alternative beaches.

318 Praslin Island, St Lucia

Small is beautiful. This tiny white-sand beach on Praslin Island on the east coast of St Lucia is perfect for a swim or perhaps a little wade before a picnic lunch. Your only company is likely to be the occasional bird and a few zandoli tè (the blue whiptail lizard found only on Praslin Island and Maria Island). The only access is by boat – about 10min from Praslin village (US$8 per person). If you can stir yourself from the idyll, nearby is the Frigate Islands Nature Reserve and just north, the Eastern Nature Trail – where you can go on a guided trail along the craggy coast.

Need to know *The boat to Praslin Island costs US$8 per person. A guided walk on the Eastern Nature Trail costs US$12 per person, plus an additional shared US$16 guide fee for groups. For reservations contact Eastern Tours (☎+758 455 3182).*

Riding in St Lucia

319 Rosalie Bay, Dominica

Dominica isn't known for its beaches: most visitors come here to hike into the island's dense jungle and visit towering waterfalls and emerald pools. Yet there are some lovely beaches so long as you're prepared to go off the beaten track. One of the most secluded is Rosalie Bay on the southeast coast: a wide, sweeping beach, backed by lush foliage, where the sand is black rather than golden – a consequence of the island's age-old volcanic activity. It faces the Atlantic so the waves are rougher than on the Caribbean coast, but the shore has a long shallow section that's ideal for a quick dip.

About a kilometre inland from the beach is Rosalie Forest Ecolodge. The camp is the brainchild of Jem Winston, an ex-London cabbie who fell in love with Dominica while backpacking and spent his twenties saving up to return to build his little patch of paradise. He learned the basics at a couple of workshops at the Centre for Alternative Technology in Wales (see p.20) and now provides guests with a choice of places to stay in Rosalie forest, including a solar-powered cottage, several wind-powered treehouses and two Mwena Carib Indian jungle cabins. Among a string of community-based initiatives, Jem organizes workshops on "sustainable living" and, with NGO funding, provides loans for locals to set up eco-friendly places of the future.

Need to know *For inter-island ferry services between Dominica and St Lucia, Martinique and Guadeloupe see p.227. Buses go from Roseau* *(opposite Jays bookstore in Kennedy Avenue) to Rosalie. For prices, reservations and directions to the lodge see ⓦwww.rosalieforest.com; ☎+1 767 446 1886.*

320 Treasure Beach, Jamaica

Away from the packed resorts of Montego Bay, Ocho Rios and Negril, tucked away in the southwest of Jamaica, Treasure Beach is a friendly, Bohemian place where you get a feel for the way of life of the local fishermen and farmers. It is in fact four loosely connected bays, which are strung out along 10km of fine sandy beaches, private coves and rocky shorelines. Though the area is not exactly unknown (in the busy months it can get crowded), there are lots of quiet spots where you can enjoy lounging on the beach without fear of being whacked by a frisbee.

Nearby is Ital Rest, two airy cottages within lush gardens that are home to over sixteen kinds of fruit trees. It's just a couple of minutes' walk from here to a secluded cove (close to the traditional fishing village of Great Bay) and beyond to several eateries at Treasure Beach where you can get pumpkin soup, salt fish, fresh lobster (in season) and jerk chicken. Think beach cafés, hammocks and a swagger in your step.

Need to know *A shared taxi from the town of Black River to Treasure Bay costs J$70 (US$1). For directions to Treasure Beach and accommodation options see ⓦwww. treasurebeach.net. For room prices and reservations at Ital Rest visit ⓦwww.italrest.com; ☎+1 876 421 8909.*

Treasure beach, Jamaica

321 ECO-CHIC AT MORGAN'S ROCK, NICARAGUA

Located in the department of Rivas, about 2hr 30min from Managua on Nicaragua's southwest coast, luxury ecolodge Morgan's Rock sits enveloped by a private nature reserve. Built as part of an extensive farming and reforestation project, the estate is home to howler monkeys, sloths, white-tipped deer and many bird species, while the protected beach is a nesting ground for sea turtles. The lodge itself is owned and run by a French family – the Poncons – who originally managed it with help from the owners of the ecolodge Lapa Rios, in Costa Rica (see p.234).

The resort comprises fifteen bungalows connected to the main lodge by a 110m

Eco-chic at Morgan's Rock;
View from the lodge of
Nicaragua's craggy coastline

suspension bridge across a forested canyon. Each luxurious bungalow has a king-sized bed, a comfortable sofa bed and a private deck overlooking the forest and ocean. Back at the central lodge there's an infinity pool and a fantastic restaurant serving wholesome meals. Many of the ingredients are

sourced from the estate – fish fresh from the estuary as well as rice, corn, wheat and fruits such as mango and papaya. Even the potent coffee comes from the Poncons' plantation, based in the north of the country. The enterprising team have also set up NicaFrance Foundation, a community scheme that has helped establish a bakery, supported a traditional folk-dance group and funded regular visits by doctors to schools in Matagalpa.

Nicaragua is fast attracting surfers and Morgan's Rock is conveniently placed close to some fantastic surf spots, such as Popoyo – you can organize a boat to take you there either from the lodge or from the nearby village of San Juan del Sur (50min). For landlubbers, there's plenty of hiking, mountain biking and horse-riding to get stuck into along the empty trails.

Need to know *Morgan's Rock is a 3hr drive south of Managua. For prices and bookings see Ⓦwww. morgansrock.com; ☎+506 232 6449. Morgan's Rock does not rent surfboards, but there are surf rentals in San Juan del Sur. The lodge works with Oceans Green – a joint UK and Nicaraguan surfing initiative, which makes surfboards from sustainable raw materials, handcrafted in Nicaragua. Order one of their "ecofoil" boards in the UK (☎+44 (0) 870 0421 712), and then collect it at Morgan's Rock for a 15 percent discount off the cost of your stay. For more information see Ⓦwww.oceangreen.org.*

322 WATCH THE CLOUDS AT RANCHO DE CALDERA, PANAMA

At Rancho de Caldera – a boutique resort in the mountains of Chiriqui on Panama's western coast – you can expect all the creature comforts of an upmarket hotel (including a swimming pool, walk-in showers and even air-conditioned rooms) yet the ranch is completely off-grid. It generates its own electricity using a combination of hydroelectric generators, solar panels and a wind turbine. It also purifies its own well water, grows vegetables in a bamboo-framed greenhouse, has its own fruit orchard (oranges,

limes, papayas, avocados, bananas) and the owners are currently growing jatropha plants to produce their own biodiesel fuel for a back-up generator and two diesel vehicles.

Close by to the ranch there are trails to five waterfalls, daily guided horse-riding excursions, white-water rafting, zip-lines through the tree canopy and coffee-farm tours, or you can spend a day at the beach (an hour away). In between all this the owners encourage you to take some time out to sit and watch the clouds. All rooms have a 6m wall of glass facing the mountains to the east, where you can catch the sunrise from the comfort of your king-size bed or just sit in the afternoon and gaze at the changing sky over the continental divide.

Need to know Minimum stay two nights. The ranch is 25 minutes' drive from Boquete. For prices, bookings and links to local activity operators in the region see ⓦranchocaldera.com; ☎+507 772 8040.

323 MEET THE MAYA AT COTTON TREE LODGE, BELIZE

Close to the small town of Punta Gorda in the remote Toledo district of southern Belize – and closer still to two Mayan villages – Cotton Tree Lodge is a jungle hideaway like few others; a place where luxury hasn't compromised involvement with the community.

A raised walkway connects the thatched *cabañas*, each with handcrafted interiors and private decks that overlook the tranquil Moho River, where guests are encouraged to take a dip or try out the rope swing. Birdsong will be your alarm call, and by day you can go on a jungle-medicine tour – on which you'll discover which plant prevents infidelity – or be shown the lodge's organic farm by its gardener, or take a hike up to and then into a nearby cave, once used by the Maya as a place of worship. After dinner in the main hotel lodge, which might include rice and beans, chicken *caldo* or fry jacks (all Belizean staples), you can swap stories over

a few beers in the adjacent bar or walk among the *cabañas* under the vivid stars amid the din of the jungle.

The environment and the Maya are integral to the philosophy behind Cotton Tree Lodge. The complex is solar-powered and a reforestation programme restores teak and mahogany trees to the area. In addition, the demonstration organic farm on the grounds has helped educate local farmers to use more efficient agricultural methods and create potable water systems. Some of the extended tours – such as the "Chocolate Week", learning about the cacao fruit in Mayan villages, visiting the growers' association and then making cocoa yourself – also directly benefit the Maya.

Get up close to some of the local wildlife from the comfort of a kayak; Kicking back at the Cotton Tree Lodge in southern Belize

A visit to Cotton Tree Lodge could involve little more than lying in your riverside hammock and kicking back in your *cabaña*, but that would be missing the point. Meeting the Maya and sharing their lives for a while – in their villages, churches, bars and daily work – is part of what makes this lodge memorable.

Need to know The lodge is about 25km from Punta Gorda; staff will collect you from there. For further info on excursions, rates and reservations see ⓦwww.cottontreelodge.com; ☎+501 670 0557.

A dive safari on board a catamaran allows you to choose the pick of the beaches away from the crowds; Scuba dive off the boat with the rays and turtles

324 SAIL AND DIVE IN THE GRENADINES, GRENADA

For many, the Grenadine islands in the Caribbean are the ultimate holiday destination: immaculate white beaches, balmy temperatures, turquoise seas and star-strewn night skies. But with such heavy tourist traffic, it's a challenge to preserve the beauty of the region. A holiday with Fab Safaris aboard the catamaran *Vaza Vezo* is a good start, however.

Equipped with a wind generator and solar panels to create all the electricity needed aboard, the sleek catamaran, powered along swiftly by large sails, is a very low-impact means of transport. Fresh drinking water is produced via a water generator and when you stop to explore an island – with the crew taking care not to damage the reefs when dropping anchor – you'll enjoy treks in the rainforest, visits to turtle sanctuaries and browsing for arts and crafts in local villages.

Back on board, it's not just plain sailing – there's scuba diving, too; whether experienced divers or beginners, guests can dive up to two times a day in the warm waters. Equipped with powerful torches, you can also dive at night, coming into contact with nocturnal creatures – such as lobsters, moray eels and octopuses – who scuttle and swim amongst the vibrantly coloured corals and anemones. After this excitement, you can relax on the deck with a potent rum cocktail before heading down to the luxurious cabins, complete with queen-sized bed.

Need to know Fab Safaris operate seven- and fourteen-day boat trips from Grenada. You can choose to cook your own food on board, or pay to have half- or full-board. For prices and more information see Ⓦwww.fabsafaris.co.uk.

325 SEE THE BIOLUMINESCENCE AT MOSQUITO BAY, PUERTO RICO

In 1688, French missionary Père Guy Tachard attempted to explain bioluminescence as: "the heat of the sun, which has…impregnated and filled the sea during the day with an infinity of fiery and luminous spirits. These spirits, after dark, reunite to pass out in a violent state". There's actually a lot more science behind it – simply speaking, it's the production of light by living organisms – but his explanation does induce some of the magic of this natural phenomenon.

Mosquito Bay, on the island of Vieques off Puerto Rico's east coast, is home to one of the brightest such displays in the world, attributed to its dinoflagellates (indigenous marine algae). Because this algae creates light only when disturbed, kayaking is the best way of seeing the light show – repeatedly dipping your paddle in the waters will summon up a mass of blue-green twinkles. Go with Travesias Isleñas Yureibo, a local bilingual tour operator, which has been organizing kayaking trips to the bay for a decade. Or Blue Caribe Kayaks, with whom you can spend the day snorkelling and then paddle through the bay at night.

You can stay at La Finca Caribe, a collection of rustic cottages with hammocks draped everywhere, or at the camp on Balneario Sun Bay – a 3km sweep of sand lined with coconut palms. Though if you time your trip right – on a moonless night (the light produced by the organisms can be disturbed if the moonlight is too strong) – you won't be doing much sleeping; you'll be transfixed by the mesmeric lights dancing above Mosquito Bay.

Need to know It's called Mosquito Bay for good reason, so take plenty of non-DEET-based repellent. Tours with Travesias Isleñas Yureibo cost US$25 per person and US$15 per child; for more information see Ⓦwww.viequestravelguide. com; ☏+1 939 630 1267. Full-day kayaking tours run by Blue Caribe Kayaks depart from Esperanza; for prices, bookings and lunar calendar see Ⓦwww.bluecaribeekayaks.com; ☏+1 787 741 2522. The Puerto Rican Port Authority runs a regular ferry service from Fajardo, Puerto Rico to Isabela Segunda, Vieques (1hr 15 min; ☏+1 800 981 2005), from where it's a short taxi ride to Balneario Sun Bay and Esperanza.

Eco labels and awards

Key in "ecolodge" or "ecotourism" into a search engine and it will throw up thousands of results, but how can you be sure that any are the genuine article? Similar search terms, such as "responsible", "sustainable" and "ethical" are becoming just as over-used (and abused) by websites and tourism companies looking to ride the green wave. Travellers' feedback forums can be useful but you'll rarely find reviews on how green a place is. After all, who wants to spend their holidays sticking their nose into recycling bins? An increasing number of websites claim to point you in the right direction yet often these are merely portals to places that claim they are green; few of them have actually sent someone to check out whether they deliver on what they promise.

So how can you tell the green from the greenwash? One of the best indicators is whether the business has been awarded an eco label. If it has then you know that a qualified inspector has certified that the business is a worthy contender for a kitemark. There are over 150 tourism ecolabels worldwide, ranging from regional schemes to pan-continental programmes, yet there is no single international body responsible for providing a standard by which they operate. The following schemes are national schemes, which are often the most reliable as they allow you to compare like with like within a country.

Green Tourism Business Scheme (ⓦwww.green-business.co.uk) has vetted over two thousand tourism businesses in England and Scotland, from small B&Bs to luxury five-star hotels and visitor centres. The scheme requires owners to provide details on over 160 criteria, such as how they minimize their use of energy and water, reduce waste, contribute to conservation and facilitate customers' use of local transport. It sends out a qualified environmental auditor to visit each property before awarding them bronze, silver or gold awards. According to the scheme's chief inspector, Jon Proctor, the most impressive place on his books is Strattons Hotel and restaurant (see p.37).

Nature's Best (ⓦwww.naturensbasta.se) is a Swedish certification scheme that works with adventure- and nature-tour operators to help minimize their impact on the environment and protect wildlife. Approved holidays include dog-sledding, sea kayaking, white-water rafting, canoeing, timber rafting, wolf-tracking and horse-riding (see p.105).

Fair Trade in Tourism South Africa (ⓦwww.fairtourismsa.org.za) assesses travel businesses on fairtrade principles, such as whether they provide adequate wages and working conditions for their staff. It has certified over thirty South African businesses, including a backpackers' hostel in downtown Cape Town, an adventure park in the Eastern Cape and a luxury lodge in the Kruger National Park. See also p.178.

Australia's Ecotourism Certification (ⓦwww.ecotourism.org.au) has developed a comprehensive list of certified tours, accommodation and attractions in Australia. The best are awarded a certificate of "Advanced Ecotourism". It also runs an ecotourism guide qualification award.

Certificate in Sustainable Tourism (ⓦwww.turismo-sostenible.co.cr) has certified over fifty hotels in Costa Rica. Only four hotels have qualified for its maximum five-star rating, including Finca Rosa Blanca and Lapa Rios (see pp.234–235).

OTHER SCHEMES

EU Flower (Ⓦwww.ecolabel-tourism.eu) and **Green Key** (Ⓦwww. laclefverte.org) are both purely environmental ecolabels that certify hotels and campsites in Europe.

Blue Flag (Ⓦwww.blueflag.org) is a certification scheme awarded to over three thousand beaches and marines in Europe, Africa, New Zealand, Canada and the Caribbean.

La Clef Verte

AWARDS

Awards can be a useful guide to find those companies that are going the extra mile, but only when the awards themselves vet their nominations thoroughly. These two international awards each send an inspector to visit and examine their shortlisted finalists:

To Do! International Contest for Socially Responsible Tourism (Ⓦwww. todo-contest.org) Organized by the German-based Institute for Tourism and Development, these awards are given to one or two organizations a year for outstanding commitment to socially responsible tourism.

Tourism for Tomorrow Awards (Ⓦwww.tourismfortomorrow.com) Organized by The World Travel and Tourism Council, which awards one winner in each of four categories: destination stewardship, conservation, community benefit and global tourism business.

NATIONAL ECOTOURISM ORGANIZATIONS

Armenia Ⓦwww.ecotourismarmenia.com

Argentina Ⓦwww.aaeta.com.ar

Australia Ⓦwww.ecotourism.org.au

Benin Ⓦwww.ecobenin.africa-web.org

Belarus Ⓦruralbelarus.by

Brazil Ⓦwww.ecobrasil.org.br

Cambodia Ⓦwww.ccben.org

Costa Rica Ⓦwww.canaeco.com

France Ⓦwww.ecotourisme.info

Indonesia Ⓦwww.indecon.or.id

Israel Ⓦwww.ecotourism-israel.com

Japan Ⓦwww.japan-ecolodge.org

Kazakhstan Ⓦwww.eco-tourism.kz

Kenya Ⓦwww.ecotourismkenya.org

Laos Ⓦwww.ecotourismlaos.com

Mexico Ⓦwww.amtave.org

Namibia Ⓦwww.nacobta.com.na

Nepal Ⓦwww.keepnepal.org

New Zealand Ⓦwww.ecotourismnz.com

Norway Ⓦwww.ecotourismnorway.org

Pakistan Ⓦwww.ecotourism.org.pk

Panama Ⓦwww.ecotourismpanama.com

Philippines Ⓦwww.ecotourismphilippines.com

Romania Ⓦwww.eco-romania.ro

South Africa Ⓦwww.community-tourism-africa.com

Sri Lanka Ⓦwww.ecotourismsrilanka.net

Uganda Ⓦwww.ucota.or.ug

United States (and worldwide) Ⓦwww.ecotourism.org

VENEZUELA

GUYANA
SURINAME
FRENCH GUIANA

COLOMBIA

ECUADOR

PERU

BRAZIL

BOLIVIA

PARAGUAY

CHILE

URUGUAY

ARGENTINA

SOUTH AMERICA

326 Hike an alternative Inca Trail, Peru

327 Be one of the family at the Black Sheep Inn, Ecuador

328 Learn to dance in Rio de Janeiro, Brazil

329 Hire a Kawsay Wasi guide, Bolivia

330 See the cock-of-the-rock, Peru

331 Trek to the lost city of Teyuna, Colombia

332 Meet the river people of the Amazon, Brazil

333 Discover "The Lost World", Guyana

334 Visit Bolivia's Mapajo Community

335 Dome sweet dome, Patagonia

336 Steppe on a horse, Patagonia

337 Explore the Lake District, Patagonia

338 Paddles and pedals, Patagonia

339 The world's highest vineyard, Argentina

340 Adrenaline-fuelled excitement in Colombia

341 Ride with cowboys in Venezuela

342 Volunteer in the Pantanal, Brazil

343 Stay at the Refugio Ecológico Caiman, Brazil

344 See fair trade in action, Peru

345 Sani Lodge, Ecuador

346 Yachana Lodge, Ecuador

347 Napo Wildlife Center, Ecuador

348 Inkaterra Reserva Amazonica lodge, Peru

349 La Selva Ecolodge, Ecuador

350 Refugio Amazonas, Peru

351 Iwokrama, Guyana

352 Cristalino Jungle Lodge, Brazil

353 Amazonat Jungle Lodge, Brazil

354 Chalalán Lodge, Bolivia

355 Travel to conserve the Galápagos Islands, Ecuador

356 Visit the cloud forests of Ecuador

357 Meet the Huaorani, Ecuador

358 Community and conservation, Ecuador

359 Watch whales feeding in the Strait of Magellan

360 The simple life in Uruguay

326 HIKE AN ALTERNATIVE INCA TRAIL, PERU

The path to Choquequirao, a lesser known yet equally stunning alternative to the trail to Machu Picchu; The main square in Choquequirao

Every year the Inca Trail sells out. It's a good thing too – where once up to two thousand people trampled every day along the sacred trail to Machu Picchu in the high season (April–Sept), causing massive erosion of the path and ruins, now only five hundred permits are available per day (and because this includes support staff, in reality that's only two hundred trekkers).

Congratulations if you're one of the lucky ones to get a ticket – it's one of the most spectacular hikes in the world. If you're not, don't worry, as there are plenty of alternative treks available, usually far less crowded and often rivalling the Inca Trail for their sheer beauty. Among these is the Salkantay Trek, which leads to Machu Picchu via the Cordillera Vilcanota mountain range. The five-day trail begins south of Machu Picchu at Mollepata (2900m) and ascends through dry Andean grasslands for the first two days, during which the scenery is dominated by the impressive peaks of Salkantay (6271m) and Huamantay (5850m). On the third day you descend through a warm cloud forest passing hot springs and waterfalls, before finally reaching Aguas Calientes, rising at dawn to trek the final stretch up to Machu Picchu.

Another alternative is to miss out Machu Picchu altogether and trek to the ruins at Choquequirao ("cradle of gold" in Quechua). It's more remote, but arguably equally as important, as well preserved and as beautiful as its famous neighbour: for forty years (1536–72) the Manco Inca dynasty resisted the Spanish conquerors from this impressive fortress in the Vilcabamba range.

The trek from the north of the ruin takes nine days and begins at Huancacalle village – a community of tin shacks approximately six hours by minibus from Cusco. The first stop south is the Vitcos ruins – a classic ceremonial plaza lined with massive, lichen-covered Inca stone – and on to the canyon waterfall of Puma Chaca, before spending the second day climbing up through forest to the high-altitude desert at Choquetacarpo (4600m). The following three days you descend to a cloud forest, then climb to the village of Yanama and further up along vertiginous mountain ridges. You'll then pass through more forests and valleys, camping out on mountain ridges, before eventually arriving at Choquequirao – a combination of a central plaza, terraced buildings, small chambers and water channels. It's an awesome

sight, not least – like Machu Picchu – because of its incredible setting, high on a ridge above the Apurimac River Valley and surrounded by towering snow-capped peaks.

This is not a trek for the faint-hearted, but if you choose your timing well and conditions are right, your reward is a spectacular adventure. Arduous it may be, but by the time you arrive at this spectacular ruin, you know it has been worth every ounce of unconventional effort.

Need to know *May to September is the dry season in Peru (April & Oct are usually dry during the day with some rain at night). Whichever route you take, ensure you include at least three days at altitude before starting the trek, to acclimatize. This should be at a minimum of 3000m above sea level – most people spend it in Cusco (3400m) or at Lake Titicaca (3800m). For details of alternative treks to the Inca Trail see Ⓦwww.apus-peru.com; ☎+51 8423 2691. Details of porters' rights in Peru and elsewhere are at Ⓦwww.ippg.net.*

327 BE ONE OF THE FAMILY AT THE BLACK SHEEP INN, ECUADOR

Most visitors to Ecuador have to make a choice between which side of the country they have time to explore: either east into the Amazon Rainforest or south and west to the Andes and the Pacific Coast. The Black Sheep Inn – perched on a hillside just outside the rural Andean village of Chugchilán in central Ecuador – is for those who choose to head for the mountains.

Whether you come here by bike, bus or taxi, the journey up to the inn is an adventure in itself – negotiating wild backroads over mountain passes, passing llamas along the way. On a clear day you'll see the imposing peak of Mount Cotopaxi (5897m), the highest active volcano in the world. There are two routes to the inn from Quito via the busy Pan-American Highway: the southern route via Latacunga, Pujilí and Zumbahua (past the emerald crater Laguna Quilotoa) and the trickier northern route via

Toacazo and Sigchos. Check with the owners about local conditions before deciding which to take, especially in the rainy season. Eventually you'll reach the village of Chugchilán and the remote setting of the inn itself, perched on a hillside with magnificent views of patchwork fields and cloud forest.

Over the last fifteen years, the inn's two American owners have developed their property into a showcase for small-scale ecotourism: each room has recycling facilities and the lodge harvests rainwater and has a permaculture garden. Black Sheep Inn also has an excellent relationship with the nearby villagers, striking a comfortable balance between using their products and services while not changing their way of life for the sake of tourism. Volunteers come here to learn how ecotourism works and staying here is like being part of one big family: everyone eats together around a large table in the main lodge, tucking into delicious vegetarian meals followed by a spot of communal stargazing.

The pick of the many local hikes is the trek to Laguna Quilotoa, which includes visiting the indigenous village of Guayama, and descends via several switchback trails down to Río Toachi, known as the Grand Canyon of Ecuador. But if you really want to experience rural Andean life, take a bus to some of the local villages – though note that you're likely to share the ride with chickens, pigs and sheep. The area is popular for horse-riding (a local from Chugchilán runs trips across the *páramo*) and for mountain biking along the canyon's edge. The inn offers a ten percent discount if you arrive by bike, but if you've managed to cycle all this way, you should demand you get first dibs on the home-made chocolate brownies and banana bread, which are free for guests. Sound like family life?

Need to know *There are twice-daily buses from Quito (4–5hr) or you could share a private 4WD taxi for around US$100. For prices, activities and details of local transport see Ⓦwww.blacksheepinn. com; ☎+593 3281 4587.*

328 LEARN TO DANCE IN RIO DE JANEIRO

Do you know the difference between Samba no Pé and Samba de Gafieira? Or when to recognize the change in tempo from the Brazilian zouk to the Lambada zouk? If not, then Jingando Holidays offers excursions to learn the stepped patterns and subtle styles of Brazilian dance – as an individual or in a couple – from ballroom dancing to street-style funk, swinging Soltinho to salsa-style Forró.

Based in locally run guesthouses in the neighbourhood of Santa Teresa, guests are transported around the city in a combi-van. You'll spend the day learning how to perfect the moves and then put it all into practice in the local nightclubs, such as Lapa 40 Graus and Cachanga do Malandro, where many of the city's best dancers go on Friday nights.

Swirls of colour on the streets of Rio

Jingando (roughly translated as "X-factor") provides 25 percent of the funds needed to help a local NGO run a community centre in Julio Otoni, one of the poorest shanty towns in Rio. For a couple of afternoons, you'll help with a painting project, at a crèche, or on an out-of-school activities programme teaching the kids some of the moves you've learned. The holiday is all about sharing – you'll learn how to embrace the grace that comes so easily to Brazilians, while giving something back to their community.

Need to know *For prices of dancing holidays and details of volunteering projects see ⓦwww. jingandoholidays.com; ☏+44 (0) 208 877 1630.*

329 HIRE A KAWSAY WASI GUIDE, BOLIVIA

Bolivia's Carrasco National Park is home to over five thousand plant species and eight hundred different birds, yet it's all too easy to miss most of these if you don't know where to look. To help you make the most of your time in the park, hire a guide from Kawsay Wasi, a partnership of naturalists from the park's local communities: Bateón, San Mateo Alto, El Palmar, Ivirizu, Km. 118, Muyurina and Bolívar.

All fifteen of Kawsay Wasi's guides have been trained as part of a Conservation International-sponsored programme. They have each had a whopping 720 hours of training, which includes site visits to other successful ecotourism projects in Bolivia, such as Chalalán (see p.267).

The guides offer two types of trips: day-trips to the park's wildlife sanctuary (15min from the town of Villa Tunari) and overnight camping tours, including a three-day hike from an altitude of 4300m down to the Amazon Rainforest. Over seven hundred species of orchid have been identified on this latter trip. They'll help you identify a fair few.

Need to know *For contact details of guides and info on tours see ⓦwww.kawsaywasi.com; ☏+591 717 89 408.*

330 SEE THE COCK-OF-THE-ROCK, PERU

Few must-see birding experiences can be as easy as this. Just twenty minutes' walk from your cabin in the heart of the Peruvian jungle, you're treated to a daily appearance (at dawn and dusk) of Peru's national bird – the male cock-of-the-rock – as it performs an elaborate mating dance to attract females, dipping its prominent fan-shaped crested head while extending its wings.

A male Andean Cock-of-the-rock

Such a dependable sighting is due in no small part to the conservation status of this elegant bird's home, the Pampa Hermosa Reserve in the heart of the Peruvian cloud forest, where a ban on tree-felling has meant its numbers are flourishing. The ten cabins at the lodge are built with local materials in the traditional style of the Ashaninca jungle tribe; each has a double bed (plus bunkbed and two twin beds in a small loft) and bathroom, with hot water and electricity provided by hydro and solar power.

The reserve is also home to a variety of unusual animals from armadillos to porcupines, as well as a 600-year-old cedar tree, reputed to be one of the largest in Latin America. If you like wildlife-watching made easy, come to this successful example of where conservation is breeding convenience.

Need to know *The best time for viewing the cock-of-the-rock is September to November. Buses go from Lima to San Ramón (7hr) from where you'll be collected and taken to the lodge, by arrangement (2hr). For details of bus companies and directions by car from San Ramón, prices and reservations see ⓦwww.pampahermosalodge.com; ☏+51 225 1776.*

Jungle lodgings; Mutanshi village, en route to the lost city; Children at the village

331 TREK TO THE LOST CITY OF TEYUNA, COLOMBIA

La Ciudad Perdida, the lost city of the Tayrona people located in the Sierra Nevada de Santa Marta in northern Colombia, may not seem so lost anymore – tour groups arrive here on a weekly basis all year round. But the arduous six-day trek it takes to get there and back across mountain, river and jungle terrain ensures that this ancient city, one of the most significant pre-Columbian archeological sites in the Americas, still retains an air of mystery and adventure.

With origins dating as far back as 700 AD, the city and its terraces – which took roughly two centuries to construct – lay abandoned until they were rediscovered by treasure hunters in 1972. Once the government had quashed the resulting flurry of looting and grave robbery, archeologists moved in and were able to reveal the full extent of the site, a sophisticated political and agricultural centre housing around four hundred families and known to its indigenous population as Teyuna, meaning "mother nature".

It's only possible to reach the lost city on a guided trek with one of three tour companies operating out of Santa Marta or nearby Taganga, about a four-hour drive from the beautiful city of Cartagena (a world-class tourist attraction in its own right). A typical trek lasts six days and five nights and leads you through some of the most spectacular scenery Colombia, if not South America, has to offer. Hiking up mountainsides, scrambling over rock faces and wading across icy rivers is not for the faint-hearted, and the night stopovers in hammocks with river baths perhaps not for those with a penchant for luxury. But by the third day of mud and mosquitoes, your efforts are rewarded when a river crossing brings you to the foot of 1200 steps, literally carved out of the mountain and drenched in thick jungle foliage.

After a breathless climb, spurred on by anticipation and tour group camaraderie, you arrive at a series of terraces marking the start of the lost city of Teyuna. Not all of the terraces have been uncovered and excavations are still in progress but the main terrace, which once belonged to the head shaman, is in full view in all its verdant glory. It is thought the Tayrona people lived in this area for around eight hundred years before the arrival of the Spanish and their devastating diseases. Intriguingly, the descendants of Teyuna, the local Arhuaca, Kogui and Sanká tribes, knew of the city's existence all along, but kept quiet.

Perhaps inevitably, this beautiful region is still home to cocaine production and all its associated problems. Not to mention a history of violence between right-wing paramilitaries and Marxist guerrillas for whom the impenetrable jungle provided the perfect hideout. But nowadays a heavy military presence along with impeccably organized tours ensures that all visitors need worry about are mosquito bites, blisters and the odd wild pig. Indeed, this is another example of tourism providing a desperately needed alternative source of income for the local community, an issue perhaps more pertinent to Colombia than anywhere else.

Need to know *Tours depart regularly from Taganga or Santa Marta. The price of the six-day, five-night tour is COP550,000 (US$250), including transport, food, accommodation (hammocks), a guide and permits. Porters and mules carry cooking materials but hikers are expected to carry their clothes and other supplies. Sturdy walking shoes, strong mosquito repellent and water purification tablets are essential. For itineraries and rates see ⓦwww.sierratours-trekking.com (Spanish only) or ⓔinfo@ sierratours-trekking.com for more details.*

Crossing the river Buritaca; Terraces once home to the head shaman of Teyuna

332 MEET THE RIVER PEOPLE OF THE AMAZON, BRAZIL

Jungle lodges are ten-a-plenty in Peru and Ecuador, but there are surprisingly few in Brazil, given that so much of the country is home to the Amazon Rainforest. One of the few gems is Pousada Uakari, a floating lodge at the confluence of the rivers Japurá and Solimões in the heart of the enormous Mamirauá Reserve in northern Brazil, the largest protected area of flooded forest in the Amazon.

The local people in this region are known as Ribeirinhos (meaning "Amazonian River People"), whose livelihoods are based on fishing and agriculture. Guests at Uakari can join day-trips to visit one of their villages, led by a local guide who will help to explain their way of life.

During the flood season (May–July) you can also paddle in a small canoe along eleven trails to see red howler monkeys, squirrel monkeys and scarlet-faced white uakari monkeys (throughout the rest of the year the trails can be walked). You can also canoe on the Mamirauá Lake, where pink river dolphins, manatees and caimans swim among the submerged trees.

The lodge has ten thatched wooden cabins, built on floating timber. Each is basic but fairly comfortable, with two king-size beds, a bathroom (with hot-water shower) and a terrace facing the forest. Dinner is served in the main lodge building (expect lots of fresh fish, fruit and juices). The lodge has been designed with various environmentally friendly technologies, such as rainwater collection, solar power for lighting and water heating, and a sewage filtration system to limit its impact on the river habitat.

The reserve is the first place in Brazil where conservationists are working with Amazonian communities to involve them actively in conservation and tourism, as an alternative income to plundering natural resources. So by staying at this floating lodge, you will not only get to meet the river people and the abundant wildlife in this remote part of the Brazilian rainforest, but you'll be helping to test the waters, literally and metaphorically.

Need to know *Tefé – the gateway town to the reserve, from where you'll be collected and taken to the lodge by boat – can be reached by boat from the jungle city of Manaus in two days. Boats depart every day (except Wed) at around 10am. For the latest departure times, prices and reservations contact Manaus Port: ☏+55 923 621 4316. For prices, activities and reservations at Uakari Lodge see ⓦwww.uakarilodge.com.br; ☏+55 973 343 4160. UK-based Tribes Travel organizes package tours to the lodge; for prices and itineraries visit ⓦwww.tribes.co.uk; ☏+44 (0) 1728 685 971.*

Top: A bird's eye view of Pousada Uskari; Bottom: The riverside lodges at Pousada Uskari are built on floating timber

333 DISCOVER "THE LOST WORLD", GUYANA

You'd be forgiven if you don't know much about Guyana. Despite its many cultural and natural attractions (its flat-topped mountains are thought to have been the inspiration for Sir Arthur Conan Doyle's novel *The Lost World*), tourism here is still in its infancy. Lying north of Brazil, east of Venezuela and west of Suriname, it is home to one of the four pristine tropical rainforests left in the world, the Guiana Shield. There are nine distinct ethnic groups and the country's culture is more Caribbean than Latin American (it helped host the Cricket World Cup in 2007). It is also Latin America's only English-speaking country.

Georgetown-based travel company Wilderness Explorers has long known of the country's potential for adventure travel. For over fifteen years, it has organized tours to some of Guyana's hotspots, such as the Kaieteur Falls (five times the height of Niagara Falls) and the Essequibo River. It also runs trips to the cattle ranches at Rupununi, such as Rock View Lodge, where you can ride out with the *vaqueros* (local cowboys) and visit both the central forest reserves at Iwokrama (see p.267) and a community of Macushi Amerindians. With support from Wilderness Explorers, the Macushi have established a hammock camp from where you can canoe along the Burro Burro River to see giant river otters, tapirs and spider monkeys.

At Shell Beach Conservation Camp in northwest Guyana, you can see the work of a scientist who has persuaded the local Amerindians to turn from turtle hunters to protectors of the 145km stretch of coast, which is the breeding ground for four of the world's eight sea turtles: leatherback, green, hawksbill and olive ridley. So as not to disturb the turtles, you stay in basic thatched huts away from the beach, and either walk with guides to the nesting sites or go by boat under the cover of darkness.

Turtles and tribes – many of the kinds of experiences you find in Guyana are similar to those in South America or the Caribbean. But what is different about Guyana is that very few tourists have been there; this is still relatively uncharted territory.

Need to know Turtle nesting at Shell Beach Conservation Camp occurs between April and August. For prices, booking and itineraries for all trips run by Wilderness Explorers see Ⓦwww.wilderness-explorers.com; ☏+592 227 7698.

334 VISIT BOLIVIA'S MAPAJO COMMUNITY

On the border of La Paz and Beni, Mapajo Lodge is owned and operated by the communities of the Quiquibey River, who offer four- to six-day guided tours through the Pilón Lajas Reserve, a dense jungle of forests, streams and unexplored mountains packed with wildlife. Itineraries on offer include boat trips along the river to indigenous villages, where guests can learn traditional fishing methods, watch locals crafting bows and arrows, baskets and textiles, or go on canoe excursions by night.

To help you understand more about the biological and cultural diversity of the reserve, the lodge runs a visitor centre with a library and a small exhibition of arts and crafts. Accommodation is rustic: there are four twin-bed thatched cabins with hot-water showers, shared bathrooms (one cabin has a private bathroom) and a hammock, while water is piped in from a natural spring. It's not exactly eco-chic, but then the focus here is not on staying indoors – it's on discovering the unknown.

Need to know As the bus route is arduous and unreliable, the easiest way to get from La Paz to Rurrenabaque is by air (daily; 1hr), from where you canoe along the River Quiquibey to the Mapajo Lodge as part of the package (3hr). For prices, booking and details on activities see Ⓦwww.mapajo.com; ☏+591 3892 2317.

GREEN PATAGONIA

In the southernmost region of South America (in both Chile and Argentina), Patagonia is one of the world's most epic locations. It is a land of extremes, ranging from the vast, steppe-like plains in the east to the fringes of the Northern Patagonia Icecap and the high peaks of the Fitzroy Massif in the Argentinean Andes. The high season runs from December to February, but go in March and early April and you'll avoid the crowds, the persistent winds will have dropped and the magnificent autumnal colours of Patagonia's native forests will be on display. Below are four ways to get the most out of this magnificent wilderness.

Ecocamp's spectacular accommodation; fleece sheets and blankets keep you warm at night

335 Dome sweet dome

A remote, futuristic camp in Chile's Parque Nacional Torres del Paine. Tucked up in an igloo-like geodesic dome (made from sturdy galvanized iron and raised above the ground on a wooden base), guests can enjoy all the creature comforts of a hotel yet still have the wind-whistling-against-the-canvas experience of camping. Inside, the domes are high enough for you to stand upright; there are double or twin beds with fleece sheets and blankets, and the "suite" versions have a private bathroom. Heating comes from a wood stove and each dome has its own hydro-turbine and solar panels to provide electricity.

Ecocamp's owner, Cascada Expediciones, organizes a circular seven-day trek in the Torres del Paine that begins and ends at the

camp, taking in Lago Nordenskjold, Valle Francés, the glacial Lago de Grey, the eastern lakes and the gigantic granite monoliths of the Torres del Paine. From the top of this awesome range you'll feel like you're at the ends of the earth, though of course you're not: the Falkland Islands are only 800km away.

Need to know *Prices, bookings, and details of walking itineraries are at* Ⓦ*www.cascada.travel;* ☏*+56 2232 9878. Wilderness Journeys (*Ⓦ*www. wildernessjourneys.com;* ☏*+44 (0) 131 625 6635) also organizes a sixteen-day trekking holiday visiting the Torres del Paine, Fitzroy range and Parque Nacional Los Glaciares.*

336 Steppe on a horse

Ride across northern Patagonia on a nine-day wilderness horse-riding adventure, galloping across water meadows and rolling hills, passing through narrow rocky gorges and climbing up to high vantage points where condors soar overhead. The trip begins and ends at Estancia Heuchahue, a working cattle farm by the Río Aluminé in the Patagonian Steppes. The *estancia* is a centre for horse-riding – there are some eighty horses here – and is almost entirely self-sufficient: water for irrigation is gravity-fed from natural springs, all the electricity is provided by a hydro-turbine and fuel for hot water and heating comes from firewood on the farm.

Need to know *The trip starts at Chapelco Airport in San Martín de los Andes, by Lago Lacar in western Argentina. For prices and itineraries see* Ⓦ*www.equineadventures.co.uk;* ☏*+44 (0) 845 130 6981.*

337 Explore the Lake District

Just 35min south of Bariloche, the Lake District is one of the most accessible parts of northern Patagonia. Peuma Hue is a ranch at the southern tip of Lago Gutiérrez within the

In the saddle: let the horse do the hard work while you admire the stunning views

grounds of Nahuel Huapi, Argentina's biggest national park, where you stay in restored log cabins overlooking a forested creek and the valley of D'Agostini. The area is popular with anglers, and there are guided treks and horse-riding in the surrounding poplar-filled hills. The short walks around the *estancia* connect with the national park trails, which you can follow on multi-day treks using the park's mountain huts, plus there's white-water rafting and kayaking at the nearby Río Manso.

Need to know *For prices, directions, booking and details of accommodation and activities see* Ⓦ*www.peuma-hue.com;* ☏*+54 9294 4501 030.*

338 Paddles and pedals

Fitzroy Adventure Camp, 17km north of El Chaltén, is a great base from which to explore the Mount Fitzroy range – its eight cabins on the shore of Río de Las Vueltas have views of Mount Fitzroy's north face. The emphasis of the camp is on low-impact activities, so you can hire mountain bikes, canoes and kayaks for the day, or join a two-day canoe-and-camping descent of Río La Leona between Lago Viedma and Lago Argentino.

Need to know *For trekking routes and expedition details see* Ⓦ*www.fitzroyexpediciones.com.ar;* ☏*+54 2293 436 424.*

339 THE WORLD'S HIGHEST VINEYARD, ARGENTINA

Wine connoisseurs will tell you there are many things you can understand about a wine from its aroma, taste and look, including alcohol and tannin content, age and "vitality". But taste a Malbec produced from Bodega Colomé and you can also taste one other vital ingredient: altitude.

Estancia Colomé is the world's highest commercial vineyard. In the foothills of the Andes, it's the vision of Swiss art collector and winemaker Donald Hess, who has transformed a former bodega and vineyard in the Calchaquí Valley (2300m above sea level) into a five-star hotel and successful organic wine estate. There are nine lavishly decorated suites, each with their own fireplace and a private terrace with spectacular views of the mountains. You can take a tour of the vineyards and gardens, walk round a contemporary art museum, swim in a large outdoor pool or take a look at the huge hydroturbine, which produces eighty percent of the estate's electricity.

Most people, however, come to Colomé to taste its internationally renowned Malbec wines and learn about the estate's particular style of winemaking. Hess practises a form of biodynamic agriculture that coordinates organic planting with cycles of the moon; the vines are also watered with a traditional irrigation system whereby water is dispersed throughout the land by gravity, rather than using power-driven pressure hoses.

But does it all make for better wine? Organic wine aficionados seem to think so. The theory behind it is that the intense sunlight experienced at high altitude produces thicker grape skins that contain lots of different phenolic compounds in the wine. So expect "intense colour, fresh acidity and silky-smooth tannins".

Need to know *To get from Buenos Aires to Salta you can either fly (6 daily; 2hr) or catch a bus (hourly; 18hr) and then take the daily bus to Molinos (a scenic 4hr trip), from where you'll be collected, by arrangement. For prices, reservations and details of activities and accommodation see Ⓦwww.estanciacolome.com; ☎+54 (0) 3868 494 044.*

340 ADRENALINE-FUELLED EXCITEMENT IN COLOMBIA

Colombia has a reputation as the world's cocaine supplier but now another white stuff is also making headlines: water. Rafting and other adventure sports have taken off in places such as the Chicamocha canyon – and now a new

Estancia Colomé: the highest vineyard in the world

venture in the north, near the Caribbean coast, takes you on a joyride down torrents of snowmelt from the world's tallest coastal mountain range, the Sierra Nevada de Santa Marta.

After spending several years living with the indigenous Koguis people and poor communities of this area, anthropologist Fernando Tovar encouraged youths of the village of Don Diego, a scruffy roadside settlement, to help themselves out of the poverty trap. They saved up to buy three inflatable kayaks and Tovar organized some professional guiding training. Now tourism plays a key part in the local economy, with visitors coming to be led downriver for a couple of hours and then hiking up through cassava plantations and villages, past areas where coca once grew. The river is most exhilarating from September to November; from December to August there are a few small rapids but it is largely a leisurely float past tree-lined shores, where indigenous Koguis people come to fish and wash clothes.

Until recently, the only employment young men such as Jonathan González could find was in the narcotics industry. They would pick and process coca leaves into paste with noxious chemicals, which were afterwards discarded into the river. Now he is a tour guide. On the borders of nearby Tayrona National Park, other villagers have been given grants to build twenty basic one- and two-roomed *posadas* (thatched lodges), near waterfalls and wave-crashed beaches. People who once had no alternative to the violence-fuelled illegal drug trade are now finding a new means of income via tourism – from cocaine to kayaking, in other words.

Need to know *From the town of Santa Marta, take a bus to Don Diego (1hr) or arrange transport from your posada. Life jackets are provided, though you should have at least basic swimming ability. Whitewater rafting on the Don Diego River costs about COP57,000 (US$25) per person. A night at one of the twenty posadas costs about COP157,500 (US$70) including breakfast, for a double room. @alema@accionsocial.gov.co; ☏+57 3132 828 790 (ask for Pilar Ruiz).*

341 RIDE WITH COWBOYS IN VENEZUELA

Saddle up and ride with the weather-hardened cowboys of Venezuela's Wild West. From Hato Piñero, an 800-square-kilometre cattle ranch and nature reserve bordered by three rivers in the vast plains of Los Llanos, you can discover some of the area's rich wildlife on horseback, led by the *llaneros* (cattle ranchers). Jaguars, occlots and pumas may be hard to spot, but you've a good chance of seeing river dolphins, howler monkeys and numerous birds, including ospreys, hoatzins, roseate spoonbills and kingfishers.

Breakfast is a combination of pineapple, melon, coffee, local honey and fresh *arepas* (fried balls of maize bread), then it's off for a day's riding via the Hato Piñero's biological research station, which has carried out important conservation work for species including jaguar and tapir. After a day outdoors, guests return to the colonial-style country house, which is more like an elegant family home than a hotel, with stone floors and furniture made from local wood. The thirteen rustic rooms each have a bathroom (though there's no hot water) and guests eat together on trestle tables in the dining room – expect simple dishes, such as pumpkin soup and grilled chicken. Conservation and cowboys is an unlikely partnership. Come here to see how it works.

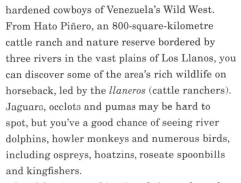

Cowboys farming Nelore cattle at Hato Pinero, Los Llanos

Need to know *Hato Piñero is in the central region of Cojedes, 350km southwest from Caracas (5–6hr by car). For prices and reservations see Ⓦwww.branger.com; ☏+58 212 991 8935. Last Frontiers (Ⓦwww.lastfrontiers.com; ☏+44 (0) 1296 653 000) organizes tailormade tours to Venezuela, including a 17-day tour of the Llanos (with 3 nights at Hato Piñero), Choroni, Quito and Galapagos Islands.*

342 VOLUNTEER IN THE PANTANAL, BRAZIL

Cattle-ranching used to be the main threat to the biodiversity of Brazil's Pantanal, the world's largest freshwater wetland (it's bigger than France). But now pollution, sport fishing and tourism (as well as a black market for exotic pets) are all contributing to the destruction of this unique habitat – a UNESCO World Heritage Site that's home to thirty million caimans alone.

You can help address these problems by joining one of four research projects organized by Earthwatch, a global conservation body that places volunteers at the heart of scientific research. You'll stay in shared accommodation on a ranch with other members of the expedition. Choose between working with: amphibians and reptiles (using a variety of methods to catch and record red-footed tortoises, false water cobras, tiny tree frogs and many other animals); bats, which involves catching them at night with mist nets (lightweight mesh netting that provides a safe technique for capturing them in flight); birds (there are 690 species in the Pantanal, including parrots, kingfishers and hummingbirds

(Clockwise from top) Caiman; Jaguar; Crested Caracara; Capybara; Parrot Snake

whose songs and calls volunteers tape); or otters (which participants video from the banks of rivers).

In an age of disappearing wetlands, proposals are in place to alter the natural flow of water in the Pantanal, which threatens to disturb its complex ecosystem. By helping to monitor the effects of human impact on its biodiversity, you will not only become familiar with perhaps the world's most amazing wetland, but also provide valuable data that could help save it from irreversible damage.

Need to know *Tours depart from Campo Grande in the state of Mato Grosso do Sul. Earthwatch has offices in the US, UK, Australia and Japan. For prices, booking and more details about each expedition see ⓦwww.earthwatch.org.*

343 STAY AT THE REFUGIO ECOLÓGICO CAIMAN, BRAZIL

Refugio Ecológico Caiman, a hotel and converted ranch, is in the south of the Pantanal, 263km from Campo Grande, the main access point into the wetland. The accommodation is suitably luxurious – thatch and adobe lodges with outdoor swimming pools and hammocks – but the Refugio is also the base for research into the ecology of the Pantanal. From here scientific projects on the jaguar, hyacinth macaw and blue-fronted parrot are managed, and you can hear presentations from biologists on their work.

Naturalist guides will take you on treks into the caiman-rich wetland of the Pantanal by Canadian canoe or on horse-riding trips, which enable you to access the marshes, impassable on foot or by vehicle. The Refugio is particularly popular with birders, who come to see the gilded sapphire, marsh seedeater, king vulture and yellow-faced parrot. The Pantanal is the natural world's equivalent of Disneyland: staying here can feel surreal at times, though always magical.

Need to know *Flights to Campo Grande can be included on a Brazil airpass, from US$411 for four flights. For prices, reservations and details of activities and projects at Refugio Ecológico Caiman see ⓦwww.caiman.com.br; ☎+55 1137 061 800. For trips elsewhere in the Pantanal see ⓦwww. pantanaltours.com; ☎+55 6733 218 303.*

344 SEE FAIR TRADE IN ACTION, PERU

Meet the people behind the products. British-based travel company Saddle Skedaddle (ⓦwww. skedaddle.co.uk) has joined forces with Fairtrade company Traidcraft to run two-week tours to Peru, among other destinations. Guests visit the suppliers of Fairtrade coffee in the Andes while stopping off en route in Lima, Cusco and the Sacred Valley (where accommodation is in a homestay as a guest of the small communities of Cuyo Grande and Cuyo Chico).

The coffee suppliers are small-scale farmers who live in the cloud-forest region of Santa María. You'll visit the coffee production area managed by the COCLA co-operative, learn from some of the workers about coffee processing and then stay overnight in their lodges. The tour continues to Machu Picchu and includes a trip on a luxury Orient Express train to Lake Titicaca, from where guests take a boat to Taquile Island to sojourn in a homestay with the Kollima and Huallani.

This trip has several purposes: visitors not only see some of the best sights in Peru but also supplement the income of farmers and rural families. A bit of give and take then; that's fair trade.

Need to know *Tours depart in August and September. For tour details, prices and booking see ⓦwww.traidcraft-tours.com; ☎+44 (0) 191 265 1110.*

JUNGLE LODGES

The Amazon Rainforest is the stuff of dreams: there are iridescent butterflies the size of your hand, deafening waterfalls that cascade into emerald pools, indigenous tribes who hunt with blowpipes, and as many different kinds of exotic plants and birds as you'll find anywhere on earth. The remoteness of most jungle lodges means they have to be self-reliant for electricity, food and water, and many now organize guided treks that promote conservation of the jungle's biodiversity. They also bring much-needed income to remote communities and provide visitors with an insight into their struggle with logging and oil companies. Below are our ten favourites.

345 Sani Lodge, Ecuador

Ten lakeside, thatch-roofed *cabañas* owned and operated by the Sani Isla community in a wildlife-rich corridor of rainforest between the Cuyabeno Reserve and the Yasuni National Park. Fredy is the general manager, Manuel the chef, and Domingo and Guillermo will take you to see some of the region's 1500 species of trees, five hundred species of tropical birds and thousand species of butterflies.
Ⓦ*www.sanilodge.com;* ☎*+593 2255 8881.*

Rope bridge at Inkaterra Reserva Amazonica Lodge, Peru

346 Yachana Lodge, Ecuador

This one is for chocoholics. Yachana ("Place of Learning"), surrounded by 17 square kilometres of protected forest, is where Yachana Gourmet cacao (Ⓦwww.yachanagourmet.com) is grown. Here you can learn how chocolate is made from freshly picked cacao beans, go river swimming, or join jungle treks with indigenous guides to nearby waterfalls and Yachana villages.
Ⓦ*www.yachana.com;* ☎*+593 2252 3777.*

347 Napo Wildlife Center, Ecuador

Owned by the Añangua Quichua community, this luxury lodge on the banks of the Napo River supports the conservation of 200 square kilometres of Yasuní National Park – a UNESCO Biosphere Reserve and the largest tract of tropical rainforest in Ecuador. There are several clay licks near the lodge where you can see parrots and macaws, and a short trek away is a 36m-high canopy tower that will get you closer to toucans as well as spider and howler monkeys.
Ⓦ*www.napowildlifecenter.com;* ☎*+44 (0) 800 032 5771.*

348 Inkaterra Reserva Amazonica lodge, Peru

Come to this luxury lodge in the Tambopata National Reserve if you like your creature comforts: hot showers, "terracotta exfoliates", robes and rubber slippers are the order of the day here. Various excursions are available, including guided treks with professionally trained guides to a canopy walkway, Lake Sandoval and a nearby indigenous farm belonging to the Ese Eja community. Ⓦ*www.inkaterra.com/en/reserva-amazonica;* ☎*+44 (0) 800 458 7506.*

349 La Selva Ecolodge, Ecuador

Owned by an American (he rents the land from the indigenous community of Pilche), La Selva is one of the longest-running lodges in Ecuador, so expect a well-polished service; the food and

accommodation are first-class. Birding – led by local guides – is popular and you can try your hand (no pun intended) at piranha fishing. Ⓦ*laselvajunglelodge.com;* Ⓣ*+593 2254 5425.*

350 Refugio Amazonas, Peru

A good choice for families. Children aged 6–12 can go on short jungle trails where they'll learn to follow a map and take part in a treasure hunt for "the lost Brazil nut". Refugio Amazonas is run by Peruvian ecotourism company Rainforest Expeditions, in collaboration with the indigenous Ese-Eja community of Infierno in the Tambopata National Reserve. It is part of three interlinked lodges. Posadas Amazonas is the easiest to access, while the more intrepid can travel upriver (2.5hr) from Refugio Amazonas to the Tambopata Research Centre – home to the world's largest macaw clay lick. Ⓦ*www.perunature.com;* Ⓣ*+51 1421 8347.*

351 Iwokrama, Guyana

See conservation in action at the headquarters of the International Centre for Rainforest Conservation and Development, which in collaboration with the Makushi people, manages 3700 square kilometres of the Iwokrama Forest in central Guyana. The field station has five cabins, but you can also stay in basic satellite camps throughout the forest, including one that is 500m from the 30m-high Iwokrama canopy walkway. Ⓦ*www.iwokrama.org;* Ⓣ*+592 225 1504.*

352 Cristalino Jungle Lodge, Brazil

The focus at Cristalino is on learning about the riches of the rainforest from local guides – especially about birds and butterflies. And no wonder: the lodge's private reserve is home to six hundred bird species, a huge variety of butterflies and moths and some unusual wildlife, including jaguars, harpy eagles, capybaras and agoutis. A room in a dormitory starts from US$135 full-board per person per night, including transfers and activities, but for those with deeper pockets there are private bungalows (US$198–$298) with ceiling fans, double beds and private outdoor rest areas. Ⓦ*www.cristalinolodge. com.br;* Ⓣ*+55 6635 127 100.*

353 Amazonat Jungle Lodge, Brazil

One of the most accessible jungle lodges, Amazonat is two hours by road east from Manaus international airport, in a 50-square-kilometre private reserve. The owners run treks deep into the jungle and include courses on jungle survival. Ⓦ*www.amazonat. org;* Ⓣ*+55 1199 872 498.*

354 Chalalán Lodge, Bolivia

Conservation International's flagship community-run ecolodge in the Madidi National Park is managed and staffed by the indigenous Quechua-Tacana people. Learn from them about the medicinal qualities of plants and go on boat trips on the River Tuichi to see caimans, turtles and peccaries. Ⓦ*www.chalalan.com;* Ⓣ*+591 (0) 3892 2419.*

(Clockwise from top left) In the swing of things at Inkaterra Reserva Amazonica Lodge, Peru; Cristalino River; Spider monkey

Marine iguana, Galápagos Islands

355 TRAVEL TO CONSERVE THE GALÁPAGOS ISLANDS, ECUADOR

The Galápagos Islands, 1000km off the west coast of Ecuador, are a living laboratory of evolution, a fragile home to a collection of unique species. It's a sad truth then that if tourism wasn't providing an alternative income to the islands' fishing industry, it's likely the surrounding waters would be fished out. And with no fish, the seabird population would plummet and the island ecology would be devastated.

So tourism helps, but it can also add to the islands' woes if not managed responsibly – and unfortunately many operators here could do better. One clear exception is UK-based operator Discovery Initiatives, which arranges a two-week cruise around the islands in partnership with the Galápagos Conservation Trust and the Charles Darwin Research Station. On board a deluxe yacht, guests sail around the islands, hike up to the famous Sierra Negra volcano, see some of the last remaining wild tortoises on Isabela and learn about the Trust's turtle conservation efforts. All funds raised through the trip go to the Charles Darwin Research Station to support its conservation work.

Alternatively, there are several volunteering initiatives with conservation projects on the islands. The Ecuadorian organization Fundación Jatun Sacha runs short-term placements on San Cristóbal island, where you'll help local NGOs eradicate non-native plants. If you can spare longer, join a Global Vision International volunteering project, which last from five to thirteen weeks. Volunteers, based at the San Cristóbal Biological Station, help conservationists on reforestation projects. You'll be given Spanish classes and, once a week, hike to one of the tourist hotspots and help teach visitors about the islands' ecological issues.

Need to know *For prices and booking for the Discovery Initiatives cruise see Ⓦwww. discoveryinitiatives.co.uk; Ⓣ+44 (0) 1285 643 333. For prices, reservations and more info on volunteering in the Galápagos visit Ⓦwww. jatunsacha.org; Ⓣ+593 2243 2240 or Ⓦwww. gvi.co.uk; Ⓣ+44 (0) 1727 250 250. Galápagos Conservation Trust: Ⓦwww.gct.org. Charles Darwin Research Station: Ⓦwww.darwinfoundation.org.*

356 VISIT THE CLOUD FORESTS OF ECUADOR

Travelling from Quito, it's easy to make a beeline along the Pan-American Highway to Cotopaxi and west to the beaches of the Pacific Coast or east to the Amazon Rainforest. But that would mean missing out on the cloud forests of Ecuador, where you'll find some of the most fascinating birdlife in the country. Head 80km northwest from Quito and you come to Nanegal, home to Bosque Nublado Santa Lucía, a community-based organization formed by local *campesino* (farm worker) families who live in the heart of the virgin cloud forests of the Chocó Andean Bioregion.

Guests stay at the twenty-room Santa Lucía ecolodge – a simply furnished timber building (there's no electricity so candles provide the light) with shared bathrooms but wonderful views of the forest. Forty-five species of mammals inhabit the area, including pumas and the spectacled bear, and with over 390 species of birds, including endangered species like the wattled guan and plumbeous forest falcon, it's a twitcher's paradise. The families organize four- and six-day hiking tours into the forest or you can help out with some of the co-operative's conservation work – planting trees, maintaining paths or monitoring wildlife. But if that sounds too taxing (you are after all on holiday) then just relax in a hammock, sip a beer and watch the hummingbirds, with your head in the clouds.

Need to know *For directions, prices, itineraries and reservations see Ⓦwww.santaluciaecuador. com; Ⓣ+593 2215 7242.*

Local Huaorani guide Omene Paa leads the way along the Shiripuno River;
Learning the art of a hunter gatherer

357 MEET THE HUAORANI, ECUADOR

Dawn is a magical time in the rainforest. Especially just before the sun rises: nocturnal creatures have gone into hiding and there's a fragile period of peace before the forest reawakens. It's at this bewitching hour when you set off through the cool morning mist in a dugout canoe along the Shiripuno River to meet the Huaorani, a tribe of native Amerindians.

The Huaorani have long inhabited the headwaters of the Ecuadorian Amazon, hunting game with blowpipes and gathering food from the forest. They were the last of Ecuador's indigenous peoples to be contacted by missionaries – in 1956 – and they now mostly live in permanent settlements, though at least one clan continues to shun all contact with the outside world. Their chronicles tell of ancestors who escaped from cannibals and moved downriver a thousand years ago from what is now Brazil. At present their territory covers "an untouchable zone" of about 6000 square kilometres of rainforest in northwestern Ecuador – about a third of the size of their ancestral lands, thanks to encroachment by logging and oil companies.

On this trip you are taken to meet the small community of Quehueri'ono ("Cannibal River"), hunter-gatherers who live in the northwestern part of the Huaorani territory. Such a unique encounter is the result of years of consultation between their chief Moi Enomenga and an Ecuadorian travel company, Tropic EcoTours (see p.272). For twelve years, Tropic has run hiking tours with Moi, employing Quehueri'ono villagers as guides – a sign of its success is that a permanent ecolodge, used as a base for village trips, has now been built, with five cabins equipped with twin bed, shower and flush toilet.

As you approach their village (an hour's walk from the ecolodge), your guide whacks a fallen tree trunk with a stick to signal your arrival. But don't expect a welcome party: there will be no beating of drums; no-one will greet you with a refreshing face towel or a piña colada. The villagers are likely to be engrossed in their daily chores, making *chucula* (a sweet drink of ripe bananas) or *tepe* (an unfermented manioc drink), or lying on a hammock in the shade. Yet when you are introduced they welcome you warmly and often invite you to spend the whole afternoon with them, showing you how they make traditional handicrafts such as bags, woven hammocks, pots and necklaces.

For several days a Huaorani guide leads you through the rainforest, demonstrating how they use plants for medicine, shelter and clothes, and how to hunt monkeys by climbing up trees and firing poisoned darts from blowpipes. He'll also point out an astonishing variety of wildlife, including blue morpho butterflies, greater and lesser kiskadees and several species of Amazonian kingfishers; quite often you'll hear howler monkeys high up in the trees. Six hours downriver by canoe, guests camp at another village, Nenquepara, where you can swim at a beautiful waterfall and return for a simple meal of mashed plantain, rice and beans, prepared by the Huaorani.

On the final day you canoe to the Huaorani's territorial border, from where you're driven back to Coca (where there's an air route back to Quito) through land taken over by oil firms. The road was built to service a pipeline and the 2.5hr journey reveals the full effects of deforestation as you come across oil leaks and vast stretches of rainforest stripped bare. It's a sobering trip, in many ways a poignant reminder of the abundance of life you witnessed earlier.

The Huaorani have the phrase "wah poh nee" for anything that conveys understanding and appreciation. During your time with them you find yourself repeating it over and over again: when you see the flash of a kingfisher; when you arrive at a beautiful natural pool for bathing; when you've eaten a delicious meal made from ingredients found in the rainforest. But it also stays with you long after you've left their beautiful, unique and threatened home.

Need to know *To get there you are taken by minibus from Quito to Shell (6hr) then fly to the Shiripuno River airstrip (40min), from where you travel by canoe to the Huaorani ecolodge (45min). For itineraries, prices and booking for transport and accommodation see Ⓦwww.huaorani.com. Journey Latin America organizes package trips that include staying at the Huaorani ecolodge and accommodation in Quito; for prices and itineraries see Ⓦwww.journeylatinamerica.co.uk; ☎+44 (0) 20 8747 8315.*

The Huaorani sell their handmade crafts, such as necklaces and bracelets, to the few intrepid travellers who reach their remote villages; Need a basket? The Huaorani can whip one up in four minutes flat

358 COMMUNITY AND CONSERVATION, ECUADOR

Central America is famous for its ecotourism, yet Ecuador is fast becoming recognized as a centre for ecolodges and tours that are managed and run by local people, often in stunning settings – in the heart of the Amazon Rainforest, high up in the Andean mountains and among the mangroves on the Pacific coast.

The pick of these community-based trips are to Sani Lodge in the Amazon Rainforest; to Santa Lucía, a lodge in the cloud forests of the northwestern slopes of the Andes; and to Oyacachi, a mountain community in the Cayambe-Coca Ecological Reserve in northeastern Ecuador.

These and other tours can be organized through Quito-based company Tropic Ecotours. Run by Welshman Andy Drumm and an Ecuadorian, Jascivan Carvalho, the company has worked with indigenous communities for over a decade, developing small-scale trips that provide guests with an insight into the life of rural communities and the threat to indigenous lands caused by logging and oil extraction.

As well as pioneering trips in the Amazon to meet the Huaorani (see p.270), Tropic runs trips to meet the Secoya people, an ethnic minority of fewer than one thousand in the upper Amazon basin. Tropic only takes small numbers of guests to visit typical Secoya houses so as not to overwhelm the local communities. As a result, these unique adventures provide guests with a raw sense of discovery time and time again, while the local communities benefit from a regular supply of income for medicine and education.

Need to know *For details of programmes, prices and reservations see ⓦwww.tropiceco.com; ☏+593 2223 4594.*

359 WATCH WHALES FEEDING IN THE STRAIT OF MAGELLAN

It's all part of the nature of things, but herring don't stand a great chance of survival when there's a group of humpback whales circling in on them. These enormous marine mammals work together to catch their prey – some blow bubbles under the herring while others grunt and scream to scare them up to the surface. When the bubbles rise up through the water, the school of herring form an inescapable tight ball, the cue for a whale to rise up and gulp down a healthy mouthful of fish. Job done.

This remarkable spectacle is known as "bubblenet feeding" and you have a good chance of seeing it in the Francisco Coloane Marine Park in the Strait of Magellan, at the southern tip of South America where the Atlantic and Pacific oceans collide. It's a historic setting, as the Strait was once an important navigable passage for mariners and explorers, especially before the Panama Canal was built. Nowadays it's home to Chile's first marine area, set up to protect the summer feeding-ground for humpback whales, sea lions and fur seals, and also to conserve the nesting areas for Magellanic penguins.

A local travel company, Whalesound, run by a group of conservationists and marine biologists, organizes three-day boat trips into the Strait of Magellan to observe the whales, other mammals and seabirds in the marine park. You stay out overnight at a campsite built with domed tents raised on wooden platforms (and connected by gangplanks) to minimize their impact on the environment. By staying at such a remote location – at the foot of the continent – you experience a strong sense of how harsh and wild a place this is, while across the continental divide lies Antarctica, one of the most fragile ecosystems on the planet. Conservation, in these parts, has a special meaning.

Need to know *Trips depart from Punta Arenas. For prices, booking and more details about Whalesound's support of scientific research see ⓦwww.whalesound.com; ☏+56 6171 0511.*

360 THE SIMPLE LIFE IN URUGUAY

Uruguay's most famous beach resort is the brash, glamorous Punta del Este, but if you prefer empty stretches of sand and utter tranquillity to yacht-filled harbours and posturing models, then head further up the Atlantic coast to the charming Cabo Polonio. A simple fishing village with just 140 residents, Cabo is comprised of small, rickety houses dotted arbitrarily among the white dunes, each facing a different direction. Seemingly fashioned from whatever was to hand at the time – patchworks of weathered driftwood and dulled corrugated iron – the hotch-potch of unique buildings appears inspired more by a child's drawing than an architect's blueprint. Designated a protected area in 2009, Cabo's makeshift allure is now safe from the reach of ill-planned development. A few homes boast electricity and out-of-place satellite dishes, but the vast majority continue to function as they have for generations, without technological frills.

A Bohemian hangout popular with musicians and artists, Cabo's calm beauty may spark your creative urges. During high season (mid-Dec to Feb) day-trippers flock in to visit the lighthouse and the neighbouring colony of sea lions smugly basking on the warm rocks. At other periods you'll have the beaches to yourself for long windswept walks, bracing dips in the ocean and cloud-gazing. Hire horses to ride up to aptly named panoramic viewpoint Buena Vista, or watch lightning fork across the horizon in distant electric storms.

To enjoy a taste of rustic life stay at Posada Santa Maradona (named in honour of Diego Maradona, Argentina's most celebrated footballer). A comfortable and solidly built house, it's a snug, off-grid retreat from the modern world. Pumping water from the well to flush the toilet reminds you to use it sparingly, and heating up a large pan of water on the stove for a bucket shower makes you appreciate every drop.

As night draws in guests gather round the crackling wood fire to play draughts, or chat to charismatic host Willy about Bob Dylan and independent cinema, before turning in to one of the three cozy attic rooms. In a spot this peaceful, the only thing that will rouse you from your sleep in the morning is the smell of freshly baked banana bread.

Need to know *Cabo Polonio is a 5hr bus ride from Montevideo. From the roadside (the driver will drop you where a dirt road to Cabo forks off the main route) a jeep awaits the bus for a 20min ride over the dunes. For rates, reservations and directions see ⓦwww.cabopolonio.com/restaurantesx.htm (Spanish only); ☎+598 9900 0305. For reservations at Posada Santa Maradona Ⓔposadasantamaradona@yahoo.com.ar or ☎+598 9418 9556.*

The small coastal village of Cabo Polonio is a popular Bohemian hangout; Enjoy the rustic vibe of the village; The all-but-deserted beach

Live with the locals

There's no better way to get to know a place than to stay with the local people. You get to experience life as they live it and benefit from their intimate knowledge of the area, while contributing to the local economy in the most direct way possible. And it's almost always cheaper than a hotel, and in some cases free. For a list of relevant websites relating to the types of accommodation detailed here see p.376.

HOSPITALITY EXCHANGES

Members of hospitality exchanges let visitors stay for free in their homes, and when they are travelling, look to stay in other people's. So if you're going to Brussels, you can log onto a site such as Ⓦwww. couchsurfing.com, discover how many members live in the city, read their profiles, get in touch with some of them and, if they are willing, stay with them while you're there. Almost all destinations have at least a few participants: at the last check Couchsurfing had 140 members registered in Azerbaijan, twelve in Papua New Guinea and two on Christmas Island.

It's one of those remarkable experiments in mutual altruism like Wikipedia that has taken off in no time at all. What sort of relationship you have with your hosts depends on the people involved. Some will simply let you in and out and leave you to yourself, while others will be keen to show you round their city and take you to their favourite bar or restaurant. Different organizations cater for specific groups, including cyclists and even Esperanto speakers. And once you start hosting in your own home, you'll begin to have the random encounters with foreigners you normally only get when on holiday, without having to leave your house.

HOUSESWAPPING

Think how many people go on holiday each year leaving their house empty. Houseswapping teams these people up, through organizations that charge an annual fee (typically less than £100/US$150) so that they can arrange to stay in each other's properties while on holiday. So, suppose you live in London and would like to go to Barcelona for a week next summer. You post your details on the site and if another member in Barcelona is keen to come to London, then you can arrange through the site to swap keys. In some cases people will even lend each other their cars or bicycles.

Less common is indirect swapping: for example you might stay in a house in Barcelona, while its owners stay in a villa in France, whose owners stay in an apartment in Prague, while the people from Prague come to stay in your home. While you don't get the direct contact with the homeowner of a direct houseswap, you may well get to meet their neighbours. And as houseswappers are generally eager for you to enjoy their home and area, they'll often leave you handy information and tips – a sort of personalized travel guide for your new locale.

HOMESTAYS

A homestay is exactly what it sounds like: living in someone's home (generally with the family there) and paying to do so. It might be an apartment similar to where you live at home, a bamboo hut in Vietnam, a thatched cabin in Fiji or a luxurious restored villa in the backwaters of Kerala. Sometimes these are intended to be long-term stays for language students or migrant workers, but short-term homestays for tourists are increasingly common, particularly in parts of the world where tourism is less developed. For many of the hosts, it is a way of profiting from tourism without the investment and commitment needed to build and run a hotel or lodge. For the visitor, experiences vary from just staying in a spare room, sometimes even with a separate entrance, to really feeling like part of the family, eating dinner with them, playing with the kids, even helping out around the house and garden. In some places (such as Wenhai in China or Ban Talae Nok in Thailand – see p.285 and p.294) villages have banded together to form a homestay co-operative, thus offering travellers more options and allowing villages to benefit from shared marketing.

AGRITURISMI OR FARMSTAYS

Farmers are increasingly supplementing their incomes by inviting guests to come and stay on their properties. In some cases it's possible to help out on the farm for a reduction in or instead of costs; organizations such as WWOOF (World Wide Opportunities on Organic Farms) run volunteer programmes that allow you to do just that. As you'd expect, the food on offer is usually fresh and organic. Some farmstays in the US and Australia are on ranches – a great chance to release your inner cowboy.

WWOOFing in Spain

RUSSIA

372

363

369

KAZAKHSTAN

368

MONGOLIA

370

374

375

TURKMENISTAN

376

UZBEKISTAN

TAJIKISTAN

KYRGYZSTAN

CHINA

N. KOREA

S. KOREA

377

JAPAN

379 378

364 365

366 367

362

373

380

361

371

HONG
KONG

CENTRAL AND EAST ASIA

361 Yangshuo Mountain Retreat, China

362 Explore the Commander Islands, Russia

363 Discover the island of Olkhon, Russia

364 Sleep at Yoshimizu, Tokyo

365 Eat organic at Mominoki House, Tokyo

366 Shop with the original green bag, Tokyo

367 Cycle round the city, Tokyo

368 Live with nomads, Mongolia

369 Volunteer at Lake Baikal, Russia

370 Discover dinosaurs in the Gobi, Mongolia

371 Pink dolphins in Hong Kong harbour

372 Take the Trans-Mongolian Express

373 Go trekking in northern Yunnan, China

374 Silk road by horse

375 Silk road by truck

376 Silk road by train

377 Explore the Snow Country, Japan

378 Build a treehouse in Japan

379 Watch dolphins with a former hunter, Japan

380 Follow the caravan route to Sideng, China

361 YANGSHUO MOUNTAIN RETREAT, CHINA

As you lie back on your balcony and wait for the heat of the day to subside, a couple under an umbrella float past on a bamboo raft. Behind them the pilot of their river taxi propels them smoothly through the water. The Yulong, a tributary of the Li River, carries them away on a gentle meander beside lush paddy fields broken by giant stands of bamboo. In the distance, domed limestone peaks reach towards the hazy sky.

Scenes like this at Yangshuo Mountain Retreat, an ecolodge in Guangxi Province, are difficult to tear yourself away from. Take one of the best rooms, overlooking the river, and you can enjoy them from bed via the floor-to-ceiling windows. Meals here don't encourage you to be active either: along with home-grown organic vegetables and fish from the river, there are local specialities such as snake hotpot or river snails.

Fortunately there are plenty of good reasons to get up. Moon Hill, a 380m limestone pinnacle with a half-moon-shaped hole through its centre, makes for a good trek. For climbers there are a further seventy thousand small peaks in this area to choose from, most little higher than a few hundred metres, and for the less energetic you can simply walk or cycle on the hotel's bikes through the paddy fields. But if all of that still seems like too much effort, you can just stick out your arm, hail a river taxi and drift off down the river.

Need to know *Yangshuo Mountain Retreat is a 70min drive from Guilin, a major stop on the train between Beijing (22hr) and Hanoi (17hr). For more on getting there, dining, local amenities and reservations see Ⓦwww.yangshuomountainretreat. com; ☎ + 86 (0) 7738 777 091.*

362 EXPLORE THE COMMANDER ISLANDS, RUSSIA

When people talk about the edge of the world, they're probably thinking of places like this. Sailing among the seventeen treeless Commander Islands in the icy Bering sea, where the only settlement has a population of 750 people, is a journey into an extreme wilderness of volcanic plateaux and legendary summer fogs which can blanket out all around for miles.

This wilderness is far from empty though. Around 200,000 northern fur seals spend their summer here to mate and give birth – a time when the islands seem covered in a squawking, writhing mass of blubber – and many humpbacks, sperm whales and orcas also migrate to these cold waters to feed. Over a million sea birds, including fulmars, guillemots, puffins and kittiwakes form huge colonies atop the coastal cliffs.

Dr Vladimir Sevostianov, a marine biologist with more then 25 years' experience

Boats and a balloon on the Yulong River in front of Yangshuo Mountain Retreat

of fieldwork in the region, leads two-week trips to discover the islands by sea and on foot. One day you might be bathing in a hot spring, the next following migrating whales or training your binoculars on colonies of sea birds on the cliffs above. Guests stay in simple cabins in Nickolskoe, the only town on the islands, or on board the research vessel, part-funded through tourist fees. As time is also spent meeting the local Aleut people you'll leave with some insight into the culture of those who make this inhospitable place their home.

In the end, though, man's impact here feels minimal. As you cruise in a dinghy along recently thawed rivers – a sea eagle circling overhead – watching brown bears come down the slopes to hunt for fish, it's the power of nature that overwhelms. These trips aim to keep it that way.

Need to know *All-inclusive fourteen-night tours (costing $4600 per person) run from July to September, with groups meeting either in Moscow or Petropavlovsk. For more on the people, art and fauna of the Commander Islands see Ⓦhome. comcast.net/~mishkabear/island;* ☏ *+7 250 598 6898*

363 DISCOVER THE ISLAND OF OLKHON, RUSSIA

When Lake Baikal freezes over, it's possible to drive from the mainland 12km over the ice to Olkhon, one of the world's largest lakebound islands. As you reach it (with a sense of relief that you didn't sink into the icy depths) you'll see the road's edge coloured with wooden poles tacked with fluttering ribbons: shamanic totems where it's customary to stop and make an offering of a few coins.

Jack Sheremetoff – a native of the nearby city of Irkutsk, where you can stay at his Baikaler Hostel – takes visitors from the hostel to explore this island, where you'll peer over precipitous cliffs and shine your torch into icicle-filled caves. Accommodation is in the wooden home of one of

Hiking over a frozen Lake Baikal

Jack's friends, where instead of running water there is a banya (a Russian sauna) to get clean. Dinners include omul, the salmon-like fish found only in these waters.

Driving around on the ice in a 4WD is an exhilarating experience, especially when you reach the vast crack below Cape Khoboy that marks where the northern Baikal and middle Baikal ice plates meet; a stark reminder of the vastness of the freezing waters below.

Need to know *Three-night or four-night tours start from Irkutsk, a major stop on the Trans-Siberian Railway, five days' travel from Moscow. Drives across the ice only take place in February and March, although tours to the island are available most of the year. For more on Baikaler Hostel as well as tour details see Ⓦwww.baikaler.com;* ☏ *+7 3952 929 686.*

GREEN TOKYO

Around five million foreigners and 420 million Japanese visit Tokyo each year, and while few come for an eco-getaway, it's perfectly possible to live green for a few days while in the city. As well as the suggestions below, you can also stay at the eco-friendly J-Hoppers backpackers' (🖰osaka. j-hoppers.com), tuck into fabulous vegetarian food at The Brown Rice Café (🖰www.brown.co.jp) or get some second-hand fashion bargains at the Togo Shrine market in Harajuku on Sundays. And don't forget to buy your own wooden chopsticks: the Japanese get through sixty million pairs of disposable chopsticks every day.

A room at Yoshimizu

364 Sleep at Yoshimizu

With no telephones, TVs or refrigerators in the rooms, Yoshimizu inn is the antithesis of the ultraconnected city on its doorstep – but then it is run by a former hippy who used to live at Woodstock in the 1960s. Right in the middle of the upmarket Ginza district, the eleven rooms combine zen simplicity with eco sensibilities, incorporating mud walls (which absorb moisture and odour), bamboo flooring and organic *tatami* mats. The traditional cuisine served up in the restaurant is organic and homely and before you realize it you'll have forgotten that you're in one of the world's busiest cities.

Need to know *For rates, reservations and info on getting there see 🖰www.yoshimizu.com; ☎+81 (0) 332 484 432.*

365 Eat organic at Mominoki House

Mominoki takes its organic principles seriously: it has its own farm and offers cooking lessons with the master chef (who is also the owner). The restaurant's simple, unfussy design makes it clear that nothing is to get in the way of appreciating the food, where dishes such as steamed organic Orara perch, fresh wakame seaweed and king prawn with sea-urchin cream sauce are all washed down with the finest organic sake or shochu.

Need to know *Mominoki is at 2-18-5 Jingūmae, Shibuya-ku; the nearest station is Meiji-jingūmae. Lunch costs around ¥1100 and dinner ¥2800. For menus and prices see 🖰www2.odn.ne.jp/ mominoki_house; ☎+81 (0) 334 059 144.*

366 Shop with the original green bag

Several hundred years before the "bag for life" became fashionable in Europe, the Japanese were using the *furoshiki*. It's essentially a large square of material, often made of cotton or silk and beautifully patterned, which you open out, put your supplies in, and then tie up using the kind of folding techniques that seem to come more naturally to the Japanese. They're having a bit of a renaissance in these eco-conscious times, and will cause more of a talking point back home than the latest reusable bag.

Need to know *Most department stores will stock furoshiki, with simple cotton fabrics selling for as little as ¥300 and pure silk anything up to ¥7500 or more. Try Matsuya in the Ginza district for everything from traditional to modern designs.*

367 Cycle round the city

It may not seem so at first glance but Tokyo is actually fairly bike-friendly, and it's highly satisfying to slowly free-wheel through the quiet backstreets and meander between serene parks such as Ueno, Yoyogi and Imperial Garden.

One of the best outfits for hire is Cool Bike (Ⓦwww.coolbike.jp), which delivers fold-up bikes to your hotel. You're allowed to take these on the metro – and if you're getting on at Shibuya station, you'll be helping the environment that little bit more, since footplates in the turnstiles harness the energy created by passengers walking over them and convert it into electricity.

Need to know *Cool Bikes rents cycles from ¥2000 yen a day. Helmets, panniers and baskets can also be hired. For cycle maps and further info on cycling in Tokyo see* Ⓦ*cycle-tokyo.cycling.jp.*

A pagoda in Ueno Park; A businessman relaxes under the cherry blossom in Yoyogi Park

368 LIVE WITH NOMADS, MONGOLIA

A hundred or so goats head off bleating their complaints in one direction, while a herd of cows tramps off in another. A boy of perhaps ten rides by on his horse, with no saddle. All around smoke rises from the fifteen or so gers spread across this high plain, surrounded by a ring of forested hills. Here in the Terelj National Park, fewer than 100km from the Mongolian capital Ulaan Bator, the only signs of industrialization are the occasional solar panel or motorbike.

A typical day on a trip with Ger to Ger, a non-profit organization that promotes grassroots tourism development, starts with a journey on horse or oxcart (typically of around 10km) from the ger where you spent the night onto your next resting post. The rest of the day – once the customary welcome of home-made biscuits, clotted cream and cups of milky tea is dispensed with – is spent doing what your new hosts do. That could mean helping them collect the sheep at dusk, milking horses (the local tipple is Airag, fermented mare's milk only slightly less alcoholic than vodka) or being taught how to use a bow and arrow.

It is highly rewarding but can be pretty exhausting. With no translator you have to communicate with a Mongolian phrasebook and any props such as family photographs you might have with you. Vegetarians may struggle with a diet that's almost exclusively meat and dairy, and are advised to bring some extra supplies along. But for anyone keen to get a taste of what travel was like before everyone spoke English and booked online, a few days riding across Mongolia should suffice.

Need to know *Ger to Ger's office is based in Ulaan Bator. Treks start with a three-hour introduction on what to expect, including a basic language lesson, before guests take a public bus to meet their first guide/host. All equipment can be hired from the main office. For itineraries and prices see ⓌWww.gertoger.org; ☏ +976 1131 3336.*

(From top) A Mongolian herder rounds up her goats; Inside a typical ger; With few roads, horses are the main form of transport

369 VOLUNTEER AT LAKE BAIKAL, RUSSIA

Called "the sacred sea" by those who live around it, Lake Baikal, in Siberia's southern steppes, is the oldest, deepest and most biologically diverse lake on Earth. To help protect it, the Great Baikal Trail Association is creating Russia's first environmental trail system round the lake's 2000km circumference, providing a focal point for ecological tourism in the region and an alternative to industrial development.

On two-week volunteer holidays throughout the summer months, the first half of each day is spent working on the trail, doing anything from clearing paths to constructing shelters, signs and other facilities for hikers. Afterwards you're free to walk around the lake, swim or just hang out with the other volunteers, a mix of locals and international visitors. Accommodation is in two-person tents (you'll need a sleeping bag) or sometimes in homestays. It's simple living – there are no showers or hot water and you cook for yourselves.

Along the way you'll get the chance to go to a Russian sauna, visit hot springs or try to spot the nerpa, the world's only freshwater seal. And while working alongside other volunteers snapping branches and clearing rocks makes for good camaraderie, this is also a wonderful place to get away from it all, a tranquil region whose vast still waters only accentuate the sense of calm.

Need to know *The programme runs from March until September in various locations around the lake at different times of the year. The Trans-Siberian Railway stops in both Irkutsk and Ulan Ude, where volunteers can be picked up. For more on what volunteering projects will involve and how to apply, see* *www.greatbaikaltrail. org.*

370 DISCOVER DINOSAURS IN THE GOBI, MONGOLIA

The chances of finding fossils in the area around the Three Camels Lodge in Mongolia's Gurvansaikhan National Park are still good, over eighty years since Roy Chapman (upon whom Indian Jones was based) first found dinosaur eggs here in 1921. The barren dunes of the surrounding Gobi are surprisingly full of animals, and not just the million-year-old ones: gazelles, camels and woolly-legged yaks can all be spotted on horse-riding, camel-trekking or hiking trips from the lodge. Or you can arrange a fossil-excavation trip to the Flaming Cliffs where Chapman made his discovery.

Guests at Three Camels sleep in traditional felt-lined gers, with organic meals from local farms and the lodge's garden served in a traditional wooden ger – built without nails. Three Camels is commited to improving locals' quality of life, running environmental conservation groups in schools and providing organic waste for use in local farms as pig-feed or compost.

When night falls you can drift off to the haunting sounds of Hoomi throat singers – who control mouth, larynx and abdomen to create multiple sounds in one voice – and hear in their strange harmonies the paradox of romance and rigour that epitomizes nomadic life in Asia's largest desert.

Need to know *The lodge is a 90min drive from Dalanzadgad, accessible by bus or air from Ulaan Bator. Accommodation costs from $120 per person a night. For more on lodging and activities see* *www.threecamellodge. com or* *www. nomadicexpeditions.com.*

Three camels in front, Three Camels Lodge behind

371 PINK DOLPHINS IN HONG KONG HARBOUR

Hong Kong – one of the most densely populated urban centres on Earth – hardly sounds like a place where you'd encounter dolphins. Pink dolphins at that: a surreal rose-coloured strain of river dolphin that became the official mascot for the handover of sovereignty in 1997.

Fantastic as they are, these fairytale creatures may not be with us much longer. Faced with chronic pollution of their waters, habitat loss and overfishing of their food sources, the population left in Hong Kong is now suspected to be fewer than a hundred. One of the best ways to help them survive is to take a boat trip with HK Dolphinwatch, which uses visitor fees to raise awareness of the dolphins' plight and demonstrate their economic value as a tourist attraction.

As you cruise through the crowded shipping lanes of one of the world's busiest harbours, your guide will explain about this curious creature and the threats it faces. All the while, everyone will be on the lookout for tell-tale flashes of pink in the water. If by chance you don't see them – and on 97 percent of tours you do – you'll get a free ride next time.

And in case you wonder why they're pink: the dolphins pump blood towards the surface of their skin to regulate their body temperature. Or less scientifically, they blush.

Pink dolphins in Hong Kong

Need to know *Trips take around three hours and run every Wednesday, Friday and Sunday; guests are picked up from Kowloon Hotel in Tsim Sha Tsui. For times, fares and bookings see Ⓦwww. hkdolphinwatch.com; Ⓣ +852 2984 1414.*

372 TAKE THE TRANS-MONGOLIAN EXPRESS

Even after seven unbroken days on a train from Moscow, nothing can prepare you for the Chinese border. As you pull into the platform, which is lit up in neon colours, a Chinese-tinged version of the Vienna Waltz comes blaring over the Tannoy. Trying to work out the cultural relevance of this is a hopeless task, as the tune soon changes – moving through the works of Richard Clayderman before finishing as you draw away with a stirring rendition of Beethoven's Fifth. As the music fades, the train rolls into a vast shed manned with soldiers and workers in hard hats. Each carriage is then separated and raised on hydraulics, the wheels removed and new narrower ones rolled into place to match the Chinese gauges – the whole process lasting almost two hours. All while the passengers are still on board.

This isn't the Trans-Siberian railway (which goes to Vladivostok) but its more tourist-friendly sister the Trans-Mongolian, which veers south just after Lake Baikal, stopping in Ulaan Bator on its way to Beijing. The first few days showcase the vastness of the forested Russian landscape, so that as you approach Lake Baikal early on day four, the sight of contours and water is a bit of relief – though it soon gives way to the barren steppe and then desert of Mongolia.

At times the train has quite a party atmosphere, with travellers playing cards, swapping anecdotes or eating and drinking in the restaurant car, which is replaced at each border by a new car serving food from and run by members of the country you're passing through. The best is the Mongolian, but more for the ornate woodcarvings and wall-hangings than because the food is much to remember.

Buy your ticket in Moscow and it is probably the best-value form of intercontinental transport imaginable, especially if you get one of the two-person "first class" cabins – en-suite and complete with armchair and writing desk. Along the way you can get off at various stations to stock up on provisions sold by women from the surrounding villages. Normally they offer fresh vegetables and fruit from their gardens, dried fish and various homemade rolls, dumplings and cakes.

Cheaper than flying, many times more fun and at a fraction of the environmental cost, the Trans-Mongolian really is the epitome of the adage that it's the journey that counts.

Need to know *The best place to start researching is ⓦwww. seat61.com. The weekly Trans-Mongolian train leaves Moscow for Beijing every Tuesday night. Fares start at around £220 one-way in a second-class four-berth cabin or £345 in a first-class two-berth. You can get tickets far cheaper than this (perhaps from as little as £150) if you buy them in Moscow but you'll have to be very time-flexible and patient. Real Russia (ⓦwww.realrussia.co.uk) is an efficient British/Russian agency that can organize the trip and process visas.*

The Moon-Embracing Pavilion at the Black Dragon Pool Park in Lijang, with snow-capped Jade Mountains behind

373 GO TREKKING IN NORTHERN YUNNAN, CHINA

The village of Wenhai, on the shores of the lake in Yunnan that shares its name, hasn't changed much since Marco Polo visited seven centuries ago. Dark wooden Naxi houses, their tiled roofs warped with age, line its cobbled streets. Women in loose-sleeved gowns and bright waistcoats laugh together in doorways, and husks of corn hang drying from racks, ready to be ground for flour.

Keen for tourists to visit but not wanting to lose the village's soul, the villagers have established several homestays, spending a portion of the income these generate on projects such as micro-hydroelectricity and improved health services. Guests can also choose to stay in the twenty-bed Wenhai Eco Lodge, a renovated Naxi house powered by solar energy and biogas.

Some of the best trekking in China can be found in this region that stretches between Wenhai Lake and the thirteen peaks of the Jade Mountains. The slopes that surround the lake are covered with the rhododendrons or azaleas for which the area is most famous. Snow leopards, red pandas and black bears also live here, but they are all pretty elusive. Unmissable, however, are the tens of thousands of migratory birds such as whooper swan and black stork that flock to the lake each year.

Wenhai village is more than just a base for setting off on walks, though. As it takes five hours on foot from Lijang, the nearest village accessible by public transport, getting to it makes for a trek all of its own.

Need to know *For details of treks, accommodation options and how to get there see ⓦwww.northwestyunnan.com; ☎ +86 (0) 139 8882 6672.*

TRAVEL THE SILK ROAD

The stories associated with the Silk Road (or rather roads, for it was never a single route but a network of interconnecting ones stretching from southern Europe to Java) have captivated travellers for centuries. Silk was the main commodity behind the foundation of the highway – made famous by Marco Polo – but porcelain, gunpowder and spices were also traded along it. Since the collapse of the Soviet Union the iconic part of this journey through Central Asia has become much easier to negotiate, but tackling bureaucracy and border controls can still be taxing, and using an experienced operator will make life easier. Below we detail the three main options for traversing the Silk Route: by horse, truck and train.

374 By horse

Over the course of two weeks on a horse-riding trek with Wild Frontiers you'll ride more than 250km through Kyrgyzstan, crossing mountain passes and narrow, densely forested canyons. One night you'll be staying with an eagle hunter on the shores of Lake Izzyk Kul, another bathing in hot water springs or staying in camps high in the mighty Tien Shan mountain range.

Wild Frontiers was founded by Jonny Bealby, a travel writer whose knowledge of the area and the relationship Wild Frontiers has developed with local hosts ensure an opportunity to discover more about Kyrgyz culture than would normally be possible. Wherever you stay, whether in a yurt or a family-run guesthouse, and wherever you go – normally far off the beaten track – this will never feel like a package tour.

Need to know *The fourteen-day Nomads Trail horse trek takes place in June and July; maximum group size is twelve.* Ⓦ*www.wildfrontiers.co.uk;* ☎*+44 (0) 207 363 968.*

375 By truck

Following roads that have developed out of the original caravan routes, an overland trip with Dragoman Adventures opens the way to the legendary Karakoram Highway that runs through China and Pakistan and a crossing of China's mighty Taklamakan desert, whose name means "go in and you'll never come out". Carrying everything on board a 4WD truck, you've the flexibility to visit whichever sites you most want to see along the way.

It's also possible to stop and volunteer on projects in the communities you pass through, for periods of up to six weeks. Participants can join the trips at various points along the way, staying for a few weeks or months. It may not suit the loner keen to set out in the footsteps of Marco

(Clockwise from top left) Son Kul, a 3000m glacial lake in central Kyrgyzstan; Horse-trekking through Kyrgyzstan; A truck on the road

Polo, but for anyone looking to muck in, make some new friends and journey as far along the Silk Road as time allows, there's no better way.

Need to know *Accommodation is in tents or homestays. Dragoman runs a variety of Silk Road itineraries, including special family trips and small-group trips in minibuses rather than trucks. For more see ⓦwww.dragoman.com; ☏ +44 (0) 1728 861 133.*

376 By train

Most people wanting to travel from Moscow to Beijing take the Trans-Mongolian or Trans-Manchurian trains. But you can also head south on trains such as The Kazakhstan or The Uzbekistan out of Moscow towards Tashkent and Almaty, and then travel east through Uzbekistan, visiting Bokhara and Samarkand en route. The journey is similar to the aforementioned trains – there are two- and four-berth sleeper wagons, plus you can step off at stations and buy everything from local sausages and vegetables to home-made dumplings or vodka. But it's much less frequented by tourists, as there isn't one train going the whole way through – you need to take at least three. This is no bad thing, with so many fascinating cities to stop in along the way.

For those with more to spend, there are also two luxury trains: the Golden Eagle from Moscow to the Kazakhstan/China border and then the Shangri-La from the Chinese side of the border to Beijing. With a DVD player in the cabin, power showers, two restaurant cars and even a bar with a pianist it's a different world from the *borscht* and boiled water out of the samovar on the public trains, but the spectacular views from the window are still the same.

Need to know *Information on planning the journey, including guidance on visas, is at ⓦwww. seat61.com/SilkRoute.htm. The Golden Eagle and Shangri-La trains are run by GW Travel (ⓦwww. gwtravel.co.uk).*

(Clockwise from top) Typical Kazakh scenery; An Uzbekistani market; A boy on a horse in Kyrgyzstan; Outside a mosque in Uzbekistan

377 EXPLORE THE SNOW COUNTRY, JAPAN

Spend summer in Sakae, a village in Japan's Kita-shinshu region, and you might wonder why all the houses have their front doors on the upper floor. Come in winter, when an average of four metres of snow falls, and you'll see why.

On a Snow Country tour with One Life Japan – run by an American/Japanese couple who live in Sakae – you will learn how people here adapt to the conditions. You could spend your time trekking on bamboo snow-shoes you've learned how to make, or build an igloo and spend the night in it. The flexibility of the tours means you can more or less choose to do whatever you want, though it's likely to include hot springs or helping on One Life's project to clear snow from the roofs of villagers unable to do so themselves. Also more or less guaranteed are copious amounts of sake to warm you up – either at home with the locals or in the traditional Japanese inn where you stay if the thought of sleeping in your recently made igloo seems too extreme.

Need to know *Sakae is 45km from Tokyo on the train (Ⓦwww.japanrail.com). Contact One Life Japan to design your own tour with them; each day is likely to cost around ¥20,000–30,000. Bike and walking tours are also offered throughout the year, along with several heritage projects in the local community. For more see Ⓦwww.onelifejapan.com; ℡ +81 090 3337 3248.*

378 BUILD A TREEHOUSE IN JAPAN

Deep in the mountainous forests of Chiba's Boso Peninsula, Gankoyama is the first "treehouse village" in Japan, offering a back-to-nature escape from the bustle of Tokyo. Eleven guest treehouses are grouped around a central treehouse/reception hall, with the whole complex surrounded by tall trees cloaked with creepers.

You could just kick back completely and swing in a hammock, but if you're up for a bit more adventure, spend a couple of days on the "Tree House Master" course learning how to build a treehouse. In between carpentry sessions you'll also get a chance to climb trees and forage for herbs and mushrooms.

The tree houses at Gankoyama are far comfier than those you may have played in as a kid: rooms are large, heated in winter and have solar-powered hot showers. Impressively, the whole village is powered by solar and wind energy, and all meals are cooked by wood-fired stove. But the childish excitement of playing in the trees is still there, as anyone who tries out the zip-slide that runs through the village will affirm.

Need to know *Gankoyama is two hours' south of Tokyo. For directions, details of tours, availability and costs see Ⓦwww.gankoyama.com*

379 WATCH DOLPHINS WITH A FORMER HUNTER, JAPAN

Staring out from the bow of the *Kohkaimaru*, skipper Izumi Ishii points at an indistinct point amid the waves. "Bottlenose dolphin", he says. It's just possible to distinguish the grey triangle of a fin – you think – before the dolphin helps you out by leaping obligingly into the air.

Izumi Ishii's skill at finding dolphins and whales comes from a life looking for them in the waters around the pretty harbour town of Futo, on Honshu's Izu peninsula. But it is only in the last few years that he has had tourists on board. Before that he was, like his father and grandfather before him, a hunter.

In 2003, however, he had a change of heart, and with the help of the American NGO Blue Voice established one of the few dolphin-watching businesses in Japan, right in the heartland of its hunting industry. One of the reasons Futo was a hunting base (and is now so ideal for watching) is that the waters are very deep, perfect for large pods of dolphins and whales, and it is not uncommon to see up to a hundred dolphins at a time. It takes more patience to spot sperm whales and orcas, but using tracking devices on the boat, you can hear their popping calls from below to help work out when and where they might surface.

In his spare time Izumi Ishii works to persuade other fishermen that his path is a more profitable one – financially and ethically. Already the volume of tourists wanting to come on his tours is too great for him to handle alone, and other fishermen are getting involved. If visitors keep coming to Futo to see the dolphins and whales, then, here at least, they will be better protected.

Need to know *Futo is two hours south of Tokyo by train (ⓦwww.japanrail.com). Guests stay in a family-run inn in Futo, eating local cuisine. Izumi Ishii's website is currently only in Japanese, but he can be emailed on ⓔohkaimaru@nifty.com or contacted through ⓦwww.bluevoice.org.*

380 FOLLOW THE CARAVAN ROUTE TO SIDENG, CHINA

For centuries the township of Shaxi, an ancient collection of sixteen villages in Yunnan surrounded by terraced paddies, was a key stopping-post on the caravan route that connected China with Tibet. Its thriving market square, trading everything from tea to horses, was lined with temples, a stage and guesthouses. That changed in 1950, when the People's Liberation Army marched on Tibet and the trade route ground to an almost instant halt. Over the following years the Communists banned private markets and Shaxi's deserted guesthouses crumbled, taken over by squatters as the marketplace fell into neglect.

Now all that is changing. As the last of its kind in China, the market in Sideng – the main village – has been recognized by the World Monuments Fund as one of the hundred most endangered heritage sites on Earth, and is being restored. Visitors can stay nearby with

Wu Yunxin, who speaks English and runs a guesthouse in an ornate three-storey opera house. It's the perfect base for arranging guided treks along the former salt route, picking wild mushrooms in season or seeing the seventh-century Buddhist rock carvings at Shibao Shan.

Or you can just step out the front door of the guesthouse and take a walk among the wooden buildings of the village, many of whose roofs are curved like the spines of upturned books. Thanks to the restoration work, paintings hidden in the soot-covered walls for over a century are being revealed and brought back to life. And there's a new buzz on the cobbled streets, especially on Fridays, when there is a market day once again and eager traders come from all around the valley.

Need to know *Mr Wu can accommodate up to ten guests and offers home-cooked meals. Shaxi is three hours south of Lijiang or four hours north of Dali via buses available daily from the long-distance bus station in either city. For more on activities, Wu Yunxin and Shaxi's history see ⓦwww.teahorse.net.*

Shaxi's old market

Volunteering

Tell me and I will forget; Show me and I may remember;
Involve me and I will understand. **(Chinese proverb)**

Volunteering can be a rewarding way to see the world: by living and working with local people on scientific, conservation or development projects, you can gain a much better understanding of their culture, develop genuine friendships and learn new skills while giving something back to the places you visit.

Hundreds of agencies offer volunteering experiences, from weekend breaks to placements that can last as long as two years. These experiences range from those whose primary focus is on the work to those that are a balance between work and a holiday. There is also a more casual (and usually short-term) form of volunteering known as "voluntourism", where you include a few hours or days of volunteering, perhaps at a school or community project, as part of your holiday. There is no governing body that regulates the volunteering industry; however, Comhlámh – an Irish association of development workers – has drawn up a Code of Good Practice for volunteers and agencies (⊛www. volunteeringoptions.org). Comhlámh's website is also an excellent resource for finding volunteering projects worldwide. The Ethical Volunteering Guide (⊛www.ethicalvolunteering.org) has some useful tips on how to choose the right agency, depending on how much time you have to give.

The huge number of options means it can be difficult to find the sort of volunteering best suited to you, and one that genuinely benefits the destination. Below are a few pointers to help you choose the right project and the right organization.

What work will I do?

Find out exactly what work you will be expected to do and for how long, and whether you need any particular skills or experience. Labouring is often suitable for weekend projects, while volunteering at community centres or on larger construction projects suits longer-term placements. One month is usually the minimum required for teaching children.

How did the project come about?

Ask whether the organization has built up a good relationship with a local NGO or charity and whether there is long-term commitment to its projects. Often, the most worthwhile projects originate within the destination where local people have sought out specific help from agencies to select volunteers.

Is there a selection process?

You can get a sense of an organization's commitment to the work it supports by checking whether it tries to match your particular skills to its programmes. If there isn't an interview and selection process, you risk not being matched to an appropriate project.

Where does the money go?

Find out what proportion of the money you spend goes on internal administration costs, staff wages, your food and accommodation, and how much actually goes towards the projects. Be wary if you are quoted more than fifteen percent for "agency admin".

What's the feedback like from other volunteers?

Either speak to someone who has been on the trip or ask to see the feedback forms of previous volunteers.

Will they give you support and training?

Good organizations usually offer pre-departure training and provide support and further training during the project. Make sure there is someone at the destination who has direct responsibility for you and that there's adequate provision in case things go wrong.

15 RECOMMENDED VOLUNTEERING AGENCIES

1. British Trust for Conservation Volunteers (@www.bctv.org). Mainly weekend conservation projects in Britain but also runs overseas conservation holidays in Europe, Japan, Nepal, USA, New Zealand and South Africa.

2. Conservation Volunteers Australia (@www.conservationvolunteers.com.au) and Conservation Volunteers New Zealand (@www.conservationvolunteers.co.nz). Voluntary projects in the Antipodes.

3. Cross Cultural Solutions (@www.crossculturalsolutions.org). Care work, teaching, healthcare and community development in Eastern Europe, Africa, Asia and Latin America.

4. Different Travel (@www.different-travel.com). Voluntourism in Asia, Africa and South America.

5. Eco Volunteer (@www.ecovolunteer.org.uk). Wildlife conservation mainly in Eastern Europe, Thailand, USA and Brazil.

6. Global Visions International (@www.gvi.co.uk). Conservation and community projects worldwide.

7. Handsupholidays (@www.handsupholidays.com). Short-term voluntourism worldwide.

8. International Volunteers for Peace (@www.ivp.org.au). Short-term (2–4 weeks) conservation and humanitarian "work camps" and medium-term (3–12 months) projects worldwide for Australians.

9. Operation Wallacea (@www.opwall.com). Scientific and conservation expeditions to Indonesia, Honduras, Egypt, South Africa, Mozambique, Cuba and Peru.

10. People and Places (@www.travel-peopleandplaces.co.uk). Community projects in The Gambia, Madagascar, Nepal, Indonesia, Pakistan, Swaziland and South Africa.

11. Projects Abroad (@www.projects-abroad.co.uk). Sends volunteers to work in over one hundred different conservation and development projects worldwide.

12. Quest Overseas (@www.questoverseas.com). Gap-year specialist that runs year-round conservation and community projects across Africa and South America.

13. Raleigh International (@www.raleighinternational.org). Highly regarded and long-established volunteering organization that currently runs expeditions (4–10 weeks) in Borneo, India, Nicaragua and Costa Rica.

14. 2Way Development (@www.2waydevelopment.com). Places skilled volunteers on development projects in association with NGOs.

15. VSO (@www.vso.org.uk). The granddaddy of volunteering has traditionally sent skilled volunteers on a one- or two-year placement in a developing country, but it now also offers short-term placements from one to six months. It recently launched an online TV channel so you can gain an insight into what life as a VSO volunteer is like: see @www.green.tv/vso.

5 DIRECTORIES FOR VOLUNTEER PROJECTS

The following agencies connect potential volunteers with organizations that arrange placements worldwide.

1) Ecoteer (@www.ecoteer.com).
2) Greenvolunteers (@www.greenvolunteers.com).
3) TimeBank (@www.timebank.org.uk).
4) Year Out Group (@www.yearoutgroup.org).
5) WorldWide Volunteering (@www.worldwidevolunteering.org.uk).

THAILAND

LAOS

CAMBODIA

VIETNAM

MALAYSIA

SINGAPORE

BRUNEI

MALAYSIA

PHILIPPINES

I N D O N E S I A

EAST
TIMOR

SOUTHEAST ASIA

381 Experience coastal village life, Thailand

382 Stay at Rivertime, Laos

383 Charity Challenge, Vietnam

384 Intrepid Travel, Thailand

385 Khammouane Ecoguides, Laos

386 Pooh Eco Treks, Thailand

387 Hill Tribe Tours, Thailand

388 Yeak Laom, Cambodia

389 Rinjani, Lombok

390 Taman Negara, Malaysia

391 Green Discoveries, Laos

392 Mount Kinabalu, Sabah, Malaysian Borneo

393 A biodiesel bus around Cambodia

394 Dive Apo Island, The Philippines

395 Take a boat up the Mekong, Laos

396 Give an elephant a bath, Thailand

397 Common sense luxury, Thailand

398 Stay in an Isan village, Thailand

399 Canoe the Ba Be Lakes, Vietnam

400 Dive at Bunaken, Indonesia

401 Surf your own wave at Nihiwatu, Indonesia

402 Enjoy a puppet show, Luang Prabang

403 Get a massage with the Red Cross, Luang Prabang

404 Make your own scarf, Luang Prabang

405 See moon bears, Luang Prabang

406 Go gourmet at Tamarind, Luang Prabang

407 Birdwatching at Kingfisher Ecolodge, Laos

408 Visit a Khmu village, Laos

409 See Cambodia by bike

410 Learn how silk is made in Laos

411 Join an elephant patrol in Indonesia

412 Balinese village life, Indonesia

413 On the rafflesia trail in Sabah, Malaysia

414 Turtle watching in Sabah, Malaysia

415 Miso Walai Homestay, Sabah, Malaysia

416 Visit an Iban longhouse, Sarawak, Malaysia

417 Face to face with an orang-utan, Kalimantan, Indonesia

418 Spot a giant ibis in Cambodia

419 Behind the scenes at Angkor Wat, Cambodia

420 Explore rice terraces, Vietnam

The sea at Ban Talae Nok;
Preparing the ingredients to
make soap

381 EXPERIENCE COASTAL VILLAGE LIFE, THAILAND

Standing on the shore by the village of Ban Talae Nok, looking past the ambling water buffalo to the rainforest-covered Gum islands a kilometre out to sea, it's hard to imagine that in December 2004 the tide suddenly receded as far as those islands, before returning as a wall of water that destroyed almost everything in its path. In the wake of the tsunami almost a quarter of Ban Talae Nok's two hundred inhabitants had perished, including fifteen children who had been rehearsing a play for New Year in the school.

Within weeks, however, the villagers had begun rebuilding their lives, and with the help of a young American who had been working in a nearby guesthouse, they set about deciding on a new future for themselves. The result was Andaman Discoveries, a community-based tourism venture that aims to provide a supplementary income to fishing in villages like Ban Talae Nok. It's a form of tourism very much on the villagers' terms: they are involved and consulted throughout, and eighty percent of a trip's cost goes direct to the village (twenty percent of this via a community fund).

Andaman Discoveries recommends that visitors opt to stay with a host family while in Ban Talae Nok. This homestay scheme is organized by the villagers on a rotation basis, and it's the best way to find out more about the locals (a translator is provided to smooth over communication problems) and sample traditional Thai cuisine. Guests can also make soap or batik (a fabric hand-dyed using wax) with the women's co-operative. There's also the opportunity to do your bit for the natural environment by planting saplings on the shore of the mangroves.

The real joy of staying at Ban Talae Nok, though, is the time spent inbetween these activities – playing with the children; picnicking with the family on the beach at sunset; listening to the villagers describe their experiences; and understanding what life is like here and how hope can spring from even the worst disasters.

Need to know *Trips cost roughly $55 per person a day including all food, accommodation, activities and services of a local guide and translator. For details see Ⓦwww.andamandiscoveries.com; ☏ +66 (0) 879 177 165.*

382 STAY AT RIVERTIME, LAOS

With its floating restaurant, fish ponds and organic vegetable garden, the slow pace of life at Rivertime Ecolodge feels far from the busy streets of Vientiane, yet it is just 30km up the Nam Ngum River – making the capital easy to reach and quick to escape. Guests staying in the wooden chalets, surrounded by forest and with balconies overlooking the river, can catch a river taxi into the city to see the monasteries and temples, or visit schools in the nearby villages that the lodge works with. Rivertime also runs its own school next to the resort, training local adults in agricultural and community skills, where you're welcome to help out teaching English. If you're keen to immerse yourself even more, the lodge can also arrange for guests to stay in the home of a local family and participate in their daily life.

Anyone wishing to escape the crowds altogether can head towards the pristine river-gorges and butterfly-filled forests of nearby Phou Khao Kwai, or simply cross the river by long-tailed boat and explore the many trails through the primary forest, accompanied by the sounds of birds and monkeys chattering in the tall, leafy trees. Rivertime pays an annual fee to the nearby villagers – most of whose income is dependent on logging – to ensure a 630,000-square-metre concession remains pristine. Yet, despite all that's available, you may still struggle to fight the temptation to sit in the restaurant with a cool drink and watch the magnificent river drift by.

Need to know *For directions, details of tours and homestays, rates and reservations see Ⓦwww. rivertimelaos.com; ☏ +856 205 513 672.*

Hmong traditional dress; The huts at Rivertime Ecolodge

TREKS AND HIKES

Southeast Asia offers some wonderful treks, spending days walking through dense rainforests, spotting spectacular wildlife, learning about the cultures of the many different tribes who live in the remoter areas, and often staying with them in their homes and sharing their meals. The following ten treks are highly recommended, and also ensure that any communities visited benefit from your presence.

Walking through paddy fields on an Intrepid Trek, Thailand

383 Charity Challenge, Vietnam

This challenging hike through the hills of northern Vietnam takes you between villages of Black H'mong, Red Dao and Tay minorities, with some nights spent in the homes of tribes and others camping. You have to raise a minimum sponsorship before you go, but because everyone is doing it for the charity of their choice, it creates a real bond among the group, with everyone supporting each other to achieve their aims. Ⓦ www.charitychallenge.com.

384 Intrepid Travel, Thailand

This three-day trek, visiting the hospitable Karen people who live in the hills around Chiang Mai, forms the middle part of a week-long trip starting and ending with visits to some

of the highlights of Bangkok, making it ideal for those on limited time. The walking is only three or so hours each day through thick forest, which leaves you plenty of time to explore the villages where you'll stop off for the night. Ⓦ www.intrepidtravel.com.

385 Khammouane Ecoguides, Laos

Escorted by a guide from the local community, this two-day journey in Phou Hin Poun explores some of the vast caves and churning rapids for which this area of forested limestone hills is famous. Bring your torch, as the biggest cave – the stalactite-filled Kong Lor – is 7km long. Ⓦ www.ecotourismlaos.com/khammouane.htm.

386 Pooh Eco Treks, Thailand

Setting off from Chiang Mai, your guides Mr Pooh and his Karen associate Mr Tee will lead you with flaming torches deep into bat-filled caves and help you get the most of a stay with Karen villagers whom they have known for twenty years. By the end of your trek, they will also have taught you how to forage for food in the jungle. Ⓦ www.pooh-ecotrekking.com.

387 Hill Tribe Tours, Thailand

Run by an NGO based in Chiang Rai, the focus of these trips is more on cultural exchange than physical endurance. As you walk only a couple of hours a day, most of your time is spent experiencing the rhythms of daily life with members of the Lahu, Akha and Karen tribes – perhaps preparing meals on the bamboo floor of your host's home, helping in the fields or volunteering in the local school. Ⓦ www.mirrorartgroup.org.

388 Yeak Laom, Cambodia

The dense forests covering the Ratanakiri district in northeast Cambodia are not easy to negotiate alone, so you'll be glad to have a knowledgeable guide who can lead you to the most remote areas. One of these is the stunning Yeak Laom Lake – which fills a disused volcanic crater – and its surrounding five Tampuen villages, where you'll learn about traditional handicrafts, customs and beliefs. Ⓦ www.geocities.com/yeak_laom.

389 Rinjani, Lombok

As the first man ever to take trekkers to Mount Rinjani over twenty years ago, no-one knows the area and its people better than self-styled "Mr John". As part of the "John's Adventures" programme, he will take you on a three-day trek up the slopes of the volcano to the sacred lake that fills it crater, known as Segara Anak ("child of the sea"). After a sweaty hike, you'll be ready for a refreshing swim. Ⓦ www.rinjanimaster.com.

390 Taman Negara, Malaysia

There are six observation hides in Taman Negara – one of the oldest rainforests on earth – where you can stay the night and experience the jungle in all its noisy nocturnal glory. During the day, you can go on river cruises, explore limestone caves with ancient wall-drawings or climb up to the canopy trail for a closer look at the wildlife. Ⓦ www.taman-negara.com.

391 Green Discoveries, Laos

In between tramping through the forests around Luang Namtha in northern Laos, gathering forest vegetables for dinner, you'll get to meet the Akha people. You'll sleep in the villagers' homes, and there's time to watch or join in with their lively songs and dances, and have a go on some of the instruments they use. Ⓦ www. greendiscoverylaos.com.

392 Mount Kinabalu, Sabah, Malaysian Borneo

It is just one day's steep uphill trek and a pre-dawn climb up a rocky ascent to see the sun rise at the summit of Mount Kinabalu, the highest mountain in Southeast Asia. To tackle it you must buy a permit for RM250 (includes fee for a local guide) at Kinabalu Park's headquarters. After the hike, soothe your muscles in the geothermally heated Poring Hot Springs. Ⓦ www.sabahparks.org.my.

Akha girl in traditional headdress, Laos

Mount Kinabalu, Malaysian Borneo

393 A BIODIESEL BUS AROUND CAMBODIA

Wat in Cambodia; False crown anemone fish, Apo Island, Negros, Philippines

A visit to the temples of Angkor Wat, followed by the Killing Fields around Phnom Penh and the idyllic islands of Ream National Park, gives you a taste of Cambodia's highlights. Do it differently with Sihanoukville-based Planet Biodiesel: guests on the seven- or twelve-day tours are transported between these attractions in a bus (or boat, for the islands) powered by biofuel manufactured from used cooking oil from nearby restaurants. So pollution is virtually nil.

There's also the chance to stop in at a sight not on most people's itineraries – the school run by the organization, which educates local children whose parents can't afford to send them to school. Unsurprisingly, the bus that picks them up each day from their homes is run on biodiesel too. Planet Biodiesel also has ambitious plans to set up microbusinesses that will recycle toxic materials into usable products; to build Cambodia's first public children's playground; and to establish a medical training centre in Sihanoukville. It's the best of both worlds: you get an eco-friendly tour guided by locals, and your fees go towards a charity working determinedly to improve Cambodia's quality of life and environment.

Need to know For details of tours, rates and reservations see ⓦplanetbiodiesel.org; ☏+855 1656 0511. The website also has info on the school and other charitable projects.

394 DIVE APO ISLAND, THE PHILIPPINES

Seven kilometres south of the island of Negros lies little Apo Island, whose crystal-clear waters harbour a thriving population of turtles, coral reefs and 650 varieties of tropical fish. What makes the richness of the marine life here all the more amazing is that a few years ago there was almost no reef, and these waters were practically devoid of fish.

By the 1970s, after years of destructive fishing practices, the situation had deteriorated so much around Apo that fishermen were forced to go to other islands, often for weeks at a time. That all changed in 1982 with the founding of the Apo Island Marine Sanctuary, which keeps ten percent of Apo's waters free of fishing, thereby providing a breeding and feeding ground for marine life. Visitors today pay a small fee to the sanctuary on top of their diving costs to be able to step off the beach and swim out to one of the best diving sites in the world.

There are no cars on the island,

and there's little to do but walk up the hill to the lighthouse and stare out to sea. Accommodation is at the fourteen-room Liberty's Community Lodge, which keeps its own impact down with solar panels and rainwater-harvesting systems, while also supporting the island's school. No TV or phone can disturb your escape: instead enjoy the sound of the sea lapping at the shore beneath your balcony and the rosy haze of the sun setting. And although almost everyone's come for the reef, it's never crowded underwater – to protect the corals and the fish that feed on them, only fifteen people are allowed in the sanctuary's waters at any one time.

Need to know *You can reach Apo in 35min by boat from Malatapay. For further info about the island, including Liberty Community Lodge, see ⓦwww.apoisland.com. For those interested in reef conservation in the Philippines, Coral Cay (ⓦwww.coralcay.org) runs an excellent volunteer project off Leyte Island.*

395 TAKE A BOAT UP THE MEKONG, LAOS

The boat journey between Luang Prabang and the Thai border at Huai Suay passes through some of the most unspoilt passages of the Mekong River. Amid the endless tracts of primary jungle that line the steep, cloud-topped hills, signs of human habitation are scarce – chances are you'll see little more evidence of civilization than rice paddies, small teak plantations or isolated wooden fishing villages, their stilted houses clinging to the hillsides.

There are many ways to take this journey – by

Fishermen's boats on the Mekong

far the most scenic route from Laos to Thailand – such as hanging on for dear life and missing the view in a six-man speedboat, or idling along in a rickety public river bus. Probably the best choice, therefore, is to travel on the Luangsuay, a 34m river barge with its own bar and lunch served onboard. It's a more peaceful, leisurely way to appreciate life on and around the river than the other two choices, plus the two-day journey is broken at the Luang Suay ecolodge. Perched on the steep sides of the bank just outside the small town of Pak Beng, this locally staffed lodge is the perfect place to sit and watch the sun set over the Mekong.

Many people stay at the lodge just for a meal and a bed for the night, but you're welcome to stay for a few days more, which will allow for a visit to the school that the lodge funds, or an extended hike into the surrounding countryside. However long you stay, this trip, from the most beautiful town in Laos deep into the Golden Triangle, is a chance to feel the romance of travelling upriver in a way that has hardly changed for almost a century.

Need to know *The journey can be done in either direction. For itineraries and booking information see ⓦwww.asian-oasis.com/Luang.html.*

396 GIVE AN ELEPHANT A BATH, THAILAND

Elephants and tourism have typically presented an uneasy mix in Asia: riding elephants is a unique experience but many visitors are understandably uncomfortable about seeing these mighty creatures reduced to pack animals.

A mahout sitting atop his beloved elephant at Elephant Hills

On the Elephant Experience at Elephant Hills, a luxury tented lodge on the edge of Thailand's Khao Sok National Park, guests can do far more than on the usual elephant trek offered elsewhere. As well as hosing and scrubbing inside the folds of the elephants' skin, you'll prepare their food and feed them, learn how they and their *mahouts* (trainers) communicate, and then watch them playing together in the pool. It's exhilarating and humbling to be so close to such mighty creatures, who love being washed and often respond with a delighted squirt of water from their trunk.

While most people would prefer that these creatures were truly wild, for two-thirds of the three thousand Asian elephants left this isn't currently feasible: they have worked in the logging or tourism industries all their lives and wouldn't survive independently. As well as giving more dignified lives to the fifteen or so elephants at its camp, Elephant Hills is establishing an elephant sanctuary in the north of the country, which will give even more elephants a better life and the opportunity to breed. For now, however, for anyone wanting to see more than the back of a pachyderm's head, Elephant Hills offers the best and most humane experience in Thailand.

Need to know *Stays of two to four days are available at the lodge. Other activities on offer include kayaking, a boat trip and a visit to the mangrove swamps. Staff will pick you up from Surat Thani, Phuket and Ranong. For package details, rates and reservations see Ⓦwww.elephant-hills.com; ☎ +66 (0) 7638 1703.*

397 COMMON SENSE LUXURY, THAILAND

It's not often a five-star hotel offers to show guests the rubbish dump. Normally it would be more likely to flaunt its infinity pool, its luxury organic spa or the restaurant with a view out over the sea. And Evason Phuket has got all of those. It's just that the hotel is more proud of its award-winning ecotrail around its grounds showcasing its many environmental initiatives, of which the compost and recycling centre is just a part.

Of course you could happily stay here and remain completely unaware that the world's first commercial biomass reactor is powering the air-conditioning system. Most guests are perfectly oblivious, as almost all the initiatives being put in place to make the hotel carbon neutral by 2020 take place behind the scenes. Few visitors leave knowing that much of the food they ate was grown organically on site, or that the water is recycled into the gardens filled with indigenous plants and herbs.

But it's not all hidden from view. A few metres out from the shore of the hotel's private island lie some of the best-preserved corals in Thailand. But because they want to keep them that way, staff explain to guests that they can only snorkel there at high tide. So, if you want do more than sip cocktails under an umbrella on the beach, check what time that is.

Need to know *Evason Phuket runs a volunteer programme that allows visitors to stay for four weeks but pay for two if they participate in various community and environmental projects while there. For directions, accommodation details, rates and booking see ⓦwww.sixsenses.com/Evason-Phuket/index.php; ☏+66 (0) 7638 1010.*

398 STAY IN AN ISAN VILLAGE, THAILAND

It's far too easy to visit Thailand and come away feeling that you never really got to see what life for Thais is like outside of the tourist centres. If you're curious, then a visit to the tranquil rice-growing village of Ko Pet in the northeastern Isan region may be just what you're looking for.

Ko Pet is a village like many others in the region, with the difference that it has built a lodge so that small-scale tourism can supplement incomes from rice and vegetable cultivation. Guests (a maximum of six at a time) stay in the locally built three-bedroom Lamai guesthouse at one end of Ko Pet, surrounded by a garden of palms and mango trees, and are always accompanied by two of the villagers on visits into the village – who are there to provide translation and keep tours unobtrusive.

The activities on offer – joining elders foraging for edible insects or mushrooms, learning how to weave baskets from raffia, seeing silk being produced – are not staged, since they comprise what the villagers would be doing anyway. Guides ensure these are rotated between the twenty or so participating families, so there is little disruption of routine and income is spread evenly.

Everything about the project has been carefully thought through. All goods and services are purchased locally; kitchen waste is composted; bicycles are used for tours; plastic bottles are collected and distributed to fishermen as traps;

and an organic gardening scheme has diversified the economy and attracted new species back to the area. Ko Pet may be in one of the more remote areas of Thailand but the scheme here is showing the way forward for rural tourism in Asia.

Need to know *The homestay will pick up guests from the train station at Bua Yai or the bus stop at Sida. For directions and details of tours and packages see ⓦwww.thailandhomestay.com; ☏+66 (0) 862 585 894.*

(Clockwise from top) Learning to weave from raffia; Woman harvesting rice; Fishing with recycled plastic bottles as traps

399 CANOE THE BA BE LAKES, VIETNAM

As your guide paddles out of the dim, stalagtite-filled cave and onto the shimmering lake, the air fills with the roar of the distant Dau Dang waterfall. On all sides the tree-covered limestone cliffs loom overhead, their dense vegetation seeming to merge into the jade-coloured water. You're a long way north of Hanoi and it feels like it.

Canoeing on the tranquil Ba Be Lakes with Footprints Vietnam (an operator staffed by local Vietnamese that works directly with the villages you visit) is a nature retreat like few others. Ba

Be means "three seas" – a reference to the three natural lakes that spread over an area 7km long and 1km wide – and three-day boat trips on this wide expanse of water typically stop by caves and waterfalls, and include a stay in the homes of the Tay people who live beside the lake. The Tay, most of whom are farmers or fishermen, live in houses on stilts perched over the edge of the water – and it's in one of these that you'll eat and sleep, looking out over the bamboo-lined lake as fishermen pass by at dusk in their wooden canoes.

Need to know *The best time to go is September to April. The lakes are around six hours' drive from Hanoi, though Footprints Vietnam and other operators will drive you from the capital. For details of tours and rates see Ⓦ www.footprintsvietnam. com; ☎ +84 43 933 2844.*

Paddling towards the cave at Ba Be Lakes; Common lionfish

400 DIVE AT BUNAKEN, INDONESIA

No one's really sure how many fish dwell in the gin-clear waters of Bunaken Marine Reserve in the north of the Sulawesi archipelago. It's probably more than 2500 different species, but the number keeps changing as more are discovered. Whatever the exact amount, with up to 45m visibility on a clear day this is one of the best places to dive not just in Indonesia, but the whole world.

And each year it gets a bit more beautiful. That's partly because the 890 square-kilometre reserve – which is spread over five small islands – is using money raised from entrance fees to end damaging practices such as coral mining and blast-fishing. Also, because the reserve employs local villagers to clean up the reefs and beaches and guard them from trespassers, live coral cover is now increasing by around five percent a year.

Most of the reserve's accommodation – mainly basic homestays – is on Bunaken Island. If you're after a little more luxury, head for the nearby island of Siladen and the Siladen Resort and Spa, with fifteen stylish villas, its own dive

The beach at Nihiwatu

centre and a spa to relax in after a day counting hundreds of different fish. There's one fish you almost certainly won't see, however – the coelacanth, which has been swimming deep in these waters for over seven million years. Thankfully with the controls the reserve has put in place, a great deal more species now stand to survive a long way into the future too.

Need to know *Bunaken is about 45min–1hr by boat from Manado; entry to the reserve costs Rp50,000 (US$6) per day. For accommodation options, dive operators and further information on Bunaken Marine Reserve, visit ⓦwww.sulawesi-info.com/bunaken.php. Siladen Resort and Spa: ⓦwww.siladen.com; ☎ +62 431 856 820.*

401 SURF YOUR OWN WAVE AT NIHIWATU, INDONESIA

Seventy metres from the shoreline the wave breaks, a lone surfer skillfully riding it in. Known as Occy's Left – after the former surfing champion Mark Occhilupo – this particular wave has achieved legendary status; all the more so because so few get to surf it. The reason for this is Nihiwatu, a luxury resort located here on the remote island of Sumba in Bali. Made up of just seven bungalows and three villas, the resort overlooks its own private beach (accessible only to residents), and while it has room for up to twenty guests, it will only allow nine surfers to stay at any one time.

Everything at Nihiwatu has been designed to maximize the feeling of exclusivity and luxury: the 2km beach is hemmed in by cliffs and headlands, while the spa, built in the style of a traditional Sumba spirit-house, offers massages, yoga and Pilates. If you want to intersperse the relaxation with action, the resort also organizes game-fishing, horse-riding and day-trips to meet Sumba's indigenous people. They are big fans of Nihiwatu, which through its Sumba Foundation has built many schools and clinics, developed organic agriculture projects and helped to protect them from less sensitive tourist developments. Whether you come searching for legendary waves, encounters with traditional cultures or just an escape from the rat race, there are few places more idyllic.

Need to know *The minimum stay is five nights and you'll need to spend a night in Bali in order to get the connecting flight. For accommodation, dining, prices and reservations see ⓦwww.nihiwatu.com; ☎ +62 361 757 149.*

GREEN LUANG PRABANG

Laos eased restrictions on foreign tourism in 1994, and the sleepy former royal capital of Luang Prabang, hidden away in the jungle at the confluence of the Kahn and Mekong rivers, was made a World Heritage Site a year later. Visitor numbers have accelerated since, and Luang Prabang now has several ventures that aim to cope with this growth sustainably. The following experiences offer the best of this magical place, and will help to preserve its soul for many years to come.

402 Enjoy a puppet show

Every Thursday and Saturday at 7.30pm the kids at Children's Cultural Centre, a project developed with Unicef, put on a traditional Lao puppet show. Throughout the year the CCC members (aged between 6 and 18) perform in rural villages, using puppetry and other traditional forms to deliver messages about children's rights and health issues. The rest of the time they learn all manner of traditional arts at the centre, and guests are welcome to learn as well, or help out. It's all part of a concerted effort to ensure interest in Lao traditional culture is carried on by the next generation. And for families whose children are bored of traipsing round temples, it provides an engaging day out.

Need to know *The 50,000K fee (US$6) for the puppet show goes towards the CCC's work. The Centre (open 8.30am– 4pm) is located between the Hmong and Dara markets. ☏+856 (0) 71 253 732.*

403 Get a massage with the Red Cross

There are plenty of places in town where you can get an invigorating massage for very little money, but choosing the Red Cross means you'll help to fund projects to provide latrines and water systems to local villagers, and train local youths and tuk-tuk drivers in first aid. It's a proper massage too: after sweating away toxins in a steam bath infused with 24 different herbs, you're kneaded and pummelled back into shape by medically trained professionals.

Need to know *The Red Cross is on Visounlath road. It costs 36,000K for 1hr (approx US$4). Open 9am–11pm. ☏+856 (0) 7125 2856 or ✉ lrclpg@ laohotel.com.*

Wat Xieng Thong, Luang Prabang

404 Make your own scarf

Laos is famous for its silk, and at Ock Pop Tok's textile gallery you can select your favourite patterns and colours from a range of hand-stitched fabrics, or have clothes made to measure. Or you can visit their weaving centre located in a traditional riverside garden just 2km from the centre of town. Here you can learn how to weave or dye your own scarf in classes lasting from a half-day to a week; you'll be taught by women working with Ock Pop Tock in an effort to keep their traditional handicrafts alive.

Need to know *The gallery is on Ban Vat Nong (open 8am–9pm), while the weaving centre is on Ban Saylom (open 9am–5pm). For more info and prices of courses see ⓦwww.ockpoptok.com; ☎+856 (0) 7121 2597.*

405 See moon bears

Tuk-tuk drivers in Luang Prabang will happily take you the 30km south to Tat Kuang Si park, where there's not only a spectacular 60m waterfall but also a less well-known sight: a rescue centre where you can get close to Asiatic black bears, known as moon bears because of the crescent markings on their chests. The bears here have been rescued from traffickers and poachers, who capture them for their bile (used in traditional medicine) or to sell to restaurants in China. At the centre the bears are free from these dangers, and you'll see them enjoying themselves swimming, climbing trees or using their long tongues to snaffle up insects in hard-to-reach places.

Need to know *It costs around 50,000K (US$6) for the 45min tuk-tuk ride to the rescue centre. Go early and you'll miss the crowds at the waterfall. For more on the centre and moon bears see ⓦwww.bearlao.com.*

406 Go gourmet at Tamarind

A welcome escape from the typical traveller fare of banana pancakes or coconut curry, Tamarind restaurant is dedicated to revitalizing interest in traditional Lao cooking and ingredients, and runs cooking classes to spread the word. Of course you can just let the chef do the work and tuck in to lunch – dried buffalo or pickled bamboo, say, or for the more adventurous, some of the stranger beasties that you may have seen on display in the markets that day – bugs, worms and frogs. Some you'll struggle with, but others, such as fried grasshopper, are far tastier than they might look. For anyone keen to challenge their tastebuds while travelling, lunch at Tamarind is a must.

Need to know *Found opposite Vat Nong temple, Tamarind is open Mon–Sat 11am–6pm. For details and prices of cooking classes see ⓦwww tamarindlaos.com.*

Asiatic black bear

407 BIRDWATCHING AT KINGFISHER ECOLODGE, LAOS

Situated in the fertile northern wetlands of a conservation area in Champasak Province, Kingfisher Ecolodge blends perfectly with the natural environment. Standing high on stilts, its six bungalows' spiky wooden roofs are enveloped in lush foliage. Each is simply equipped and solar-powered, but their best feature is the enormous glass windows: peering out over the emerald expanse from your little wooden island, the sense of space and distance is almost overwhelming.

Pavillion at Wat Phou temple; statue at Wat Phou temple

Close to the vibrant town of Pakse, the spectacular waterfalls of the Bolaven Plateau and the Khmer ruins of Wat Phou, Kingfisher is a good base for excursions. And with opportunities nearby to go mountain biking and birdwatching, there's little time to be bored. Although it would be completely understandable if you'd rather tuck into the home-made cakes in the lodge's restaurant, sit back and soak up the peace and quiet.

Need to know *Kingfisher Ecolodge can be reached by taxi or public bus from Pakse's southern bus station (Lak Pet station), around 60km away. Five percent of income from activities is added to a fund that supports the local primary school. For details of accommodation, activities, rates and booking see Ⓦwww. kingfisherecolodge.com; ☎ +856 (0) 305 345 016.*

408 VISIT A KHMU VILLAGE, LAOS

But for the Mekong River on whose banks it stands, the village of Yoi Hai is cut off from the world, with no road cut through the dense jungle that surrounds it. Living here, surrounded by the cloud-covered heights of the hills, are the Khmu – an animist tribe who worship spirits in the trees and rocks that surround them. Until recently the population was even more isolated, but in 2000 the government decreed that they, and all the other hill tribes, had to form new towns on lower ground, partly in a bid to stamp out the opium trade and partly to improve access to healthcare and education. However, many tribal peoples have struggled to adapt to these more urban communities, with alcoholism and drug abuse on the increase.

Thanks to their relationship with the nearby Kamu Lodge, however, the future doesn't look quite so bleak for the Khmu. The lodge – comprising twenty comfortable two-person safari tents and a thatched pagoda restaurant topped with solar panels – employs staff from local communities, is responsible for building a school and also pays a monthly community fund. You'll get the chance to meet the people whom the lodge is helping – they will show you round the village, teach you how to cast a net into the river or how to pan in its waters for gold.

Lit gently by the flickering of paraffin lamps, night at the lodge is accompanied by crickets singing and the earthy croak of frogs – few places feel this remote. Staying here, you'll glimpse a little bit of this wonderful place, which, thanks to the efforts of Kamu Lodge, the people of Yoi Hai are still able to call home.

Need to know *Kamu Lodge's boat leaves daily at 8.30am from Luang Prabang (arriving 12.30pm). From Pak Beng, you'll need to come by public boat, which the lodge can help arrange. For further details, including rates and booking, see Ⓦwww. kamulodge.com; ☎ +856 (0) 2126 2605*

409 SEE CAMBODIA BY BIKE

For many visitors to Cambodia, the highlight of their trip is a visit to Angkor Wat. But for those on the annual cycling tour with PEPY ("Protect the Earth, Protect Yourself") it's just the beginning – the start of a three-week biking adventure that continues around Tonle Sap Lake, down to Phnom Penh and then south to the coast. On some days you may pedal as far as 100km over dusty roads, through rice paddies and vibrant city streets. There are regular stops for an energizing bite to eat and drink – tasty noodles, fried rice, fresh coconut juice – when you'll get the chance to meet the locals. The tour also explores the darker sides of Cambodia's past, such as the notorious Killing Fields. But this is counterbalanced by visits to the many inspiring projects run or supported by PEPY, such as the development of environmental school clubs in rural classrooms, ride-to-school groups and rainwater harvesting schemes. And when you finally reach the white sands of the beaches in the south, a celebratory splash in the warm waters of the Gulf of Thailand makes for the perfect finale.

Need to know *The trip costs $1500, which includes bike rental if necessary, all accommodation and most meals. In addition participants must raise at least $1500 to support projects, which they visit on their tour. PEPY also runs several other trips throughout the year. See Ⓦwww.pepytours.com for further information.*

410 LEARN HOW SILK IS MADE IN LAOS

Holding the tiny cocoon in your fingers, it's hard to imagine it contains a fibre of silk that will be 800m long when finally unravelled. And when you consider 100,000 silk worms are being cultivated here at Vang Viang Organic Farm, you're effectively surrounded by 80,000km of silk – enough to circle the earth twice.

The farm was established in 1996, in the village of Phoudinadaong, on the banks of the Nam Song River, as a model centre of organic agriculture: mulberry trees are cultivated using natural fertilizers and predators, and their leaves picked daily to feed the silkworms or to make mulberry tea and wine. Half of each silk harvest is sold for fabric production, while the other half provides income for village women, who weave it at home and then sell silk products back to the farm. Profits from the farm are also used to run a community centre and school, where volunteers can help with English lessons.

Cambodia by bike; Angkor Wat

Travellers are welcome to visit the farm – you can stay in simple rooms if you wish – to learn about how the silk is processed or see how the fruit and veg is grown using traditional techniques. And if – having learnt that each harvest produces around ten kilos of silk which is then dyed with local plants – you buy one of the brightly coloured scarves made by the women, you'll have gained a real appreciation of what your silk is worth.

Need to know *For directions to the farm and details of projects and accommodation (dorm beds US$1, rooms without bath US$3) see Ⓦwww. laofarm.org; ☏ +856 205 523 688.*

(Clockwise from top left) Woman carrying vegetables in Danau Batur with Gunung Batur rising behind; Rice fields, Jatiluwih; Woodcarver at work, Mas; Northern Cassowary; Cottages at Puri Lumbung; Purple Water Lily

411 JOIN AN ELEPHANT PATROL IN INDONESIA

Wildlife lovers have plenty of reasons to head up to Gunung Leuser, one of Asia's biggest national parks. Located three hours north of Medan in northern Sumatra, it covers almost 9500 square kilometres, stretching from the shoreline to the top of Indonesia's tallest mountain (3381m), after which the park is named. Some wildlife is relatively easy to find, such as the rafflesia, the world's biggest flower, which also has a vile rotting smell – earning it the nickname "corpse flower". You're less likely to see the Sumatran rhinoceros or Sumatran tiger, although you might come across their tracks. Birds, however, will be your constant companions, with over three hundred species found here. But for many the big draw is the chance to see one of the world's rarest animals, the orang-utan, whose existence is threatened by the continued felling of its habitat.

There are, however, signs of hope that some habitat can be saved – epitomized by Tangkahan, a village of former loggers now making their living from ecotourism. There are only three places to stay (all simple riverside lodges) and you're free to explore the jungle by boat, foot or on the back of one of the seven elephants, who are used to patrol the area and deter loggers. Afterwards, you might like to get stuck in and wash your elephant, or rest on the beach, or even drift down the clear waters towards bat-filled caves, lazing in a rubber ring amid the chatter of toucans and leaf monkeys. Whether you're lucky enough to encounter an orang-utan or not, it's a world few get the chance to experience.

Need to know Tangkahan is five hours by car or daily bus from Medan. Accommodation can be booked through Ⓦwww.sumatraecotourism.com, which also has transport information. It's always humid, though the wet season proper occurs from October to March. Entrance to the park costs Rp20,000 (around $2).

412 BALINESE VILLAGE LIFE, INDONESIA

A world away from the frenetic hustle of Bali's tourist centres, life moves slowly in the village of Munduk. Framed by the volcanic mountains, a peaceful, bucolic scene unfolds: lumbering cows pull wooden ploughs through terraced fields, while women, encumbered with baskets of pickled cloves on their heads, stand chatting to each other.

High on a ridge in the centre of Munduk are the Puri Lumbung Cottages – sixteen converted rice granaries (lumbungs) restored by villagers using local bamboo, wood and grass. Meals, sourced from the surrounding fields, are served in the open-plan thatched restaurant whose magnificent views stretch far over the verdant rice paddies and out towards the coast.

In such relaxing surroundings, anyone needing to truly unwind could sit here for days and soak up the rhythms of rural life. But for those keen to immerse themselves in the Balinese way of life, owner Nyoman Bagiarta offers a variety of classes. These include cooking lessons, or, for the more nimble-fingered, courses in traditional weaving and woodcarving. Those with energy but less dexterity will find plenty of willing accomplices in the village's children, eager to fly their kites with you or involve you in their games. Villagers play gamelan music in the evenings and as with all else going on in this inspiring place, you're welcome to get involved. For anyone thinking there must be more to Bali than the beach, Puri Lumbung is the place to go.

Need to know Munduk is 85km from Ngurah Rai international airport. There are several other homestays in and around the village, all of which can be booked through Puri Lumbung's website. For rates, reservations, activities and accommodation details see Ⓦwww.purilumbung. com; ☏ +62 (0) 3629 2810.

INTO THE HEART OF BORNEO

The island of Borneo – which is divided between Malaysia, Indonesia and Brunei – is home to some of the world's best diving sites, along with a huge variety of plants, birds and mammals, some unique to the country. Yet it is also the land of the super-logger and oil-palm plantations that are eradicating the island's natural forests. Ecotourism is one of few economic activities that can make a convincing case for protecting these habitats while supporting indigenous communities. The following five experiences get under the skin of Borneo and demonstrate that its superb natural assets are worth more alive than felled.

413 On the rafflesia trail in Sabah, Malaysia

Sabah's Rafflesia Forest Reserve exists to protect the rafflesia – the world's largest flower. The quest to find this rare plant begins in Kota Kinabalu, where you can take a bus upwards of 1500m through thick pockets of Bornean mist to the Tambunan waterfall. Then the trail leads into the forest; scrambling through the trees, stepping round enormous buttresses and over fallen logs you come to a clearing, and there it is, lying on the ground in splendid isolation: the unmistakable blood red bloom, spotted with white markings – a lone and beautiful rafflesia.

Rafflesia flower

Need to know *Take the bus from Kota Kinabalu to The Rafflesia Information Centre at Tambunan (about 1hr). For more information about visiting the centre and guided tours contact the centre on ☏+62 (0) 8889 8500 or see ⓦwww.sabahtourism.com.*

414 Turtle watching in Sabah, Malaysia

When you see a turtle hatchling take its first steps towards the sea it becomes instantly clear what conservation is all about. You can witness this remarkable sight at the Turtle Islands National Park, which is made up of three small islands (Selingan, Bakkungan Kecil and Gulisan) in the Sulu Sea off the east coast of Sabah. Visitors may only stay on Selingan (numbers are limited to 38 per night divided between three chalets) though you can visit the two other islands during the day. At night, a ranger will take you to watch green turtles nesting on the beach and in the morning you'll get the privileged chance to see their young being released into the sea.

Need to know *The egg-laying season for turtles is between July and October. All accommodation has to be booked through Crystal Quest: ⓔcquest@tm.net.my; ☏+60 8921 2711. For entrance fees see ⓦwww.sabahparks.org.my.*

415 Miso Walai Homestay, Sabah, Malaysia

Ecotourism is a much-bandied term in Borneo, but this place fits the bill perfectly. Stay with a local host family in one of four villages in Batu Puteh Community, located in the wetlands of

Lower Kinabatangan. You'll go on river cruises and hikes into the jungle with naturalist guides, where you might come across gibbons, lemurs, tarsiers, some of the two hundred bird species or perhaps the bizarre-looking proboscis monkey, with its long, protruding nose and large belly.

Need to know *Batu Puteh is 1.5hr by road from Sandakan or 5hr from Kota Kinabalu. For prices and reservations see Ⓦwww.misowalaihomestay.com; Ⓣ+61 8955 1064.*

416 Visit an Iban longhouse, Sarawak, Malaysia

Beyond the towns and cities, the majority of the population of Sarawak lead a traditional life that revolves around the longhouse (a communal wooden house on stilts) and the river. There are several disingenuous showcase village tours, but for a more authentic experience head for the Nanga Sumpa longhouse – located a two-hour longtail-boat ride from the Batan Ai jetty on the Ulu Ai River. For the last twenty years, Kuching-based Borneo Adventure has developed tours with the owners of the longhouse, home to about thirty Iban families who provide guests with river transportation, local guides and cooks. Based at a nearby jungle lodge, you'll go fishing with the Iban, hike through jungle trails to waterfalls and visit the longhouse for an insight into today's rural Iban lifestyle.

Need to know *Three-day trips depart from Kuching. For prices and reservations see Ⓦwww. borneoadventure.com; Ⓣ+60 8224 5175.*

417 Face to face with an orang-utan, Kalimantan, Indonesia

One orang-utan has the strength of seven men. To see these rare creatures in the wild (from a respectable distance) go to the lowland rainforest of the Tanjung Putin National Park

in Kalimantan, home to one of the largest buffooneries of orang-utans in the world. Stay at Rimba Lodge, a simple and comfortable 35-room lodge by the Sekonyer River, from where you can hire guides and walk into the park...cautiously.

Orang-Utan in Tanjung Putting national park, Central Kalimantan; Iban tribe houses, Malaysia, Borneo

Need to know *For details about visiting the park either on your own or as part of a tour group, as well as information about volunteering with the Orangutan Foundation, see Ⓦwww.orangutan. org.uk. For prices, directions and reservations for Rimba Lodge see Ⓦwww.rimbalodge.com; Ⓣ+ 62 5326 710 589.*

418 SPOT A GIANT IBIS IN CAMBODIA

With only a hundred breeding pairs left in the world, the giant ibis is a twitcher's dream sighting. But as the population is confined largely to the wetlands of northern Cambodia, the only realistic prospect of sighting this elusive creature is on a birdwatching tour to the Kulen Promtep Wildlife Sanctuary. At this remote spot, the government and the Sam Veasna Centre (an ecotourism and wildlife conservation body) have established an award-winning programme that aims to link tourism, species preservation and community development harmoniously.

Four-day tours from Siam Reap to Tmatboey, a village within the wildlife sanctuary, are run exclusively through the Centre. Once in the sanctuary visitors are led by guides from the village through wetlands and deciduous forest, all the while on the lookout for the giant ibis or the white-shouldered ibis, which only nests here. A fee is paid to the village conservation fund (which goes towards schools and building fish ponds) only if you spy one of these two birds while out walking with the guides. Rather than limit the amount of funds going to conservation, this provides a clear economic incentive to the villagers – who also provide lodging and meals – to protect their prized asset.

Need to know The best time to see the ibises is January to March. For booking and details of the various birding tours offered by the Sam Veasna Centre see Ⓦwww.samveasna.org.

419 BEHIND THE SCENES AT ANGKOR WAT, CAMBODIA

Situated in the heart of Siem Reap's French Quarter, Shinta Mani hotel is just 9km from Angkor Wat, giving you a good chance to get there early enough to beat the crowds. With spacious modern rooms, a spa offering massage, body scrubs and aromatherapy, plus a swimming pool to cool off in, it's an ideal place to return to after a long day exploring the ruins. There are several boutique hotels close to Angkor but what makes Shinta Mani stand out is its Institute of Hospitality – a programme that provides young adults with nine months of culinary training, so that they can beat the poverty trap by becoming chefs. Guests can also contribute to various community projects – such as building wells or buying bicycles – and then visit the villages they have aided. It's a rare chance to meet the people who live near one of the world's great tourist attractions.

Need to know For availability, rates, directions, package offers and for details on funding students or community development projects see Ⓦwww.shintamani.com; ☎ +855 63 761 998.

The cookery school, the food and the spa at Shinta Mani

420 EXPLORE RICE TERRACES, VIETNAM

Topas Ecolodge, a solar-powered guesthouse co-owned by a Danish tour operator and local Vietnamese, has a setting to die for: perched high on a mountainous ridge near Sapa, one of Vietnam's trekking hubs, its views over the surrounding misty valleys and contoured rice paddies are mesmeric. And if you take a guided tour through these paddies – using one of the local guides who also work as waiters and carpenters at Topas – you'll discover a hidden layer of sophistication. Inside the fields an elaborate network of open pipes reveals itself, all cut like guttering from bamboo canes and connecting the paddies with mountain springs. Hydropower schemes fashioned from buckets, rocks and bamboo bring flickerings of light to the settlements hidden around.

To show you the system in more detail, your guide will take you on tiny paths you wouldn't know existed but which the hill tribes use every day, often while carrying bags of rice weighing up to 50kg on their backs. Along the way you'll stop to visit some of their homes, built of wood on the rough ground and surrounded by pot-bellied pigs, bleating goats and lumbering water buffalo.

Evening meals at the lodge (very welcome after a day's trekking) are served in the open-sided restaurant, built from a disused house that was transported in pieces to the top of this ridge, both to preserve it and bring it back to life. Ingredients are sourced from the lodge's garden and nearby food markets, and while the various Vietnamese specialties on offer are all excellent, your attention will probably still be focused on what it takes to produce a single, simple grain of rice.

Need to know *The lodge can collect you from Lao Cai railway station, about one and a half hour's drive away. Lao Cai is accessible via an overnight train from Hanoi, and as it is a border crossing with China, can also be reached from Nanning. For images and details of tours see Ⓦwww.topas-eco-lodge.com; ☏ +84 (0) 2087 2404.*

(From top) A room at Topas Eco Lodge with a view over the valley; Harvesting rice; Farmers heading home across sodden rice terraces

Local voices

Here is what tourism means to a few people who live in some of the destinations featured in this book.

ECUADOR

Moi Enomenga is president of the Quehueri' ono Association (see p.270).

"We, the Huaorani, have been around for a long time. We arrived some thousand years ago at our present location in the northeast of what is now Ecuador. "We have lived as nomadic hunters and gatherers in an extensive territory bounded by the Napo River in the north and the Curaray River in the south. Evangelical missionaries made the first contact with my family, and after them came the oil companies and loggers. Our territory suffered: pollution became a problem, the forest was threatened and our traditional lifestyle began to be undermined. In 1994 we teamed up with Andy Drumm and his tour operator Tropic Journeys in Nature, and together started a joint venture in order to work on a solution: community tourism.

"The result was a new form of ecologically friendly development sensitive to our traditions. The venture began with the development of a trek called "Amazon Headwaters with the Huaorani". That programme proved a huge success, which bought further plans – this time for a more permanent structure in the form of our new Huaorani Ecolodge. Community members were trained and plans made to produce and sell crafts.

"The project now provides work and alternative income, as well as a reason to protect the environment. As a bonus the profits pay for health and education projects to be decided on by the women of the community. There is still a lot to be done: more training, promotion and the strengthening of our tourism association are all crucial. But the creation of a new forest reserve of some 300 square kilometres will provide a boost, protecting the area's precious wildlife and providing further stimulus to tourism and protection of our land."

INDIA

Gopalan is a potter supported by The Blue Yonder's tours of Kerala (see p.348).

"Interacting with travellers who visit my pottery gives me inspiration to experiment with styles and designs in ways that I wouldn't have tried earlier. This has brought wider recognition of my work, which for me and other craftsmen has been the most important contribution of responsible tourism to our community. And in turn this brought in more orders from curious travellers, locals and even small resorts and restaurants who were trying to incorporate traditional values into their businesses."

SCOTLAND

Duncan MacPherson is Land Manager at the North Harris Trust, where Wilderness Scotland (see p.36) operates.

"We're lucky because we're not crowded out by visitors, but enough come here to put money into our pockets so that islanders can continue living here. The traditional jobs in crofting, fishing and weaving Harris tweed are no longer enough to sustain a living on their own, so tourism helps as part of the mix. But it's not like the Copacabana – you're never likely to see more than fifteen to twenty people on the beaches at any one time. That's the way we and the visitors like it!"

SOUTH AFRICA

George Dokora is a handicraft artist at Spier (see p.179).

"My journey as an artist was very tough as I could not find a place to market the artefacts and ornaments that I create out of wire and beads. I was selling them at the corner of traffic lights – at risk from car accidents and also traffic officers, who would sometimes take our wares and break them into pieces before fining us. I also had to give my products to others to sell and they were taking advantage of me.

"Finally I met Jane and Sue from Spier and they allowed me to market and exhibit my products at Spier's craft market. This has enabled me to meet clients from South Africa and abroad. Now I am able to look after my brothers and mum, and pay for their school fees, food and clothing."

THAILAND

Salamah Vejasart is from the village of Laem Naew, which is part of the Andaman Discoveries programme (see p.294).

"Before the tsunami I worked in Krabi as a door-to-door cosmetics saleswoman. After the wave took so much from my village, I decided to come back and live with my family in Laem Naew. At first I didn't understand what tourism was, but I have discovered that homestays are a way to make friends all over the world. Visitors can also help local people understand the value of the natural resources in their area and provide income for the community.

"We have no need for high technology; we do not need everything that others call 'civilized'. We have our friendships and our community. Moreover, we have the natural environment that gives us everything we need and delights all. Together, we have learned that community tourism means working with your heart."

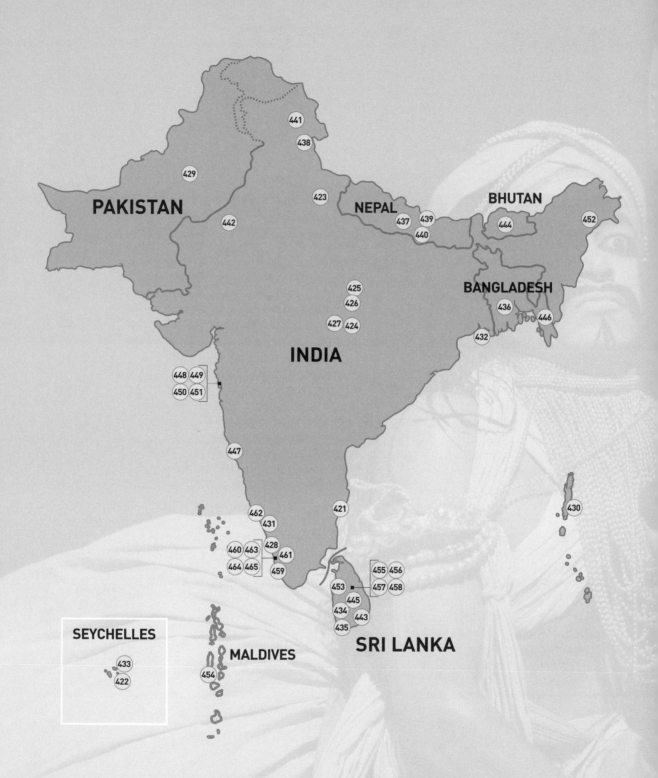

PAKISTAN

NEPAL

BHUTAN

BANGLADESH

INDIA

SEYCHELLES

MALDIVES

SRI LANKA

441
438
429
423
442
437 439
440
444
452
425
426
427 424
436
446
432
448 449
450 451
430
447
462
431
421
460 463 428
461
464 465
459
455 456
453 457 458
445
434 443
435
433
422
454

THE INDIAN SUBCONTINENT

421 Beach chic in Pondicherry, India

422 Conservation islands in the Seychelles

423 Corbett Tiger Reserve, India

424 Kanha National Park, India

425 Panna National Park, India

426 Bandhavgarh National Park, India

427 Pench Tiger Reserve, India

428 River life in Kerala

429 Go on a dolphin safari, Pakistan

430 Go barefoot on the Andamans, India

431 Take to the trees in Kerala

432 Explore the Sunderbans, India

433 Laid-back La Digue, Seychelles

434 See a rainforest being born, Sri Lanka

435 Pick a papaya in Sri Lanka

436 Travel by Rocket in Bangladesh

437 Meet the three sisters, Nepal

438 A yak safari, India

439 Journey to the centre of the world, Tibet

440 Trek through villages in Nepal

441 Track snow leopards in India

442 The real Rajasthan

443 Sleep in an elephant, Sri Lanka

444 Take the road least travelled in Bhutan

445 Tea and tartan, Sri Lanka

446 Take to the hills in Bangladesh

447 Salute the sun, Goa

448 Visit a handicraft centre, Mumbai

449 Sleep in the park with leopards, Mumbai

450 Stay in an Ecotel, Mumbai

451 Tour the slums, Mumbai

452 The Great Indian Elephant Safari, India

453 Practise your yoga at Ulpotha, Sri Lanka

454 Underwater gardening in the Maldives

455 Vil Uyana, Sri Lanka

456 Hotel Sigiriya, Sri Lanka

457 Mahoora Treehouse, Sri Lanka

458 Watch wildlife in bed, Sri Lanka

459 Go further, slower on a Keralan houseboat

460 Learn to cook, Keralan style

461 Spice up your life at Vanilla County, Kerala

462 Have Thottada beach to yourself, Kerala

463 Explore the hidden backwaters at Emerald Isle, Kerala

464 Beat stress the natural way at Philipkutty's Farm, Kerala

465 Fish for prawns in Cochin, Kerala

421 BEACH CHIC IN PONDICHERRY, INDIA

If you're looking for a different sort of beach break then try the stylish Dune Hotel, 15km from Pondicherry in Tamil Nadu. Each of its 41 rooms, spread so far among the trees on its beachfront estate that every guest is given a complimentary bike to get around, is radically different from the next. Many have been decorated with artworks by the hotel's various resident artists.

You can stay in the "Nawabi House", its four-poster bed surrounded by panelled wooden screens, which make it feel as though you're sleeping in a jewellery box. Or the two-storey "Tower", furnished like a New York loft with a jacuzzi that looks out onto the Bay of Bengal. Another has a rooftop garden, while the thatched "Baywatch" house feels more suited to Robinson Crusoe than Pamela Anderson. The resort's impact on the environment is minimal, with the rooms mostly built with reclaimed materials – and whether you've a hot tub or an outdoor shower, your water is heated with solar panels.

There's also plenty to do should you get tired of the beach or infinity pool. Families can visit the on-site organic farm that supplies the restaurant (serving French Creole–Indian fusion cuisine) and kids can milk the cows or play with a pair of noisy ducks called Sonny and Cher. There's also a catering school in the grounds training up young people who lost their parents in the 2004 tsunami. Or you can visit the quaint cobbled streets and seaside villas of the French Quarter in nearby Pondicherry, an elegant reminder that India's colonial past wasn't just about the Raj. Whatever you do and whichever room you sleep in, the Dune Hotel hints that India's beach scene is no longer just about Kerala and Goa.

Need to know *The nearest train station (Villupuram) is a 1hr taxi or rickshaw ride away, with connections from Chennai and Bengaluru. For more on accommodation, dining and reservations see ⓦwww. thedunehotel.com; ☎+91 (0) 413 265 5751.*

(Clockwise from top) Scenes at the Dune Hotel: the pool and sea; the Tower House; Lounge at the Family House; Bath at the Gramam House

422 CONSERVATION ISLANDS IN THE SEYCHELLES

Hawksbill turtle on Bird Island

The Seychelles are a celebrated honeymoon destination and as the high cost of accommodation and getting there has kept mass tourism away, you can still expect to find pristine, palm-fringed beaches and glassy waters without the crowds. Such enduring natural riches have inevitably attracted the wealthy, who come here to enjoy five-star luxury in a five-star setting. With all the excess at these exclusive hideaways, you might think there's little consideration for the environment – yet look beyond the infinity pools and you'll find that some use the income from tourism to fund admirable conservation work. These hotels match their opulence with some eye-watering prices, but if you're looking to splash out then you can live in the lap of luxury while helping to protect the exotic wildlife.

Three islands in particular are synonymous with conservation. The private island of Fregate has all you could wish for on a tropical island: beautifully crafted sea-front villas, lush vegetation and seven pearl-white beaches. Cousine Island, to the northwest, is smaller but more spacious: with only four villas (each for two persons) you're likely to have a whole stretch of sandy beach to yourself; while in the far north Bird Island has 24 spacious bungalows owned and managed by a Seychellois family.

On all three islands resident ecologists will take you on guided nature walks. Over the last decade, eighty thousand native trees have been planted on Fregate Island; you can expect to see giant tortoises wandering across the paths and exotic birds including the Seychelles blue pigeon. On both Fregate and Cousine, keep an ear out for the song of the endangered Seychelles magpie robin, which has been re-established on both islands. Cousine Island's beaches are also important nesting sites for over 250 hawksbill turtles (from mid-December to mid-February).

In terms of the sheer numbers of birds, the largest conservation work is – as you'd perhaps expect – on Bird Island, which is a breeding ground for almost two million sooty terns. The villas are in the south of the island, well away form the birds' nesting areas, but you can go on a guided tour to the north where you'll see thousands of eggs laid on the ground. All the various stages of development are on view, from the newly hatched young to overconfident juveniles attempting to fly for the first time. The island is also home to Esmeralda (aged 237), one of the largest giant tortoises in the world.

Need to know *Fregate Island:* ⓦ*www.fregate.com;* ⓣ*+49 6986 0042 980; Cousine Island:* ⓦ*www. cousineisland.com;* ⓣ*+248 (0) 321 107; Bird Island:* ⓦ*www.birdislandseychelles.com;* ⓣ*+248 (0) 224 925. Rainbow Tours organizes holidays on all three islands; for prices and reservations see* ⓦ*www.rainbowtours.co.uk;* ⓣ*+44 (0) 207 226 1004.*

TIGER SAFARIS IN INDIA

India is still the place to go if you want to see a tiger in the wild and their populations are generally healthiest in parks most visited by tourists, where there's a financial incentive to protect them. The lodges mentioned below are all committed to the preservation of the tiger, and staying at one of them ensures you the best chance of seeing this magnificent cat in the most unobtrusive way possible.

October (towards the end of the monsoons) is the coolest time to be in the parks. From October to January the land is green and lush, which makes it harder to spot tigers, but best for birdlife. The hottest months are April to June as the land gets drier before the next monsoon, when tiger sightings become more likely as wildlife gathers round the shrinking waterholes. For more on Indian tiger safaris see Ⓦwww.toftigers.org.

423 Corbett Tiger Reserve

The first wildlife reserve in India, Corbett was responsible for launching the tiger conservation scheme Project Tiger, and is well-known for its varied wildlife – keeping the striped cats company are elephants, wild boars and flying foxes. The five Raj-era rest-houses within its borders make multi-day treks through the park an attractive possibility in a country where accommodation is usually on the parks' edges. Base yourself at Camp Forktail Creek (Ⓦwww. campforktailcreek.com; ☎+91 (0) 594 728 7804), with nine spacious safari tents and two mud huts lit by candles and paraffin lamps. From there you can head on guided walks into the forest, and if you want the full wilderness experience, stay overnight in one of the rest-houses. Back at the camp, you can head down to the river and try your luck at catching the biggest game fish in the world, the mahseer.

Need to know Corbett is located in the foothills of the Himalayas near Ramnagar, in the state of Uttaranchal, an overnight train journey from Delhi.

424 Kanha National Park

Probably the most beautiful of all India's parks, Kanha – a mix of deciduous forest and savannah grassland – is reputed to have provided some of the inspiration for Rudyard Kipling's novel, *The Jungle Book*. It's particularly rich in wildlife – tigers and gaurs are regularly spotted here – and its remoteness keeps it quieter than some other parks. You couldn't get better guides to this majestic landscape than Nanda and Latika, the owners of the elegant Singinawa Jungle Lodge. Latika was the first woman to gain a doctorate in tiger conservation, while Nanda has made films for the BBC and National Geographic on the tiger.

Need to know *Located in the centre of India in southern Madhya Pradesh, the park can be reached by rail from all over India via Jabalpur. For directions, rates and reservations see Ⓦwww. singinawa.in; ☎+91 124 406 8852.*

425 Panna National Park

Covered in a mix of acacia and forest, Panna is a beautiful park with an amazing variety of birds, and plentiful wildlife from crocodiles to sloth bears. Unfortunately many of its tigers haven't fared so well in recent years, with poaching a persistent threat despite improved measures protecting tigers' welfare. Stay at Ken River Lodge, however, and you've a tiger-spotting opportunity unique in all of India – night safaris, which offer the best chance of seeing these nocturnal predators hunting. Futhermore, a stay in the park could easily be combined with a visit to the famous temples of Khajuraho – only 27km away – complete with erotic stonework.

Need to know *For information on Panna National Park visit Ⓦwww.pannanationalpark.net; ☎+91 (0) 112 794 8870. Ken River Lodge: Ⓦwww. kenriverlodge.com; ☎+91 773 227 5235.*

426 Bandhavgarh National Park

You've got to be really unlucky not to spot a tiger here. One of India's most prominent national parks, Bandhavgarh is also home to over 150 species of birds, among them purple sunbirds and golden orioles. Ancient ruins – statues, forts and man-made caves – scatter the park, making this a magnet for history-lovers and photographers. As a nature photographer himself, Satyendra Kumar Tiwari makes the ideal guide. Along with his wife Kay, he runs an intimate guesthouse in their family home – Skay's Camp, situated in a small village on the park boundary, with just five rooms for guests. He'll take you on two trips a day, looking for everything from big cats to butterflies.

Need to know *The park is in Madhya Pradesh and can be accessed by taxi from Umaria (1hr), itself accessible by train from Delhi (Utkal Express #8478). Bandhavgarh National Park: ⓦwww.bandhavgarh.net; ☎+91 (0) 112 757 0446. For information on Skay's Camp visit ⓦwww.kaysat.com; ☎+91 (0) 762 726 5309.*

427 Pench Tiger Reserve

Singinawa Jungle Lodge

Another inspirational setting for Kipling's *The Jungle Book*, Pench Tiger Reserve – now better known for its leopards than its tigers (although sightings are becoming more common as stocks improve) – is home to over 250 species of bird. Animals gather at the reservoir in the centre of the park to drink, and as the seasons get hotter and drier, this becomes an excellent spot to observe wildlife as the other water sources dry up. It's also a relaxing place to go boating. The twelve villas at Baghvan lodge each have their own private viewing decks, giving you the chance for that elusive sighting all on your own.

Need to know *Pench is open Nov–July. The nearest train station is Badnera, 110km from the reserve. For further info on the park see ⓦwww.pench.naturesafariindia.com; ☎+91 (0) 921 230 5607. Baghvan lodge: ⓦwww.tajsafaris.com.*

Getting this close to a tiger is something few forget

428 RIVER LIFE IN KERALA

To really discover the heart of Kerala, you need to leave the beach, jump off the houseboat or troop down from the hills to the banks of the River Nila, where a variety of traditional activities are on offer with The Blue Yonder. You could spend a day river-rafting with former smugglers, help out at an elephant rehabilitation centre or admire the spectacular kicks and dives of *kalari payattu*, Kerala's traditional martial art. The Blue Yonder works with local artisans and communities to promote and preserve their culture; as such they encourage you to learn how to play Keralan musical instruments, visit villages along the river and watch traditional *kathakali* (theatre) and *mohiniyattam* (dance).

The accommodation is also much more than just a place to lay your head – it's an integral part of the experience, especially if you opt for the homestay option with local families in preference to a stay at River Retreat, a former summer palace of the Maharaja of Cochin. You could stay with Praveen, retired early from the Merchant Navy to run a homestay with his wife – they both also manage the local school. Or with the Namboodris in their calm and elegant 200-year-old home. Pillars of their local rural community, the Namboodris are well-travelled and erudite companions (he's a water engineer and expert on international development; she's an excellent guide to India's spiritual traditions). You're free to wander round their beautiful, herb-filled garden and say hello to the resident – and cherished – cow. In the evenings, you'll dine on delicious, home-grown vegetarian food while conversation drifts easily between the relevance of the *Vedas* to the adventures of the Namboodris' daughter – India's first female elephant trainer – and her husband, a snake priest.

Need to know *Contact The Blue Yonder (ⓦwww. theblueyonder.com; ☎+91 8041 152 218) to customize your trip. The Blue Yonder runs similar community-focused trips throughout India; for further details see the website.*

(From top) Kerala scenes: Kathakali performance; practising kalari payattu; peppercorns growing in the sun

429 GO ON A DOLPHIN SAFARI, PAKISTAN

A devastating mix of over-hunting, dam building and declining water levels has had terrible effects on the Indus River dolphin, to the extent that there are reportedly only one thousand of them left in the world, all in Pakistan. Grey-brown, stocky and functionally blind, these dolphins have a peculiar and unique trick: swimming on their side while underwater, they use one fin to feel their way along the bottom, then roll to the surface to take in air, appearing to wave with their other fin.

Instead of hunting the dolphins for their blubber, local fishermen are now working with The Adventure Foundation of Pakistan to earn a better living by taking guests on dolphin "boat safaris". For two days aboard the fishermen's wooden sail-boats, guests glide down part of the 900km stretch of the Indus, searching for these rare mammals.

Unobtrusive hydrophones, used to pick up the dolphins' sonic communication, are dropped into the water, so unlike many other invasive and damaging tours – which might involve feeding or swimming with the dolphins – The Adventure Foundation ensures that your contact with them is as discreet as possible. Once found, you'll follow the chattering dolphins along the river, watching them dive into the murky depths and waiting for them to rise up again with that distinctive wave.

Mesmerizing as the dolphins' antics can be, it's also worth looking to the skies; among the many bird species following the migratory flight path south from Russia, you might spot Siberian cranes, flamingos and pelicans. You'll have to tear yourself away from all the action above and below water – but there's also camping by the river and a couple of visits to lively riverbank villages to fit in.

Need to know The tour starts at the Taunsa River Barrage, which can be reached from Multan by car or taxi (2hr 30min; contact the Foundation for directions). There are also half- and one-day tours available. For prices and more information, see Ⓦindusdolphin.org.pk; Ⓣ+92 (0) 512 825 805.

430 GO BAREFOOT ON THE ANDAMANS, INDIA

With perfect beaches, dense rainforests and some of the world's best diving, there's much to lure travellers to the Andaman Islands, 1000km off the east coast of India. But it would be best to steer clear of Sentinel Island: so averse to visitors are the indigenous Sentinelese that when the Indian army airlifted supplies in after the 2004 tsunami, they simply took everything, buried it on the beach, and hurled spears at the helicopters above. They remain one of the last truly isolated tribes on Earth.

Elsewhere, however, development is happening at a greater pace. The main tourist hub is the island of Havelock, where plenty of beach huts are set back among the trees that line two of its beaches. The star is Barefoot Jungle Camp, whose complex of thatched cottages and villas is one of just two resorts located in the mahua forest that fringes Radhanagar Beach. Staffed by Andaman locals, the camp has set up the only rubbish-collection operation on the island, and is educating school children on how best to protect and preserve their surrounding environment.

For those eager to get a taste of deserted island life, Barefoot offers a few overnight trips to some of the uninhabited islands. You can sea-kayak, snorkel little-visited reefs and share the beach with unperturbed and harmless monitor lizards. And as you'll be visiting one of the hundreds of islands on which no people live, you can rest assured there'll be no spears piercing your tent while you sleep.

Need to know For details on how to access the resort from the cities of Chennai or Kolkata as well as prices and further information, see Ⓦwww. barefootindia.com; Ⓣ+91 3192 236 008.

431 TAKE TO THE TREES IN KERALA

You can see your accommodation – a wooden hut housing a double bed swathed in a mosquito net, with an attached bathroom and verandah – on top of a giant banyan tree. You don't fancy shimmying up the 18m trunk to get there though. Thankfully, you're saved by an ingenious "water lift".

Babu Varghese – the owner of the treehouses at Green Magic Nature Resort 2, situated at Kalladi, in the hilly district of Wayanad in northeastern Kerala – is the inventor of this unique contraption: a giant bucket is filled with water, which is then used as a counterweight for the caged metal lift that holds the guests. As you wait several minutes for the buckets to fill, you may wish you hadn't had that extra serving of curry at dinner. But it wouldn't be easy to say no. The resident chefs prepare spectacular Keralan vegetarian specialities, with all the ingredients sourced from their own farm. Those keen to try Keralan cooking at home can even take classes in how to make delicious dishes such as pineapple curry or potato bhaji.

During their stay, every guest – whether they are staying in a treehouse or, for those suffering from vertigo, in the remote cave room or simple rooms in the lodge – is required to plant a sapling to help ensure the forest's survival. The rest of the time, the resort offers visits to the lovely Soochippara waterfalls, searches for wild elephants, or drives around the surrounding tea plantations. But with the plethora of bushy-tailed Malabar squirrels and brightly coloured song birds in the camp, it would be just as tempting to spend the day sitting in your treehouse, training your binoculars into the branches. It'll give the staff time to fill the bucket, too.

Need to know The treehouses cost US$240 full-board per night, which also includes jeep transfer to and from Kalladi. Kalladi can be reached by taxi in a couple of hours from the cities of Ooty, Kozhikode and Mysore. For further info see ⓦwww.tourindiakerala.com; ☏+91 (0) 471 232 8070.

432 EXPLORE THE SUNDERBANS, INDIA

The Sunderbans National Park is the largest mangrove forest in the world – a giant mass of trunks and spindly roots that reach deep into the salty water, enabling them to survive. The area is home to crocodiles, monitor lizards and hundreds of species of birds, including kingfishers and egrets. But the animal for which this region is most famed is the Royal Bengal tiger, of which around 270 live in the park – the highest density anywhere in India.

Help Tourism is one of the few companies offering safaris around the Sunderbans park – in their case, via a motorized boat that cruises through the park's rivers and creeks and stops at wildlife-watching towers en route. Their accommodation, the remote Jungle Camp on Bali Island, consists of six comfortable bungalows and a restaurant situated among trees and lush paddy fields. Towards the end of the tour guests visit a village and then spend an hour on rowing boats exploring the mangroves.

Four million people inhabit the Sunderbans, sharing the marshy ecosystem with the animals: a large proportion of them are fishermen and rice farmers, while some also venture far into the tangle of vegetation to collect honey, always at risk of a tiger attack. As well as being a significant source of employment for the local people, Help Tourism is committed to protecting the tigers and their prey, the spotted deer, from poaching – and they've almost achieved a complete stop to this on Bali Island. Staying here not only helps them with their continued efforts but provides one of the best chances of spotting a tiger in the wild.

Need to know Help Tourism will transfer guests from Kolkata airport to the harbour (3hr), from where a boat takes you to Jungle Camp (2hr). A three-night stay, including transfer, all food and safaris, costs R15,950 (US$330) per person. For further information and reservations visit ⓦwww.helptourism.org; ☏+91 (0) 983 103 1980.

433 LAID-BACK LA DIGUE, SEYCHELLES

Bikes are the premier mode of transport on La Digue

Hotels in the Seychelles are mainly luxurious (see p.319), but for a more down-to-earth experience head for the island of La Digue, a short ferry ride from Praslin. Here you'll find simple, locally owned guesthouses costing around R1220 (US$70) a night for two people, such as Bernique Guesthouse, a 20min walk from the village of La Passe. Surrounded by breadfruit trees, breakfast here is fresh fruit and local vanilla tea – after which you can spend a day exploring the island by bike.

Island life on La Digue retains a sense of how it's been for generations. The fishermen's fresh catch is still sold on the quayside, roadside musicians strum Creole rhythms and you'll see plenty of late-night rum-fuelled dominoes matches. Needless to say the pace of life is slow. The island is just 5km long and 3km wide, so it's easy to walk around, though most of the locals ride bikes or use ox-carts to transport goods as the roads are mostly car-free (there is only one paved road). Some of the guesthouses offer an ox-cart taxi service from the jetty (or even ox-cart tours around the island) and rent bikes.

Although the island is largely flat, you can do a fairly steep walk up to the summit of Nid Aigle ('Eagle's Nest Mountain'), 333m above sea level, where there are stunning views of the plateau and beyond, to the west, the islands of Praslin, Félicité and Marianne. Elsewhere you can visit the Veuve Reserve, the only home of the critically endangered black paradise flycatcher.

The beaches on La Digue – quietest in the morning, when you're likely to find them largely empty – are long strips of soft pinky-white sand, framed by arching coconut palms and enormous, smooth granite boulders. Source d'Argent claims to be the most photographed beach in the world (access is via L'Union Estate, which requires an entrance fee of US$5), though if you want somewhere more low-key, head further along the coastline to Anse Bonnet Carré, which has the same white sand as its famous neighbour, with fewer rocks and the same shallow warm waters.

Despite the seductive beauty of the area, La Digue has managed to resist the development of international hotels that, elsewhere, have alienated local people by blocking access to the coast. Welcoming and friendly, the guesthouses here are a different breed: inclusive and laid-back. Truly Seychellois.

Need to know *Ferries run from the island of Praslin to La Digue (20min). For prices and reservations at Bernique Guesthouse call ☏+248 234 229. For a map of the island and information on restaurants, accommodation and activities see ⊛www.ladigue.sc. You can hire bikes from Chez Michelin, just across the road from the jetty, for around R220 (US$13) per day (⊛www.seychelles.net/chezmich; ☏+248 234 304).*

Red chillies (top) and papaya (bottom) are some of the fresh produce ready to be picked and cooked at Samarkanda

434 SEE A RAINFOREST BEING BORN, SRI LANKA

Fifteen years ago the land around the village of Hindurangala, 70km from Colombo, was a degraded rubber plantation. Now, the Mahausakande forest – a swathe of dense foliage – carpets the area. This remarkable regeneration has come about thanks to the Ellawalla Foundation Trust, a non-profit organization committed to conserving and safeguarding the southwestern Sri Lankan rainforests, which are fast disappearing as tea and coconut plantations, rice paddies and new settlements are developed over them.

Ellawalla's main aim is to nurture the rainforest's endemic species, and to cast out invasive ones. It works with local communities, encouraging them to cease environmentally damaging activities such as illegal logging and overzealous farming, and to focus instead on looking after their surroundings, from which they can foster sustainable incomes. Children from nearby schools are brought here to learn about conservation and local women have formed a co-operative to make crafts from recycled paper and natural products.

To help fund all this, the Foundation has created four nature trails. The yellow trail winds you through the lush riverside habitat; the green deals with woody plants; the red shows off the forest's birds and butterflies. The fourth trail meanders through Mahausakande up to the adjoining Bambaragala Reservation, where visitors can have a picnic lunch beside a waterfall – a deafening but exhilarating experience after heavy rains.

If you want to listen to the scuffles, squawks and squeaks of the forest at night, and perhaps spot a porcupine, you can spend an hour or two in the purpose-built "night watch" tower. Or, if you prefer to catch up on your sleep after an energetic day's hike, bed down in the simple wooden hut nestled among the trees.

Need to know *The rest huts sleep twelve, but is only hired out to one group at a time, at the same price regardless of number. There are cooking facilities, or you can employ the services of one of the villagers. For directions, prices and more information, see ⓦwww.mahausakande.org; ☎+94 (0) 365 671 421.*

435 PICK A PAPAYA IN SRI LANKA

If, along with rest and relaxation, your idea of the perfect holiday hideaway involves cooking up your own meals with fresh ingredients, then a self-catering stay at Samakanda Guesthouse might be just what you're looking for.

Tucked away in the hills above the town of Galle, Samakanda comprises two comfortable, solar-powered cottages: one a restored planter's hut, the other a small bungalow overlooking lush terraced fields. As well as being an idyllic spot to cook your own food, it's a great place to pick it – guests are welcome to take what they need from the organic spice, herb and vegetable gardens that enclose each property, from fresh salad greens to delicious fruits such as papayas, coconuts, passion fruits and bananas. The estate even grows its own rare strain of red rice, while local markets can supply fresh fish.

Should you fancy a night off from cooking, call on gourmet chef, Rory, the owner and founder of Samakanda, to show you how the stone pizza-oven works, or help you prepare some of his own favourites. With all the meals you and he can rustle up, you'll also need a way to work it off; walk some of the trails laid out through the surrounding fields and forests, amble down to the river to cool off, or for the more energetic, try an exhilarating 40km cycle ride down through the jungle to the beach...and back.

Need to know *For directions, accommodation details, rates and reservations visit ⓦwww. samakanda.org.*

436 TRAVEL BY ROCKET IN BANGLADESH

More water flows through Bangladesh than in all the rivers of Europe combined, so the most logical choice of transport here is boat. One of the more unusual ones is a 1920s British-built paddlewheel steamer, known as *The Rocket*, which leisurely plies the waters between Dhaka and the southern town of Khulna. At 28 hours, the journey is not a fast one; by bus, the same trip takes eight. But while the bus is a white-knuckle ride through some of the world's most crowded and chaotic streets, where you put your life in the driver's hands, this is an unparalleled opportunity to discover life on the Ganges.

Stepping onto the deck of *The Rocket* you soon learn where third class is – it's everywhere. Every inch of space is utilized in some way. Music blares from speakers hung around a packed chai stall while cigarette sellers and food vendors jostle for business. First class is another matter, however. It's by no means luxurious (people might still be sleeping outside your door, and the dining table may have seen better days) but you get your own cabin with a fan, a sink and a small porthole. Don't spend too long squinting through it, though, as you'll get a better view of the spectacular scenery outside from on deck: men fishing among the verdant water hyacinths, women slapping saris clean against the smooth rocks, children dashing about, and maybe even a rare Gangetic dolphin breaking the surface.

Need to know Tickets for The Rocket can be booked in Dhaka or at the various ports of call, though not by internet. A tour company such as Bangladesh Ecotours (🌐www.bangladeshecotours. com) can book the tickets for you, and it's probably the best way to ensure a first-class cabin.

Pulling away from the Rocket in a wooden boat taxi; A food-seller in third class on the Rocket

SEE THE OTHER SIDE OF THE HIMALAYAS

They may cross six countries and contain many colossal mountains such as Everest and K2, but journeying through the Himalayas isn't just about making it to the top. The following five treks will give you more than just sore feet and lots of photos of snow-capped peaks.

437 Meet the three sisters, Nepal

Lucky, Nicky and Dicky are a bit of a legend in Nepal. Having opened a restaurant and guesthouse overlooking Lake Fewa in the trekking capital of Pokhara, the three Chhetri sisters broke with taboo in this traditional society by establishing their own trekking company. They and their female guides and porters take groups on a variety of different treks, including through the famous Annapurna, Everest and Langtang ranges. Some of their groups are women only, others open to both sexes; all their trips, however, are refreshingly free of the obsession with "getting there" that some testosterone-heavy hikes to the summit can exude. At a slower pace, you'll have time to really enjoy the spectacular surroundings; after all, it's a long way up.

Need to know Minimum group size five. The Annapurna Circuit (18 days) costs US$1045 per person; the Ghorepani or Poon Hill Loop circuits (both 5 days) cost US$290 per person, inclusive of meals, accommodation, transport and entry fees. For details of treks and accommodation visit Ⓦwww.3sistersadventure.com; ☎+977 (0) 6146 2066. The sisters also offer women-run rafting and safari trips to Chitwan.

438 A yak safari, India

As they seem to prefer standing alone atop freezing mountain ridges, few people ever get very close to a yak. On a "yak safari" with Spiti Ecosphere, however, you'll get to ride one. With a surefootedness suited to the rocky paths and alpine pastures, the hairy beast will transport you over the Spiti Valley in northern Himachal Pradesh. You'll stay overnight with families in remote villages, dining with them and chatting with some of the local farmers. Once the lifeline of isolated rural communities scattered about Himachal Pradesh, the yak is now slowly disappearing, as modern farming tools obviate the need for it. The emergence of yak safaris, however, has ensured that the hirsute animal has regained its value. Long live the yak.

Need to know Ecosphere also offers several walking and mountain-biking trips in the valley, plus rafting trips down the Spiti River. Ⓦwww. spitiecosphere.com; ☎+91 (0) 1906 222 724.

439 Journey to the centre of the world, Tibet

Going to Tibet (or not) is a thorny issue for travellers, as if you visit from inside China your only realistic option is a state-sanctioned tour. One way round this is to go on a trip with The Himalayan Adventure Company, which starts its tour in Kathmandu, exploring its winding lanes and ornate temples, before setting off on a long drive into Tibet. Along the way, you'll break for village visits and a dip in another deeply revered site – the salty Lake Manasarovar. The highlight of the trip is Mount Kailash, a hulking mountain of black rock from which spring four major rivers: the Indus, Bramaputra, Sutrej and Karnali.

Need to know Trips run from April to October. For prices and details of itineraries visit Ⓦwww. thehimalayanadventurecompany.com; ☎+44 (0) 845 094 0273.

440 Trek through villages in Nepal

The Himalayas are home to some of the world's most physical trekking, but if you're after a gentler approach, head for the Annapurna region. A trek here takes in spectacular views of Machaupuchare mountain and involves a morning on Poon Hill, watching the sun rise over the Daulaghiri peaks. With plenty of other trekkers on the path, you could easily negotiate the trek alone. But if you do it as part of a two-week Annapurna Trails and Homestay trip with The Responsible Travellers (who invest all their profits in local charities), you'll also spend four days visiting Kathmandu and the medieval town of Bhaktapur. The trip concludes with four nights living with a Nepalese family.

Need to know *The fifteen-day trip starts and ends in Kathmandu. For itinerary details and prices see Ⓦwww.theresponsibletravellers.com. For a similar experience, but trekking through the foothills of Everest, see Ⓦwww.handsupholidays.com/tours/ everest-bound; Ⓣ+44 (0) 800 783 3554.*

441 Track snow leopards in India

The ideal time to look for the snow leopard is late autumn and early spring, when there's enough food to tempt it out of hiding but there's still snow on the ground to reveal its tracks. After a few days acclimatizing in Ladakh's capital Leh, you and your local guide, an expert mountaineer and snow leopard researcher, head off into the Hemis Valley National Park to spend six days in pursuit of this most elusive of cats. Sightings are not guaranteed, but even if you don't spot one, the rugged mountain scenery is populated by enough other animals, including the ibex and Himalayan marmot, to keep you happy.

Need to know *Starting and ending in Delhi, the fourteen-day trip takes place in March and November. Accommodation in Delhi and Leh is in guesthouses, while trekking accommodation is in rural homes and tented camps. For tour dates and details of itineraries see Ⓦwww.discoveryinitiatives. com; Ⓣ+44 (0) 1285 643 333.*

The ideal time to look for a snow leopard is late autumn or early spring

Traditional houses and homes of Nepal

The Blue Yonder take guests to meet the people making souvenirs like this doll

442 THE REAL RAJASTHAN

The largest state in India, Rajasthan is also one of the most beautiful and exciting – home to colourful markets, welcoming cities, vibrant music and delicious cuisine. The royal palaces that pepper the state feature heavily on tourist itineraries: rich, decorative and intricate, they epitomize the luxury and decadence of the Raj. But for those who want to go behind the scenes, India-based travel company The Blue Yonder runs custom-made trips that allow you to explore what really makes Rajasthan tick.

A trip could kick off in the rose-pink city of Jaipur, famous for its magnificent sandstone Amber Fort. After staying for a night or two in an attentive, family-run hotel, you might decide to travel on to the semi-arid areas of Shekhawati or the desert city of Bikaner, where you'll meet artisans busy weaving Rajasthan's famous patterned carpets and making pretty tie-dye garments. You can even make your own bangles, like those you see dripping from most Indian women's wrists.

Elsewhere, you'll join the Makrana people, who practise puppetry not just to entertain tourists but, in conjunction with The Blue Yonder, to educate and inspire illiterate local children. You could finish your trip with a shopping expedition in market-filled Udaipur. And in the evenings you'll sit among the community and listen to folk songs and stories, watching the whirling choreography of the richly bejewelled dancers.

As well as looking behind Rajasthan's cultural scene, you could choose to go on a jeep tiger-safari in Rathambore Park, visit the Karni Mata Temple, where thousands of rats are worshipped, or hop aboard a camel for a bumpy ride among the sand dunes of the Thar Desert. Allowing visitors a large variety of ways in which to meet the local people and to see little-trodden areas of the state, Blue Yonder's trips give a vibrant taster of the real India.

Need to know *A typical two-week tour starts in Jaipur and ends in Udaipur, but it's possible to customize your visit to any length, and to any of the projects and villages involved. Contact The Blue Yonder (Ⓦwww.theblueyonder.com; ☎+91 (0) 8041 152 218) for prices and more information.*

443 SLEEP IN AN ELEPHANT, SRI LANKA

That's no misprint in the title. At KumbukRiver, an award-winning ecolodge, you really do sleep in an elephant – except this one is 12m tall and thatched, built to resemble a pachyderm and set in rural surroundings by a babbling river. It's a fabulous structure: the long thatched trunk extends down to the entrance, while the softly lit wooden interior is decorated with cartwheels on the walls and cushioned benches.

The lodge sleeps ten, but to ensure exclusivity on the estate, it's only ever let to one group at a time. Delicious Sri Lankan dishes are cooked up and served by members of the local farming village – the very members who built and run this unique hotel as an alternative to poaching and illegal logging. Should you tire of lounging by the pool, there's organized trekking and wildlife-spotting in nearby Yala National Park – where you might catch a glimpse of an elephant of the non-thatched kind.

Need to know KumbukRiver is located 250km from Colombo and can only be reached by road (car or taxi). For further info, rates and reservations visit ⓦwww.kumbukriver.com; ☏+94 (0) 773 632 182.

444 TAKE THE ROAD LEAST TRAVELLED IN BHUTAN

If any country in the world can lay claim to the word unique, it's the Himalayan mountain kingdom of Bhutan. Where every other government in the world views economic growth, measured via Gross Domestic Product (GDP), as the indicator of its success, this landlocked region nestled between Tibet, Nepal and the Indian state of Sikkim has declared that its yardstick is GNH, or Gross National Happiness.

It's the only country in the world to ban tobacco; it's compulsory for Bhutanese to wear the national dress while in public; and television was only made legal in 1999. After introducing their first-ever traffic light a few years ago, they changed their mind, decided it was too impersonal, and re-employed a smartly dressed traffic officer to direct what little traffic there is. If it sounds somewhat undemocratic, that was also true until 2008, when the king voluntarily abdicated, changed the monarchy from absolute to constitutional, and called for Bhutan's first democratic elections.

Tourists are welcome as part of groups (or escorted individuals) and account for its second-largest industry – but they are still few and far between. The government mandates that all trips charge a minimum cost equivalent to US$165 per person daily in the low season (more for individuals and in high season), which includes all accommodation, food and internal transport. It's elitist, but at least keeps hordes of backpackers at bay.

All tourism must be approved by the government as being environmentally and socially sustainable, and as such the idyllic landscape – scattered villages surrounded by terraced paddy fields, soaring snow-covered peaks and stone mountain fortresses with foreboding iron doors – remains almost untouched by industrialization. The close familial bonds, religious devotion expressed publicly in an endless array of colourful festivals, and the shifting of the seasons all still define daily life for most of the people you'll encounter.

Bhutan also has some of the best trekking in the world, from short visits to the villages in the sacred Bumthang Valley to the awesome Lunana Snowman trek – a 28-day high altitude trek into the most inaccessible parts of the country, home to yaks, yeti legends and the vast mountain of Gangkar Punsum. And as one of the world's most biodiverse countries, there's also the chance to see snow leopards, tigers, elephants and red pandas, and hundreds of species of birds. The forests they inhabit are pretty safe, too, as the king has decreed that the country will never be less than sixty percent forest – and at present it remains over 75 percent covered. Head off into the beautiful hills and you'll probably come across more yaks than fellow walkers.

Need to know Several tour companies run guided tours and treks in Bhutan. To take part in the Snowman, try ⓦwww.themountaincompany.co.uk or the Bhutanese-run ⓦwww.bookbhutantours.com. For all else, the national tourism website of Bhutan is a good place to start: ⓦwww.tourism.gov.bt.

The hills around Hunas Falls;
Women picking tea

445 TEA AND TARTAN, SRI LANKA

Hunas Falls isn't what you'd normally expect from an ecolodge in Sri Lanka. That might be down to the piped jazz in the lobby, the billiards room or the tartan extravaganza that is "the Highlander Suite". But it's worth getting past (or better still, getting into) the retro décor: high up in the cool, fresh air of the hills above the city of Kandy, Hunas Falls is the perfect place to escape the heat and humidity of central Sri Lanka.

Surrounded by a series of waterfalls and a fertile forest of bamboo, fern and avocado trees, the hotel overlooks spice and vegetable gardens and beneath them the Dumbara Valley, from where much of the food for the lakeside restaurant is sourced. Committed to conserving its lush environs for decades now, the hotel avoids the use of pesticides and grows seedlings of indigenous trees in its nursery for reforesting; guests are welcome to buy their own tree to plant.

During your stay you may like to potter about in a pedalo on the glassy lake, trek in the surrounding Dumbara Valley, make a visit to a local tea factory or try some Ayurvedic massage. Hunas Falls will certainly fulfill your expectations of an ecolodge – and it might even foster a keen interest in billiards.

Need to know *The lodge is 26km from Kandy. For prices and more information (including the lodge's environmental policies) see ⓦwww.jetwingtravels. com; ☎+94 (0) 812 470 041.*

446 TAKE TO THE HILLS IN BANGLADESH

When people talk of visiting hill tribes, Bangladesh is rarely the destination that comes to mind. Yet in the dense rainforests that line the country's southeastern border with Burma and India, there are half a million indigenous people belonging to fourteen different tribes – and unlike in Laos, Thailand or Cambodia, very few tourists make the effort to visit the villages.

For the visitors that do come, however, Bangladesh Ecotours takes guests into the Chittagong Hill Tracts region to stay with tribes, sharing in traditional feasts, shopping for handicrafts, and often finding themselves the audience for an impromptu song-and-dance given in their honour. There's usually the chance for some trekking in the surrounding hills, birdwatching, cruises down the river or visits to nearby Hindu and Buddhist temples. In return for their hospitality, the company provides the tribes with funds for education and medical aid, promoting conservation projects such as reforestation and handicraft development.

One other aspect makes these hill tours different, at least at present. A few years ago, an aid worker was kidnapped in the area and returned unharmed. As a consequence the government now insists that all foreigners have an armed guard for the entirety of their stay in the Chittagong Hill Tracts. The constant presence of a couple of rifle-laden policemen isn't ideal, but they keep themselves to themselves and it's the only way to get to see these remote places. And considering that you are likely to be the only tourist there, you're going to stand out anyway.

Need to know *Bangladesh Ecotours, based in Chittagong, will customize a trip according to individual requirements. Also available are trips to the Sunderbans and to the northern tea estates. For prices, reservations and information on how to get to Chittagong see ⓦwww.bangladeshecotours. com.*

447 SALUTE THE SUN, GOA

While much of the enlightenment on offer in Goa is distinctly ersatz, Yogamagic is the real deal. Set a couple of kilometres back from celebrated Vagator beach, the solar-powered resort is made up of several airy desert tents – complete with cool thatched roofs and earthen walls draped with colourful saris – and two luxurious suites set in the main house. Food is a highlight – a world away from the identikit menus found in many of the state's beach shacks; guests will find surprising twists on Indian classics, such as avocado *raita* and cherry tomato *sambal*, and most of the ingredients are grown in the fields that surround the tents and pool.

Yoga classes take place in the ambient "yoga temple" and are held daily in the mornings and some evenings, attracting experts and novices alike. Chanting and meditation is also on offer, as well as some philosophy, art and music classes.

If you're curious, it's easy enough to seek out the legendary Goan parties on Vagator and Anjuna beaches. But if you're looking to clear your head in Goa rather than shake it on the dance floor, this is the place to come.

Need to know Yogamagic is open between mid-November and mid-April. The nearest train station is 30min away at Thivim, on the line between Mumbai and Trivandrum. For further info on accommodation, classes and rates see Ⓦwww.yogamagic.net; ☎+91 (0) 832 652 3796.

Practising the Mountain Pose on the beach

GREEN MUMBAI

It's difficult to get bored in a city like Mumbai: you can be an extra in a Bollywood extravaganza one day, see leopards in the wild the next, and on the third, visit the Temples of Silence, where the Parsis lay their dead out for vultures to feed upon. Your own food options are rather more appetizing: you can stroll down Chowpatty beach to mix with the locals and snack on *bhel puri* (puffed rice and diced potato with chutney, onion and coriander); try every Indian regional cuisine in one of the many restaurants; or stop by the side of the road for a samosa and sweet lassi (a flavoured yogurt drink). The following four experiences give just a taste of what's on offer.

448 Visit a handicraft centre

India is home to over a billion people, more than a thousand distinct languages and countless different arts and handicrafts. Travelling across the country, you'll no doubt encounter some of these crafts, but the trouble is, in such a large place, it would take you a lifetime to trawl them all. Fortunately, since 1960, Fabindia has been collecting them and bringing them to a single location. Pay a visit to one of its stores – showcasing the finest hand-made linens, textiles, garments and jewellery, sourced directly from village craftsmen – and you're bound to find something worth taking home.

Shop for hand-made textiles at Fabindia; Woman buying a lassi from a Mumbai street vendor

Need to know *Fabindia has eleven stores in Mumbai, often open until 9pm or later. They also sell organic food. Visit* Ⓦ*www.fabindia.com for more information.*

449 Sleep in the park with leopards

Where London has Hyde Park and New York has Central Park, Mumbai has Sanjay Gandhi National Park, also known as Boravili. While the others are well-tended city parks, however, Sanjay Gandhi is, in places, truly wild. So wild that there are leopards and, reputedly, the occasional tiger lurking about – but they are shy beasts, so the chances of coming across one are pretty slim. Beloved by Mumbaikers for a stroll, the huge park provides a unique getaway from the crowds pounding the hot streets of the city. Better still, book yourself into one of the park huts, and as the hordes of people ebb away towards closing time, you'll have the park to yourself. The huts themselves are very simple – there are no mod cons – but that's of no significance as you peer through your hut window, aware that somewhere out there in the inky blackness, a leopard is prowling.

Need to know *To reserve a stay in either the forest lodge or one of the surrounding huts, go to* Ⓦ*www.tourism-of-india.comsanjaygandhi.html.*

450 Stay in an Ecotel

If the thought of leopards outside your bedroom window isn't your cup of chai, there are two great hotels in Mumbai offering alternative encounters with nature. The five-star Orchid is 15min from the international airport, has a 21m waterfall in the lobby and its own rooftop swimming pool from where you can survey the busy Mumbai skyline. The three-star Rodas, meanwhile, is located on the edge of Powai Lake, where you can take a boat out and watch the crocodiles basking on the banks. By undertaking a range of initiatives to reduce their environmental impact – from the design of the buildings, stringent water and energy conservation, composting food waste and even providing sustainably produced slippers in every room, both hotels show that if you can do it in one of the world's biggest cities, you can do it anywhere.

Need to know *For rates and reservations at Orchid see ⓦwww.orchidhotel.com, ☏+91 (0) 222 616 4040. Rodas: ⓦwww.rodashotel.com, ☏+91 (0) 226 693 6969.*

451 Tour the slums

You might not think a slum could be a tourist destination, but responsible tour operator Reality Tours and Travel aims to banish that preconception by taking visitors around Dharavi, the largest slum in Asia. It's a noisy, vibrant place – packed full of kids, people going about their daily business and scavenging goats – but Reality Tours and Travel ensures you aren't there to gawp; the people make sure that the people you meet will benefit from your trip, with eighty percent of profits going to local charities. A tour highlight is a visit to the school and community centre built with these funds.

Need to know *Reality Tours also offers market and village tours. It's possible to volunteer at the centre for periods of three months or more. ⓦwww. realitytoursandtravel.com.*

(Clockwise from top) A potter at work; the Dharavi skyline; A leather tannery; A tour around the slums of Dharavi offers an insight into daily life

Taking a break at the safari camp; Once employed as timber fellers, these elephants along with their mahouts now happily enable tourists to see the more remote parts of Arunachal Pradesh; Camp accommodation; The Khampti musicians and dancers

452 THE GREAT INDIAN ELEPHANT SAFARI, INDIA

Elephant rides are a common enough tourist activity in India, but an elephant safari – riding tamed elephants from village to village or camp to camp – is a much rarer experience, and one that benefits animals whose survival would otherwise be at risk.

For years the Khampti tribe, located in the remote northeastern region of Arunachal Pradesh, used their elephants for timber felling, but a subsequent government restriction has meant that many Khampti *mahouts* (elephant trainers) are out of a job, with little incentive to protect the animals they no longer work with. By organizing safaris, Help Tourism aims to support elephants and villagers living round the village of Chongkham. On their eleven-day Great Indian Elephant Safari, guests spend four days exploring the rivers, hills and once-felled forests with the *mahouts* as guides. To ensure their well-being, the elephants are ridden for no longer than three hours each day, with their physical and mental conditions kept under constant surveillance.

But it's not all about the pachyderms. The tour also includes birdwatching, a boat expedition on the Lohit River and plenty of nature trails to follow. A highlight is staying in the Khampti villages; here you'll learn about the villagers' Buddhist culture and customs, see intricate Khampti weaving, witness the traditional peacock dance and taste local cuisine, cooked solely with herbs and plants harvested from the forest. These distinct customs have remained remarkably intact as India has developed relentlessly around the Khampti, and now, thanks to Help Tourism, the elephants and the livelihoods of their *mahouts* are being saved too.

Need to know *The trip starts and ends in Kolkata and includes visits to both the Manas and Sundarbans reserves; likely costs are US$1500– 2000 per person. For further information visit Ⓦwww.helptourism.com; ☎+91 (0) 983 103 1980.*

453 PRACTISE YOUR YOGA AT ULPOTHA, SRI LANKA

A quiet village situated in the tropical heart of Sri Lanka three hours from Colombo, Ulpotha has been a pilgrimage site for thousands of years. In 1994, a Sri Lankan ecologist and two businessmen were drawn here to set up an organic farming community, which soon developed into a weekend retreat. Word soon spread about the tranquillity of the area, and it wasn't long before their haven blossomed into a popular yoga and Ayurveda destination.

Made up of airy and spacious adobe huts, the Ulpotha retreat lies next to a lotus-filled lake, surrounded by green paddy fields and ringed by the low Galgiriyawa Mountains. Wildlife in the area is abundant – guests will spot kingfishers, monitor lizards, mango-munching monkeys and huge butterflies, and be lulled to sleep by frog chorus. During the day, life revolves around yoga sessions at the pavilion, cleansing treatments at the Ayurvedic centre, dips in the cool lake, and the even more languid lure of the communal hammocks and huts.

There are no timetables here: the barefoot, sarong-clad hosts have a very relaxed approach to mealtimes – breakfast is a help-yourself affair, while supper is informally announced by the setting sun. Food is predominantly organic and vegetarian – vegan even, if you discount the irresistible buffalo curd and kithul treacle dessert – and based around the rich, spicy flavours of the various curries, *dhals* and *sambals* laid out on rush floor-mats in the *ambalama* ("resting place").

Any profits made by the retreat are given back to Ulpotha's agrarian community, who are encouraged to practise organic farming and to reforest the area. And in return, the retreat operates a free Ayurvedic clinic, treating over a hundred local villagers weekly.

Need to know *Trains run from Colombo and other destinations to Maho (www.slrfc.org/sri-lanka-railways-timetable), from where it's a 20min taxi ride to Ulpotha. For prices, reservations and further info see www.ulpotha.com; +44 (0) 208 123 3603.*

454 UNDERWATER GARDENING IN THE MALDIVES

Lots of people dream of sitting on a Maldives beach, soaking up the sun and gazing out to sea. Few people dream of sitting on a Maldives beach and rolling up balls of cement. But this is one of the most popular choices of activity at Angsana Velavaru, a luxury resort situated on a pristine island on South Nilandhe Atoll.

The appearances aren't deceptive – Angsana is your typical Maldives hotel, a pampered paradise offering day-long watersports, endless spa treatments, cocktails at sunset and dinner on the beach. There's a restaurant on stilts over the water, and sumptuous private villas with their own pools and bubbling jacuzzis. But the resort is also making concerted efforts to conserve its habitat: rising sea levels and temperatures caused by El Niño phenomena and global warming have put the islands at risk of flooding. This is where the (voluntary) cement-rolling comes in, as part of an ambitious project to replant damaged reefs, essential for protecting the islands they surround from the rising sea.

Once you've rolled out the cement balls, you swim out into the blue where, a few metres below the surface, new corals are being planted on a mix of custom-made frames, concrete blocks from building works, and even the odd broken air-conditioning unit. For the next hour or so, you wedge the balls into place and then stick shards of coral into their new home. You'll then swim off to see some already-established coral beds, to see what your little saplings will become.

Need to know *Angsana is 45min by sea-plane from Male. It also runs free weekly reef clean-up excursions. For prices and more information see www.angsana.com; +65 6849 5700.*

WHERE TO STAY NEAR SIGIRIYA, SRI LANKA

Sigiriya, the ruined rock fortress sitting atop the vast, ancient plug of magma of an eroded volcano, is a striking sight. But it's only up close that the architectural sophistication of the citadel – commissioned by the fifth-century monarch King Kasyapa – becomes clear. On the journey upwards you'll climb through terraced gardens – with gravity-powered fountains that still flow at the height of the monsoon – past caves subsequently used for meditation by Buddhist monks, and beautiful frescoes that reveal the advanced artistry of the time, before reaching the fortress ruins and extraordinary views at the summit. Below are our three favourite places to stay nearby.

455 Vil Uyana

A 5km drive from Sigiriya, Vil Uyana blurs the boundary between hotel and nature reserve. The resort is built over reclaimed paddy fields and is made up of 25 vaulted wooden villas. Guests can choose which ecosystem they would like their villa to look out over: there are six among the paddy fields, six over marshlands, three suspended above the water and connected by waterways, and ten – the largest and most private dwellings – nestled in the forest habitat. Each villa has its own private plunge pool and sun deck, and the restaurant serves fantastic food. So successful has this natural development

Individual huts at Vil Uyana

been that as well as the birds and lizards now settled in the hotel's grounds, wild elephants occasionally roam here and two resident crocodiles have settled down in the resort's marshes.

Need to know *For directions, excursions, rates and reservations see* ⓦ*www.jetwing.com;* ☎*+94 664 923 5846.*

456 Hotel Sigiriya

You can't beat the views from Hotel Sigiriya, the closest accommodation to the fortress: from the lounge bar or the outdoor swimming pool the citadel takes centre stage. Another plus is the abundant birdlife flitting around the grounds – you might well spot the pheasant-tailed jacana, scarlet minivet or the Malabar pied hornbill. If you're keen enough, get up early and join the resident naturalist on a short walk to nearby Sigiriya Lake, where you'll set up a telescope and watch the birds. Or try a tour of a nearby village, a cycling trip or a magical hot-air balloon ride over Sigiriya itself.

Need to know *For further details, rates and reservations visit* ⓦ*www.serendibleisure.com;* ☎*+94 662 284 811.*

457 Mahoora Treehouse

Wild elephants can be the bane of a Sri Lankan farmer's life, with their voracious appetite for crops and often aggressive behaviour. To see them in time to guard their paddies, farmers keep watch at night from thatched treehouses on stilts – and on a nature holiday with Ecoteam, you can stay in such a structure in the middle of the paddy fields, from where you'll join farmers as they rotate their elephant-watching shifts. Eyes and ears alert, you'll also share responsibility for keeping the campfire alight. Dinner is a barbecue with the villagers; a chance to swap a few songs and stories. And if you hear an elephant rumbling below, enjoy your close encounter from the safety of the treehouse – it's the best place to be.

Need to know *Up to six guests can sleep in the treehouse at one time. The only way to reach Mahoora is on foot; guides will lead you there from Hotel Sigiriya. For further details see* ⓦ*www. srilankaecotourism.com;* ☎*+94 773 088 540.*

(From top) Sigiriya Rock seen from the gardens; What remains of the frescoes in the citadel is exquisitely painted; The view from the top of this ancient, eroded plug of volcanic magma

(From top) A parakeet; The view from Kandalama Hotel; Monkeys peering into the bedroom

458 WATCH WILDLIFE IN BED, SRI LANKA

Propped up in bed, you're glad you kept the French doors to your balcony closed – there's a veritable crowd of monkeys out there, tumbling about, play-fighting, chasing each others' tails and grooming themselves. With such a free floorshow each morning, it's tempting to phone the Heritance's five-star room service and skip the breakfast buffet.

The Heritance Kandalama – designed by Sri Lanka's leading architect, Geoffrey Bawa – lies surrounded by thickly forested hills and a shimmering lake, looking as if it is on the verge of being reclaimed by the forces of nature. Built so as not to affect the course of the water that flows underneath it, and with roof-top gardens festooned with creepers that drape seven floors down to the grass below, it blends seamlessly into the rock face into which it is built. Despite having 152 bedrooms, five restaurants and bars, three swimming pools and an organic spa, its stone facade is so covered with greenery that from the other side of the lake you can hardly see it.

The hotel's environmental policy is also designed to make it fit in with the forest: waste is minimized and recycled wherever possible, noise is reduced and Heritance recently purchased a belt of virgin rainforest surrounding the hotel to prevent possible deforestation. This also ensures there's plenty of wildlife to see – as well as bird-, butterfly- and dragonfly-watching walks, guests can take part in a nocturnal snake-hike with the resident naturalist. Though if you'd rather see snakes during the day you can check out the hotel's own animal rehabilitation centre and say hello to convalescing cobras and vipers. Having seen them you'll probably want to double-check those French doors before retiring to bed.

Need to know *The Heritance Kandalama is 160km from Colombo, with the UNESCO World Heritage Sites of Dambulla and Sigiriya a 30min drive away. For further information on accommodation, dining, activities, prices and getting there visit ⓦwww.heritancehotels.net; ☏+94 (0) 665 555 000.*

459 GO FURTHER, SLOWER ON A KERALAN HOUSEBOAT

If you spend just a couple of minutes surveying the waters from the grassy banks of a Keralan river, all sorts of boats will pass you by: small wooden canoes ferrying people from one bank to another, long cargo vessels laden with sand and stone, and sporadically, the vessel for which Keralan tourism has become best known – *kettuvallam* houseboats.

In 1991 Tour India launched the first tourist houseboat – converted from an old *kettuvallam* barge (*vallam* means "boat" in Malayalam, *kettu* refers to the way the boats were made using no nails). Today it has six boats, each with up to three cabins with attached bathrooms, their windows peering out like rows of heavily lidded eyes from the distinctive woven-palm roof. Unlike many other companies which stick to the busy, tourist-packed waters around Allepey, Tour India offers longer charters – effectively, as long as you want – which allows you to take its boats to more remote areas: little-visited waterways and genuine, workaday villages.

Alternatively, you could take it still slower with Coco Houseboats. On a boat propelled slowly through the water by two men with long wooden poles, you don't cover as much ground, but your journey is more peaceful, and you'll have even more time to enjoy the passing scenery: women waist-deep working in the rice paddies, fishermen by the water's edge, bustling villages on market day and children splashing about.

A highlight of both companies is the food: served on banana leaves is an ever-changing array of Keralan delicacies such as bitter gourd fry, green mango pickle and chilli-fried fish, with the occasional unusual curry such as banana or beetroot. Days rotate slowly around these meals, the rest of your time spent idly watching the world go by from your chair on the deck. But with so much happening on the river and its bank, there's few places where sitting back and doing nothing can be quite so engrossing.

Need to know *Prices for Tour India's boats start at R6000 (US$125) for one night. Boats embark from Kollam and Allepey in the south or Thanneermukkam in the north, all of which are easily accessible by train (connecting with Mumbai in the north). Boats run all year, but the best time to visit is November to March. For more information see Ⓦwww.tourindiakerala.com and Ⓦwww.cocohouseboatskerala.com.*

Take a *kettuvallam* through the backwaters

STAY AT HOME IN KERALA

Kerala is known for dazzling beaches, luscious tea estates and the impressive houseboats that idle along its backwaters. The best way to savour these attractions is to base yourself in the homes and family-run guesthouses of its residents, where you can sample authentic Keralan food, learn a few words of the local language – the lilting, but very difficult, Malayalam – and revel in their generations-old stories and customs. Below are six of the best.

460 Learn to cook, Keralan style

Whether it's a *masala dosa*, *idli* or a fiery chutney, after a couple of days at The Pimenta on Haritha Farms, you'll be amazed at how many new vegetarian dishes you have in your repertoire. The Mathew family runs the farm, and head honcho Jacob is also in charge of the kitchen; a calm, authoritative master of Keralan cuisine, he will help you get the most from the flavoursome spices and fruits that are grown on the estate. The Pimenta offers a variety of holiday packages, combining cooking lessons with unusual trips such as visiting a small factory that produces Bombay mix and a fascinating three-woman rubber band-making enterprise. A cooking holiday here ensures you take home more than just a few new recipes.

Need to know *For directions, prices and packages see* Ⓦ*www.harithafarms.com;* ☎*+91 485 226 0216.*

Jacob Mathews and students at his cooking school at Haritha Farms

461 Spice up your life at Vanilla County

A large spice plantation surrounds this 60-year-old former tea-estate bungalow in the hills of northern Kerala, so there's little chance of you being bothered by the neighbours. And as the organically grown vanilla, pepper and cardamom are used to flavour the traditional Keralan dishes – served up here by Rani, who is head chef in the home she shares with her husband, Babi – you'll be tucking into some delicious, aromatic food too. The estate is high enough in the hills to escape both the mosquitoes and the humidity, and after a long walk through the plantations, a swim in the nearby natural rock pools is a wonderful way to cool off.

Need to know *For directions, prices and details of activities see* Ⓦ*www.vanillacounty.in;* ☎*+91 482 228 1225.*

462 Have Thottada beach to yourself

If all-night parties and banana boats are your thing, you're on the wrong beach. Here, on little-known Thottada beach in northern Kerala, you'll get a length of palm-fringed shoreline to yourself, bar a few fishermen hauling in their catch. Kannur Beach House, two minutes from the beach and next to a freshwater lagoon, is the place to stay: the comfortable rooms have wonderful views of the pristine sands, the friendly owners cook and dine with you, and will take you on various trips to hand-looming workshops and traditional Theyyam (dance) festivals – there's even a boat you can borrow, but you'll probably have to row that yourself.

Need to know *For directions, rates and booking visit* Ⓦ*www.kannurbeachhouse.com;* ☎*+91 984 718 4535.*

463 Explore the hidden backwaters at Emerald Isle

One quick glance at your surroundings will confirm that Emerald Isle is a very aptly named place. Hidden among swaying coconut palms and ringed by a complex web of water canals is the beautiful 150-year-old Heritage Villa, the family home of your hosts for generations. Sunbathe, swim and swing in your hammock – or, if you're tempted to join the river traffic drifting by, jump in a small wooden canoe with a guide and glide round some of the waterways. This way you'll meet the local people up close, see workers tending the paddy fields, and visit nearby temples and churches; a rewarding and exhilarating insight into the secret backwaters of Kerala.

Need to know *For directions, details of activities, prices and reservations see ⓦwww. emeraldislekerala.com; ☏+91 477 270 3899.*

464 Beat stress the natural way at Philipkutty's Farm

Philipkutty's farm, set on an island in the middle of Lake Vembanad, has been in the family since the 1950s, and the holidays they run here are very much a family concern; mum cooks, while the husband-and-wife team look after the guests. The warm hospitality will eliminate any stress you might still have with you, while daily activities can include fishing, a canal cruise, cooking classes or swimming in the backwaters. To really unwind, take the free 10min boat ride over to the neighbouring Ayurvedic centre. Whether you just pop over there for a massage or book in for anything up to a thirty-day course of pampering treatments, you'll be benefiting from a system of health they've been honing in Kerala for over two millennia.

Need to know *Prices on request. For directions, rates, reservations and details of activities visit ⓦwww.philipkuttysfarm.com; ☏+ 91 482 927 6529.*

465 Fish for prawns in Cochin

Kerala's prime tourist destination, and, for centuries, an important fishing harbour, Cochin is a fantastic city in which to spend a few days. Stay with Jos Byju and his wife in their converted coconut storehouse alongside the family's home, set on a promontory overlooking the lake. In the morning, Jos will take you to meet a local prawn farmer who will teach you how to cast out a fisherman's net; afterwards you'll feast on the prawns you've just caught. Once you've had your fill, there's plenty to see and do in Cochin: art galleries, boutiques, churches, boat trips and, of course, more fishing…there's dinner to eat later.

Need to know *For directions, accommodation details, prices and more information visit ⓦwww. keralagramam.com; ☏+ 91 484 224 0278.*

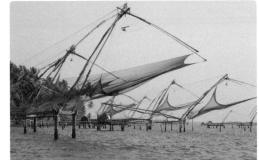

(From top) Traditional cantilevered fishing nets; The converted coconut store (now a bedroom) at Kerala Gramam; Fishing for prawns for breakfast

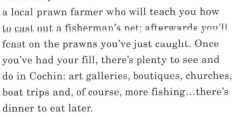

Travelling by cargo ship

ARCTIC OCEAN

NORTH ATLANTIC OCEAN

NORTH PACIFIC OCEAN

SOUTH ATLANTIC OCEAN

SOUTH PACIFIC OCEAN

SOUTHERN OCEAN

UK LIGHTHOUSES

The *Patricia*, operated by Trinity House (the lighthouse authority for England, Wales and the Channel Isles), sails around the UK coastline checking up on lighthouses, lightships, buoys and even the occasional wreck. As the ship is regularly used by members of the Royal Family (Prince Philip is Master of the Corporation of Trinity House), accommodation in its six cabins is of a high standard and the food and wine selection a highlight. Depending on the position of the vessel, embarkation and disembarkation take place at various ports around the coast of England and Wales, including Harwich, Southampton and Swansea, and voyagers can join it for periods of between one and three weeks watching essential maintenance work going on and visiting points usually only seen on the horizon.

Searching the waves for the spouts of humpback whales, or training your binoculars on a lone albatross gliding high in the sky, hundreds of miles from land. Arriving at the dead of night in ports like Piraeus and Port Said, where work carries on as if it was the middle of the day. Nothing epitomizes the joys of slow travel better than a voyage on a cargo ship, spending anything from several weeks to a few months at sea.

You need to be flexible, as schedules aren't rigidly fixed – boats may arrive late in port, leave early if they've filled with their cargo, or maybe not even stop in a certain port at all. As such, cargo trips aren't so much an alternative way of getting to specific places as an experience in themselves. On board there will probably be a pool, a gym, somewhere to watch films (and maybe a DVD player in your cabin), a bar and a dining room. Mobile phone reception and internet access are unlikely, but then this is the chance to spend days or weeks away from the cares of the world.

Despite the ships being major polluters, it is nevertheless an environmentally friendly way for an individual to travel. These vast vessels (the largest carry the equivalent freight of six thousand lorries) already ship the majority of the world's international cargo and they use no more fuel as a result of you and your luggage being onboard. Nor do they alter their schedule for you or add more boats if all the cabins are full. You are effectively a paying hitch-hiker.

This map shows some of the more frequent and interesting routes available, with rough times for the entire journey, although on many trips you can just do a part of the voyage. For further information on sailing companies and itineraries see p.376.

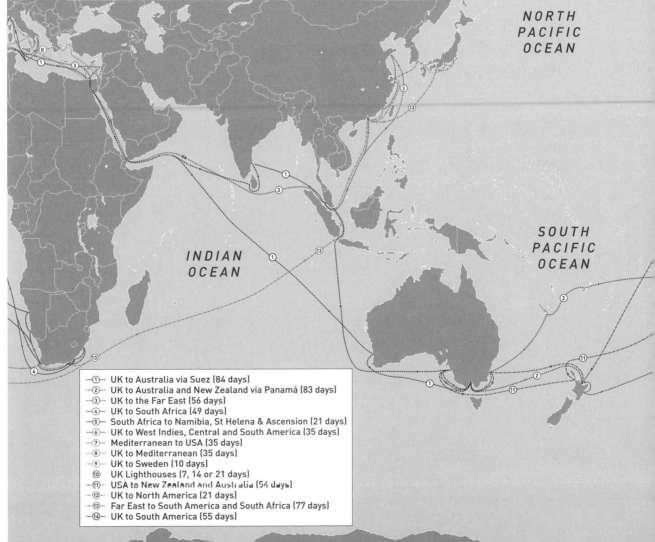

NORTH PACIFIC OCEAN

SOUTH PACIFIC OCEAN

INDIAN OCEAN

- ①- UK to Australia via Suez (84 days)
- ②- UK to Australia and New Zealand via Panamá (83 days)
- ③- UK to the Far East (56 days)
- ④- UK to South Africa (49 days)
- ⑤- South Africa to Namibia, St Helena & Ascension (21 days)
- ⑥- UK to West Indies, Central and South America (35 days)
- ⑦- Mediterranean to USA (35 days)
- ⑧- UK to Mediterranean (35 days)
- ⑨- UK to Sweden (10 days)
- ⑩ UK Lighthouses (7, 14 or 21 days)
- ⑪- USA to New Zealand and Australia (54 days)
- ⑫- UK to North America (21 days)
- ⑬- Far East to South America and South Africa (77 days)
- ⑭- UK to South America (55 days)

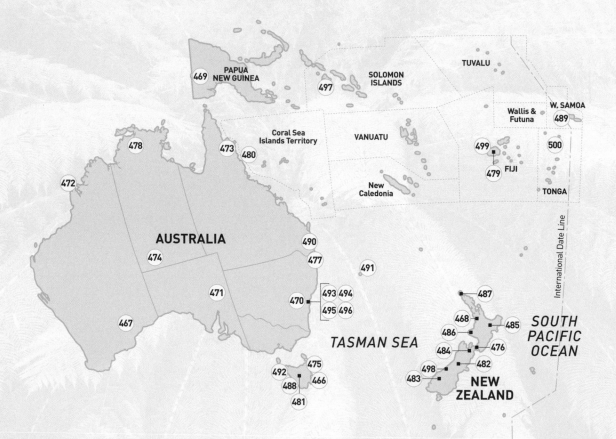

PAPUA
NEW GUINEA
469

SOLOMON
ISLANDS
497

TUVALU

Coral Sea
Islands Territory
473 480

VANUATU

Wallis &
Futuna

W. SAMOA
489

478

472

499
479 FIJI

500

TONGA

New
Caledonia

AUSTRALIA

474

490

471

477

491

467

470 493 494
495 496

International Date Line

487

468 485

486 476

**SOUTH
PACIFIC
OCEAN**

TASMAN SEA

484 482

492 475

498

483

**NEW
ZEALAND**

488 466

481

AUSTRALIA, NEW ZEALAND AND THE SOUTH PACIFIC

466 Maria Island, Tasmania

467 Take the train across Australia

468 Surf at Raglan, New Zealand

469 Birds of paradise in Papua New Guinea

470 Bushwalking in the Blue Mountains, Australia

471 Go walkabout in the Flinders, Australia

472 Take the long road to Kooljaman, Australia

473 Learn what rock art means, Australia

474 See Uluru the right way, Australia

475 The Bay of Fires, Tasmania

476 Kiwi spotting at the Karori Wildlife Sanctuary, New Zealand

477 The best in world music, Byron Bay, Australia

478 Kakadu National Park, Australia

479 In search of the real Fiji

480 Help conserve the Great Barrier Reef, Australia

481 The Walls of Jerusalem, Tasmania

482 Ski the resort-free Craigieburn, New Zealand

483 Rees Dart Track, Otago, New Zealand

484 Pelorus Track, Marlborough, New Zealand

485 Whirinaki Forest Park, Central North Island, New Zealand

486 Mount Taranaki, New Plymouth, New Zealand

487 Cape Reinga Walk, Far North, New Zealand

488 Raft the Franklin River, Tasmania

489 Stay with a Samoan family

490 Koala spotting, Brisbane

491 A view over paradise at Lord Howe Island, Australia

492 Walk the wild Tarkine, Tasmania

493 Swim in a coastal pool, Sydney

494 Have some bonza tucker, Sydney

495 Aboriginal Sydney

496 See the city by foot or bike, Sydney

497 Visit an uninhabited Solomon Island

498 New Zealand's best wilderness lodges

499 Teach rugby in Fiji

500 Sail around Tonga's Vava'u Group

466 MARIA ISLAND, TASMANIA

"No cars, no shops, no worries" was how the flyer for Maria Island National Park read a few years ago. But it forgot to mention no people. If part of the park's appeal is casting yourself adrift on an island that has barely changed since Europeans first waded through its aquamarine shallows around 250 years ago, another is that most tourists haven't yet cottoned on that it's there.

Because it's 14km offshore – and only accessible by a small ferry – Maria (pronounced "Ma-*rye*-a") remains a hauntingly beautiful Treasure Island while the much-lauded Freycinet National Park just up the coast is besieged by coach tours. And it is the isolation that saw it swing from convict sink of the British Empire to Victorian health retreat, preserving the wildlife in the eucalyptus rainforest and making it Tasmania's very own Noah's Ark for endangered species. Thank Professor Thomas Flynn, Errol's father, who proposed it as a sanctuary for the now extinct Tasmanian Tiger. Too late for the tiger, but perfect for the other indigenous species.

Take to any number of paths and Forester kangaroo, pademelons and Bennetts wallabies can be seen bouncing away into the bush. Cape Barren geese, a breed near extinction in the 1950s, trim the grass by the jetty – just one from a spotter's book of rare birdlife – while in a marine park you can see dolphins, seals or even whales in season.

Of course, you can also just loaf about on some spectacular sands such as Reidle Beach, the sort of improbably perfect arc you ache to tell friends about. Or on second thoughts, maybe not.

Need to know *The Maria Island Ferry (*🅦*www. mariaislandferry.com.au;* ☎*+61 (0) 419 746 668; reservations recommended) runs from Triabunna to Darlington on Maria Island. A Parks & Wildlife Service office at Darlington (*🅦*www.parks.tas. gov.au;* ☎*+61 (0) 362 571 420) manages accommodation in the former convict penitentiary (bunkhouse A$15; rooms A$50) and camping (A$12 at Darlington; free elsewhere); it also hires bikes (A$15 per day). Maria Island Walk (*🅦*www. mariaislandwalk.com.au;* ☎*+61 (0) 362 342 999) provides four-day luxury treks on the island from October to April.*

Sunrise on Maria Island; Kangaroos and wombats are just some of the animals you can see on the island

The Ghan train travels from
Adelaide to Alice Springs

467 TAKE THE TRAIN ACROSS AUSTRALIA

For many, crossing the vast Australian bush is all about *Flying Doctors* and *Priscilla Queen of the Desert*. A bustling network of European-style high-speed rail lines it is not. Yet it is possible to cross the length and breadth of the country by train in relative comfort, thanks to the clean, air-conditioned interstate services that provide comfortable sleeping carriages, private washrooms and a dining car. Flying is the quickest and cheapest way to get between the major cities, but take the train and you'll see the wheat fields of Victoria, the dusty outback towns and kilometres of endless white-sand beaches.

The *Indian Pacific*, from Sydney to Perth via Adelaide, is one of the world's longest train journeys. It's a three-day, 4352km trip (that's just one-way), though the train stops long enough for you to spend an evening in the gold-rush town of Kalgoorlie and to visit the remote outpost community of Cook on the Nullarbor Plain. The *Ghan* travels from Adelaide overnight to Alice Springs, where you have four hours to see the sights before heading up to Katherine for another stop and the final stretch up to Darwin; while the *XPT* travels from Sydney up the east coast overnight and arrives in Brisbane the following morning, where you can change to the sleeper *Tilt Train*, which arrives in Cairns the following evening.

None of these trips will get you from A to B quickly, but these journeys aren't meant to be purely a means of transport: they're a sightseeing trip, a hotel and a sociable holiday all in one.

Need to know *For times, fares and reservations for all Australian trains see ⑩www.railaustralia.com. au; ☎+61 882 134 592. For more information on specific rail journeys, including stopping services, from Melbourne–Sydney–Brisbane–Canberra see ⑩www.countrylink.info; for Sydney–Melbourne– Adelaide–Perth and Melbourne–Alice Springs– Darwin see ⑩www.gsr.com.au; and for Brisbane– Townsville–Cairns see ⑩www.traveltrain. au. For maps of all, see ⑩www.railmaps.com.au.*

Raglan is home to one of the world's longest left-hand breakers

468 SURF AT RAGLAN, NEW ZEALAND

Don't be surprised if you to come to the beach town of Raglan and stay for longer than intended. Many do. Experienced surfers are drawn by the reliable swells and one of the world's longest left-hand breakers, while beginners are seduced by the laid-back Bohemian atmosphere and their first taste of the addictive surfing thrill.

The town hugs the south side of the large and picturesque Raglan Harbour, 48km west of Hamilton in Waikato. Fresh-faced surfers go in search of gentle waves at the rock-free Ngarunui Beach, 5km out of Raglan, while the more experienced boarders head to the long breakers at Manu Bay and Whale Bay, both around 8km out of town.

Surfing lessons are provided by Raglan Surfing School and Solscape, who both rent boards and wet suits and provide a range of deals, from day-long starter lessons to accommodation-inclusive packages. Raglan Surfing School is based at Karioi Lodge in Whale Bay and has all the usual surfing facilities, including hammocks (of course), flat-screen TVs and hot tubs. But if you're after a more back-to-nature experience you're better off staying at Solscape, based at Manu Bay, which has an eclectic mix of accommodation ranging from tipis to recycled railway carriages and self-contained eco-cottages.

If you decide to have a break from the waves, you can go horse-riding in the area around Mount Karioi and further south at Bridal Veil Falls. Or if the wind picks up you can also try kitesurfing – the lie of the land at Raglan means it's one of the best places in New Zealand to try this. Just don't expect to leave when you thought you would.

Need to know For prices, reservations and lessons at Raglan Surfing School see ⓦwww.raglansurfingschool.co.nz; ☏+64 7825 7873; for Solscape see ⓦwww.solscape.co.nz; ☏+64 7825 8268.

469 BIRDS OF PARADISE IN PAPUA NEW GUINEA

When it comes to courtship, birds of paradise know how to do it in style. The Magnificent Bird of Paradise favours the low branches of bushes, the Blue Bird of Paradise hangs upside-down in a tree, while the Six-Plumed Bird of Paradise puts on an elaborate show in its specially prepared clearing on the forest floor. You may have seen the latter starring in the BBC series *Planet Earth*: at first it looks like a rather unglamorous crow, but then it transforms its wings into a little tutu, stands on tiptoe and hops back and forth in a coquettish dance. As one of the producers of the series remarked: "they are like two birds for the price of one".

Birds of paradise are the holy grail for birdwatchers, yet most of them live in the jungles of Papua New Guinea, one of the least-explored regions on Earth. Though tourism here is still in its infancy, birdwatching tours are relatively well-established and there are plenty of operators that will take you to reliable spots to see birds of paradise.

Local expert Samuel Kepuknai leads one of the best tours (typically six days) to Kiunga, Ekame and Tabubil in the lush virgin forests of Western Province. His Kiunga nature tours begin in a region known as KM17, where you can see the Greater and Raggianna birds of paradise performing their mating rituals on the same tree. The tour then moves on to several other well-known watching spots in the jungle, such as Frame Bower Bird Hill and the Elevara River – where you take a boat trip to see a variety of other birds, such as the azure kingfisher, great-billed heron and channel-billed cuckoo.

Those with deep pockets can head to Ambua

Lodge, a luxury ecolodge with wonderful views overlooking the lush vegetation of the Tari Valley in the southern highlands. Local guides arranged through the lodge will take you on guided nature walks into the dense forest across traditional vine bridges, and to a secluded waterfall where you can meet the local Huli clan, who wear wigs adorned with the colourful feathers of the Birds of Paradise and revere them through song and dance.

Need to know *The best time to see the birds displaying is Aug–Sept. For prices and reservations at Ambua Lodge see ⓦwww.pngtours.com; ☏+675 542 1438. For Kiunga Nature Tours ☏+675 548 1366 or ⓔkepuknai@online.net.pg.*

470 BUSHWALKING IN THE BLUE MOUNTAINS, AUSTRALIA

If you're visiting the Blue Mountains expecting them to be a) blue or b) mountains, then you may be disappointed. In fact they're better described as a kind of Australian Grand Canyon: think chiselled sandstone cliffs tumbling down into thickly forested valleys (the "blue" part of the name comes from the occasional blueish tinge in the air caused by eucalyptus trees). Covering 10,000 square kilometres of New South Wales, the whole region is a World Heritage Site and a hugely popular destination for Sydneysiders. In fact, given the amount of cosy hotels, gourmet restaurants and yoga retreats, it's possible to lose sight of what attracted people here in the first place – pristine wilderness and plenty of fresh air.

To get a real feel for "The Blues" you need to get away from the viewpoints and clearly marked paths and head down into the creeks and gorges below. The best way to do this is on a guided bushwalk exploring historic trails such as the Jamison Valley Traverse. Apart from a good day's hiking, this offers a chance to imagine what it was like for the colonial explorers who spent an astonishing twenty years hacking their way through the bush in search of grazing land to the west.

The first thing you're struck by descending into the valley is the smell – a thick perfume of tea-tree oil and eucalyptus – after which comes the buzz of cicadas and the cries of cockatoos. The trail shifts through a range of habitats from dry forest and spongy swamp to rocky mountain passes and is barely distinguishable at times. It's not hard to see why new species are continually discovered in the national park, including "living fossils" such as the Wollemi Pine, a Jurassic-era plant long thought extinct. At times the walk is hard going and you need to cling to ropes for safety, but the hard work is soon rewarded. Just as your knees are about to give way you emerge blinking in front of the cascading Wentworth Falls, named in honour of one of those hardy explorers.

Need to know *The Jamison Valley Traverse is offered by River Deep Mountain High (ⓦwww.rdmh.com.au; ☏+61 247 826 109) based in Katoomba, which is connected by regular trains from Sydney. A full day-hike costs A$175.*

The Blue Mountains are just 90min from Sydney

ABORIGINAL EXPERIENCES

Whether you are keen to learn more about their art and customs, such as the many dances of the corroboree ceremony or the songs of The Dreaming, or simply want an authentic trip to Uluru, there are no better guides to Australia's outback than the many Aboriginal peoples who have lived here for millennia. All the following experiences are run by indigenous Australians and are committed to preserving and sharing one of the world's oldest cultures.

471 Go walkabout in the Flinders

While it may look like a vast crater formed by a meteor strike, Wilpena Pound is in fact an 83-square-kilometre amphitheatre of mountains in the arid deserts of South Australia's Flinders Ranges. It's one of many natural highlights of a five-day trip through the area with Bookabee Tours, staying in remote lodges and Aboriginal communities, taking in gorges etched with 30,000-year-old rock art, and spotting kangaroos, echidnas, emus and many other of Australia's endemic animals. Bookabee is run by Hadyn Bromley, a former teacher and member of the Adnyamathanha people, who is passionate about sharing his people's understanding of the region. For him this is an essential part of sustaining his culture – for guests it is one of the best ways of grappling with such Aboriginal concepts as walkabout and Dreamtime.

Need to know Tours start and end in Adelaide, where Bookabee also offers short tours of the city from an Aboriginal perspective. For more details see ⓦwww.bookabee.com.au; ☏+61 (0) 882 359 954.

472 Take the long road to Kooljaman

Unzip your tent early in the morning at Kooljaman wilderness camp in the north of western Australia, and you can watch the sun rise over the endless white-sand beach and azure sea. Take a short walk from your tent across the sands at the point of Cape Leveque and you can watch the sun set on an equally breathtaking stretch of beach on the other side of the point. You're so far from anything and anyone here that you'll probably have both views to yourself.

Run by the two local Aboriginal communities, whose members are all shareholders in the company, Kooljaman offers a total escape into the Australian wilderness, whatever your budget – for those seeking a little barefoot luxury, there are safari tents, while those with less to splash can crash down in the rustic beach shelters. Whatever you choose, the attractions are the same – hunting for crabs with the locals in the mangroves, diving off the empty reef or simply letting your head clear in one of the most remote places on Earth.

Need to know Kooljaman has tents, cabins, beach shelters and campsites available all year round. For information on accommodation and activities visit ⓦwww.kooljaman.com.au; ☏+61 (0) 891 924 970.

One of Australia's most remote beaches, Kooljaman

473 Learn what rock art means

Standing under the heavy overhanging rocks of Wangaar-Wuri caves in northern Queensland, whose sides are covered with Aboriginal paintings representing the myths of their creation story, it's easy to forget about the modern world. All the more so when Aboriginal elder Willie Gordon, whose ancestral land this is and whose grandfather was born among these stones, begins to explain the stories and messages in the images. Willie runs Guurrbi Tours, taking visitors on short trips into the native lands of the Nugal people. And as you walk through the rainforest to get to the caves, he tells you about the animals and plants and their various uses, from the sap of bloodwood tree, used as an antiseptic, to various edible grubs. In 2007 Willie was recognized as Australia's best indigenous tour guide – if you want to understand about rock art and bushcraft, he's your man.

Need to know *Wangaar-Wuri is a 40min drive from Cooktown, where Willie will pick you up, or you can arrange to meet him nearer the caves. For itineraries, directions and conservation policies see Ⓦwww.guurrbitours.com; ☏+61 (0) 740 696 043.*

474 See Uluru the right way

No one has a deeper understanding of Uluru (Ayers Rock) than the Anangu, the name for the Aboriginal peoples of Australia's Western Desert, on whose ancestral lands Uluru is found.

While the tourist hordes clamber to the top, despite requests from the Aboriginal peoples to leave their sacred rock alone, Anangu Tours offer a respectful alternative and the opportunity to share in their unrivalled knowledge of the area.

Trips to the rock depart at sunrise or at sunset – the coolest times of the day – by foot or by camel. The company also offers workshops in Aboriginal dot painting, as well as lessons in bush survival skills, such as starting fires and hunting with spears.

Need to know *Tours collect visitors from accommodation near the rock. All tours are conducted in Western Desert languages such as Pitjantjatjara and Yankunytjatjara, and translated into English. For tour details see Ⓦwww.ananguwaai. com.au; ☏+61 (0) 889 503 030.*

(From top) Aboriginal artworks recount stories from the Dreamtime using stylised shapes to symbolise different experiences; Willie Gordon explains the meaning of rock art in Jiliburu cave, Northern Queensland

475 THE BAY OF FIRES, TASMANIA

The Bay of Fires Walk is eco-hiking for softies. Say goodbye to those trail boots and say hello to your trainers: this is wilderness without the wild. Sure, you'll still have to shoulder a rucksack for two days. But that's a small price to pay for an access-all-areas pass – only Bay of Fires Walkers get to camp in these remote areas – to the coastline of the Mount William National Park on Tasmania's northeastern tip.

And what a coastline. The Bay of Fires has wow factor even in a nation that knows a thing or two about world-class beaches. Broken only by sculptural headlands splashed by orange lichen – evidence of the air's exceptional purity – its quartzite sands are a dazzlingly white silky powder. The sea is an implausibly tropical turquoise. There's even something insouciant about the way the surf crumps lazily onto the shore.

Kilometre after kilometre of pristine sandy nothingness stretches beyond the start at Boulder Point, in the north of the national park. Yet you are not alone; not quite. At dusk marsupials graze behind Forester Beach Camp, your timber-floored, canvas-roofed home for night one, 9km from Boulder Point. And there are ghosts if you know where to look – the shell mounds of Aborigines who occupied the area for thousands of years before British explorers saw their cooking fires and coined the bay's name.

The goal of the 23km walk is the Bay of Fires Lodge, a glass-lined solar-powered outpost of eco-chic buried into a hilltop 20km from its nearest neighbours. During nearly two days here, your reward for a hard day of swimming in private bays, dipping a paddle into the Anson River or just gazing at an ocean which seems to lap your window is a hot shower plus cuisine that would not disgrace a top Sydney restaurant. Wilderness has never been so aspirational.

Need to know *The four-day Bay of Fires Walk (Ⓦwww.bayoffireswalk.com.au) runs twice a month from October to April. It costs A$2000 approx and*

(From top) The stunning quartzite-sand beaches and pristine waters of the Bay of Fires; The most contemporary of architectural styles are incorporated into the eco-chic lodges; The sculpted coastline; Paddling along the Anson River in a kayak

includes transfers from Launceston, national park passes, food and wine, accommodation and basic walking gear. The Bay of Fires Lodge takes guests from May to mid-Sept; the A$450 per night charge includes all meals, and activities such as kayaking and guided walks.

476 KIWI SPOTTING AT THE KARORI WILDLIFE SANCTUARY, NEW ZEALAND

The kiwi is New Zealand's national icon, yet there are few places in the country where you can see this elusive, flightless bird. The remote Stewart Island in the far south is one location where you have a good chance of seeing a kiwi, while Karori Wildlife Sanctuary – just minutes from downtown Wellington – is virtually the only place on the mainland where you're likely to get a glimpse of one.

The sanctuary is an ambitious project to restore native bush and provide a safe haven for endangered birds. As well as restocking the area with indigenous trees, the sanctuary's managing trust has introduced the little-spotted kiwi, brown teal, stichbird, kaka bush parrot, North Island robin and tuatara reptile, as well as New Zealand's only native land mammal – the long-tailed bat.

During the day you can walk along 35km of paths and listen to the kind of birdsong that's not often heard elsewhere on the mainland. But kiwi are shy, nocturnal creatures, so your best bet if you want to hear their short whistle (and maybe even see one) is to go on a guided night-boat trip, where you can also watch kaka bush parrots feeding, see banks of glow-worms and experience genuine conservation in action.

Need to know *Buses run from downtown Wellington to the sanctuary (⑩www.metlink.org. nz). For prices and admission times see ⑩www. sanctuary.org.nz; ☏+64 4920 9200. To log kiwi calls and sightings throughout New Zealand visit ⑩www.savethekiwi.org.nz.*

477 THE BEST IN WORLD MUSIC, BYRON BAY, AUSTRALIA

With music guaranteed from every continent, the eclectic line-up at the Byron Bay Bluesfest has something for every one of the twenty thousand people who attend each year. The line-up could range from the political hip-hop of Michael Franti to the African soul music of Angelique Kidjo or blues legend Booker T. This broadbrush approach is perhaps best summed up by one of the performers, Alabama 3, who describe themselves as "a punk rock, blues and country techno-situationist crypto-Marxist-Leninist electro band".

The festival, which takes place over the five days of Easter (it starts on Maundy Thursday), is also deeply committed to its local environment and community. As well as favouring local suppliers wherever possible and providing a focus on Aboriginal culture, the carbon-neutral event ensures that all utensils and packaging are biodegradable or recyclable. The site itself is pretty unique too – whereas most festivals just lease a few fields from a farmer and hand them back in a well-trodden state a few days later, the Bluesfest has bought (using proceeds from former events) its own organic tea-tree farm just outside Byron Bay, thus providing a permanent home for partygoers that won't disturb the neighbours.

Need to know *Byron Bay can be reached by bus from both Brisbane (4hr) and Sydney (14hr). For routes see ⑩www.greyhound. com.au. There's camping on site or around Byron should you wish to just come for a day or so. For tickets, programmes and info on accommodation and getting involved see ⑩www.bluesfest. au; ☏+61 266 858 310.*

Michael Franti

478 KAKADU NATIONAL PARK, AUSTRALIA

As you bump along in a 4WD on the way to Kakadu National Park, a World Heritage Site 150km east of Darwin part-managed by Aborigines, your guide Gerry mentions that the park alone is half the size of Switzerland and that over the next three days you'll cover over a thousand kilometres. Things in this part of Australia are clearly done on a large scale.

Gerry left home at 17 to work on a cattle-and-sheep station in the outback followed by a ten-year stint building houses and schools for Aborigines in the Northern Territory. "Cities are too tame for me," he explains. Now he leads tours with Connections, drawing on his encyclopaedic knowledge of the region's geography and indigenous culture, as well as his cooking skills.

A couple of hours later, you're working up a sweat as you walk along a trail to Ubirr Rock to view three Aboriginal art sites. Australia has one of the world's oldest indigenous people – their culture dates back fifty thousand years – and they pass down their teachings, beliefs and laws through the Dreamtime stories represented in rock art. One "gallery" at Ubirr Rock is particularly impressive – a massive wall beneath a rocky outcrop covered in 1500-year-old drawings of fish, possums and wallabies, drawn in the Aborigines' distinctive skeletal manner known as "x-ray" style (see pp.352–353).

Much of the three-day tour is spent hiking steep paths, climbing over rocks and walking through steamy tropical forest – but each time you're rewarded with abundant wildlife or tranquil waterholes for a cool swim. At the end of each day, Gerry drives you along a sandy track to Connections' exclusive tented bush camp in the heart of a remote Aboriginal community. On the way you help collect firewood but that's the end of your "work" for the day, since back at the camp there's a permanent kitchen, showers and toilets, and tents boasting wooden decks with canvas chairs overlooking a billabong.

After dinner – citrus-infused perch perhaps, or a smoky barbecue of kangaroo and buffalo – you'll sleep well, but don't be surprised if you wake later to the sound of munching outside and the magical sight of animal silhouettes as wallabies, wild horses and perhaps a feral pig or two pass by.

Need to know *Connections runs the three-day Kakadu Dreamtime Safari in the dry season (April–Oct). Tour costs cover all transport, accommodation, meals and entry tickets. For further info see Ⓦwww.connections.travel; ☎+61 282 525 300.*

479 IN SEARCH OF THE REAL FIJI

For many people a visit to Fiji simply means lying on a beach interspersed with snorkelling trips and evenings spent drinking cocktails. While this can be fun for a few days, it is completely detached from the real Fiji beyond the resort gates – a land of dramatic mountains, raging rivers and traditional villages, still governed by a fascinating tribal culture. While many resorts offer "village tours", these are generally stage-managed affairs that only visit the nearest villages, which in turn become over-dependent on tourism. You are much better off heading to one of the more remote communities and staying directly with a Fijian family. This way you'll be welcomed as a guest rather than a souvenir hunter and gain a genuine insight into island life. One of the most beautiful villages in Fiji is Navala, set deep in the hills of the main island of Viti Levu. All the homes in the village are traditional *bures*, built with woven bamboo walls and thickly thatched roofs. Several offer accommodation but perhaps best of all is Balou's Retreat, perched on a riverbank a few minutes' walk away. Here you can stay in your own en-suite *bure*, enjoy authentic Fijian food with the family and try out activities from guided treks to drifting down the scenic Ba River on a bamboo raft. In Navala and other villages it's possible to just turn up and find somewhere to stay, though you should be aware of a certain amount of etiquette; this includes dressing conservatively, removing hats and sunglasses and presenting your host with a gift when you arrive (alternatively book through an agency such as FijiBure). The most important ritual of all is also the most fun – the evening *yaqona* or *kava*-drinking session. This odd, cloudy brew, made of the roots of the *kava* plant, is Fiji's national drink and is served to guests during a welcome ceremony – when it's your turn to drink just remember to say *bula* ("cheers").

Need to know *Agencies such as FijiBure (Ⓦwww.fijibure.com; ☏+61 (0) 738 927 333) and Fiji Ecotours (Ⓦwww.fijiecotours.net; ☏+679 672 4312) can arrange village stays for around F$80 (US$42) per night including meals. Balou's Retreat can be booked by phone on ☏+679 628 1224.*

Island life, Fiji

480 HELP CONSERVE THE GREAT BARRIER REEF, AUSTRALIA

Scientists will tell you Australia's Great Barrier Reef is one continuous living structure, but to everyone else it is an enormous adventure playground. Especially for scuba divers: beneath the vivid turquoise waters lies an extraordinary world of coral gardens and tropical fish. Snorkellers exploring the shallow sections of the reef are hardly limited to a second-rate experience either, as visibility of up to 40m allows them to observe almost as much as the divers.

At around 600,000 years old, it's tempting to imagine that this World Heritage Site is resilient to the passing of time, but recently its ecosystem has become dangerously unbalanced. Irresponsible tourism and chemical pollution have been damaging, but climate change has had the most devastating impact on its coral reefs. The warming seas have caused the tiny algae zooxanthellae, which lives symbiotically with coral (providing it with food and colour) to migrate away, leaving these intricate formations white and susceptible to decay.

Coral bleaching threatens not only the reef itself but the marine wildlife that lives in abundance here. The more scientists understand about the precise effects of climate change on the coral the better they will be able to protect it in the future. By filling in a "Coral Health Chart" each time you snorkel or dive, you can combine underwater exploration with invaluable conservation work. Whenever you come across coral, match it by colour and type to a corresponding example on the chart, and your data can be used to analyze the changes occurring throughout the reef.

Sadly the issue of coral bleaching extends far beyond the Great Barrier Reef: alarming research indicates that since 1980 twenty percent of the world's reefs have already died and another fifty percent face imminent or long-term risk of collapse. Logging the extent of coral bleaching may seem inconsequential, but when you consider that almost two million people visit the Great Barrier Reef every year, then every contribution counts.

Need to know To order a Coral Health Chart and submit your recordings online visit Ⓦwww.coralwatch.org. Project AWARE has registered over five hundred coral-monitoring locations worldwide to help direct you to the most useful recording sites. For a full list of participating dive centres see Ⓦwww.projectaware.org.

481 THE WALLS OF JERUSALEM, TASMANIA

"The Walls" – a jagged ridge that walls in a plateau at Tasmania's centre – is the forgotten part of Tasmania's World Heritage wilderness. On the other side of its dolerite spine lies Cradle Mountain, the busiest bit of bush in Tasmania. What keeps the alpine wonderland of The Walls crowd-free is a stiff three-hour haul up to the lake-pocked plateau. And if that doesn't deter the happy hordes, try fickle weather that swings from snow to sunburn within the hour year-round, and verges on dangerous in winter.

Pass through Herods Gate mountain pass,

More than just a dive: recording a coral health chart

however, and you are not in a landscape so much as a realm that's as otherworldly as the Biblical names on your map. Stunted pencil pines found nowhere else ring a thousand miniature tarns and green bolster heath clumps into a sort of living cushion. So primeval is this landscape that the BBC shot it as an authentic backdrop for its prehistory nature series *Walking With Dinosaurs*.

While you can catch a glimpse of the Walls' super-sized bonsai garden on a long day-trip, a landscape sculpted by aeons of ice deserves time. With a base at the bushcamp by Wild Dog Creek near Herods Gate, you can lose days exploring a part of Tasmania much like Cradle Mountain, except that nobody knows about it. Aborigines and then itinerant fur-trappers were the first to see its fragile ecosystem. Now connoisseur trail-junkies have caught on. Tread softly.

Need to know *The track into the park begins from Lake Rowallen, 35km south of Mole Creek. Maxwell's (☎+61 (0) 364 921 431) and Outdoors Recreational Transport (☎+61 (0) 363 918 249) run on-demand bushwalker bus services from Devonport and Launceston respectively. A Parks & Wildlife Service office in Mole Creek (🌐www.parks.tas.gov.au; ☎+61 (0) 363 636 1487) sells maps and park passes. Craclair (Jan–May; 🌐www.craclairtasmania.com; ☎+61 (0) 363 394 488) and Tasmanian Expeditions (Oct–May; 🌐www.tas-ex.com; ☎+61 (0) 363 393 999) lead hiking tours into the Walls.*

482 SKI THE RESORT-FREE CRAIGIEBURN, NEW ZEALAND

Here's a fresh take on the ups and downs of advanced off-piste skiing. At Craigieburn Valley in the heart of the Southern Alps, there are no chairlifts, no two-lane road access up to the remote ski area and no groomed pistes – but nor do you have to come by helicopter. Instead, a 4WD vehicle takes you along alpine tracks – often through dense native beech forest – to

the edge of the area, where you then kit up and join three fast-moving tow ropes that pull you 500m to the top, where you'll find off-piste patrolled terrain with powder basins and steep narrow chutes, but best of all, kilometres of empty slopes of white powder that can last for days.

This backcountry ski area is one of three in the Canterbury region in South Island operated by small ski clubs for their members, though anyone is welcome

Backcountry bliss at Craigieburn Ski Area

– provided you are at least an intermediate grade off-piste skier. The Craigieburn Club Field provides basic off-grid accommodation in two huts equipped with bunks and communal showers, plus there's a bar and a generator that is on for a few hours each day.

From NZ$85 for dinner plus B&B, this economical and accessible off-piste skiing is becoming increasingly popular with skiers looking to escape the more crowded and expensive resorts. And they say your skiing will improve immeasurably – on this kind of testing off-piste terrain, it has to.

Need to know *Craigieburn Valley Ski Area is open from July to early October. Non-members pay NZ$60 a day for a tow pass. To book accommodation, lessons and week-long packages visit 🌐www.craigieburn.co.nz; ☎+64 3318 8711. For daily and multi-day ski packages, including 4WD transfers from Methven and Christchurch, see 🌐www.blackdiamondsafaris.co.nz; ☎+64 274 508 283.*

ALTERNATIVE TREKS IN NEW ZEALAND

New Zealand's reputation as a walker's paradise is thanks partly to its diversity of scenery, from the tropical beaches, hot springs and volcanic mountains in the north to the temperate forests, dramatic fjords and glacier-fed lakes in the south. But it's also due to the country's well-maintained network of backcountry trails managed by the Department of Conservation (DOC). Access to the country's nine "Great Walks" is strictly controlled via a quota system to ensure their protection, but the downside is that often you have to book months in advance to secure your place. There are, however, plenty of other DOC-maintained trails among stretches of equally magnificent scenery; the accommodation along these trails might not be as sophisticated as those along the Great Walks, but they are usually well-equipped, cheaper (typically NZ$5–10 per night) and far less crowded. Below are our five favourite alternative treks.

483 Rees Dart Track, Otago

A 4–5 day circuit that winds across two lush valleys following the course of two rivers – the Rees and the Dart – in the Glenorchy region in the south of Mount Aspiring National Park. Much of the 57km trek is well-marked, there are three DOC huts en route, and you can expect forested as well as steep alpine sections with dramatic views of mountain ranges similar to those encountered on the Routeburn, one of the nine Great Walks. However, the Rees Dart trek is more challenging, and the one to go for if you're looking for several days of mountain solitude.

484 Pelorus Track, Marlborough

This three-day trek is for those who like to combine walking with the occasional refreshing dip in a river. The 36km trail, which begins 13km along the river valley from the Pelorus Bridge Scenic Reserve in Mount Richmond Forest Park, leads to several green natural pools where you can soak your sore feet after tramping through forested valleys of matai and beech trees. The most famous bathing spot is the Emerald Pools Picnic Area – it is about an hour from the start of the trail so it's popular with day-trippers – and though it may be hard to leave this idyll, press on and you'll discover more wonderful bathing spots along the track. The further you go, the more likely it is that you'll have them all to yourself.

Off the beaten track in Mount Aspiring National Park

485 Whirinaki Forest Park, Central North Island

A feature of New Zealand's walks is its ancient forests, and there are few finer examples of this than the Whirinaki Forest Park and the adjacent Te Urewera National Park, the largest single block of native forest in New Zealand's North Island. Maori-owned Te Urewera Treks (Ⓦwww.teureweratreks.co.nz; Ⓣ+64 7366 6055) specializes in walks (1–3 days) to both areas under the guiding eye of Joe Doherty, of local Ngai Tuhoe descent, who shows guests how the Maori use native plants for medicine and food, and gives lessons on the local history and Maori legends.

486 Mount Taranaki, New Plymouth

Egmont National Park on the west coast of the North Island is about as off-the-beaten-track as it gets in New Zealand, and there are some wonderful treks in this often overlooked park. Pride of place is Mount Taranaki, a dormant volcano and the site of several walks through alpine and bush in altitudes ranging from 500m to 1500m. The five–day lower-level circuit is the easier option, though from December to February the snow melts enough for hikers to loop off the main track and do the more challenging high-level route that heads up the slopes. Those who want a quick mountain fix can walk directly up to the summit and down again in a day – it's a strenuous trek but well worth it for the wonderful views of the Tasman Sea and Tongariro mountains.

487 Cape Reinga Walk, Far North

"Ninety Mile Beach" might not sound like an easy walk to do in three days, but fear not, it is at the northern end of a wide, flat expanse of windswept sand that is the starting point of a relatively comfortable – and uncrowded – hike around the headland of the northern tip of New Zealand. The walk begins at the impressive dunes of Te Paki Stream and heads northwards along 41km of coastline, stopping off at some beautifully sited campgrounds overlooking the sea. The walk ends at Cape Reinga where the Tasman Sea and Pacific Ocean collide in a froth of foam. According to Maori legend, it is here that spirits depart to the next life. However, you might prefer to pitch your tent at the DOC campsite in the manuka woods and go for a swim in the usually deserted 7km sweep of Spirits Bay and feel very much alive.

October–May is the best time for walking in New Zealand. For details of itineraries for all the trails listed here, as well as relevant visitor centres, huts, campsites and directions to the trailheads, see Ⓦwww.doc.govt.nz. For more info on walking in New Zealand see Ⓦwww.tramper.co.nz.

Top: Crossing the stream in the Whirinaki Forest North Island; Bottom: The Tasman Sea meets the Pacific Ocean at Cape Reinga

488 RAFT THE FRANKLIN RIVER, TASMANIA

If there's a textbook method to psych up rafters for a ten-day expedition on one of the wildest white-water rollercoasters on Earth, the sign where you launch into the Franklin River isn't it. "Warning!" it shouts at the handful of adventurers who dare to tackle the west Tasmanian gorge on their own. "Several people have died on this river system." It catalogues the reasons for their aquatic ends before concluding: "Not sure of your abilities? Do not go on."

It's at this point that you should become aware that the safe option is to tackle the rapids as part of a group and turn to the guides of Rafting Tasmania. While solo paddlers may be at risk, they say, all it takes to embark on one of the world's supreme rafting adventures as a team is determination and moderate fitness. At least so long as you thrill to the idea of an occasional dunking in rapids up to Grade 4, that is – the toughest spots aren't called "the cauldron" and "the churn" for nothing.

It's not all white-knuckle water rides, though. Beyond the helter-skelter of the upper and middle sections, the tannin-stained Lower Franklin becomes a dark treacly ribbon. It's a chance to absorb surrounding rainforest that's thicker than the Amazon; a pristine pocket of the world where 4,000-year-old Huon pines line riverbanks and company comes from the occasional platypus or glow-worms that stage a lightshow at dusk.

Small wonder then the Franklin River is iconic of both Tasmania's wilderness and the value of raw nature. It took the largest mass protest in Australian history – as well as the discovery of Aboriginal caves that marked the southernmost outpost of mankind during the last ice age – to save it from a hydroelectricity dam in 1983. Even David Bellamy got himself arrested to help protect it. And if Britain's favourite botanist was man enough to dip a paddle then you've got no excuse.

Need to know Rafting Tasmania (Ⓦwww. raftingtasmania.com; ☏+61 (0) 362 391 080) runs ten-day expeditions down the length of the river, plus shorter trips from the river's lower sections from Nov–March. The price includes transfers from Hobart, national park passes, all equipment, and food and wine.

489 STAY WITH A SAMOAN FAMILY

Robert Louis Stevenson, the author of *Treasure Island*, spent his last days in the South Pacific in Samoa's tropical heat. In many ways, not much has changed since his time in this Polynesian island. Life still centres on the extended family and the community; the chief-based system is strong and traditional tattoos mark out those born to lead. Nearly all villages are on the coast where people have simple thatched shelters, or *fales*, on the beach, in which to rest and enjoy the cooling trade winds.

Customary Samoan hospitality has helped simple, family-run tourist lodges to prosper as locals have turned their beachside huts into guesthouses. Now, on both of the two main islands (Upolu and Savaii), for US$40 or so, you can spend the night on a mattress on the floor of a little open-sided *fale*, with a mosquito net and maybe a locker for valuables. Your hosts will prepare dinner and a tropical breakfast and can arrange for you to go off on hikes or join in with cousins and aunties in their chores if you wish.

During the day the men venture off into the milky blue sea to spearfish from outrigger canoes, a coconut-leaf basket ready for the catch. Women weave mats from sun-dried pandanus leaves or hack at coconuts to extract the flesh for copra. Perhaps, if you're lucky, you may get to witness a traditional tattooing session, using sharpened pigs' teeth and ink made from candlenut soot. By night, as the sea laps at the stilts of your simple *fale*, you can sit and read Stevenson under the wide and starry sky.

Need to know For contact details, directions and further information on the various fales, visit Ⓦwww.samoa.travel/acc.aspx.

A fire dancer on the island of Upolu, Samoa

A cuddly koala: these shy creatures spend up to 18 hours a day asleep

490 KOALA SPOTTING, BRISBANE

If there's an A-list of Australian wildlife then the koala is right at the top of it, and many tourists arrive in the country hell-bent on hugging one at a zoo or wildlife park. You can't blame them: koalas seem almost as if they've been designed to appeal to humans, all cute fluffy ears, thick fur and big brown eyes; colonial settlers first coined the term "koala bear" as these animals reminded them of childhood teddies. These are not bears at all though but wild marsupials – closely related to the wombat – and seeing one in its natural habitat is an altogether more rewarding experience.

One of the best places to spot koalas is in the eucalyptus forest surrounding Brisbane, just an hour's drive from the city. The only catch is that these animals are notoriously shy and very well camouflaged – so if you're with a guide who knows their hangouts your odds of seeing one will be much improved. One such expert is Dr Ronda Green of Araucaria Ecotours. A trained zoologist, Ronda and her son Darren and have been tracking koalas for years. They'll soon have you peering through binoculars looking for freshly stripped branches and tell-tale claw marks, while watching your step for dry, cigar-shaped droppings – all clues to koalas being in the vicinity. With luck, you'll spot the star of the show diligently chomping its way through the forest canopy or dozing way up above (koalas spend up to eighteen hours a day asleep so don't expect them to pose for photos).

During the rest of the tour you'll encounter a range of other Aussie icons including wallabies and kookaburras (probably the country's loudest bird, with a piercing laughing call). As dusk descends there's another treat in store – the sight and sound of thousands of fruit bats taking flight to forage; the noise is so intense it's enough to wake a koala.

Need to know *Araucaria Ecotours (⊛www. learnaboutwildlife.com; ☏+61 755 441 283) runs wildlife day tours of one to three days from Brisbane (A$99) and Gold Coast resorts (A$130), which include lunch and refreshments. Longer tours into the outback and specialist bird-watching trips are also available.*

491 A VIEW OVER PARADISE AT LORD HOWE ISLAND, AUSTRALIA

A small speck in the Pacific, 600km from the nearest landmass, Lord Howe Island is one of Australia's best-kept secrets. With its lush tropical forests, white sandy beaches and lack of other people, you could be forgiven for thinking you'd arrived at a tropical Eden or perhaps the set of the TV show *Lost*. In fact the island is part of New South Wales (Sydney is "just" 700km southwest) but thanks to its World Heritage status and strict limits on visitor numbers (no more than four hundred at a time, which is still more than the island's population of 350) its unique environment has been preserved.

As soon as you set foot on Lord Howe your eye is drawn to Mount Gower (875m), pretty much all that remains of the now extinct volcano that formed the island. One of only two guides approved to lead the exhilarating trek up it is Jack Shick, a fifth-generation islander. For A$40 he can get you to the top and back in approximately eight hours. Along the way he'll point out some of the island's rarest plants and sea birds, demonstrate how to climb a palm tree and throw in a bit of local history. Shick's father was one of the first conservationists on the island and was instrumental in saving the endemic Lord Howe Island woodhen – if you're lucky you may spot one of these small flightless birds during the walk.

The scenery varies rapidly throughout the ascent; one minute you're peering out over the entire span of the island, the next you're scrambling through dense and misty subtropical rainforest, clinging to ropes for a fair portion of the trek. But once you reach the summit, the near-vertical ascent will seem well worth the effort as you look out over the island's thickly forested slopes and turquoise lagoon, framed by an azure ocean stretching to the horizon.

Tree ferns in the Tarkine, Tasmania

Need to know: *For more background on the island, including accommodation and directions, visit ⓦwww.lordhoweisland.info. Jack Shick's guided walks to Mount Gower take place every Monday and Thursday; for further info on tours see ⓦseatosummit.googlepages.com. Bookings can be made by phone (☏+61 265 632 218) or email (ⓔseatosummit@gmail.com).*

492 WALK THE WILD TARKINE, TASMANIA

The little known Tarkine region in the remote northwest of Tasmania is almost certainly the next big thing in Australian wilderness. In 2004 the Worldwide Fund for Nature described the state's last frontier as "a world beyond human memory, a living link to the primeval supercontinent of Gondwana". Three years later Australian TV's Channel Nine called it "the last unknown wilderness in Australia".

Except that the Tarkine does not exist, or at least not on official maps. Inspired by the Aboriginal group known as the Tarkiner that once roamed in the area, conservationists coined the name to refer to the blank space in the northwest whose swathe of raw coast and old-growth rainforest was threatened with commercial exploitation. Among them were the founders of Tarkine Trails, whose trekking operation funds a protection campaign.

Only on foot do you appreciate the epic quality of the Tarkine. To traverse the southern hemisphere's largest temperate rainforest, camping beneath moss-bearded myrtles and bathing in waterfalls of chilled spring water, is to timewarp into a world of myth forged when mankind was just a glint in evolution's eye. To hike 30km up its empty coastline is to be humbled, whether by evidence of tens of thousands of years of Aboriginal existence or by waves that travel unopposed from Patagonia.

Everyone loves a travel secret. Yet after a moratorium on logging was lifted in 2003, the Tarkine is "still wild, still threatened", as the conservation slogan puts it. This may be one secret to shout about.

Need to know *Tarkine Trails (ⓦwww.tarkinetrails. com.au; ☏+61 (0) 362 235 320) operates the six-day Rainforest Track (2–3 monthly) and five-day Wild Coast trip (monthly) from November to April. The price includes transfers (from Hobart, Launceston, Devonport or Burnie), tent accommodation, food and wine. Only experienced bushwalkers should attempt the Tarkine Trails independently.*

GREEN SYDNEY

Australia's best-known city may be home to two of the world's most famous landmarks – the Sydney Opera House and Harbour Bridge – but it has much to offer away from the crowds drawn to these icons, and with an ambitious city-wide sustainability plan aimed for 2030, a lot of the attractions are distinctly green.

493 Swim in a coastal pool

Along with world-famous beaches like Bondi, Sydney's other coastal institutions are its pools. There are seventy of them lining the harbour and the suburban shores, ranging from glamorous see-and-be-seen lidos to Olympic-size pools. Often the pool itself is the attraction, such as Bronte, carved into the cliffs and so close to the Pacific that you can jump over the edge and into the ocean that laps at the pool's side. Wylies, meanwhile, is covered in algae and filled with tiny fish so that it is somewhat like swimming in an aquarium. And if you're feeling brave, there's Mahon – known as "the impossible pool" because of the intensity of the waves that crash over the side from the open ocean. To dip your toe in a few of them, you can walk the cliffs from Bondi's famous Icebergs

pool to Bronte in about an hour and a half. Whichever pool you try along the way, it's the best way to enjoy swimming at Sydney's shores – without any worry about the sharks.

Need to know *All of Sydney's and New South Wales' coastal pools can be found at ⓦwww. nswoceanbaths.info. For maps and information on the walk from Bondi to Bronte see ⓦwww. waverley.nsw.gov.au/council/parks/parks/coastwalk. asp.*

494 Have some bonza tucker

With the perfect climate for farming, the Hunter Valley and other world-renowned wine areas a few hours away, and of course the vast Pacific Ocean to one side, Sydney has all the conditions for fantastic food, whatever your budget. There are nine branches of the whole-food chain Iku, which serves biodynamic, organic and vegetarian food, such as mushroom, leek and thyme pie or spicy vegetable, tofu and lime-leaf laksa. For a more special occasion, try New South Wales' only climate-neutral restaurant, Billy Kwong's (ⓦwww. kyliekwong.org; ☎+61 (0) 293 323 300), where you can dine on organic dishes like seared calamari, rocket and Asian herb salad or Sichuan pepper beef with pickled cucumber and watercress. Slow Food fans should saunter over to Peasants' Feast (ⓦwww. peasantsfeast.com.au; ☎+61

Putting in the lengths at the ocean-filled Bronte baths

(0) 295 165 998) or Danks Street Depot (ⓦwww.danksstreetdepot.com.au; ☎+61 (0) 296 982 201), which both focus on providing the finest ingredients from nearby specialist farms and producers.

Need to know *For those keen on cooking (or grazing) there are also regular gourmet food and farmers' markets all across the city. Go to ⓦwww.slowfoodsydney.com.au to find out when and where.*

495 Aboriginal Sydney

Many people think Sydney's history began with the arrival of Captain Cook in Botany Bay in 1770. Take a boat cruise with Tribal Warrior (ⓦwww.tribalwarrior.org; ☎+61 (0) 296 993 491) around the famous harbour, however, and while seeing the monuments from their best viewpoint, you'll learn about the life of the area's Aboriginal people, who were here for thirty thousand years before the arrival of the "whitefella". You'll also learn the original names for places – Botany Bay was once Kamay, and the land where the Opera House now stands was known as Jubgalee.

On board the ship, built in 1899 and the oldest working ship in Australia as well as the only Aboriginal-owned boat tour, the crew will explain about the fishing practices of a people better known for eking out a life in the dry Australian bush. The highlight is a stop on Clark Island, once a significant Aboriginal meeting place, where tribal elder Uncle Max and others will welcome you with a traditional corroboree dance. The sight of these millennia-old rituals against the backdrop of one of the world's most modern skylines is one few forget.

Need to know *Tribal Warrior runs Tues–Sat. To see the harbour on your own you can hire a kayak through ⓦwww.sydneyharbourkayaks.com.au or an electric motorboat at ⓦwww.ecoboats.com.au. For more on the wildlife and Aboriginal history of the harbour, go to ⓦwww.livingharbour.net.*

496 See the city by foot or bike

As the most populous city of one of the most outdoorsy and fitness-focused people in the world, Sydney is best seen on two feet – or two wheels. One of the most interesting routes is the 38km Green Ring that connects coastal trails, cycle paths and other green routes and includes some of the city's highlights, including Darling Harbour, Cooks River, Botany Wetlands and Sydney Harbour at Cockle Bay. With several gentle hills around the harbour, you guarantee yourself a workout along with the iconic view.

Need to know *The Green Ring can be found at ⓦsydneygreenring.blogspot.com. Info on walking the coastline is at ⓦwww.walkingcoastalsydney.com.au. For info on hiring bikes, visit ⓦwww.cyclehire.com.au.*

(From top) The Tribal Warrior is Australia's oldest working ship; The Bondi to Coogee coastal walk; Going for an early morning cycle around Daves Point Reserve at the foot of the Harbour Bridge

497 VISIT AN UNINHABITED SOLOMON ISLAND

The Solomon Islands is one of the least-visited nations in the world: as a consequence there is barely any tourism infrastructure and what exists is basic. But those adventurous enough to visit this scattering of tropical islands are guaranteed a memorable trip: with hardly anyone else around you can paddle in dug-out canoes, hike through virgin rainforest, dive some of the most spectacular reefs in the world and stay in simple village guesthouses, such as those built on stilts above the waters of the world's longest lagoon, Marovo. Conservation organizations, such as WWF, have been working with village landowners to encourage them to start small tourism enterprises based around these activities, rather than give way to foreign logging companies intent on taking valuable and rare timber.

One of the islands under threat, Tetepare, is the largest uninhabited island in the South Pacific. Over 150 years ago its residents fled, for reasons unknown, but their descendants (who still own the island) continue to visit the island to hunt and fish. Rare skinks, turtles and birds nest on this safe haven, where, so far, the loggers have not been welcome. Small numbers of hardy tourists can visit and stay overnight in a handful of simple palm-and-wood chalets, with visitor fees used to create jobs and provide improved healthcare for Solomon Islanders. You must be accompanied by a guide at all times, who will come across with you in the boat.

You can help the island's wardens (who are also the resident chefs, making simple fish and rice suppers for guests) with scientific research like counting coconut crabs or monitoring turtles; snorkel over giant clams and coral gardens or hike through one of Earth's last untouched island wildernesses. If you like your experiences removed from urban life, then this may be the perfect getaway.

Need to know *Visitors pay a daily fee of A$70 approx, plus a one-off fee of A$10, and are expected to cover their fuel costs. The turtle-nesting season is from October to January. For directions from Honiara, reservations, a list of what to bring and prices see Ⓦwww.tetepare.org; ☎+677 62163.*

The Solomon Islands are one of the least-visited nations on Earth

Arthur's Pass Wilderness Lodge
is between the Waimakariri River
Valley and the Southern Alps

498 NEW ZEALAND'S BEST WILDERNESS LODGES

Tucked away in the middle of the 27,000-square-kilometre New Zealand World Heritage Area, 300km from Queenstown, Lake Moeraki Lodge is one of the great places to get away from it all. The light, airy rooms have views out to the surrounding rainforest, while four more luxurious suites overlook the churning rapids of the Moeraki River. From here you can kayak through orchid-filled rainforests, go on nocturnal hikes to look for glow-worms or make the short trek to Robinson Crusoe beach, a suitably deserted stretch of tree-fringed sand.

The lodge is one of two established by the former director of New Zealand's Royal Forest and Bird Society – the other, Arthur's Pass Wilderness Lodge, is 130km from Christchurch. Perched between the Waimakariri River Valley and the Southern Alps, the accommodation here has panoramas that are hard to beat. During the day guests can have a picnic on mountain meadows carpeted in subalpine flowers, or trek to the many waterfalls that cascade down Mount Arthur. The lodge even has a working merino-wool sheep farm, and depending on the time of year you can help out with the lambing, weaning or shearing.

Meals at both lodges make the most of New Zealand's bounty of fresh fish, wild venison and vegetables. Washed down with fine wines at the end of a long day's hiking or kayaking, it makes for a pretty perfect day. And to turn it into an amazing week, it's easy to journey between the two lodges either by car or on the coast-to-coast *Tranzalpine Express*, considered one of the world's great train journeys, which passes through spectacular mountains, gorges and rainforests.

Need to know *Both lodges are open Aug–May; for rates, reservations and activities see ⓦwww.wildernesslodge.co.nz; ☏+64 3750 0881 (Lake Moeraki) or ☏+64 3318 9246 (Arthur's Pass). Several activities are included in the price of a stay, although half- and full-day excursions are extra. You can reach Lake Moeraki by coach from Queenstown, or driving from Greymouth (4hr), from where the Tranzalpine train goes to Arthur's Pass. From Christchurch you can get to Arthur's Pass via the Tranzscenic train (ⓦwww.tranzscenic.co.nz).*

499 TEACH RUGBY IN FIJI

Known for their ferocious tackling and some of the most imaginative play in the sport, the Fijians wouldn't seem to be much in need of rugby tuition. But while the nation's raw talent is undeniable, there is little to no coaching at junior level and as a result many children never get the chance to nurture their skills. It's one of the reasons that although the country excels at the more free-flowing sevens version, it struggles to translate this into the fifteen-a-side union game.

On a Madventurer two-week coaching holiday, you'll work with kids between the ages of 6–14, passing on what you learned at school or your club about the increasingly complicated (and ever-changing) rules and tactics of rugby union. Accommodation is at the organization's base in a house in the suburbs of Lautoka, the second-largest town on the islands. You'll share a room with up to five other people and tuck into traditional Fijian meals, such as sweet potato and pineapple bake or lentil and potato curry, courtesy of Madventurers cook Mere. Outside of training – which starts at noon on weekdays and continues for most of the afternoon – there's plenty of time to indulge in other Fijian pastimes, such as heading down to the beach, diving, swimming or drinking *kava* with the locals.

From time to time, Madventurer also takes guests to spend a few days in the village of Nakavika, occasionally doing some training there. Should you get the chance, it's a wonderful opportunity to live for a few days in a rural home, fishing with the family and perhaps learning to cook a few Fijian dishes. And if, in a few years' time, you're watching the World Cup when one of your protégés scores a try, you can nod sagely and say to your friends: "I taught him everything he knows."

Need to know *Two-week rugby training trips take place between February and September. You can combine this with one of the other Fijian trips Madventurer runs, such as teaching or constructing buildings in a village. For further information see* Ⓦ*www.madventurer.com;* ☎*+44 (0) 845 121 1996.*

Young Fijian rugby players

The islands of Tonga's Vava'u Group are one of the best places for sailing in the South Pacific

500 SAIL AROUND TONGA'S VAVA'U GROUP

Reliably warm weather, calm waters with good visibility and over fifty well-protected anchorages are just some of the reasons why sailors head for Vava'u – the most northerly of Tonga's three island groups and one of the best places for sailing in the South Pacific. Several yacht-charter companies operate out of Neiafu, the main town on Vava'u Island, whose Port Refuge Harbour is the best-protected in Tonga and the gateway to over fifty offshore islands within the archipelago.

One of the features of the offshore islands is the sea caves dotted along the coastline. The most well-known is Mariner's Cave – a couple of hours' sailing southwest of Neiafu at Nuapapu Island. The cave can't be seen above water and its location is not marked by any signposts (its whereabouts is described in terms of the topography of nearby cliffs), but if you manage to locate the entrance, you can free-dive underwater for about 3m then cross under a tunnel for 4m before you surface inside the cave. Inside, the swell from the sea causes a build-up of fog and pressure and it can become quite claustrophobic, but the sensation lasts only a few seconds and when it subsides, you are left to enjoy the eerie stillness.

The Vava'u Group is also excellent for whale-watching from July to October when humpback whales come to bear their young before heading back to Antarctica. But the best aspect of sailing here is hauling up in a protected anchorage, spending the evening alone watching the palm trees sway in the breeze and looking out over the turquoise waters of the lagoon and beyond to the big blue. The world will seem far, far away.

Need to know *You can hire small yachts (min 3 days) from operators based at the Port of Refuge in Neiafu. Sailing Safaris (*⊛*www.sailingsafaris.com) rents a 26ft yacht for US$160 per day; SailTonga (*⊛*www.sailtonga.com) has a 45ft ketch for US$250 per day full-board; Manu-o-ku (*⊛*www. manuoku.com) runs skippered cruises on board a 37ft trimaran for US$415 for two people per night full-board. For details of other activities, such as kayaking and whale-watching, see* ⊛*www.vavau. to. It is also possible to crew on yachts sailing from New Zealand to Tonga (for details see p.376).*

MAKE THE MOST OF YOUR TRIP

MAKE THE MOST OF YOUR TRIP

Selected resources to help you plan your next Clean Break

TRANSPORT

Let the walking do the talking

Ⓦwww.walkit.com
Stroll the streets and you get a much better feel for the local history, culture and vibe than you would on a bus or metro. This website shows how to get from A to Z – and everywhere in between – in ten different UK cities.

Using public transport in cities

The following sites help you navigate your way through the urban jungle.

Ⓦimetro.nanika.net
Provides free public transport maps for over four hundred cities worldwide (downloadable for PDAs, Blackberrys and iPhones).

Ⓦwww.tubemap.com
Detailed guide to the London Underground network but also has links to the official websites (with maps and ticket information) of urban transport in cities worldwide.

Hiring a city bike

Ⓦbike-sharing.blogspot.com
The success of the credit-card controlled "Vélib" cycle-hire scheme in Paris has made the traditional coin-operated schemes look outdated. Nearly a hundred cities now offer some kind of bike hire. This blog has links to all of them and covers the latest developments.

Lift-sharing

A modern, co-ordinated version of hitch-hiking, millions of people are now joining and using lift-sharing schemes as a convenient and carbon-efficient means to get around.

UK

Ⓦwww.isanyonegoingto.com
Includes a search facility for events as well as locations.

Ⓦwww.liftshare.org
The pioneering lift-sharing site now has a membership of over 300,000 participants who buddy up on their journeys.

EUROPE

Ⓦwww.ride4cents.org
Car-pooling site in 42 European countries.

WORLDWIDE

Ⓦwww.pickuppal.com
Has members in 105 countries, so as its website says: "With millions of vehicles on the road, someone is definitely going your way!"

Car-sharing

For short hops: pick up a car and you can return it to various points around the city. Most schemes are designed for residents, but they can be worth looking into if you are staying long enough or if you only need a car for a short period. For a list of schemes worldwide see Ⓦworldcarshare.com.

Hitch-hiking

For those who prefer the good old-fashioned method of thumbing a lift.

Ⓦwww.digihitch.com
Find a sidekick to join you on the side of the road, learn the do's and don'ts of different countries, and chat with other hitchers.

Ⓦhitchwiki.org
A global collaborative project to guide users through the challenges and opportunities of hitching, featuring tips on juggling roadside pebbles and how to look like you're a person who really does deserve a lift.

Driving and car hire

Car firms are at last beginning to offer the option to drive cleaner cars. There are now an increasing number of outlets where you can hire a lower-emissions car at both specialist eco car-hire firms (which usually have a range of hybrid and electric cars) and traditional hire firms offering greener alternatives to their standard cars. For the latter try Ⓦwww.hertz.com, Ⓦwww.avis.com and Ⓦwww.enterprise.com (in the US). A car that emits less than 120g of CO_2 per km is generally considered to be a greener option.

UK

Ⓦwww.eta.co.uk
The website of the Environmental Transport Association includes a "green route finder", which provides directions, journey time, map and carbon emissions so you can choose the greenest route.

Ⓦwww.whatgreencar.com
Find out how green your car is using this site's ratings for carbon dioxide emissions for every car available in the UK.

US

Ⓦwww.autodriveaway.com
Not quite car hire, Autodriveaway is a car relocation service covering the US. If you are planning on making one of the necessary journeys, you can get a fuel allowance and drive the car for free to its destination.

Ⓦwww.evolimo.com
Hybrid and gas-powered limousines, jeeps and cars in LA.

Taking a taxi

UK

Ⓦwww.greentomatocars.com
London's trailblazing hybrid car-hire firm, which claims its fleet of Toyota Prius emit less than half the carbon dioxide of black cabs over journeys of the same length.

US

Ⓦwww.plannettran.com
Hybrid taxis in Boston and San Francisco.

Taking the bus and coach

National and international coach services

UK

Ⓦwww.biggreencoach.co.uk
Bus services specifically to festivals and events in the UK.

Ⓦwww.nationalexpress.com
The UK's most extensive intercity coach operator.

Ⓦwww.megabus.com
Budget rail and coach operator, which runs services between selected major towns and cities. Also operates in US and Canada.

EUROPE

Ⓦwww.eurolines.com
Coaches connecting over five hundred destinations in cities and towns across Europe.

NORTH AMERICA

Ⓦwww.gotobus.com
For urban and intercity buses throughout the US.

Ⓦwww.greyhound.com
The largest intercity bus operator in the US, Canada and Mexico.

WORLDWIDE

Ⓦwww.busstation.net
Links to national bus and coach sites and endless enthusiasts' pages, which include a range of memorabilia from photographs of old trams to accounts of their favourite trips. Unwieldy and inelegant, but if you want to find out how to travel anywhere in the world by coach, this is probably the best place to start.

Hop-on hop-off buses

For popular long-distance routes:
buy a pass and then hop on or off wherever you want. Some are more likely to appeal to younger travellers only.

EUROPE AND NORTHERN AFRICA

Ⓦwww.fezbus.co.uk
Australian-run company offering 39 routes around the coast and interior of Turkey, connecting with ferries across the Greek islands to Athens and further into Greece.

Ⓦwww.radicaltravel.com
Routes range from within the Scottish highlands to the Moroccan Sahara.

Ⓦwww.ze-bus.com
Routes run from Paris and through France's most popular western and southwestern regions, including Bordeaux and Biarritz. Also tours to Italy, Portugal, Spain and Eastern Europe.

AMERICAS

Ⓦwww.bambaexperience.com
Routes throughout mainland Central America, often visiting more out-of-the-way areas with an emphasis on supporting the economies of rural areas, particularly in Mexico.

Ⓦwww.greentortoise.com
Adventure-themed coach trips across the US, targeted at all ages. Its coaches are increasingly run on biofuels.

Ⓦwww.moosenetwork.com
Routes across Canada for all ages, picking up and dropping off at hotel or hostel of your choice.

Ⓦwww.ticabus.com
Site in English and Spanish for routes connecting Tapachula in southern Mexico with Panama City, travelling through all the mainland countries in between, except Belize.

AUSTRALIA AND NEW ZEALAND

Ⓦwww.ozexperience.com
Tours throughout Australia, with accommodation included for everywhere except the classic Sydney
to Cairns route, where you can stay where you want.

Ⓦwww.straytravel.com
12-month passes throughout New Zealand, with stops at hostels along the way.

SOUTH AFRICA

Ⓦwww.bazbus.com
A backpackers' favourite running up from Cape Town to Durban, which then loops around Natal (including Drakensberg) to Swaziland and inland to Johannesburg.

WORLDWIDE

Ⓦwww.oz-bus.com
The original Oz bus runs from London to Sydney through Asia, though the company now operates a second route from New York to London via Asia. It also runs bus trips from Turkey to Nepal (Ⓦwww.hippie-trail.com); around Australia (Ⓦwww.oz-busdownunder.com); and overland tours throughout Africa (Ⓦwww.oz-busafrica.com).

Train

Ⓦwww.bahn.de
The German national railway site includes all the schedules for the main rail journeys throughout Europe. Just type in the necessary "from and to" and it shows you all the best train routes and even how to factor in time spent in a city; for example, if your route passes through Paris around lunch time, you can allow yourself a few hours for a salad Niçoise and a bottle of Bordeaux before hitting the tracks. Also includes an online booking facility.

Ⓦwww.interrail.net
For various rail passes in 29 European countries plus Morocco, including discounts on selected ferry journeys. Supplements have to be paid for certain services, such as overnight trains and ferry services.

Ⓦwww.seat61.com
The most comprehensive website for information on train travel throughout the world. Read more on p.154.

Ticketing agents

UK

Ⓦwww.raileurope.co.uk
For all rail tickets within Europe, including interrail passes.

Europe

Ⓦwww.tgv-europe.com
Rail Europe Continental's portal: select your home country and you're directed to a specific website for booking European high-speed trains.

Boat

UK

Ⓦwww.electric-boat-association.org.uk
The website of the Electric Boat Association provides a list of companies that run river cruises on electric boats in the UK.

Ⓦwww.waterscape.com
Discover Britain's rivers and canals, including how to book barges, find riverside pubs or where to go fishing.

Ferry

EUROPE

For a map of ferry routes to the Mediterranean Islands see p.90.

Ⓦwww.aferry.to
For booking ferry trips throughout Europe and across to North Africa.

Ⓦwww.greekferries.gr For booking inter-island ferries and from the Italian mainland to Greece.

CARIBBEAN

Ⓦwww.travellerspoint.com/guide/Caribbean_ferries
Has links to ferry operators running services throughout the Caribbean.

WORLDWIDE

Ⓦwww.youra.com
Worldwide ferry links – particularly good for the US, Canada and Mexico.

Cargo boat

A world map showing the major cargo routes and stopping points is on p.344. For further insight from other cargo-boat travellers see Ⓦwww.geocities.com/freighterman.geo.

Booking agents

UK

Ⓦwww.strandtravel.co.uk
UK-based site offering freight trips all over the world.

US

Ⓦwww.freighterworld.com
Worldwide trips, categorised by durations, ranging from fifteen days or fewer to journeys lasting over three months.

Work for free passage

Find yacht owners and skippers looking for crew:

Ⓦwww.crewfile.com
Ⓦwww.crewsearcher.com
Ⓦwww.cruiserlog.com
Ⓦwww.findacrew.net
Ⓦwww.floatplan.com
Ⓦwww.partnersandcrews.com

Flying

Flying is the fastest-growing contributor to climate change. You can see how the different airlines are responding to this, and choose a cleaner airline by checking Ⓦwww.seatguru.com/articles/green_aircraft_and_airlines.php. You can also consider "offsetting" your emissions: it's not a solution but if you are taking any form of polluting journey (particularly flying), why not pay a little more and contribute to projects that try to balance the equation? See p.186 for further info on carbon offsetting.

ACCOMMODATION

General

The following websites include reviews written by inspectors who have visited the featured accommodation.

UK

Ⓦwww.ecoescape.org
A comprehensive list of green accommodation in the UK and Ireland. Has recently added a "tours" section for low-impact adventures.

EUROPE

Ⓦwww.sawdays.co.uk
The website of book publisher Alastair Sawday (who champions owner-run, characterful places to stay mainly in Britain, France, Ireland, Italy and Spain) includes an "ethical collection" of over three hundred accommodations that score well in one or more of the publisher's self-administered criteria for "environment", "community" and "food".

Agriturismi and farmstays

Some are working farms, others are farms that have been converted to lodgings. All should offer an escape from the city and a chance to get closer to rural life.

UK

Ⓦwww.farmstayuk.co.uk
Accommodation in and around working farms all over the UK.

EUROPE

Ⓦwww.agritourismeurope.com
Individual entries of farmstays with pictures, mostly European.

Ⓦwww.ecvc.eu/agrotournetwork
A huge country-by-country network linking to regional and national sites.

US

Ⓦwww.agritourismworld.com
Find farms (categorized by what they grow or rear) and vineyards across the US, as well as ranches.

Ⓦwww.ruralbounty.com
As well as finding farm accommodation all across the US, this site allows you to search for wineries, farmers' markets and farm shops.

AUSTRALIA AND NEW ZEALAND

Ⓦwww.australianfarmstay.com.au
Accommodation and tours across Australia.

Ⓦwww.truenz.co.nz/farmstays
Details of farmstays in New Zealand wth information on activities and guides.

Homestays

Stay in people's homes and get to meet the locals and benefit from their knowledge, while saving money on hotels.

Ⓦwww.homestaybooking.com
Booking site for homestays worldwide.

Ⓦwww.homestayweb.com
Over two thousand homestays worldwide, from Nicaragua to New Caledonia.

Ⓦwww.womenwelcomewomen.org.uk
A membership site (with members in over seventy countries) for women who wish to travel the world and stay with other women.

Hospitality exchanges

Find people willing to have you stay in their homes for free and perhaps show you around their local area (see also p.274).

Ⓦwww.couchsurfing.com
With over a million members, this is the biggest hospitality exchange site – and with thorough vetting procedures one of the safest.

Ⓦwww.hospitalityclub.org
Along with Couchsurfing, pobably the best port of call for general hospitality exchanges. Has tailored parts of the site so you can search for everything from indigenous hosts to a special section for Mensa members keen to ensure brainy chat.

Ⓦwww.warmshowers.org
People offering to host those travelling by bicycle.

Home swaps

Registered members stay in each other's home while they are away.

Ⓦwww.geenee.com
Focused on the world's most popular cities. Whereas most home swaps operate as notice boards for members, Geenee also visits and rates many of the houses on its site.

Ⓦwww.guardianhomeexchange.co.uk
A worldwide home-exchange site run by the UK's *Guardian* newspaper.

Ⓦwww.homeforexchange.com
Over ten thousand worldwide listings, including camper vans and yachts to swap.

Ⓦwww.homelink.org.uk
Facilitating home exchanges for over fifty years, Homelink has properties in over 75 countries and also publishes a twice-yearly directory.

Camping

Ⓦcampingcoop.org
Blog on the world of camping, with reviews of campsites, equipment and favourite trips.

Ⓦwww.campingo.com
Find campsites all across the world, with a search engine customizable by 150 criteria such as "near beach", "shady" and what activities are available.

Ⓦwww.thehappycampers.co.uk
Recommends campsites in the UK and Ireland and includes a discussion forum for topical issues such as campfires and wild camping.

Ⓦwww.ultimatecampresource.com
For ideas on how to keep you and the family entertained around the campfire.

Alternative

Alpine mountain refuges, bothies, huts and trekking cabins

UK

Ⓦwww.camping-bods.co.uk
Former fishermen's huts in the Shetland Isles run as basic shelters.

Ⓦwww.lakelandcampingbarns.co.uk
Camping barns in the Lake District.

Ⓦwww.mountainbothies.org.uk
Find remote huts in the hills of Great Britain.

EUROPE

France: Ⓦwww.gites-refuges.com

Italy (Italian only): Ⓦwww.cai.it

Switzerland: Ⓦwww.sac-cas.ch.

NORTH AMERICA

Ⓦwww.huts.org
A network of 29 backcountry huts in the Colorado Rocky Mountains.

Ⓦwww.alpineclubofcanada.ca
A membership organization that runs 28 backcountry huts in the Canadian Rocky Mountains.

Restored buildings

Ⓦwww.landmarktrust.org.uk and Ⓦwww.landmarktrustusa.org
The Landmark Trust rescues derelict historic properties across the UK and US, restores them and then rents them out as self-catering accommodation.

FOOD AND DRINK

Organic and locally produced food

In many non-industrialized countries, local food is the norm. Elsewhere, choose locally produced food and you'll help reduce food miles and support local economies. For slow food producers and events see Ⓦwww.slowfood.com.

UK

Ⓦwww.localfoodadvisor.com
Links to four thousand local food producers, restaurants, fairs and markets throughout Britain.

NORTH AMERICA

Ⓦwww.eatwellguide.org

Key in the zip code of where you are and it will tell you what organic farms, restaurants and markets are in your area.

AUSTRALIA

ⓦwww.organicfooddirectory.com.au
A directory of organic food producers, restaurants and other businesses.

Farmers' markets

The following sites help you find the location and opening times of markets that sell fresh locally produced food.

UK

ⓦwww.farmersmarkets.net

NORTH AMERICA

ⓦwww.farmersmarketscanada.ca

ⓦwww.localharvest.org

AUSTRALIA & NEW ZEALAND

ⓦwww.farmersmarket.org.nz

ⓦwww.farmersmarkets.com.au

Vegetarian

ⓦwww.happycow.net
Find a vegetarian restaurant or health food shop anywhere in the world.

ⓦwww.veggieheaven.com
Find a vegetarian restaurant in the UK, Europe, US, Canada and Australia.

ⓦwww.vegguide.org
Vegetarian lodging, restaurants and shops worldwide.

Drink

UK

ⓦwww.camra.co.uk
For drinkers keen to taste the local brew rather than identikit imported lagers, the Campaign for Real Ale's website lists authentic British pubs and events serving real ales.

ⓦwww.english-wine.com
Provides contact details and links to websites of those vineyards that are open for tastings (some provide overnight accommodation).

US

ⓦwww.discovercaliforniawine.com
Click on the "discover green wines and wineries" link on the homepage and find sustainable vineyards across America's most famous wine-producing state.

WORLDWIDE

ⓦwww.localwineevents.com
Find wine events and tastings all across the world.

MEETING PEOPLE

Local guides

ⓦwww.leaplocal.org
A new site that puts travellers in touch with local guides in Europe, Southeast Asia, North America and South America. The guide profiles include language(s) spoken, information about their tours and how much they charge for their services. Registered users of the site are provided with contact details for each guide.

ⓦwww.ourexplorer.com
Connects travellers with independent local tour guides all over the world, with ratings given by users online and money back if you aren't happy.

Greeters

A volunteer-led scheme of locals willing to show you the sights (often for free), giving you the inside track on the best places to visit and helping you explore beyond the normal tourist trails and group tours.

ⓦwww.globalgreeternetwork.com
A hub of greeter services, in cities including New York, Toronto, Buenos Aires and Adelaide.

ⓦwww.meeturplanet.com
A greeter network across 140 countries where members can meet up all over the world and discover one another's home areas, chat and share travel information online.

ⓦwww.visitjamaica.com/about-jamaica/meet-people.aspx
Set up by the Jamaican tourist board, volunteers introduce guests to Jamaica away from the tourist trails, introducing you to families, churches, markets or whatever other activities you are looking for.

ⓦwww.yoursafeplanet.com
For £45 for each trip (including volunteering), you get a vetted local contact to ensure you (or often, your globetrotting child) is never truly alone in a strange city. What you pay upfront you'll save in local knowledge and peace of mind.

Travel companions

If you don't want to travel by yourself, the following websites can help you find like-minded companions to share the journey.

ⓦwww.companions2travel.co.uk
UK-based site for worldwide travel. Has a broad age range of users and lots of discount offers for members with tour operators and suppliers of travel accessories.

ⓦwww.meetup.com
With five million members worldwide, this is the largest online network of local groups for helping anyone from kayakers to dog owners meet other like-minded individuals.

ⓦwww.retiredbackpackers.com
For those who still want to travel independently but no longer want to slum it on a diet of bread and cheese.

ⓦwww.thelmaandlouise.com
Specifically for women looking to travel with other women. Meeting Brad Pitt is not guaranteed.

ⓦwww.travellersconnected.com
Well-designed site that allows you to categorize the sort of traveller you are and are looking to go travelling with.

Customs and manners

ⓦwww.cyberpassport.org
A wiki project on etiquette and manners worldwide.

Ⓦ www.kwintessential.co.uk/resources/country-profiles.html
Avoid offensive gaffes and learn about local manners and customs throughout the world.

ACTIVITIES

Walking

UK

Ⓦ www.ramblers.org.uk
The Ramblers' Association has an extensive set of routes, and also covers hiker-friendly accommodation and transport information for the UK and major European routes.

Ⓦ www.walking-routes.co.uk
A directory of trails throughout the UK.

EUROPE

Ⓦ www.walkingontheweb.co.uk
Web directory of walking resources throughout Europe.

US

Ⓦ www.americanhiking.org
Trails guides throughout the US with links to the homepage of every national forest or park, organized by state.

Ⓦ www.trails.com
A subscription site offering over forty thousand trail maps and guides for every state in the US.

WORLDWIDE

Ⓦ www.everytrail.com
User-generated site enabling people to store and share trails on Google Maps.

Ⓦ www.traildatabase.org
Extensive database of hiking trails.

Cycling

UK

Ⓦ www.bikely.com
Search for cycle routes recommended by local cyclists.

EUROPE

Ⓦ www.bike-express.co.uk
Coach tours with special bike trailers to take you and your wheels wherever you want to go.

US

Ⓦ www.adventurecycling.org
Download maps for cycle routes across the US and find cycling buddies.

WORLDWIDE

Ⓦ en.wikipedia.org/wiki/List_of_cycleways
Extensive list of links to cycle routes across the world.

Ⓦ www.imba.com
The International Mountain Biking Association (IMBA) has members throughout the US and forty other countries worldwide.

Horse-riding

Ⓦ www.equineadventures.co.uk
Tour operator that runs horse-riding holidays across the globe.

Ⓦ www.hiddentrails.com
Worldwide horse-bound holiday directory and booking agent.

Winter sports

Ⓦ www.snowshoemag.com
US-based online magazine dedicated solely to snow-shoeing, including monthly features on fitness, nutrition and snow-shoeing clubs. Also links to other websites where you can search for nearby trails throughout North America.

Ⓦ www.respectthemountain.com
Information on how to minimize the environmental impact of your ski trips, provided by Ski Club of Great Britain. Also includes a "Green Resort Guide", which lists the eco-initiatives of over two hundred resorts worldwide so you can see which ones are doing their bit and which ones offer little more than tokenism.

Bushcraft and survival

UK

Ⓦ www.bushcraftuk.com
The main site for bushcraft in the UK, featuring courses, expeditions and forums.

Ⓦ www.naturalnavigator.com
Founder Tristan Gooley's UK-based courses teach you how to navigate using nature as a guide, from puddles to trees to stars. His techniques might not be as quick as using a map and a GPS, but you'll learn to look at the world in a new way.

NORTH AMERICA

Ⓦ www.trackersnw.com
The Wilderness Survival Institute runs courses in Oregon and San Francisco on survival techniques in the wilderness backcountry.

Ⓦ www.survivalinthebushinc.com
Outdoor survival courses based in Ontario, Canada.

Beaches

UK

Ⓦ www.goodbeachguide.co.uk
Run by the Marine Conservation Society to help you find clean and safe beaches in the UK.

WORLDWIDE

Ⓦ www.wheresthebeachdude.com
Compiled by members who recommend beaches all across the world, and add satellite images and directions for how to get there.

Watersports

Ⓦ www.nauticfriend.com
Worldwide directory of links related to watersports, from surfing spots to kayak hire and scuba-diving charters.

Surfing

Ⓦ www.surf-forecast.com
Wave, wind and weather forecasts as well as webcams of surfing spots worldwide.

Sailing

ⓦ**www.nonstopsail.com**
For yacht chartering around Britain and the Caribbean as well as trans-Atlantic crossings.

Diving

ⓦ**www.projectaware.org**
Find a dive operator or school certified by the environmental arm of PADI, the world's largest diving certification scheme.

ⓦ**www.reefcheck.org**
Non-profit organization protecting and rehabilitating reefs worldwide.

Canoeing and kayaking

UK

ⓦ**www.canoekayak.co.uk**
A magazine on canoeing and kayaking in the UK including features on the best paddling spots overseas.

NORTH AMERICA

ⓦ**www.americanwhitewater.org**
As well as campaigning for protection of American rivers, the site also has an extensive directory of links to kayaking clubs across the US.

ⓦ**www.sanctuaries.noaa.gov**
The web directory for all the US national marine sanctuaries, the aqueous equivalent of national parks, from the Everglades to Thunder Bay and the Hawaiian Islands.

Local events

ⓦ**www.whatsonwhen.com**
Type in a country or city for a wide selection of upcoming events.

Gigs and festivals

For a guide to some of the greenest festivals in the UK see p.44.

ⓦ**www.loco2travel.com**
Guide to how to travel to some of the biggest festivals in Europe without flying, such as Exit in Serbia and Sonar in Barcelona.

ⓦ**podbop.org**
Type in the city you're visiting (or live in) and it tells you about forthcoming concerts; you can also download podcasts of bands you like.

ⓦ**www.songkick.com**
Exhaustive directory of concerts in the US, UK, Canada, Australia and New Zealand. Alerts you when your favourite bands are coming to town.

ⓦ**worldparty.roughguides.com**
Allows you to search for festivals worldwide by theme, country or date.

PROTECTED AREAS AND WILDERNESS

UK

ⓦ**www.aonb.org.uk**
Information about Areas of Outstanding Natural Beauty in England, Wales and Northern Ireland.

ⓦ**www.natureonthemap.co.uk**
Find the nearest nature reserve to where you are using this website's postcode search facility.

ⓦ**www.wildernessfoundation.org.uk**
The UK's Wilderness Foundation along with its sister organizations in South Africa (ⓦ**www.wildernessfoundation.org.za**) and in the US (ⓦ**www.wild.org**) run wilderness trails programmes mainly for schools and groups, though individuals can join "open trails" (with a maximum group size of eight and two guides).

EUROPE

ⓦ**www.europarc.org**
The website for parks and protected areas in 39 European countries.

ⓦ**www.panparks.org**
Information about some of Eastern Europe's most spectacular and wild national parks, protected as part of a WWF project.

US

ⓦ**www.lnt.org**
The Leave No Trace Center for Outdoor Ethics is a non-profit organization that runs courses for outdoor guides on how to minimize the impact of their trips on wilderness areas.

ⓦ**www.nps.gov**
The website of the US National Park Service can help you find your nearest park or trail, and also find out more about its opening hours, amenities and how and whether you need to book to enter it.

ⓦ**www.sierraclub.org**
The oldest and largest environmental organization in the US, which also runs trips and holidays into some of the country's most wild places.

Tour Operators

Some of the experiences in this book can be arranged as part of a package holiday organized by a tour operator. The website of the Association of Independent Tour Operators (ⓦ**www.aito.co.uk**) is a good place to start looking for specialist travel companies.

Below is a selection of those companies that go the extra mile to make sure their trips benefit the places where they take visitors.

AFRICA

Expert Africa (ⓦ**www.expertafrica.com**). Experienced company with knowledgeable staff who specialize in holidays to sub-Saharan Africa.

Rainbow Tours (ⓦ**www.rainbowtours.co.uk**). Tailor-made holidays to Africa and the Indian Ocean.

AFRICA AND ASIA

Dragoman (ⓦ**www.dragoman.com**). Off-the-beaten-track overland holidays.

Tribes (ⓦ**www.tribes.co.uk**). The leading "fair trade tourism" operator in Africa and several countries in South America and Asia. It recently launched a website showcasing its budget holidays (ⓦ**www.down-to-earth-holidays.com**).

LATIN AMERICA

Journey Latin America (ⓦwww.journeylatinamerica.co.uk). Upmarket holidays throughout Central and South America.

Last Frontiers (ⓦwww.lastfrontiers.com) Tailor-made trips throughout Latin America.

SE ASIA

Symbiosis Travel (ⓦwww.symbiosis-travel.com). Adventure holidays and expeditions.

WORLDWIDE

KE Adventure (ⓦwww.keadventure.com). Trekking, climbing and biking holidays.

Discovery Initiatives (ⓦwww.discoveryinitiatives.co.uk). Nature-watching holidays in partnership with conservation organizations in 35 countries.

Intrepid (ⓦwww.intrepidtravel.com). Australian-based company that runs small-group adventure holidays including voluntourism trips.

CHARITIES AND CAMPAIGN GROUPS

ⓦwww.bornfree.org.uk
International charity working to protect wild animals around the world.

ⓦwww.ippg.net
The International Porter Protection group works for fairer treatment of mountain porters worldwide.

ⓦwww.irresponsibletourism.info
Online forum to whistle-blow on bad practices.

ⓦwww.sas.org.uk
Surfers Against Sewage campaigns against marine pollution along Britain's coastline.

ⓦwww.survival-international.org
Survival campaigns for the rights of indigenous people worldwide.

ⓦwww.thetravelfoundation.org.uk

The UK-based Travel Foundation raises funds through voluntary contributions from travellers booking with leading tour operators, such as First Choice and Thomas Cook, which it uses to support specific projects that help to make tourism more sustainable.

ⓦwww.toftigers.org
Travel Operators for Tigers is an Indian organization working to ensure Indian tiger-viewing tours help to save the remaining tigers.

ⓦwww.tourismconcern.org.uk
The vocal UK-based charity (with partners in over twenty countries) that campaigns against exploitation in tourism, particularly regarding labour conditions.

ⓦwww.wdcs.org
The Whale and Dolphin Conservation Society campaigns for the protection of whales and dolphins worldwide.

OTHER USEFUL SITES

ⓦwww.aboriginal-ecotourism.org
Well-researched guide to two hundred examples of community-based tourism worldwide.

ⓦwww.ecoclub.com
Online ecotourism magazine and membership organization for ecolodges worldwide.

ⓦwww.ecotourism.org
The long-established Washington-based International Ecotourism Society has links to ecolodges and holidays worldwide.

ⓦwww.greentravelguides.tv
Online TV channel dedicated to green travel.

ⓦwww.greentraveller.co.uk
UK-based online portal for green travel worldwide. It features the latest reviews of places to stay and trips written by this book's authors as well as their tips on how to go green, including low-carbon journeys, advice on booking rail and ferry journeys and links to green holidays worldwide.

ⓦwww.maketravelfair.co.uk
Cutting-edge online magazine that covers the latest innovations and issues in environmentally and socially aware travel.

ⓦwww.nationalgeographic.com/travel/sustainable
The website of the National Geographic Center for Sustainable Destinations is a comprehensive resource on "geotourism" – defined as "tourism that sustains or enhances the geographical character of a place". It also partners with Ashoka's Changemakers (ⓦwww.changemakers.net) to run "Geotourism Challenge" awards whereby users vote online for their favourite "geotourism changemaker".

ⓦwww.planeta.com
Excellent online journal on ecotourism, primarily focused on the Americas but including recommended trips worldwide.

ⓦwww.stuffyourrucksack.com
Ever visited a local charity or school and wanted to help? This site (supported by TV wildlife presenter Kate Humble) enables to you find out the sort of things local organizations really need, so that you can stuff your rucksack with the most appropriate supplies (such as pencils, maps and toys) and drop them off when you visit.

ⓦwww.sustainabletravelinternational.org
Washington-based non-profit organization that includes a travel directory of hotels, lodges and other green tourism businesses.

ACKNOWLEDGEMENTS

We would like to thank Aaron, Ahmed, Alex, Auden, Bogi, Brother Max, David, Dawid, Dean, Do Yo Min, Icham Bair, Ivan, Jabulani, Jerome, Lindile, Mohammed, Moi, Moses, Mossie, Mr Bold, Mr Chuka, Myles, Neil, Nelson, Noi, Oi, Omene, Petri, Pink, Rudi, Superman, Tour, and all the other guides who shared with us their own corners of the world.

We would also like to thank our editor, James Rice, for meticulously editing this book; Diana Jarvis for her sympathetic design; the experienced team at Rough Guides – including Ed Wright, Nicole Newman, Jo Kirby and Lucy White – for their guidance throughout the project; and our supportive agent, Nicola Barr, at The Susijn Agency.

Jeremy's acknowledgements

I would like to thank the following for their time, advice and support: Carol and Mark Smith; Melissa Williamson; Lindy Bolt; Hilary Wooley at Lewes Travel; Lorraine Forbes; Angela Moore; Sophia de Meyer at Whitepod; Roy Watt; Ince Erasmus from Ecoist; Helen Turnbull from Serendipity Africa; Susan Stouffs at Hertz SA; Noel de Villiers at Open Africa; Ben de Boer and Lisa Martus at Kurisa Moya; John Rosmarin at Leshiba; Jennifer Seif and Lolla Meyer at Fair Trade Tourism South Africa; Dave Martin at Bulungula; Dabe Sebitola and David Dugmore at Kalahari Kavango; Enrico Soresini at Wandrian and Trenitalia for providing my Interrail tickets across Europe; Gavin and Andreea Bell at Fundatia Adept; Natasha and Natalya at Real Russia; Simon Albert at Charity Challenge; Brian Smith at Exotissimo; Andy Teague at Intrepid; Jonathan Chell at Elephant Hills; Bodhi Garrett at Andaman Discoveries; Didar and Mostafa at Bangladesh Ecotours; Ashish and Ruscha Gupta at Barefoot India; Babu Varghese at Tour India; Gopi, Arun, Namboo and Uma at The Blue Yonder; Jos Byju at Keralagramam; Jacob Mathews at Haritha Farms; Sujit and Angie at Jetwing Travel; Mirta Moraitis and Abdul Azeez; Abdul Hakeem at Angsana Velavaru. Most of all, my thanks to my fellow passenger Gail Perkins for making the journey so worthwhile and so much fun.

Richard's acknowledgements

I am particularly grateful to Amanda Monroe and Nicola Grossfield at Rail Europe who facilitated many of my train trips. I would also like to thank the following for their recommendations and support:

Alison Rice; Amanda Marks at Tribes Travel; Ann-Charlotte Carlsson of West Sweden Tourist Board; Arild Molstad; Betony Garner at Ski Club of Great Britain; Bob Carter at Nature Travels; Bob Trevelyn, BBC Middle East correspondent; Cath Urquhart; Catherine Mack; Chris McIntyre of Expert Africa; Christopher Hammond; Dan Linstead at Wanderlust Magazine; Dilwyn Jenkins; Ed Paine at Last Frontiers; Emma Heal; Gerhard Buttner; Hannah Bullock at Green Futures Magazine; Hannah Wilde and Lyndall de Marco, formerly of the International Tourism Partnership; Harold Goodwin and Xavier Font at the International Centre for Responsible Tourism; Heather Mollins and Joanna Cheok at Tourism New Zealand; Ian Belcher; Isabel Choat and Andy Pietrasik at the Guardian; Jamie Drummond at DATA; Jeff Gazzard at Green Skies; Jeremy Lazell; Dr Jonathan Keeling at the BBC Natural History Unit; Jonny Bealby at Wild Frontiers; Julian Mathews at Discovery Initiatives; Kate Shepherd; Katherine Tubb at 2Way Development; Katie Fewkes at Audley Travel; Laura Burgess at Ecoescape; Laura Rendell-Dunn at Journey Latin America; Liz Bourke at Visit Scotland; Lone Lamark at Ecotourism Norway; Luulea Lääne at Tallink; Mark Ellingham; Mary Mulvey at Greenbox; Matthew Teller; Michael Cullen; Neil Birnie at Wilderness Journeys; Nick Maes; Nigel Tisdall; Nim Singh at Canadian Tourism Commission; Patrick Thorne; Paul Miles; Polly Rodger Brown; Rebecca Hawkins; Roger Diski and Judith de Witt at Rainbow Tours; Ron Mader at Planeta.com; Rupert Fausset at Forum for the Future; Sally Broom of Your Safe Planet; Sally Shalam; Sarah Dean at Innovation Norway; Simon Heyes of Senderos; Sophia de Meyer at Whitepod; Sophie Campbell; Stephen Tuckwell at Brittany Ferries; Steve Jack at Inntravel; Toby Sawday. And finally, I'd like to thank my parents, Michael and Jenny Hammond, for their unfailing support and encouragement.

CONTRIBUTOR CREDITS

Thanks to the following contributors for writing the experiences marked:

Zoe Bradshaw: (Lord Howe Island); Lara Dunston: (Kakadu, Adrere Amellal, Al Badia, Ecotours in Iran, Walking in Lebanon); Jo Kirby: (Lost City, Colombia); Melanie Kramers: (Cabo Polonio, Uruguay); Olivia Lacey: (Trek in the Ethiopian Highlands); Wendy Martin: (Conservation islands in the Seychelles); Paul Miles: (Samoa, Solomon Islands, Pueblos Mancumanados, San Blas Islands, Rafting in Colombia, La Digue); James Rice: (Live with the Maya, Cotton Tree Lodge); James Stewart: (Bay of Fires, Maria Island, Rafting Franklin, Tarkine, Walls of Jersualem); Andy Turner: (Koala spotting, Bushwalking in the Blue Mountains); Stephanie Wienrich: (Ulpotha)

PICTURE CREDITS

INDEX – by country

ANDORRA

Walk in the Parc National
des Pyrenees 62

ANGOLA

Be one of the first to visit
Kissama National Park 173

ARGENTINA

Dome sweet dome, Patagonia 260
Explore the Lake District, Patagonia ... 261
Paddles and pedals, Patagonia 261
Steppe on a horse, Patagonia 261
The world's highest vineyard 262

ARMENIA

Ride towards Mount Ararat 118

AUSTRALIA

A view over paradise at
Lord Howe Island 364
Aboriginal Sydney 367
Bushwalking in the Blue Mountains 351
Go walkabout in the Flinders 352
Have some bonza tucker, Sydney 366
Help conserve the Great
Barrier Reef 358
Kakadu National Park 356
Koala spotting, Brisbane 364
Learn what rock art means 353
Maria Island, Tasmania 348
Raft the Franklin River, Tasmania 362
See the city by foot or bike, Sydney ... 367
See Uluru the right way 353
Swim in a coastal pool, Sydney 366
Take the long road to Kooljaman 352
Take the train across Australia 349
The Bay of Fires, Tasmania 354
The best in world music, Byron Bay 355
The Walls of Jerusalem, Tasmania 358
Walk the wild Tarkine, Tasmania 365

AUSTRIA

Cycle the Heritage Trail in Bohemia 119
Schwoich's banana lake 52

BAHAMAS

Monitor whales 241

BANGLADESH

Take to the hills 332
Travel by Rocket 327

BELIZE

Live with the Maya 230
Meet the Maya at Cotton Tree Lodge ... 245

BHUTAN

Take the road least travelled 331

BOLIVIA

Chalalán Lodge 267
Hire a Kawsay Wasi guide 255
Visit Bolivia's Mapajo Community 259

BONAIRE

Shore dive off Bonaire 222

BOTSWANA

Take a mekoro through the
Okavango Delta 168
Watch the zebra migration 184

BRAZIL

Amazonat Jungle Lodge 267
Cristalino Jungle Lodge 267
Learn to dance in Rio de Janeiro 254
Meet the river people of the Amazon 258
Stay at the Refugio
Ecológico Caiman 265
Volunteer in the Pantanal 264

CAMBODIA

A biodiesel bus 298
Behind the scenes at Angkor Wat 312
See Cambodia by bike 307
Spot a giant ibis 312
Yeak Laom 297

CANADA

Cross-country skiing in Québec 193
Dog-sledding in the
Canadian Rockies 193
Eco-chic in the mountains of
Québec 204
Fresh air in Nova Scotia 208
Go green in Vancouver 209
Log off in a log cabin 204
Meet a moose in Algonquin 215
Shadow Lake Lodge, Alberta 191
Skoki Lodge, Alberta 190
Stock up on food at
St Lawrence market, Toronto 208
Stretch your legs in Jasper
National Park 209
Surround sound in a
Free Spirit Sphere 201
The bear necessities of
life on Vancouver Island 194
Visit Montréal's Biodôme 208
Visit the totem poles of
Gwaii Haanas 210
Whale-watching in Québec 214

CARIBBEAN

Island-hopping in the Caribbean 227

CHANNEL ISLANDS

See the light on Sark 42

Train and ferry to the Scilly Isles 26

CHILE

Watch whales feeding in the
Strait of Magellan 272

CHINA

Follow the caravan route to Sideng 289
Go trekking in northern Yunnan 285
Pink dolphins in Hong Kong harbour ... 284
Take the Trans-Mongolian Express 284
Yangshuo Mountain Retreat 278

COLOMBIA

Adrenaline-fuelled excitement 262
Trek to the lost city of Teyuna 256

COSTA RICA

Bosque del Cabo 235
Cerro Escondido 235
Danta Corcovado Lodge 235
Finca Rosa Blanca Country Inn 235
La Cusinga Lodge 234
Lapa Rios 234
Luna Nueva Lodge 234
Pacuare Lodge 234
Rara Avis Rainforest
Lodge and Reserve 235
Treehouse Lodge 235

CROATIA

Help to save Europe's largest bird,
Croatia 87
Sea kayaking along the
Dalmatian Coast, Croatia 88

CUBA

Get under Cuba's skin 229
Las Terrazas 230

CZECH REPUBLIC

Cycle the Heritage Trail in Bohemia 119

DENMARK

Become a light camper 107
Fresh herring and hippy herbs,
Copenhagen 101
Get on your bike, Copenhagen 100
Sleep somewhere green, Copenhagen 101
Take the no-fly route to Scandinavia 94

DOMINICA

A different Caribbean experience 232
In tune with the moon 240
Rosalie Bay 242

ECUADOR

Be one of the family at the
Black Sheep Inn 253
Community and conservation 272

La Selva Ecolodge 266
Meet the Huaorani 270
Napo Wildlife Center 266
Sani Lodge 266
Travel to conserve the
    Galápagos Islands 269
Visit the cloud forests 269
Yachana Lodge 266

EGYPT

Camel trekking in southern Sinai 144
Go on a dive safari in the Red Sea 136
Relax in the desert sea at
    Adrère Amellal 128

EL SALVADOR

The beginnings of tourism in
    El Salvador 238

ENGLAND

A day at The Eden Project, Cornwall 18
A long weekend on
    Lundy Island, Devon 28
Acorn House restaurant, London 25
Ardfern Tipis, Scotland 35
Autumn in the Lake District
    at Southwaite Green 32
Barefoot Yurts, Kent 35
Bushey Heath Farm,
    Buxton, Derbyshire 16
Cornish Yurt Holidays 34
Cornwall Tipi Holidays 35
Create some energy at
    Club Surya, London 25
Deepdale Campsite, Norfolk 17
Down on the farm at
    Higher Lank Farm, Cornwall 29
Eat out at Brighton Beach 19
Eco-chic at Strattons Hotel and
    Restaurant, Norfolk 37
Eco-steering at
    Lusty Glaze, Cornwall 21
Explore the North Pennines 38
Full Circle Yurts, Lake District 34
Go easy on yourself and the
    planet at Titanic Spa, Yorkshire 39
Huntstile Organic Farm, Somerset 16
London Wetland Centre, London 24
Ludlow Food Festival, Shropshire 31
Milden Hall, Suffolk 23
Retreat to Lincolnshire 19
Ride the National Cycle Network 10
Spend a week at Ecocabin,
    Shropshire 11
Spot whales and Dolphins on
    board the ferry to Spain 70
Stay in an eco cottage on the
    Trelowarren Estate, Cornwall 40
Surfing in Cornwall 41
Tamar Village Tipis, Devon 35
The Duke of Cambridge pub, London ... 25

Volunteer on a National Trust
    working holiday 27
Yurt Village, Dorset 35

ESTONIA

Bog walking 112
Sea kayaking the Baltic 112

ETHIOPIA

Trek in the Ethiopian Highlands 127

FIJI

In search of the real Fiji 356
Teach rugby 370

FINLAND

Swim across Finland's
    lakes and rivers 94
Cross-country skiing in Kuusamo 99

FRANCE

A day's sightseeing in Paris, by bike 50
Bathe in a natural spa 63
Chaumarty, the French Pyrenees 53
Explore Avignon and Ardèche 48
Go walking with a donkey 56
Hôtel les Orangeries,
    Lussac-les-Chateaux 56
Keycamp 72
Le Camp 53
Orion B&B 73
Perché dans le Perche 72
See Chamois in Chamonix,
    French Alps 58
Snow-shoe shuffling in the
    French Pyrenees 58
Take the slow boat to Béziers 57
Take the train to the mountains 63
Take the train to Vizzavona, Corsica 78
Take the train-hotel from
    Paris to Madrid 55
Walk across Corsica's
    Désert des Agriates 82
Walk in the Parc National
    des Pyrenees 62

GABON

See wildlife 147

GEORGIA

Explore Borjomi-Kharagauli
    National Park 114

GERMANY

Cocktails in Freiburg 51
See Germany on two wheels 48
Winter workouts in the Ammer Valley,
    Bavarian Alps 58

GREECE

Eat in Crete 89
Head into the mountains of Crete 88
Live among birds of prey at Dadia 118

Stay at Milia Mountain
    Retreat in Crete 89
Turtle power in Zakynthos 115

GRENADA

Get back to the roots 229
Hideaway in the hills at Kido 225
Sail and dive in the Grenadines 247

GUATEMALA

Discover Mayan ruins at
    Lago de Petexbatún 221

GUYANA

Discover "The Lost World" 259
Iwokrama 267

HONDURAS

La Ruta Moskitia 230

ICELAND

Whale-watching off the
    coast of Iceland 103

INDIA

A yak safari 328
Bandhavgarh National Park 321
Beach chic in Pondicherry 318
Beat stress the natural way at
    Philipkutty's Farm 343
Corbett Tiger Reserve 320
Explore the hidden backwaters
    at Emerald Isle 343
Explore the Sunderbans 324
Fish for prawns in Cochin 343
Go barefoot on the Andamans 323
Go further, slower on a
    Keralan houseboat 340
Have Thottada beach to yourself 342
Kanha National Park 320
Learn to cook, Keralan style 342
Panna National Park 320
Pench Tiger Reserve 321
River life in Kerala 322
Salute the sun, Goa 333
Sleep in the park with
    leopards, Mumbai 334
Spice up your life at Vanilla County 342
Stay in an Ecotel, Mumbai 334
Take to the trees in Kerala 324
The Great Indian Elephant Safari 336
The real Rajasthan 330
Tour the slums, Mumbai 335
Track snow leopards 329
Visit a handicraft centre, Mumbai 334

INDONESIA

Balinese village life 309
Dive at Bunaken 302
Face to face with an orang-utan,
    Kalimantan 311
Join an elephant patrol 309

Rinjani, Lombok 297
Surf your own wave at Nihiwatu 303

IRAN

Ecotours in Iran 137

IRELAND

Action and adventure at
    Delphi Mountain Resort 33
Cycle the Kingfisher Trail 21
Rail and sail from London to Dublin 33
Whale-watching in Cork 42

ISRAEL

Follow Jesus to Nazareth 136

ITALY

Casanuova, Tuscany 52
Cycle across Sardinia 81
Feast at Salone del Gusto 66
Feast your way through southern Italy ... 55
Horse-riding in Tuscany 66
Kayak around the Maddalena
    Archipelago, Sardinia 84
La Piantata 73
Lunch with shepherds in Sardinia 85
Monitor whales and dolphins in the
    Ligurian Sea 80
Port side at the Petit Hotel, Sicily 86
Stay in a traditional Sicilian farmhouse ... 87
Stay in an agriturismo in Le Marche 61
Under the volcano, Mount Etna
    National Park 86
Walk in the Riserva dello
    Zingaro, Sicily 85

JAMAICA

Get an "overstanding" of Rasta 228
Great Huts 224
Root veg and culture 228
Treasure Beach 243

JAPAN

Build a treehouse 288
Cycle round the city, Tokyo 281
Eat organic at
    Mominoki House, Tokyo 280
Explore the Snow Country 288
Shop with the original
    green bag, Tokyo 280
Sleep at Yoshimizu, Tokyo 280
Watch dolphins with a former hunter 288

JORDAN

A trip to the sewage works 141
Bedouin and breakfast all the
    way to Petra 131
River trekking in the Mujib
    nature reserve 135

KAZAKHSTAN

Silk Road by train 287

KENYA

Amboseli Porini Camp 139
Gaze at the galaxy from a star bed 144
Go on a horse-riding safari 149
Il N'gwesi Lodge 139
Koiyaki Wilderness Camp 139
Lewa Safari Camp 138
Live with the Maasai 143
Pool with a view 129
Tassia Lodge 139
Trek to the roof of the world 148
Walk with camels 149

KYRGYZSTAN

Silk Road by horse 286

LAOS

Birdwatching at Kingfisher Ecolodge ... 306
Enjoy a puppet show,
    Luang Prabang 404
Get a massage with the Red Cross,
    Luang Prabang 304
Go gourmet at Tamarind,
    Luang Prabang 305
Green Discoveries 297
Khammouane Ecoguides 296
Learn how silk is made 307
Make your own scarf, Luang Prabang 305
See moon bears, Luang Prabang 306
Stay at Rivertime 295
Take a boat up the Mekong 299
Visit a Khmu village 306

LEBANON

A long walk through the mountains 150

LESOTHO

Pony-trekking in the mountains 176
Ride to the top 164

MADAGASCAR

Voluntary services underseas 166

MALAWI

Kayak on Lake Malawi 173
Plant trees with Ripple Africa 172

MALAYSIA

Miso Walai Homestay, Sabah 310
Mount Kinabalu, Sabah 297
On the rafflesia trail in Sabah 310
Taman Negara 297
Turtle-watching in Sabah 310
Visit an Iban longhouse, Sarawak 311

MALDIVES

Underwater gardening 337

MALI

Hear the music of the desert 134

MAURITIUS

See the pink pigeons 167

MEXICO

Birdwatching at Celestún
    Biosphere Reserve 220
Day-trips with a difference at
    Puerta Verde 236
In the wake of the Maya 226
Pueblos Mancomunados 236

MONGOLIA

Discover dinosaurs in the Gobi 283
Live with nomads 282
Take the Trans-Mongolian Express 284

MOROCCO

A trip to the Berbers in Morocco's
    Atlas mountains 142
Take the train and ferry to Morocco 151
The Kasbah du Toubkal 140

MOZAMBIQUE

Arrange a trip on a dhow 163
Have the reef to yourself at Guludo 170
Relax by the Lake of Stars 162

NAMIBIA

Kayaking with seals at Walvis Bay 165
Meet the Bushmen at Nhoma 185
See the fairy circles in the
    Namib Rand 175
Stay at a community-run camp 158
Track cheetahs on foot 159

NEPAL

Meet the three sisters 328
Trek through villages 328

NETHERLANDS ANTILLES

Discover Saba 237

NEW ZEALAND

Cape Reinga Walk, Far North 361
Kiwi spotting at the Karori
    Wildlife Sanctuary 355
Mount Taranaki, New Plymouth 361
New Zealand's best wilderness lodges ... 369
Pelorus Track, Marlborough 360
Rees Dart Track, Otago 360
Ski the resort-free Craigieburn 359
Surf at Raglan 350
Whirinaki Forest Park, Central
    North Island 361

NICARAGUA

Eco-chic at Morgan's Rock 244
Follow the coffee route to Finca
    Esperanza Verde 222
Learn Spanish 241

NORTHERN IRELAND

Orchard Acre Farm,
    County Fermanagh 35
Volunteer on a National Trust
    working holiday 27

NORWAY

Follow in Shackleton's footsteps at
Finse 102
Go on a dog-sledding safari in Svalbard...
102
Group together at Ongajok 96
Join the Sami Reindeer Migration 96
Paddle and Pedal around the
Lofoten Islands 104
Stay under the turf at Gålå 94
Take the no-fly route to Scandinavia 94

PAKISTAN

Go on a dolphin safari 323

PALESTINE

A reality tour of the Holy Land 128

PANAMA

Meet the Kuna 238
Watch the clouds at Rancho
de Caldera 244

PAPUA NEW GUINEA

Birds of paradise 350

PERU

Hike an alternative Inca Trail 252
Inkaterra Reserva Amazonica lodge 266
Refugio Amazonas 267
See fair trade in action 265
See the cock-of-the-rock 255

POLAND

Stay on an eco ranch in Bieszczady
National Park 113

PORTUGAL

Party in the sun at Boom 65
The alternative Algarve 65

PUERTO RICO

See the bioluminescence at
Mosquito Bay 247

ROMANIA

Be the guest of a count
in Transylvania 120
Canoe the Danube delta 114
Hike in Retezat National Park 119
Wildflowers and Saxon villages 116

RUSSIA

Discover the island of Olkhon 279
Explore the Commander Islands 278
Take the Trans-Mongolian Express 284
Volunteer at Lake Baikal 283

RWANDA

Face to face with a mountain gorilla ... 153

SAMOA

Stay with a Samoan family 362

SCOTLAND

Bag a Munro on Rannoch Moor 31
Camping and kayaking in the
Summer Isles 36
Get out into the wilds of Scotland
at Alladale 12
Ride the National Cycle Network 10
Sleep out in a remote bothy 14
Take the sleeper train from
London to the Scottish Highlands 26
Volunteer on a National Trust
working holiday 27
Wild camping on the
Knoydart Peninsula 38

SENEGAL

Boating the Bolongs 132

SEYCHELLES

Conservation islands 319
Laid-back La Digue 325

SLOVAKIA

Take to the waters at Aquacity 120

SOLOMON ISLANDS

Visit an uninhabited Solomon Island ... 368

SOUTH AFRICA

A night on Long Street, Cape Town 179
Become a game ranger at
Kwa Madwala 160
Conservation in action, Phinda 177
Drink with locals in a township 179
Fair game at Umlani 179
Go birding in ancient forest 174
Go local on the Wild Coast 158
Help save the chimpanzee
from extinction 172
Hide away in the treetops of
Knysna forest 185
Kayak with whales in
Plettenberg Bay 178
Live the high life at Tsala Treetops 182
Natural heritage at
Isimangaliso Wetland Park 170
Ride a bike in a township 179
Ride the Cederberg Heritage Route ... 161
See hippos near Cape Town 179
Stay in Soweto 179
Stay the night in one of
South Africa's National Parks 176
Take an eco wine-tour 164
Take the kids to Madikwe 174
Taste fine Cape wines at Spier 179
Tembe Elephant Park 181
The Midlands Meander 182
Track wild dogs in the Limpopo 167
Trek the Drakensberg 183
Visit the world's richest
floral kingdom 168
Wake up with meerkats 166

Walk with rastas in Knysna forest 180
Walk with rhinos at Leshiba 178
Walk with the Chacma baboons 164
Whizz through the forest at
Storms River 178

SPAIN

A slice of Mongolia in Andalucía 51
Canyoning in the Sierra de Guara 63
Chill out in Ibiza 78
Cycle around the island of
Formentera 83
Cycle mountain highs in the Alpujarras ... 60
Discover the quieter side of Mallorca ... 81
Go on a Green Ibiza Tour 78
Hut to hut across the
Spanish Pyrenees 59
Spot whales and dolphins on
board the ferry to Spain 70
Stay on an organic farm in Ibiza 80
Take the train to the mountains 63
Take the train-hotel from
Paris to Madrid 55
Walk in the Parc National
des Pyrenees 62

SRI LANKA

Hotel Sigiriya 339
Mahoora Treehouse 339
Pick a papaya 326
Practise your yoga at Ulpotha 337
See a rainforest being born 326
Sleep in an elephant 330
Tea and tartan 332
Vil Uyana 338
Watch wildlife in bed 340

ST LUCIA

Praslin Island 242

SWEDEN

Car-free on Koster 104
Cycle along the Göta Canal 98
Learn to ride a horse the natural way ... 105
Rafting on the Klarälven 97
Stay in a charcoal hut at Kolarbyn 99
Take the no-fly route to Scandinavia 94
Track red foxes in Vålådalen
nature reserve 107

SWITZERLAND

Ski-touring in the Swiss Alps 59
Tomorrow's tourism today
in the Swiss Alps 70

SYRIA

One steppe at a time 146

TANZANIA

Diving in Mnazi Bay Marine Park 135
On foot in the Serengeti 148
Snorkel around
Chumbe Island, Zanzibar 133

Meet the Maasai 126
Wake up and smell the
    coffee at Kahawa Shamba 142
Walk on the wild side 148

THAILAND

Common sense luxury 300
Experience coastal village life 294
Give an elephant a bath 300
Hill Tribe Tours 296
Intrepid Travel 296
Pooh Eco Treks 296
Stay in an Isan village 301

THE GAMBIA

Sleep on the water 141
Tumani Tenda 151

THE NETHERLANDS

Food, glorious food, Amsterdam 68
Generate some watts in Rotterdam 60
Green spaces, Amsterdam 69
Pedal your way around, Amsterdam 68
Stay on a canal boat, Amsterdam 69

THE PHILIPPINES

Dive Apo Island 298

TIBET

Journey to the centre of the world 328

TONGA

Sail around Tonga's Vava'u Group 371

TRINIDAD AND TOBAGO

Contribute to the Earthdive log 224
Find the soul of Trinidad 229
Marvel at birds 232

TURKEY

Hide away in a Turkish lighthouse 121

TURKMENISTAN

Silk Road by truck 286

UGANDA

Easy access to the Bwindi
    Impenetrable Forest 147
Get a taste of the real Africa 144

UKRAINE

Stay in a Ukrainian village 116

UNITED STATES

A dip in a natural pool,
    Yosemite 199
Away from the trail in Alaska 207
Bite around the Big Apple,
    New York 202
Canopy life at Cedar Creek Treehouse,
    Washington 196
Discover the roots of hip-hop,
    jazz, gospel or salsa, New York 202
Eat your way round California 200
Follow in the footsteps of
    Sitting Bull 211
Follow the trail to anywhere,
    Yosemite 198
Get a bird's-eye view from
    the harbour, New York 202
Humpbacks off Hawaii 212
Meander along the
    Merced, Yosemite 198
Moonlit meanders in Oregon 192
Mountain biking along the
    Kingdom Trails, Vermont 212
Off-grid at Treebones, California 196
Party with a purpose at
    Rothbury Festival, Michigan 205
Room with a view at
    Camp Denali, Alaska 206
Ski cross-country, Yosemite 198
Ski-touring in Jackson Hole,
    Wyoming 193
Slow ski at Lake Placid 192
Stay in your own private Idaho 193
Sweet dreams in Sugar Hill,
    New York 203

Take a walk on the wet side, Florida ... 197
To shop, or not to shop? 203
Watch lava become land in Hawaii 213

URUGUAY

The simple life 273

UZBEKISTAN

Silk Road by train 287

VENEZUELA

Ride with cowboys 263

VIETNAM

Canoe the Ba Be Lakes 302
Charity Challenge 296
Explore rice terraces 313

WALES

Caerfai Campsite, Pembrokeshire 17
Fforest 35
Larkhill Tipis 35
Mountain biking at Coed
    Llandegla Forest 29
Photograph seabirds on Skomer Island,
    Pembrokeshire 23
Ride the National Cycle Network 10
Sleep out in a remote bothy 14
Spend a weekend "Under the Thatch" ... 13
The Centre for Alternative Technology ... 20
Volunteer on a National Trust
    working holiday 27

WORLDWIDE

Go Wwoofing 33
Hunt a Geocache 19
Wild swimming 43

ZAMBIA

See the rare sitatunga deer 180
Stay in an African village 163

ZIMBABWE

Camp Amalinda 161

INDEX – by theme

ABORIGINAL PEOPLE

Amazon River People............................258
Amerindians................................. 266–267
Australian Aborigines ..352, 353, 356, 367
Bedouin.............131, 136, 144–145, 146
Berbers 140, 142
Bushmen 185
Haida 210
Huaorani..270–271
Huli 351
Kuna...238
Maori...361
Maasai.................126, 138–139, 143, 144,
    148–149
Maya 230-231
Native Americans 210–211
Sami.. 96

ABSEILING 182

ACCOMMODATION

Agriturismi.................................. 61, 85, 376
Backcountry huts.................190–191, 193
Boats 247, 278, 327, 341
Bothies 14
Bunkhouses.. 15
Cabañas.....................170, 220, 245, 266
Cabins 94, 176, 204, 206, 278
Cabins, floating...................194, 258, 311
Cabins, ski 190-191
Cottages and villas............. 12, 13, 32, 40,
    89, 115, 118, 225, 232, 273, 309, 323,
    324, 326, 342, 350
Eco-chic 37, 70, 204, 244, 260, 354
Ecolodges ..11, 19, 86, 113, 131, 132–133,
    138–139, 142, 145, 159, 168, 174, 175,
    178, 180, 213, 234–235, 237, 240, 242,
    253, 269, 270–271, 278, 283, 284, 285,
    295, 298, 299, 306, 313, 318, 330
Farmstays/farmhouses ..86, 87, 160, 161,
    307, 376
Guesthouses................................89, 119,
    120, 132, 136, 182, 203, 280, 289, 320,
    321, 325, 352
Homestays...................114, 116, 126, 132,
    143, 144, 228, 229, 279, 282, 283, 285,
    294, 296, 297, 301, 302, 310, 312, 322,
    328, 330, 333, 342–343, 356, 362, 377
Hostels.....................................31, 101, 179
Hotels.............................37, 42, 51, 56,
    86, 129, 140, 147, 220, 221, 230, 233,
    240, 262, 265, 332, 333, 339
Huts 158, 162, 163,
    164, 171, 173, 176, 183, 224, 309, 326,
    334, 337
Igloos 288
Jungle lodges 266–267
Lighthouse 121
Logcabin 204

Luxury 12, 168, 177,
    182, 300, 303, 312, 319, 321, 336,
    338, 340
Mud houses....................................151
Pods 70, 210, 260, 272
Safari lodges....138–139, 144, 149, 161,
    167, 172, 174, 179
Safari tents/bushcamps 171, 173,
    176, 180, 181, 182, 184, 185, 300, 306,
    320, 352
Self-catering...................11,19, 23,
    28, 32, 40, 80, 88, 174, 176, 179, 185,
    225, 326
Tents (see also camping)... 131, 145, 333
Tipis 34–35
Treehouses ...72–73, 182, 185, 196, 201,
    288, 324, 339
Village stays 230–231, 236, 238
Yurts........ 34–35, 51, 193, 196, 213, 282

AGRITURISMI see Accommodation

AIRLINE EMISSIONS............108–109

AWARDS 248–249

BEACHES 19, 40, 42, 78, 82, 85, 115,
    132, 158, 162, 170, 171, 172, 173, 219,
    224, 239, 242–243, 294, 300, 303, 318,
    323, 325, 336, 342, 352, 354, 368, 379

BEARS

Black.. 194, 210
Grizzly... 194, 206
Moon...305

BIKES, CITY HIRE SCHEMES........50

BIRDWATCHING

Australasia, New Zealand
    and the South Pacific.............. 350, 355
Central America and
    the Caribbean 220, 232
Eastern Europe & the Aegean....112, 114,
    118
Great Britain and Ireland................. 23, 24
Indian Subcontinent.....................319, 323,
    332, 336, 339, 340
Mediterranean Islands 87
North America................................202, 210
Northern Africa and the
    Middle East 141, 144, 147
South America 255, 264, 269
Southeast Asia....................306, 309, 312
Southern Africa........... 173, 174, 182, 183

BLOGS...154–155

BLUE FLAG AWARDS.....................249

BOATS

Canal barges.....................................57, 376
Cargo boats 344–345, 376

Houseboats 340
Safaris 249, 324
Solar-powered boats 57
Travelling by................................. 259, 269,
    270–271, 299, 306, 311, 327, 341

BOG WALKING 112

BOTHIES see Accommodation

BUNKHOUSES see Accommodation

BUSES AND COACHES...................375

BUSHCRAFT 379

CAMEL TREKKING AND RIDES........
    136, 138, 144, 145, 283, 353

CAMPAIGN GROUPS........................ 381

CAMPING 16–17, 34–35, 36, 38, 72,
    107, 131, 148, 168, 283, 376

CANALS.. 57, 98

CANOEING AND KAYAKING ....
    36, 84, 88, 104, 112, 114, 132, 158, 162,
    168, 171, 173, 180, 202, 204, 210, 215,
    226, 247, 258, 261, 262, 302, 380, 354

CANYONING/RIVER TREKKING
    .... 63, 135

CAR HIRE..374

CAR-SHARING see Lift-sharing

CARBON EMISSIONS....108-109, 376

CARBON OFFSETTING 186–187

CARGO BOATS/SHIPS see Boats

CERTIFICATION see Eco labels

CHARITIES.. 381

CHARITY CHALLENGES 296, 307

CHIMPANZEES.................. 147, 153,172

CLIMBING 33

COASTEERING see Ecosteering

CONSERVATION

Australia, New Zealand
    and the South Pacific.....348, 355, 358,
    360–361, 364
Caribbean and Central America 244
Eastern Europe and the Aegean....116, 120
Great Britain and Ireland............. 12, 27, 42
Indian Subcontinent..319, 323, 324, 326,
    329, 338
Mediterranean Islands 87
Northern Africa and the Middle East..129,
    131, 135, 138–139, 153

South America 259, 263, 264, 266–267, 269, 270–271, 272
Southeast Asia 300, 305, 310, 312,
Southern Africa 159, 161, 166, 167, 170, 172, 173, 176, 177, 182, 184

CONSERVATION, MARINE see Marine conservation

COOKING COURSES...............89, 121, 280, 305, 309, 342, 343

CORAL REEFS
Australia, New Zealand and the South Pacific 358, 368
Caribbean and Central America.....................222, 224, 237, 247
Indian Subcontinent.....................323, 337
Northern Africa and the Middle East 132–133, 135
Southeast Asia.............................. 298, 302
Southern Africa.................. 166, 170, 171

COURSES............................16, 288, 309

CROSS-COUNTRY SKIING see Winter Sports

CRYOTHERAPY 120

CYCLING
Australia, New Zealand and the South Pacific.............................367
Central and East Asia...........................281
City bikes hire schemes 50, 374
Eastern Europe and the Aegean..........119
Great Britain and Ireland.. 10, 21, 29, 379
Mediterranean Islands 81, 83
North America.. 379
Scandinavia............................ 98, 100, 104
Southeast Asia.......................................307
Southern Africa.....................................179
Western Europe.................. 48, 49, 60, 68

DANCE 25, 44–45, 65, 254

DESERT 82, 128, 134, 145, 159, 175, 185, 283

DIVE SAFARIS see Safaris

DIVING, SCUBA.................................. 135, 136, 166,170, 171,173, 222, 224, 237, 247, 298, 302, 323, 358, 380

DOG SLEDDING see Winter Sports

DOLPHINS 70, 80, 165, 212, 258, 284, 288, 323

DONKEYS............................56, 65, 161

ECO LABELS...............................248–249

ECOLODGES see Accommodation

ECOSTEERING.......................................21

ELEPHANTS 138–139, 147, 181, 300, 309

EMISSIONS see Carbon emissions and carbon offsetting

EU FLOWER.. 249

FAIR TRADE 142, 265

FAIR TRADE IN TOURISM, SOUTH AFRICA.............158, 168, 176, 178-179, 183, 248

FAMILY-FOCUSED HOLIDAYS 29, 120, 158, 178, 182, 185, 224, 318, 213, 300, 304

FARMERS' MARKETS.............208, 378

FARMS, ORGANIC...............80, 86, 222

FARMSTAYS see Accommodation

FERRY JOURNEYS 33, 151, 376
Around the Caribbean 227
Around the Mediterranean 90–91
To Scandinavia 94

FESTIVALS 31, 44–45, 65, 66, 134, 205, 228, 355, 380

FISHING 158, 163, 171, 320, 343

GORILLAS 144, 146, 147, 153

GPS see Maps

GREEN KEY 248–249

GREEN MAPS see Maps

GREEN TOURISM BUSINESS SCHEME... 248

GREENWASHING............................. 248

GREETERS...378

HERBAL MEDICINE 126, 158, 163

HIKING see Walking

HILL TRIBES 296, 297, 313, 333

HIRE CAR see Car hire

HITCH HIKING 374

HOME-GROWN FOOD ... 89, 113, 116, 120, 213, 278, 324, 326, 333

HOMESTAYS see Accommodation

HORSE-RIDING...............................66, 73, 105, 113, 118, 120, 142, 164, 168, 176, 183, 261, 263, 282, 283, 286, 379

HOSPITALITY EXCHANGES...........................154, 376

HOSTELS see Accommodation

HOTELS see Accommodation

ICE-FISHING see Winter Sports

IGLOOS see Accommodation

INDIGENOUS PEOPLE see Aboriginal people

KAYAKING see Canoeing and kayaking

KICKSLEDDING................................... 112

KITEMARKS see Eco labels

LANGUAGE COURSE, SPANISH.. 241

LIFT-SHARING.............................44, 374

LIONS...138–139

LOCAL GUIDES 378

LOCAL VOICES 314

LUXURY ACCOMMODATION see Accommodation

MAN IN SEAT 61 155

MAPS, GREEN.......................... 216–217

MARINE CONSERVATION 42, 115, 132–133, 166, 212, 214, 222, 224, 237, 259, 269, 272, 284, 336, 368

MARKETS 31, 200, 289

MAYAN RUINS 220, 226

MEERKATS.. 166

MOOSE 99, 107, 206, 215

MOUNTAIN BIKING 204, 212, 306

MUD HOUSES see Accommodation

MUSIC 44, 45, 65, 104, 202, 205, 355

NATIONAL ECOTOURISM ORGANIZATIONS 249

NATIONAL PARKS
Australia, New Zealand and the South Pacific 348, 354, 356, 360–361
Central America and the Caribbean.......................222, 237
Eastern Europe and the Aegean............ 112, 113, 114, 119, 380
Great Britain and Northern Ireland......380
Indian Subcontinent..................... 324, 334
Mediterranean Islands 86
North America........................... 191, 196, 197, 198–199, 206-207, 209, 380
South America 255, 260, 261, 266–267
Southern Africa...................................... 176

NATURAL SWIMMING POOLS........52–53, 129, 199, 230, 366

NATURE'S BEST 248–249

NIGHTCLUBS.............................25, 60

ORANG-UTANS........................ 309, 311

OVERLANDING 134, 286

POOLS, NATURAL see Natural Swimming Pools

PUBLIC TRANSPORT 374

RAFTING 33, 97, 112, 224, 362

RAIL JOURNEYS see Train journeys

RAMBLING see Walking

RASTAFARIANISM 180, 228, 229

REEFS see Coral Reefs

REINDEER 96, 107

RHINOCEROS 138, 178

RIVER TREKKING see Canyoning

ROCK ART 159, 161, 182, 352, 353

ROCK CLIMBING see Climbing

RUGBY 370

SAFARIS 143, 148–149, 161, 175, 177, 178, 180, 184
Camel 144, 149
Cultural.. 126
Diving 136
Elephant 336
Horse-riding....................................... 149
Tiger.................................... 320–321, 324
Walking 148–149, 159, 178, 180
Yak 328

SAIL AND RAIL 26, 33, 90–91

SAILING 115, 163, 170, 202, 225, 247, 371, 380

SELF-CATERING see Accommodation

SHEPHERDS................................. 85

SHOPPING 66, 182, 203, 280, 305, 307, 334

SKI RESORTS 74–75

SKI TOURING see Wintersports

SKI TRAIN....................................... 74–75

SKIING, ALTERNATIVE see Winter Sports

SLOW FOOD 19, 31, 37, 55, 61, 66, 85, 89, 116, 200, 367, 377

SNORKELLING 132–133, 145, 173, 222, 358

SNOW TRAIN................................... 74–75

SNOW-SHOEING see Winter sports

SNOWBOARDING see Winter sports

SPAS AND TREATMENTS .. 33, 39, 63, 120, 300, 302, 303, 304, 312, 340, 343

SUB AQUA see Diving, scuba

SURFING................................41, 65, 224, 244, 303, 350, 379

SWIMMING POOLS see pools

SWIMMING, WILD................ 43, 94–95

TAXIS.. 374

TIGER SAFARIS see Safaris

TIPIS see Accommodation

TOUR OPERATORS................ 380–381

TOURISM FOR TOMORROW AWARDS 248–249

TOWNSHIP TOURS 179

TRACKING 159, 167, 185, 379

TRADITIONAL ARTS 118, 134, 182, 185, 282, 304, 305, 309, 322, 330, 334, 341, 342, 343, 353

TRAIN JOURNEYS ... 26, 48, 55, 63, 74, 75, 78, 94, 151, 155, 208–209, 284, 287, 349, 369

TRAVEL COMPANIONS 378

TREE PLANTING 186–187

TREEHOUSES see Accommodation

TREKKING see Walking

TURTLES 115, 147, 171, 225, 229, 244, 259, 310, 319

VEGETARIAN 13, 113, 121, 225, 228, 322, 337, 378

VINEYARDS see Wine tasting

VISITOR ATTRACTIONS..............18, 20, 24, 78, 208

VOLCANOES 213

VOLUNTEERING 14, 27, 33, 87, 115, 136, 158, 160, 161, 166, 172, 177, 180, 212, 225, 237, 254, 264, 269, 283, 286, 290–291, 335, 370

VOLUNTOURISM......................132, 163, 290–291, 294, 298, 300, 307, 328, 358

WALKING 374, 379
Australia, New Zealand and the South Pacific 351, 358, 360–361, 364, 365, 366, 367, 369
Central America and the Caribbean.... 237
Central and East Asia................... 278, 285

Eastern Europe and the Aegean..... 113, 114, 116, 120, 121
Great Britain and Ireland 12, 14, 15, 31, 38, 379
Indian Subcontinent...326, 328, 329, 331
Mediterranean Islands 82, 84, 87
North America...197, 198, 200, 202, 204, 209, 213, 379
Northern Africa and the Middle East.. 131, 134, 136, 142, 145, 148–149, 150–151
South America 252, 256–257
Southeast Asia.....................296, 297, 313
Southern Africa........................... 164, 165, 174, 176, 178, 180, 182, 183, 185
Western Europe................................ 56, 62

WATER SPORTS 379
and see individual sports

WHALE-WATCHING 42, 70, 80, 103, 168, 178, 196, 212, 214, 272, 288, 376

WHITE-WATER RAFTING see Rafting

WILD CAMPING see Camping

WILD DOGS... 129

WILD SWIMMING see Swimming

WILDERNESS 12, 14, 31, 119, 139, 158, 210, 278, 279, 352, 369, 380

WILDLIFE-WATCHING 12, 113, 115, 159, 166, 172, 175, 176, 178, 179, 180, 184, 194, 197, 202, 212, 213, 278, 284, 285, 288, 309, 320–321, 324, 329, 330, 331, 340, 352

WINE TASTING/VINEYARDS 66, 114, 119, 164, 179, 200, 262

WINTER SPORTS................ 58–59, 359
Cross-country skiing........59, 96, 99, 102, 190–193, 198, 204
Dog sledding........................ 102, 193, 215
Ice fishing 96
Skiing.. 119
Ski-touring 59, 193, 204
Snow-shoeing 58, 70, 107, 112, 190–193, 204, 215 288, 379
Telemark skiing 192, 193, 204

WOLVES..99, 194

YOGA................................... 65, 333, 337

YOUTH HOSTELS see Accommodation, hostels

YURTS see Accommodation

ZIP SLIDES................................... 288